T0157481

London Marine Insurance 1438–1824

London Marine Insurance
1438–1824

Risk, Trade, and the Early Modern State

A.B. Leonard

THE BOYDELL PRESS

First published 2022
The Boydell Press, Woodbridge

ISBN 978 1 78327 692 9

The Boydell Press is an imprint of Boydell & Brewer Ltd
PO Box 9, Woodbridge, Suffolk IP12 3DF, UK
and of Boydell & Brewer Inc.
668 Mt Hope Avenue, Rochester, NY 14620–2731, USA
website: www.boydellandbrewer.com

A catalogue record for this book is available
from the British Library

The publisher has no responsibility for the continued existence or accuracy of URLs for
external or third-party internet websites referred to in this book, and does not guarantee
that any content on such websites is, or will remain, accurate or appropriate

This publication is printed on acid-free paper

Contents

Illustrations

Tables

Figures

Preface

This book examines the role of institutions, broadly defined, in shaping markets. It does so through the lens of marine insurance in London, from its introduction in the late medieval period to the early nineteenth century. Its focus rests on a series of attempts to resolve the challenges created when newcomers participated in this established commercial market, particularly through initiatives which either introduced novel institutions, or changed, moderated, or cemented existing ones.

To achieve this, the book explores the evolution of marine insurance practice in London, based largely on an exploration and analysis of primary sources. Its particular approach examines specific attempts to accommodate newcomers to the practice of marine insurance who may not have understood or wished to follow the prevailing rules of the game. Such initiatives included regulation, legislation, precedent, organisational structure, and others. They met with various degrees of success. The dynamics of the multiple parties involved, and the interests they pursued, lie at the core of the discussion, and influenced the longevity of their interventions.

The period reviewed coincides with a critical era in the formation of the English state. The marine insurance case study sheds light on ways in which English governments, national and local alike, experimented through executive, legislative, and judicial actions to support the effective functioning of London's open market for marine insurance, to the benefit of trade. In so doing, state servants hoped, often outwardly, to promote economic growth. Ultimately a self-governing institution of insurers was established, but it was able to function at greater efficiency in conjunction with public-order institutions such as the common law, which supported the market when the entry of outsiders presented challenges. Such institutions were not necessary for the very functioning of the market, as has been suggested, but they allowed it to function incrementally more smoothly and efficiently, amidst reduced uncertainty, as they matured.[1]

Following an introductory chapter, Chapter 1 of this book discusses the origins and development of insurance before its introduction to London, when the fundamental structures of the market and its institutions were developed. It shows how merchants' system of insurance and the rules that govern practice evolved in Italy before being exported to multiple commercial centres, including London. There, by the end of the sixteenth century, a mature and well-organised market operated, but it was beginning to be stretched by buyers from outside the system. Chapter 2 analyses actions by the state to support the incumbent system, and the institutions

---

[1] Ogilvie, Sheilagh and Carus, A. W.: 'Institutions and economic growth in historical perspective', in Durlauf, S. and Aghion, P.: *Handbook of economic growth*, Vol. 2A, Amsterdam: Elsevier, 2014, p. 404.

of dispute resolution introduced to do so. The intervention comprises a series of institutional initiatives intended to respond to problems arising from outsider-buyers, and includes Privy Council actions in the 1570s, and the first parliamentary act related to insurance, which was passed in 1601. The chapter then analyses the impact of these innovations on the market, and the weaknesses which led them to recede before the end of the seventeenth century.

Chapter 3 considers developments during and following the Glorious Revolution, and focuses upon the second major intervention into the operation of London's insurance market: that of financial capitalists who, for their own enrichment, wished to establish an entirely new institutional structure for the insurance market. In 1720 they succeeded in launching, under royal patent, two joint-stock companies which were granted an exclusive duopoly over all marine insurance underwriting, except by individuals. This book reveals and explains their critical connection to the South Sea Company. Chapter 4 analyses the third intervention, a series of actions which includes relatively narrow legislative initiatives with very broad consequences, the development of a body of sympathetic common law principles (which became a form of Braudellian 'world-law'), and the rise of Lloyd's as the major institution of trading and practice, as well as its underwriters' role in financing British state borrowing. Chapter 5 concludes.[2]

The book builds upon academic work I completed during my undergraduate, masters, and doctoral studies. After spending two decades of my professional life closely connected to London's global marine insurance marketplace, I returned to education and found historical analysis of marine insurance was sorely lacking, and chose to pursue it. This book is the culmination of that work.

As such, I owe a debt of thanks to my academic supervisors, Sir Christopher Bayly, Martin Daunton, and D'Maris Coffman; to the various examiners and other academics who supported me through those projects; to the scores of fellow academics who reviewed or contributed to the various ideas and evidence this work presents; to the journal editors and other reviewers who helped with feedback along the way; and to the many archivists who helped me find what I was looking for when I didn't quite know what it was. Special thanks to Nuela Zahedia, Peter Spufford, Edmond Smith, Guido Rossi, Nick Radburn, Duncan Needham, Larry Neal, Anne Murphey, David Ibbetson, Sabine Go, Maria Fusaro, Hannah Farber, James Davey, Guy Chet, Giovanni Ceccarelli, Richard Blakemore, and to all the other people I have forgotten to mention.

---

[2]   The concept of a world-law for insurance rests on the ideas of Fernand Braudel. See his *Afterthoughts on material civilization and capitalism* (Ranum, P., trans.), Baltimore: Johns Hopkins University Press, 1977.

Glossary of marine insurance terms

Abatement. A portion of cover retained by the insured, usually expressed as a percentage.

Adjusting. The process of determining the value of an indemnity.

Agent. An individual or firm that sells insurance on behalf of underwriters.

Average. The calculations by which each insured owner's share (and therefore each underwriter's share) of an indemnity is calculated.

Barratry, barretry. Theft or embezzlement by members of a vessel's crew, particularly the captain.

Bottom. A ship, from the shipper's perspective.

Broker. An individual or firm which arranges insurance cover on behalf of insureds.

Claim. 1) Money paid to an insured party to compensate for insured losses; also an indemnity. 2) To apply for an indemnity.

Convoy. In insurance law, a group of vessels protected by a government-appointed naval escort. Contemporaneously, the escorting vessels.

Court of Assurances. The seventeenth-century court for settling insurance disputes brought by insureds over cargo policies registered at the Office of Assurances.

Cover. 1) Insurance, often of a specific value. 2) To insure.

Cross risk, cross voyage. A voyage which neither originates nor terminates in the port where it is insured.

Follower. An underwriter who accepts risk under a policy at terms set by another underwriter, the leader.

Indemnity. A financial payment to compensate for a loss.

Insurable interest. A financial or other stake in an insured risk which extends beyond the possession of an insurance policy on that risk.

Insurance. A financial product designed to reduce by sharing or to transfer the risk of economic loss arising from the various perils faced when moving goods from source to market.

Insured. The buyer of an insurance policy.

Insured loss, insured event. A cause of damage which is covered by an insurance policy.

Insurer. The seller of an insurance policy. Often the underwriter.

Interest or No Interest. A policy clause which indicates the insured may have no financial interest in the object of cover.

Leader. An underwriter who sets the contractual terms of an insurance agreement which other participating underwriters comply with.

Line. An underwriter's share of the sum insured on a specific risk or policy, expressed as a monetary amount.

Lloyd's of London, Lloyd's Coffee-shop. An insurance marketplace (but not an insurer or an underwriter).

Lost or Not Lost. A standard policy clause which means the policy remains valid even if the vessel was lost at the time of underwriting.

Marine Insurance. Insurance on ships and cargo.

Merchant-insurer. A merchant who underwrites insurance.

On Risk. Having underwritten a specific risk.

Peril. A category of threats to property.

Policy. A contract of insurance.

Premium, praemium, premoi. 1) The money paid or received for insurance. 2) The cost of insurance.

Public Office, Public Insurance. In the seventeenth century, the Office of Assurances; from 1720, the Royal Exchange Assurance or the London Assurance. Insurances issued by them.

Rate. The price of insurance, measured and expressed as a percentage of the cover. The rate of two guineas per cent for £100 of cover yields a premium of two guineas.

Reinsurance. Insurance granted by one insurer to cover risks insured by another.

Risk. 1) An object or adventure to be insured. 2) The perils faced by a buyer of insurance.

Risk Book, Risk Journal. A ledger in which an underwriter records the details of risks underwritten.

Risk Pool. The collection of all risks available for underwriting.

Risk Portfolio. The collection of risks underwritten by a single underwriter.

Scratch. An underwriter's name on a policy.

Slip. A document passed between Lloyd's underwriters to collect commitments to underwrite a policy.

Sum Insured. The total value of insurance granted under a policy, expressed as a monetary value, and equalling the total possible indemnity under the policy.

Terms and conditions. The specific details of an insurance contract.

Underwriter. An individual or corporate body agreeing the acceptance of insurance risk.

Underwriting. The act or occupation of accepting insurance risk on one's own account, as an agent, broker, or correspondent, for a syndicate, or for an employing corporation.

Warranty. A clause in a policy which must be followed by the insured.

Introduction

Ocean-going trade in the early modern period was fundamentally precarious, unpredictable, and fraught with peril.[1] Merchants often had no choice but to bear the dangers – to 'run the risk' – of naked threats which, at worst, could mean the complete destruction of a season's invested capital, spelling ruin for an individual merchant adventurer. The rage of the oceans often caused the total loss of ships and their cargoes, or inflicted extensive damage before goods reached markets. The violence of men, in the form of warships, pirates and privateers, raiders, thieves, and brigands, was sometimes an even greater danger. Especially in wartime, human risks to trade were recurrent and grave. At their height, enemy onslaughts against seaborne trade could endanger the whole commerce of a country, imperilling its military success, and potentially its independent survival.

Happily for merchants and nations, disasters arising from the manifestation of the intrinsic perils of the seas, *mare*, and of men, *gentium*, could be eased. Marine insurance could ensure that losses arising from such hazards were indemnified, and that the insured merchant's capital would be restored. A mature insurance system, such as that developed and honed in London during the period reviewed in this book, could underpin seaborne trade, and mitigate the risk of national catastrophe arising from enemies' ocean-borne predation. The importance of London's marine insurance system to the expansion and success of England's trade was paramount, but its impact was much greater than this immediate function.[2] It made far-reaching contributions to Britain's divergence from her Continental peers, both directly by spreading risk among the members of the merchant community, especially in the eighteenth century and particularly when beleaguered by formidable and repeated assault, or enthused by offensive opportunity, and indirectly from a much earlier period, through its continued contribution to the formation of the English state, as a conduit for the introduction of merchant approaches to institutions to the process of state formation.

Marine insurance became a critical component of national development, and of Britain's rise to great power and imperial status, most directly by extending private capital to the public projects of the state (including, towards the end of the nineteenth century, directly through the investment of merchants' capital, accumulated

---

[1] For a discussion of the perils of oceanic trade, see Musgrave, Peter: 'The economics of uncertainty: the structural revolution in the spice trade, 1480–1640', in *Shipping, trade, and commerce: essays in memory of Ralph Davis*, Leicester: Leicester University Press, 1981, pp. 9–22.

[2] Hereafter 'England' will be used for references to the country before 1707, and 'Britain' for references to the country after the Act of Union, unless in references specifically to England, such as to law.

by insurers as a reserve to pay claims, in state borrowing instruments). Marine insurance increases the amount of money invested in trade, by transferring to others the risk of financial losses arising from the various perils faced when moving goods from source to market.[3] It provides contingent capital, through a promise to reimburse the purchaser for the financial cost of unforeseen, actual, incurred losses arising from insured events. This allows merchants to conduct business with less trade capital than the unavoidable perils of seaborne commerce prudently demand. The possibility of specified future large losses is swapped for a predictable, and much lower, current expense. This, in turn, allows merchants to invest the absolute maximum possible amount of cash and credit in trade goods and commercial voyages, since none need be retained to compensate for fortuitous losses at sea.

In this way, marine insurance has acted as a catalyst of international trade in England since at least the early fifteenth century, following its introduction by Lombard émigrés. By making the threats of the seas and men more tolerable, it allowed London and London-resident merchants' international business to proceed and expand. By financing the extended risk-capital required when merchants faced extraordinary wartime perils, insurance provided an important underpinning of Britain's international political adventures. It dispersed war risks by employing the capital of a broad section of the nation's commercial class to finance the monarch's foreign policy.

The individuals who introduced insurance to London used it as an instrument of mutual benefit. In the language of legislation of 1601 (assumed to have been written by Francis Bacon), 'by meanes of Policies of Assurance... upon the losse or perishing of any Shippe there followethe not the undoinge of any Man, but the losse lighthe rather easilie upon many, then hevilie upon fewe'.[4] In common with other major European seafaring nations with an insurance tradition, London insurance was underwritten primarily by sole traders, and sometimes by commercial partnerships, who were also active merchants. They were both buyers and sellers of the product. Such individuals are referred to throughout this book as *merchant-insurers*, the nomenclature contemporaneously used.[5] Concrete examples of buyers who were also sellers appear in the earliest evidence of underwriting in London, such as the Borromei Bank's ledgers of the 1430s.[6] Merchant-insurers survived into the nineteenth century and beyond. In 1818, the India merchant Stewart Majoribanks

---

3   Hereafter, simply 'insurance', except for clarity.

4   Anno 43 Eliz. c. 12, 'An Act Conc'ninge matters of Assurances, amongste Merchantes', 4 Statutes of the Realm, 1547–1624, pp. 978–979.

5   For example, in the name of the 1693/4 *'Bill to enable divers Merchants-Insurers, that have sustained great Losses by the present War with France...'*.

6   See p. 48. Bolton, J. L. and Bruscoli, Francesco Guidi (eds and transs), *The ledger of Filippo Borromei and Co. of Bruges, 1438*, London: History Department, Queen Mary University, 2007: online only, www.queenmaryhistoricalresearch.org [Accessed 3 Dec. 2021].

underwrote £50 on Sarah Wilde's share of the vessel *Frances*, returning from Quebec; in 1824 he purchased numerous policies at Lloyd's for goods he was shipping to China.[7]

The merchant-insurers' product can be characterised as a 'club good' (or, perhaps, a club service) which they used to improve the commercial experience of all the participants. Buchanan defines club goods as those which fill the 'gap between the purely private and the purely public good… the consumption of which involves some "publicness", where the optimal sharing group is more than one person or family, but smaller than an infinitely large number'.[8] The clear benefits of insurance to the nation and society notwithstanding, merchant-insurers used their club good to make more secure the trade both of individuals, and of the community, despite commercial rivalries. In a theoretical perfect underwriting environment, all merchants would share in the losses of the community proportionally to the risks which they brought to its risk pool. In practice, when underwriting was profitable, some of the cost was defrayed, but loss-costs ultimately had to be covered. Insurance made paying more manageable. This club good nature of marine insurance provided the strengths of London's underwriting system during the period under review. It also gave rise to challenges. When the optimal size – or nature – of the group sharing the club good was exceeded, problems could and did emerge.

Recent scholarly work has challenged the positive economic impact of clubs, since they can lead to inflexibility and exclusion, serving primarily the distributional interests of powerful groups. For example, Ogilvie has found that 'the historical evidence provides no support for the view that merchant guilds were the efficient institution for guaranteeing commercial security, ensuring contract enforcement, solving principal-agent problems, correcting failures in information markets, or stabilising prices'. Ogilvie goes on to outline four implications of her work which impact the explanation and analysis of economic institutions, including the 'recognition that any institution is embedded in a broader institutional framework that itself requires economic analysis'.[9] The institution of marine insurance, as a club good, must be considered in this context. London marine insurance was transacted between a relatively small group of merchants, including buyers and sellers, but unlike the guilds which Ogilvie analyses, it was no closed shop: anyone could underwrite insurance according to any rules they wished, a fact which is central to the arguments of this study. Nor did the formation of Lloyd's as a members-only institution for insuring preclude others from underwriting. Nor can overseas competition be ignored: mobile merchants naturally could and frequently did procure coverage from abroad directly or through agents. Indeed, it is in the context of the broader institutional framework that London marine insurance was to thrive, as this book will show.

---

7   Then, as today, Lloyd's was a marketplace for insurance traders, rather than an insuring corporation. ALC (uncatalogued), policy underwritten for Sarah Wilde, 27 Nov. 1818; LL (uncatalogued), *Clagett & Pratt Risk Book 1824*.

8   For the seminal explanation of the idea of club goods, see Buchanan, James M.: 'An economic theory of clubs', *Economica*, New Series, Vol. 32, No. 125 (1965), pp. 1–14.

9   Ogilvie, Sheilagh: *Institutions and European trade: merchant guilds 1000–1800*, Cambridge: Cambridge University Press, 2011, pp. 417, 426.

Further, as the institutions of marine insurance evolved, so too did they influence the evolution and actions of the institutions of state.

The methodology of insurance was dictated by merchant-insurers' custom, a fact contemporaneously recognised.[10] This customary practice was a component of the Law Merchant, an uncodified and flexible body of international rules embraced by merchants trading between national legal jurisdictions. The Law Merchant provided the rules of the game followed by merchant-insurers, and was widely recognised as a third body of English law, alongside common and civil law.[11] Within London's early underwriting community, this framework was usually sufficient to ensure the smooth operation of the market. Typically, when disputes arose they were resolved through a process of arbitration, and according to the judgements of members of the community disinterested in the specific case. The perceived intentions of the participants in specific situations, rather than rigid prescriptions of statute or ordinance, were given most weight. Specific custom was typically deemed to have been applied 'time out of mind', which in practice meant that applicable precedent was limited to the earliest which could be summoned from the knowledge and memory of the oldest adjudicator in the room.[12] Principles governed decision-making, which built flexibility into the system. When merchant practice changed in response to circumstances, the principles underlying merchant-insurers' customary practice could be invoked to respond in a way which reflected the nature of their product as a club good. When the merchant-insurers were the only buyers and sellers participating in the market for their club good, this system proved efficient at sharing loss-costs at the lowest price. The involvement of third-party adjudicators was rarely necessary.

London's market for insurance was an open one. Although closed risk-sharing insurance organisations (which can be characterised as mutual insurers) existed in London from at least the eighteenth century, and open insurance markets were active in other centres of trade (notably Liverpool), the main subject of this book is the merchant-insurers' broad, public market in London. Individuals could participate in this market as buyers, sellers, or both without being members of the merchant-insurer community. Because diversification of the underlying risks which comprised the insured risk pool was of benefit to all, and because every additional underwriter accepting risk from the pool spread insured risk more widely, the participation of outsiders as buyers and sellers was of general advantage. This occurred increasingly over the period under review, as both London's customer-base and the general take-up of insurance expanded.

However, outsiders were not always willing to play by the merchant-insurers' rules of the game, or to abide by arbiters' decisions. Such non-observance of these institutions defines the category of market participants hereafter called *outsiders*. Some outsider-sellers were merchants who also subscribed to insurance policies as underwriters. Others were merchants whose interest in insurance was purely as

---

[10] Rossi, Guido: *Insurance in Elizabethan England: the London code*, Cambridge: Cambridge University Press, 2016, p. 4.

[11] On which, much more below.

[12] Such as in the above-referenced 1601 'Act Conc'ninge matters of Assurances, amongste Merchantes'.

a financial speculation, even though they may also have been merchant-buyers of insurance. Some outsider-buyers were foreign merchants whose understanding of the Law Merchant relating to insurance was different from that of London's merchant-insurers. Others did not wish to observe the rules of the game, and sought satisfaction through the royal courts. Still other outsider-buyers wished simply to perpetrate fraud.

This division between insiders and outsiders is not new in the field of economic history. The classic usage is by Kindleberger and Aliber in their essential work *Manias, panics, and crashes*. They delineate 'two groups of speculators, the insiders and the outsiders', although they do so in a very different context.[13] Nor is the division simply theoretical. It was recognised by contemporaries. For example, in testimony to a parliamentary enquiry in 1810, the insurance-buying merchant John Inglis identified outsider-sellers: 'I perceive that the true principle of insurance is that of merchants meeting by some means or another to participate in their risks by insuring each other, and that a professional underwriter coming to Lloyd's without a known capital, is not of that class of insurers that merchants would wish to take upon their policies.'[14] Ceccarelli showed, based on the testimony of intermediaries during judicial proceedings in Italy, that outsiders seeking insurance were often required, as a sort of test, to underwrite a share of another merchant's policy in order to attract established underwriters to their risks. Quantitative evidence of this interplay can be found in Renaissance Florence, as well as in several other Italian markets during the fifteenth to seventeenth centuries. Ceccarelli explains that 'subscribing a policy is like buying the ticket to enter a "club-like" market'.[15]

Trust was a key element in relationships between merchant-insurers. Writing in 1622, Gerard Malynes, the merchant, mint-master, and government advisor on insurance and other matters, stated that 'Merchants Assuring each to other, may rescounter [settle through offset] their Premio's [premiums], in the accounts kept thereof between them; for herein is used great trust and confidence between them: And this appeareth also by every mans underwriting in the said Policy of Assurance, in these words, I *A. B.* am content with this Assurance (which God preserve)'.[16] Trust was the underpinning of credit, which Muldrew describes as 'a currency of reputation... the means by which such trust was communicated beyond local face-to-face dealing between people who knew each other'. Muldrew maps the trust-reputation-credit link onto the general population, noting, critically, that 'as the market expanded in the late sixteenth century such trust became harder to maintain, leading

---

13 Kindleberger, C. P. & Aliber, R. Z.: *Manias, panics, and crashes: a history of financial crises*, 5th edn, Hoboken: Wiley, 2005, p. 45.

14 *Report from the Select Committee on Marine Insurance (Sess. 1810)*, 5 March 1810, House of Commons, reprinted 11 May 1824, testimony of John Inglis, p. 50.

15 Personal communication; *Un mercato del rischio. Assicurare e farsi assicurare nella Firenze rinascimentale*, Venice: Marsilio, 2012, pp. 276–283.

16 Malynes, Gerard: *Consuetudo, vel, Lex Mercatoria: or, The Ancient Law-Merchant*, London: printed for T. Basset and R. Smith, 1685 (first published 1622), p. 112.

to an explosion of debt litigation'.[17] Problems could develop in the merchant-insurers' market when such trust began to break down. The resort to litigation became an increasingly common outcome.

A theoretical conception of the division between merchant-insurers and outsiders can be drawn from Braudel, who describes a two-tiered system of commerce. The lower tier, he proposes, is characterised by routine transactions of transparent but competitive exchange governed by a set of rules, and which involve only the buyer, the seller, and sometimes an intermediary. Such was the market of the merchant-insurers. In Braudel's higher tier, transparency, control, and the rules which limit profitability are sometimes avoided, or are not enforced. Transactions of great sophistication may be based on arbitrary financial arrangements. Chains are longer, and exchange may be unequal. Different mechanisms and agents govern the tiers.[18] During the later sixteenth century, as England's trade expanded in reach and complexity, a higher-tier insurance market comprising both buyers and sellers collided with that of the lower-tier merchant-insurers. Established institutions were shown to be inadequate to meet challenges posed by outsider-merchants. Disputes could not always be managed within the framework of custom and the Law Merchant. External mechanisms, principally those of the state, were found wanting.

Another useful and more recent historiographical categorisation can be drawn from Janeway's description of participants in what he dubs the 'three-player game' of enterprise. In it, sovereign *states* interact constantly with the *market economy* (which Janeway defines as the institutions enabling production) over resource allocations, while *financial capitalism* exploits discontinuities that may arise.[19] The distinction is useful since it neatly bisects the mechanisms of the market from speculations. The merchant-insurers, underwriting primarily to share risk, are part of the nuts and bolts of the market economy. Those underwriting purely for profit, or investing passively in insurance companies, are credit-providing financial capitalists, at least when their activity is not routine. Thus, they constitute another type of market outsider, distinguished by their motivations (rather than by their choice to reject the merchant-insurers' rules of the game). Their pursuit of economic rents made them the type of men Inglis saw as the wrong sort.

Recent historical analyses of insurance markets have employed the categorisation of individualists and collectivists to segment the players.[20] The approach can provide a useful framework for understanding relationships between market participants, but has several shortcomings.[21] The most significant of these is the fact that the range of behaviours of actual individual actors very often defies theoretical

[17]　Muldrew, Craig: *The economy of obligation: the culture of credit and social relations in early modern England*, Basingstoke: Palgrave Macmillan, 1998, p. 7.

[18]　Braudel, Fernand: *Afterthoughts on material civilization and capitalism* (Ranum, P., trans.), Baltimore: Johns Hopkins University Press, 1977, pp. 49–56, 62–64.

[19]　Janeway, William: *Doing capitalism in the innovation economy*, Cambridge: Cambridge University Press, 2013, pp. 3–5.

[20]　For example, Ebert, Christopher: 'Early Modern Atlantic trade and the development of maritime insurance to 1630', *Past & Present*, no. 213 (2011), pp. 87–213.

[21]　For a full discussion, see pp. 91 ff.

separation into black-or-white categories. Applying rigid, binary divisions can result in misleading interpretations, as will be shown below. Thus, the self-defining category of outsiders will be employed hereafter. It includes all those who do not play by the insiders' rules of the game. They may fall into the relatively subtle divisions set out by Braudel and Janeway. Others were simply criminals.

At the root of the entry of multiple groups of outsiders into London's insurance sector was a significant increase in demand. The patterns of England's international trade changed dramatically in the late sixteenth century, and overall volume increased in the seventeenth. These structural changes, along with the wartime perils arising from the English Civil and Anglo-Dutch wars, prompted many English merchants to begin to purchase insurance regularly. Demand was met with supply, as new underwriters entered the market. The capital cushion they provided was widely understood and broadly appreciated. The West Indies merchant William Freeman, for example, explained that 'it's my general custom to insure when adventures are anything considerable, whether at peace or war. When the danger is least, premium is low, and so I look upon it as a safe way.'[22]

By the time Freeman was writing, in 1680, insurance prices in London had already fallen dramatically in a much-developed market. Writing in 1716, Joseph Cruttenden, an apothecary of London, wrote to his New York correspondent that: 'For the time to come I resolve to ensure all I send out, which, in times of peace is not above 2 and ½ p Ct., which I think you nor noe other person can thinke much to allow'.[23] A century and a half before Cruttenden wrote, the cost of insuring cargoes from London to America was usually 6%. In the interim, a revolution in marine insurance pricing had taken place, reducing the cost of insuring vessels and cargo substantially, sometimes by as much as 75%.[24] This striking reduction in transaction costs over time must have contributed to economic growth. The unfettered entry of underwriting capital into the marine insurance business has had a significant impact on insurance pricing ever since. Similarly, the widespread withdrawal of capital, or its destruction due to major loss events, has had a similar but opposite effect, which continues to the present day. In 2018, for example, the withdrawal of multiple international speciality insurers (including numerous syndicates at Lloyd's of London as a direct result of an institutional intervention by the market's governing authorities) from various subclasses of the global marine insurance market following years of losses immediately forced a significant rise in prevailing international prices.

The tensions arising from the participation of groups of outsiders, both as buyers and as sellers, in this expanded market required institutional interventions into the otherwise obscure operation of the merchant-insurers' system. This book focuses on such interventions, which played an important role in the evolution of London

---

[22] William Freeman to John Bramley, 16 July 1680, in Hancock, David (ed.): *The letters of William Freeman, London Merchant, 1678–1685*, London: London Record Society, 2002, p. 162.

[23] Joseph Cruttenden to Thomas Barton, 28 September 1716, Letter book of Joseph Cruttenden, BOD MS Rawl Lett 66, 242.

[24] Leonard, A. B.: 'The pricing revolution in marine insurance', working paper presented at a general meeting of the Economic History Association, 2012.

marine insurance. Three interventions took place between 1547, the date at which the earliest extant insurance policy was underwritten in London, and 1824, when the market was reopened to the participation of corporate insurance bodies. The first of these was a series of initiatives made by the Privy Council and parliament between 1574/5[25] and 1601. It established new, formal institutions to govern practice, and was launched at the request of merchant-insurers in response to the actions of outsider-buyers. Ultimately the new institutions failed, in part because they inhibited the efficient operation of the market they were intended to support, but nonetheless they dominated the market for a relatively long period.

The second intervention was made for the profit of a subset of the outsider-sellers, men who fit Janeway's category of financial capitalists, rather than to improve governance of the market itself. The state's contribution to the intervention – the prohibition of further competitors against the merchant-insurers (which survived until 1824) – served to entrench the latter's position. However, it did not solve the outsider problem. A third intervention, comprising multiple initiatives, was made in the decades between the mid-eighteenth century and, roughly, the end of the American Revolutionary War. Parliament passed limited laws to govern practice, a series of common law principles were methodically established to provide certainty in situations which escaped the insiders' system, and the merchant-insurers themselves embarked upon a process of institution-building to form their own organisation to govern underwriting according to custom. The third intervention provided an enduring remedy to the escalating outsider problem.

Institutional changes arising from these interventions were implemented either by the merchant-insurers themselves or by the state at their behest. Here the state has several faces, including the monarch, the Privy Council, parliament, and the judges of various courts, whether of civil or common law. Relieving outsider challenges was the state's usual motivation, but parliament sometimes intervened to serve what could be described as the national interest (although agreement upon the substance of this interest was disputed). Ultimately, the institutional changes wrought by the state must account for an important proportion of London's forthcoming success as an international insurance centre, but that success owes as much or more to the state's lack of involvement in the functioning of the market. State interventions were few over the long period reviewed herein. When they were made effectively, they served to reinforce the old institutions of the merchant-insurers. It is characteristic of the origins and development of London marine insurance that custom was reintroduced or reinvigorated by interventions, including state interventions.

Such reaffirmations of merchant practice furnished certainty, the quest for which characterises the institution-building presented and analysed in this book. As London insurance expanded from its founding circle of merchant-insurers who traded based on trust and mutual interest to encompass the trading risks of the world's seaborne adventurers, the delivery of certainty became increasingly important. The old system worked when it was perceived to deliver certainty of outcomes. Because

---

[25] Events and documents from the period before the adoption of the new calendar and which occurred on days between 1 January and 25 March are rendered throughout this book in this fashion.

it was based on custom, uncodified law, and, in cases of dispute, judgments which could be enforced only through honour on the part of the participants and ostracism on the part of the community, it was unable always to deliver certainty when the market began to grow beyond the small community of London merchant-insurers, let alone when it began to serve foreign buyers. It was uncertain which courts would hear cases, or what judgments they would make; it was uncertain if the security of London institutions was sufficient to withstand large-scale losses, or if an alternative structure would be more robust; it was uncertain if measures to prevent abuse of the system were adequate, or if strengthened defensive systems would limit market flexibility sufficiently to render it uneconomic. All that appears to have been certain to contemporaries was that marine insurance was essential to trade, and that trade was critical to the common good.

It is worth here considering the nature of risk, especially in contrast to the more elusive property of uncertainty. The distinction, although often ignored, is well established. As is widely understood from a different context, the world is full of two kinds of mysteries – the unknown things that we are aware of, and the things we don't know that we don't know: the famous 'unknown unknowns'. A more elegant distinction between these two epistemological states of uncertainty and risk was set out by the economist Frank Knight in 1921. It yields striking practical implications for marine insurance. In principle, to render insurable an outcome – the manifestation of one of the perils named in an insurance policy – the characteristics of the uncertainties surrounding such an event must be known with sufficient confidence to transform them into risks. In other words, in principle, calculable risk can be transferred economically through conventional premium-based insurance, while uncertainty cannot. Knight stated that, in the case of risk,

> the distribution of the outcome in a group of instances is known (either through calculation *a priori* or from statistics of past experience), while in the case of uncertainty this is not true, the reason being in general that it is impossible to form a group of instances, because the situation dealt with is in a high degree unique … The application of the insurance principle, converting a large contingent loss into a smaller fixed charge, depends upon the measurement of probability upon the basis of a fairly accurate grouping into classes.[26]

Writing at almost exactly the same time, J. M. Keynes, in his masterful *A treatise on probability*, made the same distinction in a slightly different way. It is not possible, Keynes showed, to assign a numerical value to every instance of probability.

> Whether or not such a thing is theoretically conceivable, no exercise of the practical judgement is possible, by which a numerical value can actually be given to the probability of every argument. So far from our being able to measure them, it is not even clear that we are always able to place them in order of magnitude. Nor has any theoretical rule for their evaluation ever been suggested.[27]

---

[26] Knight, Frank: *Risk, uncertainty and profit*, Boston: Houghton Mifflin, 1921, pp. 233–235.

[27] Keynes, J. M.: *The collected writings of John Maynard Keynes, Vol. VIII: A treatise on probability*, Cambridge: Royal Economic Society, 1973 (1921), p. 29.

Keynes used legal and insurance-market examples to illustrate this point, and given the current topic, the latter is worth repeating. The 'arbitrary element' in some underwriting scenarios is great, he states, citing reinsurance rates offered in the Lloyd's market on the missing vessel *Waratah* in the summer of 1909.[28]

> The lapse of time made rates rise; the departure of ships in search of her made them fall; some nameless wreckage is found and they rise; it is remembered that in similar circumstances thirty years ago a vessel floated, helpless but not seriously damaged, for two months, and they fall. Can it be pretended that the figures which were quoted from day to day – 75 per cent, 83 per cent, 78 per cent – were rationally determinate, or that the actual figure was not within wide limits arbitrary and due to the caprice of individuals? In fact underwriters themselves distinguish between risks which are properly insurable, either because their probability can be estimated between comparatively narrow numerical limits or because it is possible to make a 'book' which covers all possibilities, and other risks which cannot be dealt with in this way and which cannot form the basis of a regular business of insurance – although the occasional gamble may be indulged in.[29]

The rigorous Keynes rather lets his analysis slip near the end of this illustration. While underwriters do indeed distinguish between risks which are properly insurable and those which are not, his description of the difference is flawed. Knightian risks, which can be probabilistically determined, are insurable. For uncertainties (such as the missing vessel) where this is not possible, at best a wager can be made. If it is possible to collect sufficient wagers to make a 'book' (a piece of terminology borrowed by Keynes directly from the jargon of gambling), the underlying act remains one of wager, not of insurance. The nature of the uncertainty has not changed. Further, it seems only a remote possibility that a 'book' covering all possibilities could ever be made in the practical world of insurance. Keynes offers the example of underwriters' offers on an election outcome in 1912:

> 60 per cent was quoted at Lloyd's to pay a total loss should Dr Woodrow Wilson be elected, 30 per cent should Mr Taft be elected, and 20 per cent should Mr Roosevelt be elected. A broker, who could effect insurances in equal amounts against the election of each candidate, would be certain at these rates of a profit of 10 per cent. Subsequent modifications of these terms would largely depend upon the number of applicants for each kind of policy.[30]

Even if a broker could balance his portfolio of contracts as Keynes describes, such an activity is 'in principle one of bookmaking', he concedes.[31] It is market-making in wagers, rather than genuine insurance. When the Bristol underwriter Abraham Clibborn accepted the 'risk' of 'Peace till 14th May 1772', however, he did not have

---

28 The insurance of insurers, or reinsurance, is an instrument to further spread exposure to underwriting losses.

29 Keynes, *Probability*, p. 25.

30 Keynes, *Probability*, p. 24.

31 Ibid.

an offsetting policy to pay out if war were declared.[32] It may be that the contract was called an insurance policy, the bookmaker an underwriter, and the market Lloyd's of London, but that does not make such wagers into insurance. English law specifies that such contracts are not insurance, because the beneficiaries possess no insurable interest in the outcome. Section 4 of the *Marine Insurance Act* 1906 specifies that: 'Every contract of marine insurance by way of gaming or wagering is void'.[33] This follows controversial legislation of 1746, which prohibited certain speculative insurances by requiring that buyers of policies possessed an 'insurable interest' in the object of the insurance.[34] In other words, from that year it was no longer legal to insure an outcome in which the buyer would have nothing beyond the policy itself to do with the object of the insurance.

The distinction between risk and uncertainty, and thus the insurability of a given outcome, was understood long before Knight's formal distinction was expressed. According to this distinction, insurance can operate only in the areas of uncertainty that have been translated into risk through quantification and statistical or probabilistic analysis, and where a sufficient number of homogeneous individual risks can be assumed by an individual risk-bearing entity – the underwriter – to ensure that pricing reflects actual likelihood of loss. In London's marine insurance market this was possible in the seventeenth and eighteenth centuries – leading to a steady decline in marine insurance pricing. The greater number of voyages undertaken and insured in the period allowed underwriters to undertake probabilistic assessments of the likelihood of loss (albeit in a crude, frequentist way), instead of relying on pure judgement alone. This resulted in more accurate, risk-based pricing, and thus a more affordable product. Second, the larger risk pool allowed underwriters to offer lower rates due to the simple advantages of risk diversification. Cheaper insurance attracted a larger, increasingly diverse group of customers, which in turn further increased the size of the risk pool. It was these pricing factors which were responsible for the increased uptake of marine insurance, and for its institutional evolution during the period.[35]

Law and lawmaking, and rules and rulemaking, are central to the discussion. As such, a hierarchy of illegality and prohibition is illustrative. On a continuum, the merchant-insurers' system involved the most minimal level of prohibition. Under voluntary adherence to the Law Merchant and decisions at arbitration, compliance to the rules is compelled only by the risk of lost honour, or ostracism by the merchant community. The resulting loss of credit could be catastrophic for an individual. The state may prohibit certain practices by deeming them illegal, but provide no sanction beyond their making void the offending contract. This renders it unenforceable at law, but does not prevent individuals from abiding by its terms. A higher level of legal sanction imposes civil penalties, typically monetary fines, for prohibited actions. At

---

[32] TNA C107/12, Risk books of Abraham Clibborn & Co., II, 10.

[33] 1906 c. 41, Reg 6 Edw 7.

[34] 19 Geo. II c. 37.

[35] And not exclusively, or even particularly, the growth of transatlantic trade, as has recently been asserted. Ebert, 'Early Modern Atlantic trade', pp. 87–213.

the highest level of illegality, punishment of criminal offences may include imprisonment or execution.

Merchant-insurers embraced the Law Merchant, but some of the handful of historians who have explored marine insurance in detail, and some contemporary commentators, have argued that the business lacked necessary regulatory structures. Bindoff, for example, claims that 'its unsystematic character is something to wonder at… it developed… with a minimum of control and was riddled with abuse and fraud'.[36] Outsiders sometimes challenged the merchant-insurers' system in this way, but the Law Merchant was indeed up to the job of governing routine market transactions, and even most exceptional cases. Some recent historians and economists have denied the very existence of the Law Merchant, an interpretation which can only fuel historiographical perceptions of the insurance market as unconstrained. In practice, the rules of the game which it provided constituted a comprehensive and very real dispute resolution framework, albeit one which for much of the period under review remained voluntary, which meant that some outsiders chose to ignore it.

Conferring appropriate exogenous enforcement authority for the insurance market by incorporating the Law Merchant into the formal practice of the royal courts proved a long and difficult challenge. The deterrence and punishment of fraudsters should have been addressed with relative simplicity through statute administered under the common law. However, dealing with this subset of the outsider-buyers was complicated by the extremely arcane nature of marine insurance contracts. It was very difficult for non-specialists to know if a criminal act had actually occurred. Even more difficult was providing judicial teeth to the Law Merchant customs which governed practice, without reducing the flexibility which contributed significantly to London underwriters' success. Circumstance multiplied this challenge: over the period under review, England's relatively flexible courts of civil law, which were most suited to deciding mercantile disputes, were in effect subsumed by her more rigid common law courts.

Supported by its flexibility and competitive pricing, London's insurance sector advanced to international leadership during the eighteenth century, as underwriters attracted foreign customers in increasing numbers, and London practice spread around the world. Before this, insurance was a multi-local sector. Convenience had been, for many buyers, the primary factor in their choice of market. Cover was often purchased at ports of lading. Before agency networks were established to enable the purchase of insurance from distant underwriters, local purchase was the only practical option in many places. Still, local markets could become leaders of practice. Antwerp was an important underwriting centre in the sixteenth century because its underwriters' customs provided an international standard, even though insuring in the city's bourse was a service supplied almost entirely to support the local trade of others: Antwerp's own merchant fleet was negligible.[37] Later, attracting foreign insurance risks benefitted London's insurers, as it had for Brabant underwriters.

---

[36] Bindoff, S. T.: 'The greatness of Antwerp', in Elton, G. R. (ed.): *New Cambridge Modern History, Vol. II: The Reformation*, Cambridge: Cambridge University Press, 1965, p. 65.

[37] Ibid., p. 62

Under basic portfolio theory, such risks fuelled a virtuous circle of price declines.[38] By increasing the diversity of London's risk pool, they helped to reduce the cost of the city's insurance product, which attracted more foreign risk. This circularity was not lost on contemporaries. 'The Cheapness of Insurances, and the Eagerness of Foreigners to insure here, reciprocally contribute to each other; we are often applied to, because we insure at an easy Rate, and we can insure at an easy Rate, because we are often applied to,' the parliamentarian William Guidott told the House of Commons in 1742.[39]

International leadership elevated London's insurance market into Braudel's higher commercial tier. The city and her insurance market (which during the middle of the eighteenth century had begun to concentrate physically in Lloyd's Coffee-house) had become what he describes (in translation) as a 'world-economy', one of several co existent and coherent economic zones. Braudel identifies such international markets through three defining characteristics: operation within a defined but large multinational space; a known pole, usually a city, which lies at the centre of the economy; and radiating subordinate zones.[40] This book takes the division further, perceiving world-economies within single sectors. As London merchant-insurers' reach extended, their version of ancient practice was strengthened, and grew to be widely understood, respected, and adopted. By the middle of the eighteenth century they controlled a world-economy in insurance. At this time London was emerging as the centre of Braudel's comprehensive European-centred world-economy, but her merchant-insurers had already established their international primacy. Ultimately, alongside this achievement, a world-law was adopted for insurance. It incorporated the merchant-insurers' medieval customs, and performed the Law Merchant's function of providing cross-border certainty.

London's insurance system thrived because it was effective (it worked), efficient (it was more affordable than alternatives), and flexible (its governing institutions allowed practice to match circumstances). Perhaps uniquely, London's leadership endured long after her place at the head of a broader Braudellian world-economy was relinquished. In 2018 London insurers underwrote roughly 19% of the world's international conventional marine hull insurance, nearly 11% of global cargo insurance, and 62% of its 'protection and indemnity' (mutual liability) insurance.[41] Measured by both volume and practice, London underwriters continue to hold an international lead, based on an inheritance of the institutional developments outlined in this book. The world-law for marine insurance also remains in place. It is not entirely

---

[38] First set out in Lowenfeld, H.: *Investment an exact science*, London: Financial Review of Reviews, 1907.

[39] Johnson, Samuel (attributed): 'Debate in the House of Clinabs, on the second reading of a bill to prevent inconveniences arising from the insurance of ships', *Gentleman's Magazine*, Vol. XII, January 1742, p. 12.

[40] Braudel, *Afterthoughts*, pp. 80–83.

[41] Seltmann, Astrid: 'Global Marine Insurance Report 2019', *Annual Conference Presentation*, International Union of Marine Insurers, September 2019, pp. 11, 22, 33.

global, but reaches far beyond the limits even of Britain's lost informal empire.[42] In many respects, marine insurance is transacted in the same way today as it was upon its introduction to London in the fifteenth century, although important technical, institutional, and exogenous developments have been introduced or imposed.

This book explores early developments in this continuum. It shows how the inward-looking, self-governing market of the merchant-insurers, in tandem and sometimes cooperation with the evolving authorities of the state in which it operated, responded to dramatic change. It argues that, over a period of more than two centuries, a series of major interventions which affected the market's ability to operate successfully in the face of change show, in retrospect, that neither a purely state solution nor a purely market solution constituted sufficient response. Instead, to ensure the continued smooth operation of a sector which all believed was critical to the nation, sympathetic state intervention, which both supported market initiatives and formalised established market solutions within state channels, ultimately created an environment in which London's marine insurance market was able to flourish. State involvement was essential, but it was useful only when it was limited, and when it backed tried-and-tested merchant institutions which suited the peculiar nature of marine insurance. The evolution of marine insurance in London thus provides an example of a mutually beneficial cooperation between merchants and the state. Together, in a virtuous circle, their institution-forming efforts contributed to the evolution of both. This was achieved in spite of noise from financial capitalists, and the ambitious greed of politicians.

Marine insurance and historiographical orthodoxies

The impact of marine insurance has reached well beyond its immediate effects: the protection and extension of merchants' capital, and the resulting increase in trade which that protection allows. The simple fact that insurance was seen to nurture trade ensured its general support during an era dominated by mercantilist economics. Broad consensus asserted that insurance was positive, and beneficial to the common good. Francis Bacon, that most practical of Elizabethan ministers, told parliament in 1601 that through insurance 'the safety of goods is assured unto the merchant. This is the lodestone that draws him out to adventure, and to stretch even the very punctilio of his credit'.[43] Around the same time the Privy Council declared that insurance 'moche importuneth the continewance and increase of trade within this realme'.[44] This was the received wisdom over centuries, such that in 1720, Attorney General Nicholas Lechmere advised the king that 'Insuring Ships and Merchandizes, especially in Times of War, is of the utmost Consequence to the

---

[42] As understood by Gallagher, John and Robinson, Ronald: 'The imperialism of free trade', *Economic History Review*, NS Vol. 6, No. 1 (1953), pp. 1–15.

[43] d'Ewes, Sir Simonds (ed.): 'Journal of the House of Commons: December 1601', *The Journals of all the Parliaments during the reign of Queen Elizabeth* (1682), London: History of Parliament Trust.

[44] TNA PC 2/26 f. 138, *Privy Council letter book*, 29 Mar. 1601.

Security and Encouragement of Trade'.[45] The English merchant John Weskett, in his 1781 *Complete digest of the theory, laws, and practice of insurance*, declared that trade could not continue without insurance: 'Commerce is indubitably the grand Source, from whence is derived all that enriches, strengthens, and adorns a State; and without Insurance, that commerce could never have been promoted, nor carried on; --nor can it ever proceed, unsupported by insurance.'[46]

Notwithstanding this high-level consensus about the importance of insurance, alternate views about how it ought to be transacted emerged and receded over the years. Defoe proposed, in his *Essay on Projects*, that insurance should be made compulsory, and rolled into his scheme for nationalisation and state coordination of England's shipping. Under his plan the Customs House, in exchange for a variable premium, would 'be obliged to pay and make good all losses, damages, averages, and casualties whatsoever, as fully as by the custom of assurances now is done'.[47] Defoe's plan attracted no recorded support. Other proposals sought to place insurance in the hands of a corporate enterprise, or a group of companies. The earliest in England dated from 1660, when royal approval was sought for a proposed 'Society for Sea Insurance'. It was to have a joint stock of £500,000. The proposal gained official approval, but a monopoly was refused, and without it, the petitioners abandoned their idea.[48] Other proposals of varying natures and ambitions were advanced, but the merchant-insurers' system prevailed.

War was nearly constant in the period under review. Britain was involved in major military actions for eighty-seven of the 125 years between 1689 and 1814, usually with countries which, during times of peace, were major trading partners.[49] Much of the conflict was at sea, and merchant shipping was targeted relentlessly. The ability to sustain trade during conflict was essential. Marine insurance had a critical role to play, although it has been largely overlooked in the relevant historical work. Commerce and conflict have not been so neglected, and lie at the centre of six factors which, in combination, form the core of the current historiographical orthodoxy

---

45 *The special report from the committee appointed to inquire into, and examine the several subscriptions for fisheries, insurances, annuities for lives, and all other projects carried on by subscription...* London: House of Commons, printed by Tonson, J., Goodwin, T., Lintot, B., and Taylor, W., 1720, Attorney General's Report, p. 40.

46 Weskett, John: *A complete digest of the theory, laws, and practice of insurance*, London: Printed by Frys, Couchman, & Collier, 1781, p. vi.

47 Note that Defoe did not propose a fixed premium of 4%, as stated by Barbour in her seminal article. Instead, he suggested a rate of 4% for voyages to Barbados, to be 'enlarged or taken off, in proportion to the voyage, by rules and laws to be printed and publicly known'. Defoe, Daniel: *An essay on projects* (1697), Project Gutenberg edition (unpaginated), www.gutenberg.org/cache/epub/4087/pg4087.html [Accessed 3 Dec. 2021]; Barbour, Violet: 'Marine risks and insurance in the seventeenth century', *Journal of Economic and Business History*, Vol. 1, 1928–1929, p. 577.

48 Bogatyreva, Anastasia: 'England 1660–1720: corporate or private?', in Leonard, A. B. (ed.): *Marine insurance: origins and institutions, 1300–1850*, Basingstoke: Palgrave Macmillan, 2016, pp. 183–185; for sources, see BOD MS Rawlinson A 478, Council of Trade report, 23 Jan. 1660/1, ff. 81.

49 Davis, Ralph: *English overseas trade, 1500–1700*, London: Macmillan, 1973, p. 49.

of Britain's divergence from her Continental rivals, and her advancing commercial primacy. These factors are the adoption of a 'blue-water' policy of national defence; the development of the 'fiscal-military state' characterised by a professional, transparent tax-raising bureaucracy; the establishment of a 'credible commitment' on the part of the king-in-parliament to respect property rights; the advance of a 'financial revolution' which provided the tools for military finance, capital formation, and overseas trade on a new scale; the rise of 'gentlemanly capitalism', a practical alliance of the landed gentry with a new commercial elite; and the evolution of the English state's relationship with the Dutch, which shifted from the open physical and commercial hostilities of three Anglo-Dutch trade wars to the anti-Bourbon alliance that followed 1688.

Blue-water policy

English governments from the later Tudors to the restored Stuarts favoured naval superiority in the Channel and the North Sea as England's primary instrument of defence against invasion. The royal fleet was augmented by merchantmen sufficiently armed to participate in the line of battle, and by lesser merchantmen which freely plundered rival trade under the state sanction of letters of marque. For example, Williams describes 'all' naval expeditions of Elizabeth's reign as 'joint-stock enterprise, mounted principally for profit, with the strategic safety of the realm as a secondary, but still important, objective.'[50] Intervention on the mainland, on the ground, to sway the European balance of power was a last resort. Requisite naval forces were funded through the profits of maritime trade.[51] Subsidising a Continental ally to divert nemeses on land was often an adjunct, minimising the need for standing armies. This 'blue-water policy' was 'cost-effective, practical, and mundane'.[52]

It was also cheap. Between 1585 and 1603, during sustained conflict with Spain, England spent an annual average of £55,000 on her navy, with which she crippled Spain's fleet, foiled an invasion, and destabilised the Spanish bullion *flota*. In contrast, Spain spent £500,000 per year in the Low Countries alone.[53] The combination of these tactics into a 'blue-water strategy' may well be a 'modern rationalisation of what had more to do with atavistic prejudice than rational calculation', as Rodger describes it, but William III retained its key characteristics, which were employed for over a century, while stepping-up land-based expeditionary action.[54] William III

---

[50] Williams, Penry: *The later Tudors, 1547–1603*, Oxford: Oxford University Press, 1995, p. 320.

[51] Davis, Ralph: *The rise of the English shipping industry in the seventeenth and eighteenth centuries*, Newton Abbot: David & Charles, 1962, pp. 300–304.

[52] Baugh, D. A.: 'Great Britain's "Blue-Water" policy, 1689–1815', *International History Review*, Vol. 10, No. 1 (1988), p. 41.

[53] Downing, B. M.: *The military revolution and political change: origins of democracy and autocracy in early modern Europe*, Princeton: Princeton University Press, 1992, p. 165.

[54] Rodger, N. A. M.: *The command of the ocean: a naval history of Britain, 1649–1815*, London: Penguin, 2004, p. 179.

and Anne began to express a desire to behave as a European power, which was manifest in their participation in those alliances intended to check the power of Louis XIV and the Bourbon dynasty. The Nine Years' War (1688–1697) and the War of the Spanish Succession (1701–1714) contributed significantly to the development of the English (soon British) state.[55] As Brewer has argued, few English contemporaries 'envisioned the transformation that the wars would wreak on the nation's institutions'.[56]

One institution so affected was marine insurance, as naval action caused increased loss to English shipping, and began to prompt greater take-up of marine insurance. It was during this period that England consolidated its naval and oceanic trade supremacy. England encouraged and sometimes paid for European allies to engage France on the Continental battlefield, while concentrating herself on naval warfare. The policy saw trade fuel naval growth, and in the early eighteenth century 'power followed profit', with the growing importance of mercantile interests, and a widespread ideology supporting aggressive commercial expansion. The War of the Spanish Succession saw Britain add the expansion of commercial interests to its goal of damping French power; the Treaty of Utrecht brought new colonial possessions, which extended Britain's ability to protect her worldwide trade. France made up ground in the 1730s, but reinvigoration of Britain's blue-water policy had contributed significantly, by the end of the Seven Years War, to her naval and trade dominance.[57]

The role of insurance in this strategy is significant. Insurers worked indirectly to encourage the safe execution of trade, through a system of incentive pricing. Underwriters charged a lower rate, or returned a portion of the premium paid, when in wartime vessels travelled in convoy. Underwriters' role in the promotion of merchant convoys was widespread and much discussed.[58] Insurers also supported the offensives. Merchantmen acted as a de facto naval auxiliary, supported by the insurers who supplied the contingent capital which allowed men to venture comfortably beyond commerce and into conflict. Whether in the line of battle or in the harrying of enemy shipping under letters of marque, the private capital of merchant-insurers was levered to underwrite the public project of naval warfare during the period of Britain's blue-water approach to European relations. With these measures, passive trade was doubly insulated from the heightened risk of financial disaster during wartime, while the capital invested in aggressive action against enemy commerce in the form of privateering – state-sanctioned commerce-raiding perpetrated against the enemy's merchant marine, which was rampant in wartime throughout the period of review – was similarly protected.

---

[55] For a full discussion of this argument, see Brewer, John: *The sinews of power: War, money and the English state, 1688–1783*, London: Routledge, 1989.

[56] Brewer, *Sinews*, p. 138.

[57] Ibid., pp. 168–175.

[58] See pp. 173–174, 190–191. For a thorough analysis, see my Masters dissertation: Leonard, A. B.: *Marine insurance and the rise of British merchant influence, 1649–1748*, unpublished Masters dissertation, University of Cambridge, 2011.

Taxing seaborne trade, the business supported by insurance, to fund naval activity had been royal practice since Edward I imposed the *maltote*, a wool export tax, in the late thirteenth century. This distant arrangement is relevant to the later evolution of London's insurance market. The tax was granted by merchants in exchange for trade protection, and was intended for naval finance.[59] The original bargain was more complicated than a simple fee-for-service deal. The *maltote* was usually accompanied by export monopolies granted to a cadre of merchants, the Company of the Staple, in exchange for loans. The commercial community was divided between these merchant-financiers and the remaining merchants, who were excluded from monopolies. The latter, a great majority, sought influence indirectly through Members of Parliament. Eileen Power argues that 'a complete antagonism grew up between financial capitalists, on the one hand, and the main body of wool merchants on the other'. The result was a Commons 'enormously strengthened' through the addition of merchant interests and their consolidation with those of the 'knights of the shires'.[60] Both this division, and the trading merchants' alliance with country gentry, foreshadowed debates following the Glorious Revolution over the structure of marine insurance. The schism was not between rivals, but between groups representing different economic interests, which falls neatly into Braudel's characterisations of a two-tiered economic system.

The fiscal-military state

Financing the blue-water policy through trade levies required an effective collection system. England developed a sophisticated and relatively transparent state bureaucracy, one which served the interests of the new institutions of representative government, rather than the monarch and individual patent-holders. Brewer encompassed this achievement in his construct of the 'fiscal-military state'. Borrowing for military purposes was 'both comparatively cheap and relatively simple' due to the effective tax system, which was free from ubiquitous venality, and was levied against both internal and external trade.[61] Against this robust revenue stream, government borrowing increased. From 1688/9, the crown was able to raise income and expenditure to unprecedented levels, despite the political independence of the Commons. The proportion of wartime expenditure funded through debt was 31% during the War of the Spanish Succession, and reached 41% during the American War.

However, Brewer underplays the role of private merchants, including the contribution of merchant-insurers, in the new system, which he describes as a '*public fiscal-military apparatus remarkably untainted by private interests*'.[62] He argues

---

[59] Mann, M.: *The sources of social power, vol. I: a history of power from the beginning to A.D. 1760*, Cambridge: Cambridge University Press, 1986, p. 427.

[60] Power, Eileen: *The wool trade in English medieval history*, Oxford: Oxford University Press, 1941, pp. 78–85.

[61] Brewer, *Sinews*, pp. 114, 137–138.

[62] Brewer's italics. Ibid., p. 139.

that 'states had to depend on domestic resources, in the form of money and men'.[63] Insurance multiplied those resources. The merchant-insurers' contingent capital extended enormously the risks which could be borne by those commercial actors venturing into danger to pursue projects, such as privateering, in which their interests were aligned with those of the state. In addition, the capital accumulated by merchant-insurers and conserved to fund the payment of future claims was very often invested in state debt instruments, such that by the time of the French and Napoleonic Wars, insurers were among the largest groups of lenders to the state.[64]

Brewer sees the combination of naval and fiscal power, with the navy as the mechanism and international trade as the object of military strategy, as unique and critical to British development.[65] O'Brien and Duran expand upon the theme, arguing that Britain did not achieve naval supremacy through the superiority of her vessels, armaments, or administration, but rather through better finance. Her advantage was the 'scale, scope, and persistence of investment by the state in fleets of warships and their onshore infrastructure', augmented by successful cooperation between the merchant and military marines. Britain both possessed the institutions and the political consensus required for sustained capital creation in her fleet.

These factors were also sufficient to develop and consolidate a maritime sector which at once was protected by the navy, and which generated trade profits adequate to maintain Europe's largest battle fleet.[66] However, the authors ascribe no credit to the critical role of the contingent-capital instrument provided through insurance as a component of this ability to maintain capital creation in the merchant fleet, despite its primary importance. They also miss its role in financing the king's armies. For example, comptrollers of the army paid military victualling contractors an allowance for the purchase of private insurance to cover military supplies while in shipment. The peacetime rate of 1.5% rose to 4% in 1741, and to 10% in 1744.[67]

Observed more broadly, insurance served to spread the war losses of the few over the capital of the many. Brewer observes that during the wars of 1689 to 1713 'the French seemed to have the better of the battle against seaborne trade'.[68] This is true in terms of absolute vessel numbers and values, but does not consider the impact of the losses. He notes that ransom of vessels, a widely insured peril, 'inflicted serious financial losses on those who had invested in a voyage. And, because any individual vessel was owned by a substantial number of investors, shipping losses

---

[63] Ibid., p. xviii.

[64] See pp. 206 ff., also Leonard, A. B.: 'Marine insurers, the City of London, and financing the Napoleonic Wars', in Hoppit, J., Needham, D., and Leonard, A. B. (eds): *Money and markets: essays in honour of Martin Daunton*, Woodbridge: Boydell, 2019, pp. 55–70.

[65] Brewer, *Sinews*, p. 172.

[66] O'Brien, P. K. and Duran, X.: 'Total factor productivity for the Royal Navy from victory at Texal to triumph at Trafalgar', Working Paper No. 134/10, London School of Economics, Feb. 2010, pp. 2, 36.

[67] Bannerman, Gordon E.: *Merchants and the military in eighteenth century Britain: British army contracts and domestic supply, 1739–1763*, London: Pickering & Chatto, 2008, pp. 54–55.

[68] Brewer, *Sinews*, p. 198.

were widely felt.'[69] The latter point is true, but the whole misrepresents the situation. Ownership was widely spread to make losses which occurred less painful to more sufferers. The insurance of each of those ownership shares, which was commonplace by the middle of the eighteenth century, spread the pain even more widely, perhaps between scores of individual underwriters. France may have got the better of the battles, but the significance of the financial damage inflicted was not commensurate to the blows landed, since the cost was shared widely due to the efficacy of the London marine insurance market. Britain did not enjoy naval dominance for the first half of the long eighteenth century, but the insurance system supporting her merchant navy acted as a defender of the continuity of commerce which was at least as important as convoys, and should be recognised as one of the important factors contributing to the achievement of that dominance (partly because her strategic competitors paid much more for cover, as will be shown).

Credible commitment

Britain's ability to raise state finance has been extensively investigated and debated, and linked to relations between monarch, state, and the commercial community. North and Weingast's seminal work on the subject argues that a 'sovereign or government must not merely establish the relevant set of rights, but must make a credible commitment to [maintain] them'. They claim that the evolution, after 1688/9, of 'institutions of representative government' critical to controlling the levers of state power revealed, in their being grasped, a merging of interest between the landed and merchant classes. 'The success of the propertied and commercially-minded interests led to institutions that simultaneously mitigated the motive underlying the crown's drive to find new sources of revenue, and also greatly constrained the behaviour of the government (now the "king-in-parliament" rather than the king alone).'[70] O'Brien doubts the significance of 1688/9, arguing that constitutional and administrative changes implemented between the Civil War and the revolution provided the foundations of the emerging 'fiscal state'.[71] Other work questions the entire credible commitment theory.[72] Hoppit argues that property rights became *less* secure under post-revolutionary parliaments, as increasing 'compulsory alienation', enacted by parliaments to satisfy private commercial opportunities, led to

---

[69] Ibid.

[70] North, D. C. and Weingast, B. R.: 'Constitutions and commitment: the evolution of institutions governing public choice in England', *Journal of Economic History*, Vol. 49, No. 4 (1989), pp. 803, 829–830.

[71] O'Brien, P. K.: 'Fiscal exceptionalism: Great Britain and its European rivals from Civil War to triumph at Trafalgar and Waterloo', Working Paper No. 65/01, London School of Economics, Oct. 2001, pp. 3–4.

[72] For a sustained critique, see Coffman, D., Leonard, A., and Neal, L. (eds): *Questioning 'credible commitment': perspectives on the rise of financial capitalism*, Cambridge: Cambridge University Press, 2013. See especially Leonard, Adrian: 'Contingent commitment: The development of English marine insurance in the context of New Institutional Economics, 1577–1720', pp. 48–75.

more 'flexible' property rights. It was these *eroded* rights that were critical to divergence, and not an imagined new commitment to uphold them rigidly.[73]

While the power to usurp property rights might simply have shifted from palace to parliament, merchants certainly did increase their sway over national institutions, as Acemoglu, Johnson, and Robinson argue.[74] An example is the merchant-insurers' success, apparently achieved simply by voting with their feet, in reverting from the governance of the state-convened Court of Assurance to the long-established Law Merchant.[75] Such examples of institutional development are not related to commitments underpinning property rights, but instead to the gradual decline of an economic approach characterised by royal self-interest and prerogative, and their eventual replacement by parliamentary power, a process which Ekelund and Tollison argue began in the mid-sixteenth century, and attribute to the oppressive costs the former system brought.[76] However, the latter approach was not necessarily respectful of private property rights, as Hoppit shows, nor did it end monopoly privilege under royal prerogative, as proved by the 1720 grant of exclusive rights under royal charter to the corporate underwriting of marine insurance.[77]

Overall, when facing the outsider challenges critical to the institutional development of London insurance, the state's responses map a journey *away* from commitment until about the middle of the eighteenth century. The departure gathered pace as the Glorious Revolution receded into history. The pre-revolutionary monarch behaved in a way which was neither rent-seeking nor confiscatory, and instead responded constructively to the challenges faced by merchant-insurers. In 1720, the crown returned to naked rent-seeking behaviour. As Britain's fiscal-military state developed, the security of merchant shipping, fundamental to the sustained flow of customs revenue which underpinned an important share of state debt repayment, was an important backstop to credible commitment. Still, the actions of the king-in-parliament did not always exhibit credibility to those who ventured their capital in support of that security.[78] Further, in the example of marine insurance North and Weingast's unity of interest between the ruling landed and financing merchant classes is shown also to reflect a concrete level of mutually beneficial interaction. Merchants and the state cooperated actively in the arena of institutional development to ensure merchant-insurers' business could be transacted more efficiently – for example through the shaping of law – to benefit the insurance market (rather than insurers or their customers specifically; logically since together they comprised, for the most part, the same body of merchants). As has been shown, this

---

[73] Hoppit, Julian: 'Compulsion, compensation and property rights in Britain, 1688–1833', *Past and Present*, No. 210 (2011), pp. 93–95.

[74] Acemoglu, D., Johnson, S., & Robinson, J.: 'The rise of Europe: Atlantic trade, institutional change, and economic growth', *American Economic Review*, Vol. 95, No. 3 (2005), pp. 546–579.

[75] See p. 106.

[76] Ekelund, R. B. and Tollison, R. D.: *Politicized economies: monarchy, monopoly, and mercantilism*, College Station: Texas A&M University, 1997, p. 223.

[77] See p. 151.

[78] For the complete argument, see Leonard, 'Contingent commitment'.

underpinned the finance of trade, and therefore the finance of the state. This inter-action introduces a new dimension to our understanding of the fiscal-military state by revealing a new, deeper layer of cooperation between merchants and state actors.

The financial revolution

Financial market developments of this period, likewise often regarded as products of 1688/9, are widely accepted as a 'financial revolution'. The financial settlement of 1690 set down the monarch's income, and parliament subsequently held 'the power of the purse'.[79] Thereafter, the use of annuity-based debt instruments was expanded, and they were traded in a robust secondary market. By facilitating borrowing under liquid, long-term instruments against public, rather than royal, income streams, these developments allowed Britain to spend substantially more on warfare than had previously been possible under the unleveraged taxation system. Government debt instruments were continuously refined until the issue in 1751 of the 'nearly ideal security', the 3% consol.[80] This, Dickson argues, allowed Britain to withstand the French onslaught of the long eighteenth century.[81] It certainly helped, but the refinement of financial instruments for risk transfer – marine insurance – was also essential. It kept merchants from bankruptcy. Their survival meant that, despite war, the British economy grew in the decades after the revolution,[82] and customs income continued to flow.

The importance of the merchant-insurers' extension to seaborne traders of con-tingent capital in wartime, both to finance their commerce and their sanctioned raiding, is enormously under-represented when compared to the attention lavished by historians upon the post-revolutionary systems of public credit granted to the state to finance similar activities. Both involved the raising of private capital in liquid markets, from private sources motivated by returns, to fund the public projects of the state. A strong link between the two, the investment of insurance funds in public debt instruments, has rarely been discussed in the context of the financial revolu-tion, and never in depth. It was a strong link, as the connection between the South Sea Company and London's corporate marine insurance duopolists, the London Assurance and the Royal Exchange Assurance, proves. Like the South Sea Company itself, the companies of 1720 became so embroiled in the politics of the financial rev-olution – bound inextricably as those politics were to the financing of Britain's eight-eenth-century military adventures – as to be diverted from the primary commercial purposes indicated by their names. The link appears with even greater solidity through insurers' substantial investments in government debt instruments, which

79   Roberts, C.: 'The constitutional significance of the financial settlement of 1690', *Historical Journal*, Vol. 20, No. 1 (1977), p. 76.

80   Neal, L.: *The rise of financial capitalism: international capital markets in the age of reason*, Cambridge: Cambridge University Press, 1990, p. 14.

81   Dickson, P. G. M.: *The financial revolution in England, a study in the development of public credit 1688–1756*, London: Macmillan, 1967, p. 9.

82   John, A. H.: 'War and the English economy, 1700–1763', *Economic History Review*, New Series, Vol. 7, No. 3 (1955).

constituted a second, robust contribution by underwriters to the fiscal-military state, in this case facilitated by the liquid debt instruments which formed a centrepiece of the financial revolution in England.[83]

Gentlemanly capitalism, informal empire, and the imperialism of free trade

Long before the financial revolution, 'trade capitalism' had created, in towns across Europe, a new class of individuals who possessed power disconnected from the rule of established patrician families.[84] Harris has described the 'appearance of a new force in politics, that of the "monied interest", men who had made their fortunes' in financial capitalism.[85] But the body of wealthy merchants emerging in England was not completely distinct from the aristocracy, as commercial classes were in some societies elsewhere. An evolving practical link between the landed and merchant classes is observed by Cain and Hopkins, in what they describe as 'gentlemanly capitalism'. Invoking Schumpeter, they argue that Britain's rulers changed their ' "profession and function" ' in the seventeenth and eighteenth centuries, through a commercial 'union between land and the market' based, in part at least, on shared gentlemanly ideals.[86] The financial services sector lay at the heart of this alliance.[87]

The theoretical framework appears to dismiss the influence of industrial capitalists, which is not supported by the evidence.[88] However, the contention that a series of partnerships between merchants and members of the gentry asserted increasing dominance over commerce from the later seventeenth century bears much scrutiny. As wealth arrived, alongside rank, as a determinant of class, the capitalist and political interests of the two groups often coincided. By 1700, landowners and prominent London merchants had formed 'interconnexions' – alliances often based on common interests in trade, finance, or both, forged to advance such concerns in parliament, and which sometimes broadened government's view of 'the national interest'.[89] Such cross-class interconnections are evident in early eighteenth-century

---

[83] On these investments, see pp. 206 ff.

[84] Pohl, H.: 'Economic powers and political powers in early modern Europe: theory and history', in Cavaciocchi, S. (ed.): *Poteri economici e poteri politici, secc. XIII–XVIII*, Florence: Le Monnier, 1999, p. 61.

[85] Harris, Tim: *Politics under the late Stuarts: party conflict in a divided society, 1660–1715*, London: Longman, 1993, p. 162.

[86] Citing Schumpeter's 'Sociology of imperialism', in *Imperialism and the social classes*, 1951. Cain, P. J. and Hopkins, A. G.: *British imperialism: Innovation and expansion, 1688–1914*, Harlow: Longman 1993, pp. 15, 32.

[87] Explicitly including insurance, although the authors failed to employ any of the abundant examples.

[88] See, for example, Daunton, M. J.: 'Gentlemanly capitalism and British industry 1820–1914', *Past & Present*, No. 122 (1989), pp. 119–158.

[89] Mingay, G. E.: *English landed society in the eighteenth century*, London: Routledge, 1963, pp. 11, 263.

enterprises intended to win monopoly rights over underwriting.[90] As joint-stock companies proliferated and the South Sea Company affair approached its climax, two gentlemanly capitalists, the Lords Onslow and Chetwynd, joined with leading financial capitalists to raise subscriptions for joint-stock insurers which, they argued, would support trade, and thus benefit the nation.[91]

Later, as London's underwriting practices were spread by merchants throughout the British commercial realm, comprising its formal empire and the 'informal empire' defined by Gallagher and Robinson, foreign capitalists were drawn into new, fundamentally British insurance ventures. Gallagher and Robinson saw trade as the great driver of imperial expansion, arguing that 'British industrialisation caused an ever-extending and intensifying development of overseas regions', which they characterised as the 'Imperialism of Free Trade'. They noted too that such expansion was not always successful, as in China, where 'spectacular exertions of British policy… did little to produce new customers'.[92] Yet much was gained. British merchants established enduring commercial bodies and networks, including for insurance underwriting, which brought local elites into their commercial realm as multilevel participants. I have characterised this as 'peripheral gentlemanly capitalism'.[93] Bayly called historians to look beyond the imperialism of free trade to the finance of the military-industrial state, which bankrolled its growing garrisons by capturing local wealth. He points to the opium trade of the India agency houses as a source of pay for Bengal officers, a trade facilitated by the risk transfer achieved through insurance.[94]

The English & the Dutch

To the west, the expanding Atlantic economy fuelled England's divergence through a process of Smithian growth which Ormrod emphasises was 'induced and backed by strong state support, including armed force'. By the end of the seventeenth century, Dutch merchants, who had not enjoyed unambiguous state backing of commerce, became reliant on English trade networks. Many chose to stay in the game by funnelling their trade capital through mercantile joint-ventures in London.[95] Over the next century the city, which had successfully emulated Amsterdam's methods of international commerce, accepted sufficient Dutch financial investment to help

---

[90] See pp. 136 ff.

[91] As, for example, in the anonymous pamphlet *Reasons humbly offer'd by the Societies of the Mines-Royal, &c. who Insure Ships and Merchandize, with the Security of a Deposited Joint-Stock*, London, *c.*1720.

[92] Gallagher and Robinson, *The imperialism of free trade*, pp. 5, 10.

[93] Leonard, A. B.: 'Underwriting British trade to India and China, 1780–1835', *Historical Journal*, Vol. 55, No. 4 (2012), p. 998.

[94] Bayly, C. A.: 'The first age of global imperialism, *c.*1760–1830', *Journal of Imperial and Commonwealth History*, Vol. 26, No. 2 (1998), p. 41.

[95] Ormrod, David: *The rise of commercial empires: England and the Netherlands in the age of mercantilism, 1650–1770*, Cambridge: Cambridge University Press, 2003, pp. 336–351.

Britain sustain its Continental wars with minimum economic dislocation.[96] By the mid-eighteenth century the nations' capital markets were closely integrated.[97] London had modified aspects of its fundamentally Italian insurance practices with custom received from Antwerp and Amsterdam, but the insurance markets of the Low Countries were overtaken by competition from London. Amsterdam's market was disturbed by financial crises, war, and political and naval events which led, by the later eighteenth century, to 'commercial acatalepsy' among her underwriters.[98] In 1720 two Englishmen launched *Maatschappij van Assurantie*, which became Rotterdam's municipal insurer, and survives to the present day.[99] In combination, the result of these developments in Anglo-Dutch relations was that 'the English merchant class was able to grow rich [and] to accumulate capital... in the century after 1660'.[100]

The lurching but continuous development of London's insurance institutions, the products of a cooperative approach between merchants and the state, should be added to the six factors discussed above. Like each of them, it overlaps with and supports each of the others. It was of equal importance to British divergence, linking and supporting these established branches of orthodox historiography at various and converging levels. Insurance allowed the nation's international commerce to proceed profitably, especially during wartime, by protecting merchants from financial ruin due to the total loss of their trading capital. In the face of conscious attempts to destroy Britain's military capacity through persistent attacks on her trade, insurance kept goods moving. The advantage traders gained through competitive insurance pricing was significant. Few historians have acknowledged this advantage, although it is hinted at by Price, who observes in passing that 'the regularity and low rates of insurance in peacetime, not only reduced transaction costs but made forward calculations much easier' for British merchants.[101]

It was, however, thoroughly understood by contemporaries. Alvise Contarini, Venetian ambassador to the Dutch Republic, wrote *c.*1625 that the Dutch, whose aim was 'to secure the command of the sea everywhere' through their improved navy, employed better-quality vessels and better-trained seamen. 'This hits the English, Hamburgers and others hard, because insurance on Dutch vessels is two or three

---

[96] John, 'War and the English economy', p. 343; O'Brien, P.: 'Mercantilism and imperialism in the rise and decline of the Dutch and British economies 1585–1815', *De Economist*, Vol. 148, No. 4, 2000, p. 472.

[97] Neal, *Rise of financial capitalism*, pp. 145–146.

[98] Spooner, Frank: *Risks at Sea: Amsterdam insurance and maritime Europe, 1766–1780*, Cambridge: Cambridge University Press, 1983, p. 115.

[99] Crowhurst, Patrick: 'Marine insurance and the trade of Rotterdam 1755–63', *Maritime History*, Vol. 2, No. 2 (1972), p. 140.

[100] Davis, Ralph: 'English foreign trade, 1660–1700', *Economic History Review*, New Series, Vol. 7, No. 2 (1954), p. 163.

[101] Price, J.: 'What did merchants do? Reflections on British overseas trade, 1660–1790', *Journal of Economic History*, Vol. 49, No. 2, *The Tasks of Economic History* (1989), p. 279.

per cent less than on those of other nations.'[102] This English disadvantage was rapidly inverted: insurance became a distinct advantage. London's insurers ruled the marine insurance roost, while her foreign competitors paid more, to the benefit of London underwriters. 'At this Time, the *Præmiums* given in *London* for insuring Ships and Goods are much lower than in any other part of *Europe*, and therefore many Orders for insuring in *London* are sent from foreign Parts, whereas formerly [the] great part of our Adventures were forced to be insured abroad', the Attorney General wrote in 1720.[103]

In following the development of insurance in London, this book directly modifies the six historiographical orthodoxies, and touches too upon others, such as the evolution of English commercial law. The evolution of jurisdiction over insurance disputes reveals new dimensions of the contest between common and civil law, and the fundamental importance of the Law Merchant to England's foundational commerce. Overall, it shows how the state and the market, together in cooperation, ultimately dealt satisfactorily with significant challenges, in a way that allowed the business of insurance to thrive and expand. A danger of whiggishness lurks, but the story is one of enduring success.

This conclusion moves towards a broader one which can be drawn from the study of early modern marine insurance in England. From 1649, the country was stepping towards economic and political divergence, the phenomenon marked by England's advance into empire and precocious industrialisation along a path taken neither by Asia nor Africa, nor, later, by western European countries. 'Adventurers' routinely turned, in growing numbers, to London's unparalleled concentration of underwriting capital and expertise to insure their ships and cargoes. During wartime, when enemies preyed upon commercial shipping, the financial protection provided by marine insurance was not always sufficient on its own. The physical defence of merchantmen became essential to the operation of Britain's insurance system, and thus to the continuation of her international trade.

The intersection of insurance and trade protection is clear at the point of underwriting: premium rates escalated during conflicts, but if ships sailed in government-organised convoys escorted by navy vessels, prices were dramatically reduced. This made wartime marine insurance both financially viable for underwriters, and affordable for buyers. A powerful English navy dedicated to trade protection was thus crucial to merchants. They used their emerging cooperation with the state, garnered through mutual interest in the profits and benefits of burgeoning overseas trade, to secure allocations of naval vessels for the defence of their ships and goods. It was never enough – many thousands of merchantmen were captured by privateers and belligerent navies – but as this book shows, London's superior marine insurance system prevented her enemies from achieving their strategic objective of destroying her capacity to wage war by ravishing trade. English merchants flourished.

---

[102] Bibl. Comunale di Treviso. MS. 996, Busta 4: 'Some extracts from a Relation of the Netherlands by Alvise Contarini, Appendix II', *Calendar of State Papers Relating to English Affairs in the Archives of Venice*, Vol. 19: 1625–1626 (1913), pp. 609, *British History Online*, www.british-history.ac.uk [Accessed 3 Dec. 2021].

[103] Emphasis in original. *The special report of 1720*, Attorney General's Report, pp. 25–26.

The role of insurance in changing relationships of control over the navy shows how underwriting practice fuelled merchants' use of their developing political power to effect the institutional modifications which contributed to British divergence.[104] The development of a world system of capitalist commerce is no longer embraced as an entire explanation of the economic growth gap which developed between western Europe, especially Britain, and the rest of the world in the modern era, yet the international trade pursued by the rising merchant class was undeniably important. This was known even in the seventeenth century, when English merchants evolved from a small group whose efforts were exploited by monarchs for immediate gain into a larger, more influential class, whose economic role was understood to be critical to national welfare. The merchants used their new importance to mount a sustained challenge to feudal power structures rooted in land ownership. The profits and benefits of trade allowed them to foster the development of capitalist institutions of commerce and politics necessary for modern economic growth.[105]

This book shows not only that marine insurance was a lynchpin upon which the system turned, but reveals complex ways in which the development of the emerging institutions of the state was influenced by merchant practice, consensus, and input. When the state created legal institutions to govern marine insurance practice, it did so with merchants' active participation and counsel, a practice only occasionally mirrored in other nations. That this occurred so consistently in the case of insurance can be attributed to the near-complete acknowledgement that it was beneficial to the nation, and that the incumbent system built during the late medieval period was efficient and efficacious.

Acemoglu, Johnson, and Robinson argued that income arising from commerce 'strengthened new merchant groups, and opened the way for changes in political institutions'. Profits accruing to the expanding merchant bourgeoisie allowed them to 'demand and obtain significant institutional reforms protecting their property rights'.[106] Under their influence, English society was developing such that wealth, rather than social rank alone, could determine class.[107] By the mid-eighteenth century, great merchants 'could now vie with duke or earl' in material respects.[108] Brenner outlined the advance of influence among London's new class of international traders that began during the Commonwealth.[109] More recently, O'Brien argued that

---

[104] Leonard, A. B.: *Marine insurance and the rise of British merchant influence, 1649–1748*, unpublished Masters dissertation, University of Cambridge, 2011.

[105] Acemoglu, D., Johnson, S., & Robinson, J.: 'The rise of Europe: Atlantic trade, institutional change, and economic growth', *American Economic Review*, Vol. 95, No. 3 (Jun. 2005), pp. 546–579; Allen, R. C.: *The British industrial revolution in global perspective*, Cambridge: Cambridge University Press, 2009, p. 4.

[106] Acemoglu *et al.*, 'The rise of Europe'.

[107] Wilson, C.: *England's apprenticeship 1603–1763*, second edition, Harlow: Longman, 1984, p. 5.

[108] Mingay, G. E.: *English landed society in the eighteenth century*, London: Routledge, 1963, pp. 11, 264.

[109] Brenner, R.: 'The Civil War politics of London's merchant community', *Past & Present*, No. 58 (Feb. 1973).

reconstruction of the English state following the Civil War 'forged political consensus among England's wealthy elites for an altogether stronger and more centralised state, above all to maintain order and political stability, but also to afford greater protection for the economy's growing commercial interests overseas'.[110] This book shows that marine insurance was a critical component of such protection, and constituted a specific national advantage. Further, O'Brien noted a critical connection overlooked by Acemoglu *et al.*: 'gains from overseas trade… from the mid-seventeenth century onwards flowed from the creation of conditions for the reconstruction of the realm's fiscal constitution and a massive uplift in expenditures by the state upon a standing navy'.[111] Marine insurance played an essential role in underpinning the profits of overseas trade.

This book shows not only a cohesion within rising merchant influence in a period of rapid political and commercial change, but reveals the pragmatic, non-pecuniary explanation for the developments which indeed allowed traders' sons, by the eighteenth century, to dance with the daughters of dukes and earls. It was not only that they had acquired a material wealth through commerce which vied with that of the landed gentry, and had developed enterprise from which they could profit. It was not simply that their influence expanded. Merchants and their ways – their institutions – presented those who were forming the English state (whether consciously or otherwise) with a set of institutional approaches which would add value if adopted more broadly and were in part applied (along with a host of others, of course) to create hybrids which mirrored its success. Indeed, as the period progressed many merchants were able to join the ranks of those who were actively to steer English state formation. The merchant-insurers' institutional system was efficient, practical, and flexible. Its principles, applied more broadly, would and could advantage the state. Championed by individuals such as Bacon, who in turn were influenced (or perhaps informed) by merchants such as Malynes, the merchants' institutional approaches were infused into the state-building process. This exploration of the way that merchant-insurers effected their business and managed the impacts of others who chose to enter the market shows how merchants' example, as well as their developing political power, was used to effect the institutional modifications which contributed to the broad global success of the later British state.

The environment

This book focuses particularly on institutional changes directly related to the practices of insurance trading which drove the success of the London insurance market, and on the wider impacts of that success on Britain and its eighteenth-century divergence. The former include primarily the evolution of the legal and organisational structures which governed market practice and dispute resolution. However, several exogenous, environmental factors were also critical to the growth and suc-

---

[110] O'Brien, P.: 'The nature and historical evolution of an exceptional fiscal state', *Economic History Review*, Vol. 64, No. 2 (2011), p. 426.

[111] Ibid., p. 438.

cess of the market. One of those is geography. London insurance owes a large and direct debt to the city's physical characteristics. It was positioned for trade success, both nationally and on the larger global map. A thriving and accessible port at the western extreme of northern Europe, the city was well-situated to profit from the new oceanic commerce, but also from the larger Baltic and Mediterranean trades. More important, perhaps, its access to nearby ports in France, the Low Countries, and Germany was easy. The city also possessed geo-institutional characteristics which were beneficial to the development of insurance. It was not only the centre of English trade, but it was also the nexus where the royal court, the parliamentary government, the courts, the national civil administration, the Admiralty, and the Church were based, and where national commerce, culture, finance, and consumption were most focused.

London had a great population advantage over regional English cities and most Continental ones. Her population of perhaps 70,000 in the middle of the sixteenth century was then rivalled by only about a dozen European cities. The fifteen next-largest English cities had no more than 12,000 inhabitants. By 1600 London's population had reached 150,000, ten times larger than any other English town, and was matched by only perhaps six Continental cities. Her manufacturing also increased over the period, as did consumption throughout the land.[112] Largely arising from her historical exports of wool and woollen cloth, London had strong commercial links with the successive major mercantile centres of the Low Countries; first Bruges, then Antwerp, and later Amsterdam. Like the latter two, London's merchant community was relatively tolerant in religion, and welcoming to commercial refugees and their talents.

Other English cities active in mercantile commerce, such as Bristol and later Liverpool, were important to trade, but London was dominant. Over the period of review the city typically controlled between two-thirds and four-fifths of the nation's international trade.[113] London 'virtually became England'.[114] In combination, her geographical, political, and demographic endowments had allowed London to supersede her rivals and to garner and retain pole position. Equally, these factors were critical to England's divergence from her European competitors.[115] Epstein shows that the establishment of clear property rights for both the state and individuals arose from centralised political authority (in contrast with the fragmented and diverse city-state authorities of, for example, the Italian peninsula, where insurance was invented); from strict and precocious division of legislative, executive, and

---

[112] Williams, *The later Tudors*, pp. 10, 28.

[113] Smith, Alan G.: *The emergence of a nation state: the commonwealth of England, 1529–1660*, London: Longman, 1984, pp. 176–178.

[114] Braudel, Fernand: *A history of civilisations* (Mayne, R. trans.), London: Penguin, 1995 (1987), p. 324.

[115] Ramsay, G. D.: *English overseas trade during the centuries of emergence*, London: Macmillan, 1957, p. 247.

judicial powers, within clear jurisdictions; and from the abolition of decentralised rent-seeking based on social privilege.[116] England possessed these characteristics.

London's location drove marine insurance-market development in another, less obvious way. At the heart of western European international commerce during the period of mercantilism, and close to rival trading powers (at various times France, the Low Countries, and Spain), England was often involved in naval warfare. In the later sixteenth century her ships were, in the words of Williams, 'a match for any hostile fleet', and her navy 'essentially a joint-stock concern formed from the ships of the Queen, the merchants and the privateers'[117] (of whom the latter two groups were essentially one and the same[118]). However, her future naval supremacy was not yet secured. The Port of London was vulnerable to naval and privateering attacks, and her merchant vessels often had to traverse dangerous waters before proceeding to the safer open seas. Perhaps the most ignominious of these attacks was the taking, in 1667 during the second Anglo-Dutch War, of Charles II's flagship by the Dutch Admiral de Ruyter, who sailed brazenly up the Medway and sank or captured much of the king's navy. This geographical danger, as will be shown, was a significant driver of demand for insurance, as merchants sought more cover, more often, and paid higher prices for it.

Pundits since the sixteenth century have argued that insurance fuels trade. It is beyond the scope of this book to rehearse the reasons for English, and subsequently British, trade expansion, but trade's increase clearly was the single greatest driver of rising marine insurance demand. The enlargement of Britain's merchant fleet over the period under review, enumerated in Table 1, and the presence of extensive and growing trade at British ports, in Table 2, were of course significant catalysts to the rise of her insurance sector.

Calculations of merchant tonnage figures are fraught with difficulty,[119] and an index-number problem means that growth rates must be considered with caution,[120] although in the case of early trade and shipping data, choice is often dictated by availability. Nonetheless, the clear picture presented in Table 1 is one of a merchant marine growing significantly and relatively steadily over the long term. While the insurance of ships was important in London, insurance of cargoes was even more so, drawing a broader range of buyers into the market, and presenting much greater total values to be insured. The period under review saw rapid and significant growth in English trade. This included a new dominance of English merchants over the

---

[116] Epstein, S. R.: *Freedom and growth: The rise of states and markets in Europe, 1300–1750,* London: Routledge & LSE, 2000, pp. 174–175.

[117] Williams, *The later Tudors,* p. 29.

[118] Chet, Guy: *The ocean is a wilderness: Atlantic piracy and the limits of state authority, 1688–1856,* Amherst & Boston: University of Massachusetts Press, 2014, p. 92.

[119] Since no standard definition of tonnage has been adopted. See Davis, *Rise of the English shipping industry,* pp. 395–406.

[120] The choice of the starting value may have significant impact on later comparative values. For the seminal discussion of index-number problems, see Gershenkron, Alexander: *Economic backwardness in historical perspective,* Cambridge, MA: Belknap Press, 1962 (esp. Chapter 9).

Table 1: British merchant tonnage, 1572–1829

Year	Merchant tonnage	Change
1572	50,000	
1629	115,000	130%
1686	340,000	196%
1702	323,000	-5%
1755	473,000	46%
1786	752,000	59%
1815–9	2,461,000	227%
1825–9	2,262,000	-8%

Source: Data 1572–1786 from Davis, *Rise of the English shipping industry*, pp. 27, 115–134; five-year rolling averages, from Palmer, Sarah: *Politics, shipping, and the repeal of the navigation acts*, Manchester: Manchester University Press, 1990, p. 1.

Table 2: English (British) imports, exports, and re-exports, 1622–1824, official values, £ million

	Imports	Exports	Re-exports
1598–1600*	n/a	0.22	n/a
1622	2.32	2.62	n/a
1663/69	4.4	4.1	n/a
1700	5.84	3.73	2.08
1725	7.10	5.67	2.81
1750	7.77	9.47	3.23
1775	13.55	9.72	5.48
1800	30.57	24.30	18.85
1824	37.5	48.7	10.2

Source: For 1598–1600, Fisher, F. J.: 'London's export trade in the early seventeenth century', *Economic History Review*, Vol. 3, No. 2 (1950), p. 153; for 1622, Ormrod, *Commercial empires*, p. 56; for 1663/69, Davis, 'English foreign trade', p. 154; for 1700–1824, Mitchell, B. R.: *Abstract of British historical statistics*, Cambridge: Cambridge University Press, 1962, pp. 279–282.
Note: * London only.

country's own imports and exports, a growing role of English shippers in the carrying trade, an enormous extension of the geographical reach of significant English trade, and a multiplication of English re-exports.[121] Foreigners' trade transacted through London also increased. Ormrod estimates English domestic exports were valued at £2.32 million in 1622, and imports at £2.62 million.[122] Davis has tentatively estimated that total national exports, including re-exports, were £4.1 million in 1663–1669; imports were £4.4 million. Over the period to the turn of the century, the value of manufactured goods exported from London alone increased from £222,000 to £420,000. The component of non-European exports among the total tripled, from £86,000 to £259,000.[123] Having roughly doubled over the course of the seventeenth century, a rapid escalation of British overseas trade saw official values of total international trade increase almost ten-fold in the next 125 years, from nearly £11 million in 1700 to £96.4 million in 1824.[124] Estimating the precise share of these cargoes which was insured is impossible, but the thriving insurance market in London, developed over many centuries, clearly covered the lion's share, and allowed trade to proceed and expand.

[121] Davis, 'English foreign trade', pp. 150–166.
[122] Ormrod, *Commercial empires*, p. 56.
[123] Davis, 'English foreign trade', pp. 154, 160.
[124] Mitchell, *Abstract*, pp. 395–406.

1.

The merchant-insurers' system: London marine insurance to the 1570s

London's original institutions surrounding the business of insurance were shaped according to its character as a club good traded among merchant-insurers for their mutual benefit. The merchants agreed to and accepted the complex rules governing contracts. Interpretation and modification of the rules based on circumstance usually remained in the hands of the same merchant-insurers. England did not formally adopt a codification of insurance regulations during the period under review.[1] Instead, insurance contracts and markets operated under the principles of the relevant *Lex Mercatoria*,[2] the Law Merchant, a body of commercial rules of conduct inherited from Italy and elsewhere in Continental Europe. Enforcement of the rules of the game was typically carried out within the community of merchant-insurers through arbitration.

This chapter describes the introduction of insurance into London in the fifteenth and sixteenth centuries, and shows how the Law Merchant, developed elsewhere to govern its usage, was both flexible and regularly amended and adapted to suit merchants' needs. These origins are important to understanding the future interventions which shaped the ongoing development of London insurance, and contributed to its primacy. The rules in London evolved slightly differently from those of other underwriting centres, which was one source of the city's advantage. Despite these modifications, however, the basic institutional structures and customary practices developed by the late medieval Italian merchant-insurers continued to be employed by London underwriters throughout the period of review. Ensuring the continuity of these practices was a key goal (or, in one case, the unintended consequence) of the interventions described in this book. While authorities in other important local marine insurance trading centres adopted fixed legal codes to govern market practice, London merchant-insurers were not constrained in this way. Their institution-building cooperation with the state prevented this, sometimes privately but often publicly, as will be shown. Further, merchant experts, rather than a state

---

[1] The first formal legislation was the *Marine Insurance Act 1906*. Methodical creation of common-law principles did not occur until the last third of the eighteenth century. The 1574 '*Booke of Orders*', which set down the prevailing customs governing marine insurance in London, has been described by Rossi as the first codification of a body of law in English history. Rossi, Guido: 'The Book of Orders of Assurances: a civil law code in 16th century London', *Maastricht Journal*, Vol. 19, No. 2 (2012), p. 241.

[2] As it was sometimes contemporaneously called.

judiciary, were typically called upon to interpret and enforce the body of customary mercantile law in use in London.

As the city's insurance market grew in size, volume, and importance, weaknesses in the adopted system of self-governance became apparent, revealing the merchant-insurers' inability to manage the actions of outsiders in a market which had evolved to facilitate trade in a club good. In response, legislators of the late sixteenth century established for London a more formal set of regulations and dispute resolution procedures. These institutional developments, the first major intervention into the practices of the London insurance market, are described in Chapter 2. Despite them, many merchant-insurers opted to retain the customary practice described in this chapter, in preference to newly established institutions. By the end of the seventeenth century, the state-backed framework that resulted from the first intervention had been abandoned. In its wake, the practices developed elsewhere, adopted by London, and described in this chapter once again became predominant. In this way, London's marine insurers retained the flexibility imparted by a system operating under merchant custom, although the system's inherent inability to cope with large numbers of outsiders was to remain problematic.

The nature of marine insurance, and its predecessors

Marine insurance is a Mediterranean invention. It arose in that complex of seas and mountainous peninsulas, described so eloquently by Braudel, to support the commerce which linked western Europe with Africa and the Levant. Its intimate connection with seaborne trade meant that the basic model spread quickly throughout European merchant communities, and that refinements of techniques and conventions followed merchants from port to port. For the same reasons, the key centres of insurance underwriting typically coincided with any given entrepôt's rise to commercial prominence, and similarly fell with it, as another centre gained in importance. Genoa, Venice, and Florence initially led. Their commercial decline saw Antwerp emerge as the insurance-market leader, as dominance of European trade shifted from the Mediterranean to north-western Europe, although as described above, insurance at this time remained a multi-local sector.[3]

Antwerp was a leader in trade and finance from the time that foreign merchants selected it as the European mart of choice. England's merchant adventurers had vented wool there since 1338, but its dominance began when, in 1499, the Portuguese chose Antwerp as their European staple for pepper. The number of ships paying local port fees rose ten-fold from a mean of twenty-one per year in the 1520s to 204 the following decade. To support this trade, the city became a leading financial centre. Bills could be drawn there on multiple countries, and a thriving insurance market developed at the city's bourse.[4] As will be shown, it was to make a lasting

---

[3]   For a description of this shift from Italy to Europe see Rapp, Richard T.: 'The unmaking of the Mediterranean trade hegemony: international trade rivalry and the commercial revolution', *Journal of Economic History*, Vol. 35, No. 3 (1975). For multi-local underwriting, see p. 12.

[4]   Bindoff, *Antwerp*, pp. 51–53, 59.

imprint on underwriting practice in London. Upon the decline of Antwerp, first Amsterdam and later London assumed a leading position, following the path of trade, and driven by the exogenous impetus of political machinations. Importance in insurance underwriting accompanied shifts in international commercial leadership of the kind characterised by Braudel's conception of 'world-economies' from Italy to Flanders, then to Brabant, Amsterdam, and finally to London, as merchants pursued trading opportunities.[5]

Insurance is neither the only nor the oldest way of dealing with the risks of trade. The dangers faced by ocean-going merchants, and indeed all risks, can be eased in one of three ways: through mitigation, management, or transfer. Mitigation constitutes the intentional and strategic avoidance of the hazards that present risks, for example by altering the usual route a vessel takes from one port to another in order to bypass an area where piracy has flared up. In 1710, as French privateers preyed upon British merchant shipping during the War of the Spanish Succession, the London merchant Joseph Cruttenden wrote to a client in Boston, Massachusetts to explain that the vessel carrying his goods would depart early, because it was 'sayling sooner than the others, the design to go Northabout' to avoid the enemy peril: rather than sailing through the English Channel, the ship's master was to circumvent the privateers by sailing through the North Sea and around Scotland to reach the Atlantic.[6] Mitigation is almost certainly the original way of dealing with risk.

In contrast, risk management measures constitute efforts to reduce the impact of risks. For early modern merchants, division was perhaps the most common. They often split large cargo shipments destined for the same port between several vessels, so that if one should be lost, the balance of the cargo may arrive safely. For example, in 1560 Thomas Gresham, as an agent of the Crown but trading on his own account, directed Michel von Dorovy, his agent at Hamburg, to load gunpowder onto three ships for carriage to England, rather than aboard a single vessel. He procured insurance to the limit of £1,000 for each, although the value of each cargo was closer to £2,000.[7]

Division was also a widespread risk management strategy among ship owners: fractional vessel ownership was practised around the world. Ship ownership was typically divided into equal shares, usually with divisors of four. In England, since the 1854 *Merchant Shipping Act*, vessels have been divided into ownership shares of 64ths. As well as assisting in fundraising for the purchase of vessels by facilitating wider investment, the risks of vessel ownership were managed by spreading an individual's investment over several ships. Fractional ownership was, according to Davis, 'the original means adopted to spread the risks of ship owning', and is very much older than insuring.[8] A 1703 inventory of the assets of Samuel Pinder

5   See p. 13; Braudel, *Afterthoughts*, pp. 80–83.
6   MS Rawlinson Letters 66, Letterbook of Joseph Cruttenden, Fol. 17, Cruttenden to Habijah Savage, Boston, 27 Jun. 1710.
7   Martin, Frederick: *The history of Lloyd's and of marine insurance in Great Britain*, London: Macmillan, 1876, p. 12.
8   Davis, *Rise of the English shipping industry*, pp. 82–87.

of Whitby shows the spread of his ownership of Greenland fishing vessels. He possessed shares of 6/16ths, 1/3rd, and 1/64th of his own ship, and 1/32nd each of eight others, each valued separately in the record.[9]

Insurance is a form of risk transfer, the third approach to dealing with risk. The mechanism was and remains contractual agreements (*policies*) struck with third parties (*underwriters*) who agree to assume a portion, denominated in currency, (the *line*) of specified risks (*insured perils*) to vessels or cargoes (confusingly, *risks*) in exchange for a fee (*premium*) calculated as a percentage of the total amount (the *rate*) of the maximum possible indemnity (the *sum insured*) to be paid in case of a declared insured loss (a *claim*). The details of a policy (its *terms and conditions*) often varied, which can invalidate direct price comparisons based on rates only.

The focus of this book is the type of financial arrangement sometimes referred to as 'premium insurance', which is granted under a contract known widely from the later sixteenth century as a policy. It provides, in exchange for payment of the premium, a promise of contingent, replacement capital to indemnify an actual insured loss. It is distinct from mutual insurance, which is a closed, historically non-commercial system. However, other forms of commercial risk transfer for trade were widely used long before premium insurance was commonplace.[10] They were suited to merchants who travelled abroad alongside their trade goods, and wished to raise loans or investments constituting advances of trade capital, which were used to finance individual voyages. Thus, the predecessors of premium insurance were fundamentally different, in that they offered a dual function of advancing capital and transferring risk. Premium insurance fulfilled only the second of these functions. While a detailed description of the development of insurance before its introduction into England falls outside the scope of this book, its early progress, and that of predecessor instruments for the division of maritime trade risks, is important to understanding the evolution in London of insurance custom which, under the Law Merchant, governed underwriting practice.[11]

Probably the earliest form of such dual instruments is the sea loan, a simple arrangement under which a financier would loan to an adventurer the capital required to finance trade goods and voyages, but forgive the loan in case of casualty. Sea loans were used by the ancients: the instrument is mentioned by Demosthenes, in Justinian's *Digest* (the Emperor, in AD 533, fixed the price of sea loans at 12%), in Basil I's *Basilica*, and in Roman law as *nauticum foenus*.[12] Widespread among Italian

9   Young, Rev. George: *A history of Whitby, and Streoneshalh abbey*, vol. II, Whitby: Clark & Medd, 1817, p. 563, *n.*

10   For a brief and cogent description of predecessor instruments involving marine risk transfer, see van Niekerk, J. P.: *The development of the principles of insurance law in the Netherlands from 1500 to 1800*, two volumes, Kenwyn, Cape Town: Juta, 1998, I, pp. 16–59.

11   The most comprehensive chronological account of the development of marine insurance in Europe is found in Leonard, A. B. (ed.): *Marine Insurance: origins and institutions, 1300–1850*, Basingstoke: Palgrave Macmillan, 2016.

12   Hoover, Calvin: 'The sea loan in Genoa in the twelfth century', *Quarterly Journal of Economics*, Vol. 40, No. 3 (1926), pp. 495–496; Pryor, John: 'The origins of the commenda contract', *Speculum*, Vol. 52, No. 1 (1977), p. 6; Huebner, Solomon: 'The development and

merchants from the eleventh century, sea loans conveniently usurped usury laws, with attendant interest styled as a risk premium, or simply held back from the cash advanced.[13]

A slightly more sophisticated alternative was the 'insurance loan', which comprised an advance made by a shipowner to sedentary freighter-borrowers, usually equal to about a quarter of the value of the goods shipped (with the balance of value sometimes insured separately). Like sea loans, insurance loans were forgiven if the goods failed to reach their destination. The instruments appear to have been short-lived, and raised obvious principal–agent hazards, but they are of interest because a variety, the first known example of which survives from Genoa in 1362, involved a promise by the lender, under a formal contract of sale, to purchase the goods if they did not arrive safely at their destination.[14] This is perhaps the earliest extant contractual formalisation of salvage rights, which are an important and surviving characteristic of marine premium insurance, and of the custom and later codified law which governs its practice. Accordingly, upon the payment of insurance indemnities related to losses, title to insured goods and vessels is transferred to the insurers. Salved goods and vessels may therefore be used to recoup claims paid. Insurers' salvage rights are firmly established under the Law Merchant.

The chain of development of risk transfer products moved through more complex arrangements, such as the *cambium nauticum*. This intermediate instrument combined the loan-forgiveness characteristic of sea loans (the risk transfer component) with the time-and-currency provisions of the simple *cambium*, which was intended to combat usury rules, and which, by the later middle ages, was exercised regularly through bills of exchange.[15] Developed in the thirteenth century, the *cambium nauticum* was exchanged for money advanced for the finance of trade, and was repayable – usually in a different place and currency – upon the safe arrival at their market destination of the trade goods purchased with the investment. Like the sea loan, the instrument shifted sea risk from the borrower to the lender, and masked within currency exchange rates any interest levied on the loan. However, the financially elegant dual function of the *cambia nautica* made these contracts more costly, both in terms of exchange rates and brokerage, than normal *cambia*.[16] In addition, they required borrowing to effect risk transfer, repayment in a different currency, and the engagement of an overseas agent, any or all of which may not have been desired by the merchant seeking risk transfer. These limitations, alongside the price differential, soon urged merchants to seek a further evolution.

present status of marine insurance in the United States', *Annals of the American Academy of Political and Social Science*, Vol. 26 (1905), p. 423.

[13] Hoover, 'The sea loan', p. 500.

[14] Piccinno, Luisa: 'Genoa 1340–1620: early development of marine insurance', in Leonard, A. B. (ed.): *Marine insurance: origins and institutions, 1300–1850*, Basingstoke: Palgrave Macmillan, 2016, p. 32.

[15] de Roover, Raymond: *The rise and decline of the Medici Bank, 1397–1494*, New York: Norton & Co., 1966, p. 9.

[16] de Roover, Florence Edler: 'Early examples of marine insurance', *Journal of Economic History*, Vol. 5, No. 2 (1945), p. 176.

One such advance was the *commenda* contract, under which the sedentary capital provider, or *commendator*, acted as an equity partner, sharing in the profits of a voyage, but forfeited his claim against the travelling merchant, or *tractator*, in case of a loss at sea.[17] By the thirteenth century this type of marine risk transfer had overtaken the sea loan in popularity among Mediterranean merchants, but both remained common.[18] De Roover argues that *commenda* was a necessary development of sedentary Italian merchants, who adapted earlier financial instruments to manage the attendant risks of maritime trade, while also dealing with the challenge of ecclesiastical restrictions upon loans at interest.[19] Perhaps because of their dual function, these instruments were not perfect solutions to the risks of seaborne commerce. De Lara argues that 'the sea loan and the *commenda* sustained the efficient allocation of risk', but that indemnity for actual losses could not be total, because 'indivisible ventures subject to aggregate risk limited the ability to diversify, and prevented financiers from effectively becoming risk-neutral'.[20] However, all of these instruments share two important characteristics: they necessitate trust and mutual agreement, both upon the rules which govern the underlying contracts and upon the methods of resolving any disputes arising under them, since formal regulation rarely governed their interpretation. Custom, and for international trade, the Law Merchant, were essential to their effective use.

The *commenda* did not separate risk transfer from capital advance, and did not offer complete indemnity for actual losses, as de Lara shows, and as is depicted in Figure 1. A more useful solution would divide and perfect these functions. Regular *cambia*, bills of exchange, provided capital advances if necessary (masking usurious charges), but left borrowers obliged to repay loans unconditionally. A new instrument was needed to effect risk transfer, whether accompanying borrowing, or free-standing. Conventional marine premium insurance emerged to answer this need at least as early as the first decades of the fourteenth century. It was soon in use in the major trading centres of western Europe. This development is traced comprehensively in Edler de Roover's unsurpassed 1945 article 'Early examples of marine insurance', and is rehearsed in brief below.

The development of premium-based marine insurance in medieval Italy

For much of the middle ages, Italian merchants held a commanding position in Mediterranean trade. During this period of trade dominance, they developed and refined the practices of insurance, which were quickly employed throughout their

---

[17] Pryor, 'Origins of commenda', p. 6–7.

[18] de Lara, Yadira Gonzalez: 'Institutions for contract enforcement and risk-sharing: From the sea loan to the commenda in late medieval Venice', *European Review of Economic History*, No. 6 (2002), p. 260.

[19] de Roover, 'Early examples'. See also Culp, Christopher: *Risk transfer: derivatives in theory and practice*, Hoboken, NJ: Wiley & Sons, 2004, pp. 33–34.

[20] de Lara, 'Institutions for contract enforcement', p. 259.

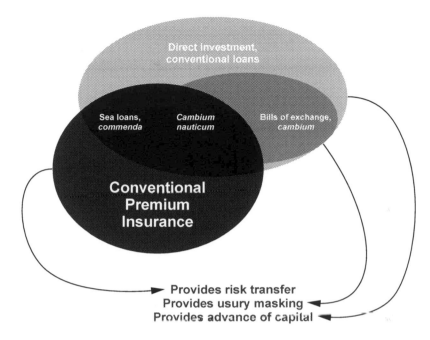

Figure 1. Forms of capital provision for merchant adventurers

trading world, including in London. De Roover states that 'there is no doubt that genuine insurance was a product of the commercial revolution which occurred during the period from 1275 to 1325', following the maturation of the commercial-ly-minded Italian city communes.[21] Spufford has attributed this revolution to the 'liberation' of large quantities of cash, increased demand for luxury goods from distant places, and the growth and specialisation of the businesses that supplied them.[22] This revolution focused on Italy, and involved, additionally, the develop-ment of bills of exchange and double-entry bookkeeping.

The earliest surviving documentary evidence of conventional insurance arises from Italy at the end of this period of commercial revolution. In the 1880s Enrico Bensa identified several early fourteenth-century Italian documents deposited in Florentine and Genoese archives as concrete evidence of the use of premium insurance policies in Genoa at least by 1347. They led him to conclude that 'it is no longer in doubt that, from the first two decades of the fourteenth century, insur-ance was routinely transacted in major Italian commercial cities', and he asserted that they stood as 'indubitable' proof that Italy was the birthplace of conventional

---

[21] de Roover, 'Early examples', pp. 173.

[22] Spufford, Peter: *Power and profit: the merchant in medieval Europe*, London: Thames & Hudson, 2002, pp. 16–19.

insurance.[23] Later Federigo Melis discovered a policy issued in Genoa and dated 20 February 1343. Both of these contracts were disguised as interest-free loans from the insured to the risk-taker which would be forgiven in the case of loss, but with no loan actually advanced, and no mention of the premium which surely must have been accepted by the underwriters.[24]

A 1384 policy underwritten in Pisa survives in the Datini archive (which contains documents of the Pisan merchant Francesco Datini, the well-known 'Merchant of Prato'). Datini was a regular user of premium insurance in the late fourteenth century, and was sometimes an underwriter, a term derived from the practice, developed by this time, of individual insurers *writing* their names and insurance commitment at the foot of the policy, *under* the main body of the contract.[25] The same practice gives us the term 'subscriber'. Datini is a model merchant-insurer, and by this time, insurance was commonplace among such men. Bensa's examination of the records of the Genoese notary Theramus de Majolo shows that between 21 August and 15 September 1393 he was involved in more than eighty insurance transactions.[26] Stefani argues that the earliest Italian 'policies did not differ very much even at the end of the fourteenth century from either those of the subsequent centuries or, we might even say, from those of the present day'.[27] The basic structure of insurance underwriting and the policies which support it, as they were employed throughout the period of review, appear to have been developed fairly rapidly, during a period when Italian merchants originated many enduring business practices, which soon found their way to London.

This early Italian insurance practice was not immediately standardised. Instead, conventions developed differently in various Italian trading cities, just as practice would, in future, vary between northwest European underwriting centres. For example, Genoese, Neapolitan, and Sicilian merchants employed notaries to draw up policies, in Latin, for each participating underwriter, although they later adopted the practice of preparing a single contract which all of the underwriters signed, a convention which became the norm. In contrast, merchants in Pisa, Florence, and Venice engaged brokers to prepare policies, a practice which was to endure. By 1397, at the latest, brokers were contracting with multiple underwriters on a single policy. However, the form of contract employed in the latter cities was

---

[23] Bensa, Enrico: *Il contratto di assicurazione nel medio evo: studi e recerche*, 1884. Translated into French as Valéry, Jules (trans.), *Histoire du contrat d'assurance au moyen age*, Paris: Ancienne Librairie Thorin et Fis, 1897, p. 20 (author's English translation).

[24] Piccinno, *Genoa 1340–1620*, p. 31.

[25] His life and business are described at length in Origo, Iris: *The merchant of Prato, Francesco di Marco Datini*, revised edition, Harmondsworth: Penguin, 1963. For his underwriting, p. 89.

[26] Bensa, *Il contratto* (Valéry, trans.), p. 47.

[27] Stefani, Giuseppi: *Insurance in Venice from the origins to the end of the Serenissima, vol. I*, Amoruso, A. D. (trans.), Trieste: Assicurazioni Generali, 1958, I, pp. 60–61.

not the same as that employed in Genoa and Sicily. It was written in the vernacular, and the terms were identical.[28]

One of the fundamentals established during this period was the breadth of cover offered, which usually included threats arising from acts of nature (typically, 'the seas'), and those arising from men, often styled *maris* and *gentium*. The insured perils named in the Florentine policies were, in translation to modern English, 'of God, of the seas, of men of war, of fire, of jettison, of detainment by princes, by cities, or by any other person, of reprisals, of arrest, of whatever loss, peril, misfortune, impediment or [catastrophe] that might occur'.[29] Some policies additionally listed barratry (theft or embezzlement) by the master of the vessel as an insured peril. The wording of Italian policies of the late fourteenth century was to set a precedent which has endured for 600 years. A 1582 policy underwritten in London bears remarkable similarity. It proffered cover against 'the seas, men of warre, fyer, enemyes, pyratts, rovers, theeves, jettozons, l[ett]res of marte, & countermarte [letters of marque and reprisal], areste, restraynte, & deteinem^ts, of kinges & princes, & of all other p'sons, barratrye of the m^st and maryn's, and of all other p[er]illes, losses, & misfortunes, whatsoe'r they be, or howsoe'r the same shall chance, happen, or come to the hurte, detrym^t, or damadge, of the' insured cargo.[30] An almost identical list of perils appeared in London insurance policies until the 1980s, including the catch-all 'all other perils, losses, and misfortunes whatsoever' conclusion (although debate within different local merchant communities, sometimes involving formal judicial opinion, has often centred on the interpretation of this apparent mopping-up clause).[31]

Italian fourteenth-century policies also show the early development of a key principle of insurance: the buyer of cover must have an interest in the safe completion of the voyage which extends beyond the policy itself. The absence of such an interest renders a policy void.[32] The Italians who developed insurance practice recognised the need for 'insurable interest' to be present for the smooth functioning of the insurance market. In its absence, the act of insuring is transformed into simple wagering (although in certain periods 'interest or no interest' policies were underwritten in London, in part due to the flexibility they granted to merchants, as described elsewhere in this book).[33] Underwriters' salvage rights, secured in the 'insurance loan' instrument described above, were further entrenched at this time.[34]

---

[28] For a comprehensive description of the early development of marine insurance in Italy, see Leonard, A. B. (ed.), *Marine insurance*, chs. 2 & 3.

[29] De Roover incorrectly translated the Italian '*sinestre*' as 'sinister'. It is correctly translated as 'catastrophe'. De Roover, 'Early examples', p. 198.

[30] GHL 062/MS22281, Policy of Bartholomew Corsini, 24 Sept. 1582.

[31] van Nickerk, *Principles of insurance law,* I, pp. 349, 357–358.

[32] Bensa, *Il contratto* (Valéry, trans.), p. 34.

[33] For a discussion of insurance versus wagering and the flexibility of interest-or-no-interest policies, see p 169 ff.

[34] Bensa, *Il contratto* (Valéry, trans.), p. 28.

The practice of engaging multiple underwriters to secure a single risk is an obvious methodology of risk-sharing, and lies at the heart of insurance practice. It constituted a divisional technique of risk management both on the part of the underwriters, since they shared risks between multiple members of the underwriting community, and on the part of insurance buyers, since it minimised the threat of an individual underwriter's insolvency. As described above, it was present in the fourteenth century. Analysis by Leone of eight Italian policies underwritten between February 1485 and August 1487 for five different insurance buyers, all of whom were Florentines, shows the extent of risk-spreading among the merchant community in Naples, where the policies were drawn up. The underwriters are identified by Leone as comprising forty-five Catalans, eighteen Neapolitans and other southern Italians, seventeen Florentines, two Venetians, one each from Genoa, Pisa, Sienna, and France, and a single Jew (who no doubt resided somewhere).[35] This had the obvious impact of creating a geographical dispersal of the assumed risk, as well as a spread between individual merchant-insurers. Leone describes most of the men as major merchants, but notes that among the Neapolitan underwriters, most were not. Instead, they were prominent men from other fields, a finding which provides early evidence of the spread of insurance risk beyond the merchant community, and of the sector proving an attractive investment. In this way merchant-insurers were joined by outsider-sellers, who appear to have worked in concert to spread risk beyond the merchant community by employing a broader capital base.

Examination by de Roover of Datini's extant account books, and those of the Constantinople-based Venetian merchant Jacomo Badoer, and of the Florentine Bernardo Cambi, who was underwriting in Bruges, has revealed another late medieval Italian insurance convention which was to endure. The underwriters involved – at least some of whom were active merchants – charged rates which varied based on the characteristics of both the vessel and the voyage, on loss experience, and on perceived exogenous threats. Like the contractual wording of the Pisan insurance policies, the early Italians' practice of calculating a premium which varied according to the characteristics of the object of the insurance (the risk), as well as its route and vessel of transport, was to endure until the present. Finally, de Roover has shown that agency was at least sometimes practised, and that the commission agents charged was calculated as a percentage of the value of the goods insured.[36] These practical conventions surrounding insurance were soon to spread to north-western Europe, including to London.

As insurance practice developed in Italy, so too did its regulation by authorities outside the insuring community. Bensa has shown that insurance regulation made its first appearance in Italy, in the form of a decree made by Gabriel Adorno, the Fourth Doge of Genoa, in 1369. The law prohibited the insurance of foreign vessels and cargoes,[37] which created a disadvantage for local underwriting by prevent-

[35] Leone, Alfonso: 'Maritime insurance as a source for the history of international credit in the Middle Ages', *Journal of European Economic History*, Vol. XII (1993), pp. 363–369.

[36] de Roover, 'Early examples', pp. 189–196, 199.

[37] Bensa, *Il contratto* (Valéry, trans.), p. 51.

ing geographical risk diversification (the decree also set out fines for abuse of the ambiguous loan contracts intended to circumvent usury laws, as described above). Florence adopted a similar prohibition against the insurance of foreign vessels in 1393, and a Venetian senatorial decree of 1421 made the same restriction. Also in Venice, insurance policies could be made a matter of public record through transcription in the *Avogaria di comun*, which could aid future litigation under a policy, but could also reveal merchants' potentially commercially sensitive trading activities to competitors.[38] Here, then, is evidence of state intervention into a marine insurance market which did not work to the benefit of merchant-insurers, but instead targeted protectionism.

Early regulation of insurance can be considered a feature of Italian insurance markets, but some of the various laws passed restricted the flexibility allowed to underwriters, such as prohibitions against underwriting foreign-owned ships and cargoes. Ordinances (the *Statuti di Sicurtà*) adopted in Florence in 1523 included provisions which prohibited insurances to be made on unnamed vessels, and required adjudication by a panel of appointees before claims could be made for goods jettisoned to save a vessel. This body has been considered to be the first dedicated insurance court, and held a place for a foreign representative.[39] The Ordinances allowed the panel, comprising five 'deputies' appointed 'for the regulation of insurance', even to fix rates to be charged by Florentine underwriters. Further, the Ordinances prescribed a policy wording, which required, among other restrictive clauses, that insurers must pay claims in cases where no 'certain news' had been heard of a vessel for a period of six months, that agreed claims must be paid within two months, and that, in cases of disputed claims, insurers were to pay up, then seek reversal in the courts within eighteen months. In such cases, should the magistrates find in favour of the insurers, the policyholder was to repay at the rate of 120%.[40]

A 1468 decree of the Florentine Grand Council transferred all insurance-related cases from the *Corti di Palazzo* to the *Consoli dei Mercanti*, where cases could be heard more quickly, and where merchant knowledge was close to hand for application. A further Ordinance of 1526 required that certain insured commodities must be specified in an insurance policy, or else the policy would be deemed void. The insured was liable to a fine for breach of this regulation.[41] The obvious drawback of such a restriction is that insurances made in advance of the purchase of a cargo may later be invalidated by the unforeseen loading of prohibited cargoes. As will be shown below, the flexibility of insurance underwriting in London, unfettered by such decrees, was much less restricted by regulation, limitation, and prohibition.

---

[38] Stefani, *Insurance in Venice*, pp. 87–89.

[39] Addobbati, A.: 'Italy 1500–1800: cooperation and competition', in Leonard, A. B. (ed.): *Marine insurance: origins and institutions, 1300–1850*, Basingstoke: Palgrave Macmillan, 2016, p. 51.

[40] Stefani, *Insurance in Venice*, p. 90.

[41] Magens, N.: *An essay on insurances*, two vols, London: J. Haberkorn, 1755, II, pp. 1–7.

Between Lombardy and Lombard Street

Marine insurance practice, like all merchant practice, followed the routes of trade. Its local fortunes rose and fell with those of the trading centres it reached and in which it took hold. If the developmental journey of the leadership of successive marine insurance centres was drawn on a map, it would link sequentially the Italian city states (beginning with Genoa, and plying a coastal route) to Barcelona, Burgos, Bruges, Antwerp, then Amsterdam before its arrival in London. The catalysts for this transmission were the nations of expatriate Italian merchants who made their home in these various trading cities. Naturally, the practice of marine insurance in one state or port has never precluded its use or enormous success in another, but in each of these places the evolution of marine insurance made strides. Some became, for a time at least, the western European epicentre of insurance practice. What follows is a very brief synthetic account of those insurance centres' institutional developments, which occurred in parallel, and never in isolation. Changes in one market were observed, and sometimes imitated, in others, as merchants cooperated with (and sometimes struggled against) state authorities to ensure insurance business could be transacted, and most importantly, disputes resolved, as smoothly, quickly, and cheaply as possible.[42]

Barcelona was one of the first cities outside Italy to embrace marine insurance, and is believed to be the first to adopt regulation governing its practice (in contrast to, for example, the 1369 Genoese Ducal decree which novated policies insuring foreign vessels and those underwritten following a casualty, but did not set out the rules of underwriting).[43] Barcelona's merchants had resolved insurance disputes through the local maritime courts, *los consols de la mar*, where they were adjudicated by leading merchants according to current norms. This practice was compelled under an Ordinance of 1435, the first of a series of regulations passed in 1436, 1458, 1461, and 1484; collectively the *Ordinances of Barcelona*. These comprised the first consistent set of rules governing insurance contracts, including the form of the contract, the requirement for a public register held by notaries, and the necessity of a specified self-insurance share (akin to a deductible or abatement), as well as setting jurisdiction: the 1458 Ordinance gave the consular courts exclusive jurisdiction over marine insurance claims disputes. The Barcelona ordinances are believed to be the first to codify insurance customs, the unwritten rules of the Law Merchant, and the experience of a century and a half of underwriting. They were appended to the Catalan *Book of the Consulate of the Sea*, and as such stood as a quasi-legal authority used throughout the Mediterranean, including in Italy (although the rules were sometimes in contradiction to local custom – a common challenge of codification of merchant practice, even in a single jurisdiction). The *Ordinances of Barcelona*

---

42 For a much more comprehensive account, see Leonard, A. B. (ed.), *Marine insurance*, on which much of what follows is based.

43 Addobbati, 'Italy', p. 48.

provided the basis for many future legislative efforts in western Europe and elsewhere, including London.[44]

The Atlantic city of Burgos, a longstanding trading centre and the capital of Castile, was home to a powerful merchant guild, the *Universidad de Mercaderes*, which in 1494 was granted jurisdiction over all the nation's foreign trade. A model policy was adopted by the market in 1509, and General Ordinances covering practice proclaimed in 1546. These were revised in 1572 under the General Ordinances of the Consulate, the body which succeeded the *Universidad*. Occasionally the Consulate would publish standard rates for existing sea routes, and would calculate rates for new voyages, in part based on the intelligence it gathered from its own international postal network, and the information delivered through it by the numerous Burgalese merchants resident in trading centres around the world. As the city's norms of marine insurance were transmitted to various European ports, and across the Atlantic, Burgos became an international insurance centre, although innovation in the market may have been stifled by the inflexibility of local regulation. The city's insurance market began to decline at mid century, and had receded significantly in importance by 1565.[45]

Competition between insurance underwriters in Burgos and Antwerp occurred throughout the mid sixteenth century, until the primacy of Antwerp won out with its rise in importance as a European centre of seaborne trade, following the decline of Bruges, whose merchants had underwritten insurance locally since about 1450, based on Italian practices, and possibly much earlier among expatriate Italians. Antwerp's broker-driven insurance market was thriving by 1560. A single broker there, Juan Henriquez, placed coverage of 487,000 Flemish pounds in 1563 alone, when he was broking three policies each day, in a market where about 600 individuals, roughly half the merchant community, were underwriting at least occasionally. Disputes were typically settled in the City Court, but despite the high levels of activity formal regulation was not swiftly promulgated in Antwerp. An initial ordinance was passed in 1550, with merchant input apparent, although it focused on coverage restrictions.[46]

In 1555 a resident Italian merchant, Giovanni-Baptiste Ferrufini, had called for the Spanish authorities to impose legislation which would require adherence to local insurance customs and, to reduce fraud, create a state registry of insurances underwritten in the city, the monopoly insurance office. The registry was to fall, for a fee, under his lifetime supervision. Opposition from the local merchant community

[44] van Niekerk, *Principles of insurance law*, I, p. 199, II, p. 1529; Addobbatia, 'Italy', p. 49; Piccinno, *Genoa 1340–1620*, p. 42.

[45] Casado Alonso, H.: 'Los seguros marítimos de Burgos: observatorio del comercio internacional portugués en el siglo XVI', Revista da Faculdade de Letras, *História*, Porto, III Série, Vol. 4, 2003, p. 215; Spufford, Peter: 'From Genoa to London: the places of insurance in Europe', in Leonard, A. B. (ed.): *Marine insurance: origins and institutions, 1300–1850*, Basingstoke: Palgrave Macmillan, 2016, pp. 283–284; De ruysscher, Dave: 'Antwerp 1490–1590: insurance and speculation', in Leonard, A. B. (ed.): *Marine insurance: origins and institutions, 1300–1850*, Basingstoke: Palgrave Macmillan, 2016, p. 89.

[46] De ruysscher, 'Antwerp 1490–1590', pp. 85–95; van Niekerk, *Principles of insurance law*, I, pp. 202–207, II, p. 1528.

stifled the proposal until 1559, when a municipal ordinance to erect the office was written, but not acted upon (a drama to be replayed with greater success for the insurance entrepreneur Richard Candeler in London, twenty-five years later). Marine insurance dispute resolution and vessel inspection was addressed in the 31 October *placcaat* of Philip II, and in 1569 a heavy-handed Duke of Alva prohibited insurance underwriting in an effort to reduce fraud, but withdrew the proscription eleven months later.[47]

Ultimately Antwerp *placcaaten* on *contracten van assurantien* were introduced in 1570/1, 1582, and 1609, the first requiring the registration of all marine insurance policies underwritten in the city, without which they would forfeit the right of adjudication in the local merchant *Schepenen* courts, and setting out a model policy form. The Antwerp Registration Office was under the supervision of Alva's secretary, rather than a merchant-insurer, but the efficacy of the office cannot be established. It is not mentioned in the 1609 regulation, a compilation of local insurance practice (the *Compilatae*, akin to London's earlier *Booke of Orders*). However, it may have served as a forum for the resolution of policy and coverage disputes, until the municipal court again resumed its jurisdiction over marine insurance disputes. Despite its loose legal framework, the practices of Antwerp became a standard. Policies written there, and in markets including Hamburg and London, frequently included a 'force and effect' clause which referenced the Bourse of Antwerp.[48]

Political tumult led to the flight of many merchants and the decline of Antwerp as an international insurance centre from the 1580s. Much of the dislocated business was taken to Amsterdam by merchants fleeing the arrival of the Spanish. Antwerp custom and practice was followed, including dispute resolution through the *Schepenen* courts and adherence to the *placcaaten*, and Amsterdam was soon to become the world's premier marine insurance market, alongside its rise to the position of European pre-eminence in trade and finance.

An insurance ordinance, which drew heavily on Antwerp practice and particularly the Antwerp regulations of 1563, 1570, and 1571, was drafted and adopted in 1598, following merchant petitions for reform. Notably, the Ordinance declared that any policies which did not comply with its provision were void, that each policy was required to specify a 10% deductible (or abatement) – a provision frequently ignored – and, more successfully, outlined the parameters and formation of Amsterdam's Chamber of Insurance (*Kamer van Assurantie*). The Chamber would relieve overloaded *Schepenen* courts and accrue relevant expertise. It was chartered in 1612, but as Go has shown, it had begun to operate almost immediately after the ordinance was adopted, and heard its first recorded case in 1598. Its decisions were made by a panel of three commissioners, or *Assurantiemeesters*, selected from among the leading members of Amsterdam's merchant, ship-owning, and banking communities – most of whom were, or later would be, *Schepenen* judges – and serving an average of six years, which provided the Chamber both with knowledge and continuity. Some

47 Ibid.
48 Ibid.

commissioners had close ties to underwriters, and in some cases had been underwriters, although to act as an insurer while a commissioner was prohibited.[49]

Nine decades after its formation, the Chamber issued a set of standardised insurance policies, based on a bylaw of 1688. The use of any other form of policy language was prohibited, and a three-penny fee was levied for each policy endorsed (as was now mandatory) by the Secretary of the Chamber, although the only penalty for using alternate policy forms was unenforceability before the Chamber. Although disputes over the Chamber's jurisdiction had widened its authority to cover 'all questions of insurance', including disputes brought by foreigners, merchants by this time had begun to renew their preference for arbitration, which was faster and cheaper. Policies sometimes included a clause which required disputes to be taken in the first instance to arbitration, rather than to the much more formal Chamber of Insurance. No formal organisation of underwriters existed, and the practice of underwriting remained individual, typically as an adjunct to other commercial and trade activities. Brokers were usually appointed to manage transactions, and were heavily regulated, although many operated outside the formal registration process, about which their merchant-customers showed little or no concern.[50]

Early marine insurance in London

By the mid sixteenth century, conventional marine premium insurance was already well established in London. Rossi reports a 1554 Italian source which states that 'many insurances are made in London, and the policies have much strength, perhaps more than elsewhere. Merchants trust them, and there is no difficulty in collecting the money [i.e., claims]; there is little problem in covering as much as £2,000 on an English ship.'[51]

However, old conventional wisdom that the practice of insurance in London dates only from this period (such as Raynes's statement that 'there is no documentary evidence of the practice of marine insurance in England before the sixteenth century') post-dates its regular use by at least a century.[52] The earliest record yet encountered of an insurance transaction in London reveals a resident Florentine merchant, Alexander Ferrantyn, buying insurance from other resident Italians in 1426. The transaction led to a dispute, the details of which are recorded in the

---

[49] van Niekerk, *Principles of insurance law*, I, pp. 207–209, 212; Go, Sabine: *Marine insurance in the Netherlands: a comparative institutional approach*, Amsterdam: Askant, 2009, pp. 95–122; Go, Sabine: 'Amsterdam 1585–1790: emergence, dominance and decline', in Leonard, A. B. (ed.): *Marine insurance: origins and institutions, 1300–1850*, Basingstoke: Palgrave Macmillan, 2016, pp. 110, 113.

[50] Ibid.

[51] The source, BL ADD MS 48,082, is described as 'a brief compendium on English commerce'. Rossi's translation. Rossi, *Insurance in Elizabethan England*, p. 53.

[52] Raynes, H. E.: *A history of British insurance, second edition*, London: Pitman & Sons, 1964, p. 22; see also, for example, the entry 'Lloyd's of London' in Weinreb, Ben and Hibbert, Christopher (eds): *The London Encyclopaedia*, Second Edition, London: Macmillan, 1993, p. 478, which states: 'marine insurance [is] a practice which seems to have been introduced into England by the Lombards in the 16th century'.

Plea Rolls of the City of London.[53] Ferrantyn's insurance-buying was not isolated. The translation and presentation by Bolton and Bruscoli of the ledgers of Filippo Borromei & Co. of Bruges and London, one bank of many in the extensive network of the eponymous Italian merchant-banking family, shows that the Borromei made regular and routine insurance transactions in London.[54] For example, on 10 January 1438 a clerk in the London office (a branch of Bruges) recorded a transaction with its parent as follows: 'credited to their *conto a parte* [account] for cloth for 50 pieces of Essex streits [a broadcloth one yard wide] bought for £st 31.5.0; insurance at £st 1.16.8'. The entry is sound evidence that insurance was being used in London at this time, and with the Ferrantyn case, constitutes unequivocal proof of its routine practice. It also provides evidence of the first known use of a broker to arrange insurances in London, one Giovanni Diversi.

The identity of the underwriters has, in some cases, survived. An entry in the Borromei ledgers of 7 November 1438 refers to 'insurance underwritten by us on the cargo and ship of Giovanni Tanzo', indicating that the bank itself would sometimes assume insurance risk; the Borromei were merchant-insurers. The bank's Bruges ledger of the same year identifies as underwriters Girolamo Lomellino, Giovanni Tanzo, Simon Francesco Maggiolini, and Lorenzo Damiani & Co, all of whom appear to be Italian. The seventeen London merchant-insurers named as defendants in the Ferrantyn case include two each who were natives of Venice, Genoa, and Florence, and eleven who are unidentified, but whose surnames also indicate Italian origin.[55] Further fifteenth-century evidence of regular insurance practice appears in the City of London's Memoranda Rolls, which record, for example, an insurance transaction between two of London's leading Italian merchants. In 1480 a resident Genoese merchant, Antonio Spynule (almost certainly Antonio Spinola of the ancient Genoese political and trading family), and his English attorney appeared before the Lord Mayor and aldermen to attest to the receipt of an insurance premium of £6.13s.4d from the merchant Marco Strozze (Strozzi), a member of the Florentine commercial family who had remained in London after his family's business there collapsed in the 1560s. The policy, here described as a 'bill of assurance', had been lost.[56] It is safe to conclude from this evidence that the community of Italian merchants in London insured regularly in the early fifteenth century, and did so primarily, but not exclusively, internally. They comprised London's earliest

53 For more on the case, see pp. 56–58. For Ferrantyn's nationality, see TNA SC 8/111/5523. For his insurance suit, see Thomas, A. H. (ed.): *Calendar of plea & memoranda rolls of the City of London preserved among the archives of the Corporation of London at the Guildhall, AD 1413–1437*, Cambridge: Cambridge University Press, 1943, pp. 208–210.

54 Bolton and Bruscoli, *Ledger of Filippo Borromei*, online: www.queenmaryhistoricalresearch. org [Accessed 3 Dec. 2021].

55 The six identifications were made by Lewin, C. G.: *Pensions and insurance before 1800: A social history*, East Linton: Tuckwell Press, 2003, p. 86.

56 Roll A99, 6 June 1480, in Jones, Philip E. *et al.* (eds): *Calendar of plea and memoranda rolls preserved among the archives of the Corporation of London at the Guildhall, A.D. 1459–1482*, Cambridge: Cambridge University Press, 1961, pp. 208–210; Mallett, M. E.: 'Anglo-Florentine commercial relations, 1465–1491', *Economic History Review*, Vol. 15, No. 2 (1962), p. 253.

generations of merchant-insurers, and their practice was typical of its time. As Origo observes, 'traders in foreign parts formed tight little natural communities, dealing and associating almost exclusively with their fellow-countrymen, and obeying the rule of their own consuls… this custom was favourable to the integrity of trade, since… the whole merchant community had an interest in the honesty of each of its members.'[57]

A story in the *Great Chronicle of London* shows that, at this very early stage in the development of the city's underwriting, dishonest outsider-buyers were already attempting to gain advantage in the insurance marketplace. In this case, a fraud was perpetrated against underwriters. The anonymous chronicler recounted the story of a rogue trader who, at some point before 1509, thought

> To stuff Shyppis, wyth ffals crafty balauncis
> As blokkys & stonys, and countyrfayt dalyauncis
> And afftyr assure, the said shippys w' theyr ffeyghth
> For grete Summys, tyll they cam on the heygth
> Of the Occean, and then cawse theym to drowne
> That the assuraunce, mygth ffor nowgth be payd.[58]

According to the *Great Chronicle*, the criminal was found out. However, such frauds, while not common in the day to day practice of insurance, were to occur again, often with equal celebration. For example, Pepys recounted the trial of a malfeasant who spread butter over a shipment of tallow, then scuttled the vessel, making a claim for the higher-value, falsified cargo.[59]

When undiscovered, such fraudulent claims would be treated by underwriters in the same way as any other, thereby inflating the loss experience they would consider in future pricing. However, the chronicler's story illustrates a challenge which can distort interpretations of historical insurance: stories of malpractice, and especially the records of disputed insurance contracts, are much more likely to have survived from the earliest period of insurance in London, and indeed until the middle of the eighteenth century.[60] Since very little evidence survives of policies which were undisputed, completed successfully, and presumably discarded, it is very difficult to garner an idea of the total volume or value of insurance underwritten in the early period, or of the incidence of disputes and malpractice.

References to insurance are frequent in surviving merchant papers of the six-teenth century. Very few comprehensive bodies of such records contain no mention

---

[57] Origo, *Merchant of Prato*, p. 40.

[58] Thomas, A. H. and Thornley, I. D. (eds): *The great chronicle of London*, Gloucester: Alan Sutton, 1983, p. 360.

[59] Latham, R. and Matthews, W. (eds): *The Diary of Samuel Pepys*, Vol. IV – 1663, London: Bell & Sons, 1971, pp. 401–404.

[60] Selective retention of insurance documents continues. The author is in possession of several London-issued insurance policies issued to the Atlantic Refining Company during the 1920s and 1930s. All record claims. I have concluded not that the said company was exceptionally claims-prone, but that it preserved the policies in question because they detailed the claims, and destroyed the others.

of insurance. Together they show that the practice was widespread, and not limited to high value or luxury goods, as has often been asserted. For example, in 1539 the Bristol merchant John Smythe insured '195 k. iren in the ships of Anto de Asteacu & Jn P de Arana cost abord 107,614 M. & for assurance made apo p't of same 1990 M'.[61] The ledger entry shows Smythe insuring iron weighing 195 *kyntalls*, or roughly 8,800 kilograms, and valued in *maravedi*, a Spanish currency worth, by Smythe's reckoning, 1,500 to the pound sterling. The iron, imported from San Sebastian in Spain, was loaded onto two ships, as was common as a risk mitigation measure. It was valued at roughly £71.15.0; the insurance, which covered only part of the value of the iron, cost about £1.6.0. Further evidence from Smythe's ledger shows that he insured often, although not always, on cargoes ranging from wine to wood.

A series of a dozen policy documents issued to the London merchant Bartholomew Corsini in the 1580s have been preserved among his papers; work by Rossi has found in Florence an additional series of London policies underwritten for Corsini.[62] Further evidence shows that insurance was underwritten at other English ports, but London merchants already enjoyed a distinct pricing advantage in this period, when most English trade was conducted over short routes to the nearby marts of the Continent. An objection to a petition of 1582, which requested the establishment of a staple of cotton at Chester, states that 'the Charge of transportacion thether [to Rouen, France] from Chester is so great a difference that it will muche alter the price of so lowe priced ware, for that which may be assured from London to Roane for thre in the hundred will not be assured from Chester for xij in the hundred, the voiage is both so long and dangerous'.[63]

Documents related to the resolution of insurance disputes provide a second important source of evidence of the practice of insurance in London in the sixteenth century. These include more than a dozen cases in the High Court of Admiralty, nearly a score heard by the Privy Council, and a handful each in the courts of Chancery and King's Bench.[64] The formal courts were rivals, and none had exclusive jurisdiction over insurance cases. The earliest known to have reached the common law courts was *Mayne & Poyn* v. *De Gozi*, which was heard at King's Bench in 1538.[65] Baker suggests that by hearing it, the common law court had managed to 'bring within its purview... even marine insurance'.[66]

However, its success was far from complete. *Vivalde* v. *Sheriff of London* was held before the Mayoral Court at Guildhall, which almost certainly was the most frequent

---

[61] Vanes, Jean (ed.): *The ledger of John Smythe, 1538–1550*, London: HMSO, 1974, p. 85.

[62] GHL CLC/B/062/MS22281, CLC/B/062/MS22282, the Corsini papers, policies issued to Bartholomew Corsini; Rossi, *Booke of Orders*, p. 244 ff.

[63] TNA SPD Elizabeth Vol. CLVII, f. 5, 'Objections advanced by Shrewsbury', cited in Tawney, R. H. and Power, E. (eds), *Tudor economic documents*, three volumes, London: Longmans, Green & Co., 1924, I, p. 206.

[64] All of which are discussed below.

[65] Ibbetson, D.: 'Law and custom: Insurance in sixteenth-century England', *Journal of Legal History*, Vol. 29, No. 3 (2008), p. 293.

[66] Baker, Sir John: *The Oxford history of the laws of England, Vol. VI, 1483–1588*, Oxford: Oxford University Press, 2003, pp. 215, 211, n. 18.

arena for such disputes, at roughly the same time (and later would argue that it, not the Admiralty, was the rightful home of insurance disputes).[67] Civil lawyers and their Roman law tradition gained renewed jurisdictional importance under the Tudor monarchs, in parallel to a rise in importance of the prerogative courts. In 1540 Henry VIII, in an attempt to revitalise the Admiralty's scope of authority, and thus his prerogative power, extended its traditional jurisdiction (which since Edward II had covered only matters related to actions on the high seas) to include pleas over contracts written on English soil but related to actions on or beyond the seas, especially over freight and charter-party disputes. Later, under legislation of 1547, the High Court of Admiralty was granted power to try summarily matters of damage to cargo.[68] While insurance disputes are not mentioned specifically in the Act, they began to reach the Court with relative frequency shortly after its passage. Marsden's first volume of *Select pleas in the Court of Admiralty*, which includes pleas from the period 1527 to 1545, includes none related to insurance, but the second volume, covering 1547 to 1602, reproduces several, the earliest dating from 1547.[69]

However, in the same year the case *Crane v. Bell* was deemed 'not determinable in the Admiralty' because the policy was concluded on land.[70] Some actions proceeded in parallel both in the High Court of the Admiralty and in the Court of Chancery, and the Admiralty sometimes brought proceedings of contempt against individuals who sued over insurance matters in competing courts, as it attempted to cement its jurisdiction over insurance actions.[71] In 1558, the Admiralty sued plaintiffs for contempt for presenting an insurance case before Chancery.[72] Meanwhile, in a dispute between the merchants Adam Wyntropp and John Combes of France, the Chief Justice of King's Bench made an 'attachment' against the Judge of the Admiralty 'upon the pretence that he had intermeddled in his jurisdiccion' over commercial disputes. When the Privy Council finally ruled, in 1558/9, they referred the case back to several aldermen and merchants for arbitration, depriving both courts of the business.[73]

Records of perhaps half a dozen discrete insurance cases from the mid sixteenth century survive in the Chancery archives; most were heard before the Lord Chancellor, rather than the Court proper, but the Admiralty seems to have been the

---

[67] TNA C 1/914/31, *Vivalde v. Sheriff of London*; Rossi, *Insurance in Elizabethan England*, p. 6.

[68] Steckley, George F.: 'Merchants and the Admiralty Court during the English revolution', *American Journal of Legal History*, Vol. 22, No. 2 (1978), p. 141; 32 Hen. VIII c. 14, par. 10, 'The Mayntenaunce of the Navye'.

[69] Marsden, R. G.: *Select pleas in the Court of the Admiralty*, two vols, London: Selden Society, 1897.

[70] Zouch, Richard: *The jurisdiction of the Admiralty asserted against Sir Edward Coke's Articuli admiralitatis, XXII chapter of his jurisdiction of courts*, London: Printed for Tyton, F. and Dring, T., 1663, p. 89.

[71] Ibbetson, 'Law and custom', pp. 293–294.

[72] Marsden, *Select pleas*, II, p. lxvii.

[73] Dasent, John R.: *Acts of the Privy Council of England, New Series*, thirty-one volumes, London: HMSO, 1893–1906, VII, pp. 12, 62.

preferred jurisdiction.[74] This seems logical since it was the only royal court routinely administering the Law Merchant (which was the primary law governing matters of the high seas), and since, according to Aylmer, civil lawyers' training left them better-disposed to deal with commercial matters, and especially with those related to foreign trade.[75] Together with the evidence of merchants' papers, these courts' records are sufficient to draw the conclusion that insurance was widespread among London merchants by the middle decades of the sixteenth century. Many individuals from both sides of these transactions are identifiable by surname as foreign merchants or resident merchant strangers, but many too were English.[76]

Disputed agreements preserved in court records provide the most numerous extant examples of sixteenth-century insurances, but it is unlikely that they represent more than a very small share of the total number of insurance agreements that were reached. Most contracts would not have led to a claim, and therefore would have expired without scrutiny, and may have quickly been discarded. It seems obvious that if even a large minority of cases led to formal dispute resolution, the market would have ceased to function. The methodical preservation of court documents means disputed transactions are much more likely to be known than others, but merchant preference means that surviving documentation probably represents only a small percentage even of disputed claims: insurance disputes were usually resolved through arbitration, under the tenets of the Law Merchant.[77] No cache of documents relating to historical insurance-related arbitrations in England has been found, but together these factors lead to the safe conclusion that the surviving evidence related to disputed claims under insurance policies must represent only a very small percentage of those underwritten in London in the sixteenth century. While it is impossible to calculate or even reasonably estimate the percentage of cargoes passing through London's ports which were insured, or to measure London underwriters' export of insurance to non-resident merchants, it is clear that by the sixteenth century, insurance was solidly established in the city, and regularly practised.

It has long been believed that insurance practice was introduced into London by resident Lombard merchants such as those described above, and more recent discoveries remove all doubt.[78, 79] But marine insurance customs differed between the originating Italian states, and London insurers did not initially adopt a single set of rules. At first the practices of Genoa were important, due largely to the city-state's

74 For details of Chancery cases, see Jones, W. J.: 'Elizabethan marine insurance: the judicial undergrowth', *Business History*, No. 2 (1970), pp. 58–62.

75 Aylmer, G. E.: *King's servants: the civil service of Charles I, 1625–1642*, London: Routledge, 1961, p. 53.

76 For the names of many merchants involved in insurance disputes in the Elizabethan period, see Jones, 'Elizabethan marine insurance', pp. 58–62 (esp. notes).

77 For more on arbitration, , see pp. 64–68; van Niekerk, *Principles of insurance law*, I, p. 245; Jones, 'Elizabethan marine insurance', p. 53.

78 See, for example, Martin, *The history of Lloyd's*, p. 25.

79 For an in-depth discussion of the Italian origins of London insurance, see Rossi, Guido: 'England 1523–1601: the beginnings of marine insurance', in Leonard, A. B. (ed.), *Marine insurance*, pp. 13–148.

early role in trade with London, but Florentine practice overtook Genoese insurance custom as London usage evolved, probably due, as Rossi concludes, to the inflexibility of Genoa's policy structure. Later still, the influence of the insuring customs of Antwerp began to overtake those of Florence in London underwriting, which critically introduced greater flexibility to the market.[80]

As the foregoing sections show, the basic institutional characteristics of the London insurance market were established by the mid sixteenth century. The Ferrantyn case and the Borromei records show that, among the community of Italian merchants resident in London, conventional insurance was in use by the third decade of the fifteenth century. A premium, representing a percentage of the contingent indemnity promised under a policy, was paid to multiple insurance underwriters based on the size of the indemnity they were obliged, under contract, to pay in case specified losses occurred. In this way, some of the risks of seaborne trade were spread among multiple members of the merchant community. These early examples of insurance also show that information including the voyage, the vessel and its master, the nature of the cargo, and the time and duration of the adventure were disclosed to the underwriters, and at least sometimes specified in the contract of insurance.

According to an anonymous commentator writing in the 1570s, until the 1530s only 'strangers' in London used insurance, but in the early 1540s English merchants began to 'translate and make policies into English'.[81] By the mid sixteenth century, the English native and resident merchant community was regularly purchasing and underwriting insurance, in the outports as well as in London (as were some English merchants resident abroad, as Ceccarelli has shown[82]). Already, too, some London insurance was exported. The oldest two policies identified in the archives of the High Court of Admiralty, drawn up in London in 1547 and 1548, are written in Italian (alongside contemporary English translations, prepared for the Court).[83] Both policies insure Italian merchants, but were underwritten by men whose surnames, such as Lodge, Maynard, and Webb, reveal them to be English, reflecting the common London practice of drawing policies in languages other than English, to suit clients' needs.[84]

Marine insurance and the Law Merchant

Within markets, enforcement mechanisms and the institutions which support them are critical to the reduction of transaction costs, and thus to the continuous

---

[80] Rossi, *Insurance in Elizabethan England*, pp. 31, 59–60.

[81] Rossi, *Insurance in Elizabethan England*, p. 56.

[82] Ceccarelli, Giovani: *Un mercato del rischio: assicurare e farsi assicurare nella Firenze rinascimentale*, Venice: Marsilio, 2012, p. 283.

[83] TNA HCA 24/27 f. 147, policy underwritten for Giovanni Broke, 20 Sept. 1547; TNA HCA 24/18 f. 131, policy underwritten for Tonamaso Cavalcanti and Giovanni Girale, for the account of Paulo Cicini of Messina, 26 Nov. 1548; f. 132 (translation).

[84] BL Lansdowne MS 113/9, 'Some Merchants, Notaries, and Brokers petition Sir James Hawes, Lord Mayor of London, against Rich. Candler's grant for registering policies of assurance' (undated, 1574?).

improvement of any body involved in economic exchange.[85] For London marine insurance among the merchant-insurers, the primary institutions of enforcement were the merchant community itself, sometimes embodied in the city's Lord Mayor and aldermen, and its body of governing rules, the Law Merchant. In 1781 the underwriter Weskett published his encyclopaedic *Complete digest*. It describes the Law Merchant as follows:

> Law Merchant, or *Lex Mercatoria*. No municipal laws can be sufficient to order and determine the very complicated affairs of traffic and merchandise; neither can they have a proper authority for this purpose: for as these are transactions carried on between subjects of independent states, the municipal laws of one will not be regarded by the other:– for which reason the affairs of commerce are regulated by a law of their own, called the Law Merchant, or *Lex Mercatoria*, which all nations agree in and take notice of: and in particular it is held to be a part of the law of England, which decides the causes of merchants by the *general* rules which obtain in all commercial countries.[86]

The Law Merchant provided the rules of the game for insurance both before state judicial oversight, and, in practice, afterwards as well. It operated alongside the civil and common laws of the nation, and functioned – according at least to some contemporary observers and current commentators – as a distinct third branch of the law. Like marine insurance itself, the genesis of the Law Merchant was in Italy, and was based on customary practice.[87] Despite a clear division between lawyers of the civil and common law, the place of the Law Merchant as a branch of English law was relatively widely acknowledged. As the common law jurist Sir John Davies argued early in the seventeenth century, 'laws as be common to other nations as well as us, have been received and used time out of mind by the king and people of England in divers cases, and by such ancient uses are become the laws of England in such cases, namely the general law of nations and the Law Merchant, which is a branch of the law, the imperial or civil law'.[88] The customary practice it outlines for marine insurance was incorporated methodically into English common law only in the latter half of the eighteenth century, and was not formally codified or enacted through statute until 1906. Tellingly, the 1906 Act (6 Edw. VII cap. 41) is sub-titled *An Act to codify the Law relating to Marine Insurance*, indicating recognition of the pre-existing body of marine insurance law. The market operated successfully, and indeed reached international predominance, long before this occurred.

Davies, who served as both Solicitor and Attorney General for Ireland (1603–1619), and was a member of the Virginia Company, observed the impact of the Law

---

[85] North, Douglass: *Institutions, institutional change and economic performance*, Cambridge: Cambridge University Press, 1990.

[86] Weskett, *Complete digest*, p. 321.

[87] For a concise history of the development of the law merchant, see Benson, Bruce L.: 'The spontaneous evolution of commercial law', *Southern Economic Journal*, Vol. 55, No. 3 (1989), pp. 664–661.

[88] Cited in Levack, B.: *The civil lawyers in England 1601–1641: a political study*, Oxford: Clarendon Press, 1973, p. 146.

Merchant system as practised by the merchant-insurers of London. Richard Zouch, a seventeenth-century Admiralty Judge, recorded a manuscript admission of Davies, who

> saith... 'That until he understood the difference 'betwixt the Law-Merchant and the Common Law of *England*, he did not a little 'marvel that *England*, entertaining Traffick with all Nations of the World, having 'so many Ports, and so much good Shipping, the King of *England* also being Lord 'of the Sea, what should be the cause that, in the Books of the Common Law of '*England*, there are to be found so few Cases concerning Merchants or Ships: but 'now the Reason thereof was apparent, for the Common Law of the Land did 'leave those Cases to be ruled by another Law; namely, the Law-Merchant; which 'is a branch of the Law of Nations.'[89]

Authorities over centuries regularly referred to the body of rules encompassed by the Law Merchant when called upon to intervene in insurance-related disputes. In some major maritime centres, its main tenets were compiled and codified as a corpus of marine regulation, during an era in which, Dickson reports, some contemporary English writers 'suggested that mercantile law should be codified, and administered by special courts so as to speed up the resolution of commercial disputes'.[90] Barcelona adopted insurance ordinances in 1484; they are regarded as the first insurance code.[91] Florence set out an insurance ordinance in 1523. Burgos adopted ordinances in 1538 and 1572, perhaps based on earlier codifications. Seville and Bilbao followed in 1556 and 1560 respectively. Philip II approved insurance regulations for Antwerp in 1563, and for the insurance in Spain of vessels to the Indies between 1556 and 1588. Amsterdam adopted broad ordinances in 1598, leaning heavily on Antwerp practice. Rouen's *Guidon de la Mer* was adopted probably in the 1580s. Genoa passed regulations in 1610, Middleburg in 1689, Rotterdam in 1604 and 1721, and Amsterdam in 1598 and 1724.[92] Codification of the rules of the game of insurance, as established under the Law Merchant, was widespread in the major western European trading port cities and nations from the sixteenth century, as customary law was written into the statute books.

The codification of any local Law Merchant transforms it into something else, however. It becomes the fixed law of the proclaiming authority, rather than the flexible, customary law of the merchant. This is problematical for some scholars. Ogilvie, for example, states

> If a coherent body of merchant law existed at all, it must have been customary and oral. But that means it is all but impossible to establish its existence. The absence of merchant law from contemporary written collections and legal manuals raises

---

[89] Zouch, *Jurisdiction of the Admiralty*, p. 79.

[90] Dickson, *Financial revolution*, p. 4.

[91] Rossi, *Insurance in Elizabethan England*, p. 16.

[92] Rossi, *Booke of Orders*, p. 241, n. 2; Magens, *An essay*, I, p. 1 ff.

the question of how significant or widely used it can have been, given that other bodies of law did appear in written form at the same period.[93]

This opinion, drawn from a recent school of Law-Merchant deniers such as Sachs (who describes the Law Merchant as 'fictional'), is caught upon two fundamental flaws.[94] First, it ignores much secondary evidence of the existence of the Law Merchant. This evidence includes pleas in the 1426 Ferrantyn case, described below,[95] which refer repeatedly and specifically to the Law Merchant, and Gerard Malynes's 1622 tome entitled *Lex Mercatorta: or, the ancient Law-Merchant*, a manual self-described as 'necessary for statesmen, judges, magistrates, temporal and civil lawyers, mint-men, merchants, mariners, and all others negotiating in any parts of the world'.[96] The opinion denies extremely competent authorities such as Richard Zouch, cited above, and the barrister Charles Molloy, who wrote in 1676 that 'The Law concerning merchants is called the Law Merchant from its universal Concern, whereof all Nations do take special Knowledge, and the Common and Statute Laws of England, takes notice of the Law Merchant, and leave the Causes of Merchants in many Instances to their own peculiar Law.'[97]

Second, Law Merchant deniers miss a basic characteristic of the uncodified body of rules: its flexibility. While a newly codified selection of Law Merchant customs may initially be identical to the Law Merchant itself, it probably would not be for long. This is evident in the two extant copies of England's *Booke of Orders*, drafted in the 1570s at roughly the same time, but which differ significantly, if not dramatically.[98] It was in the nature of the Law Merchant to change over time and distance, in a manner suited to those applying it in and at a specific place and occasion, and, especially, as new circumstances arose. This flexibility allowed the rules of the game to be altered to account for evolving trade scenarios, and thus was of particular importance as the nature of European trade developed.

Flexibility was one of the characteristics of insurance regulation, especially as practised in London, which made it such an effective tool for meeting the uncertainties of early modern merchant adventurers. As will be shown below, the first semi-formal codification of insurance law in London sought to remain flexible through frequent modification based upon changes in practice and the decisions of arbiters. In this way, it represented a meeting of the English common and civil law traditions. Underlying this flexibility was England's longstanding sympathy for flexibility in the legal interpretation of regulations, such that intent, rather than the rules themselves, should guide dispute resolution. The Norman jurist Glanvill, writing

---

93 Ogilvie, *Institutions*, p. 266.

94 Sachs, Stephen E.: 'From St. Ives to cyberspace: the modern distortion of the medieval "Law Merchant"', *American University International Law Review*, Vol. 21, No. 5 (2006), p. 695.

95 See p. 58; Thomas, *Calendar of plea & memoranda rolls*, pp. 209–210.

96 Malynes, *Lex mercatoria*, 1686.

97 Molloy, C.: *De jure maritimo et navali: or, A treatise of affairs maritime, and of commerce*, eighth edition, London: J. Walthoe (printer), 1744 (first published 1676), p. 461.

98 See pp. 85 ff.

*c.*1188, stated in his chapter regarding 'purchase and sale' that 'it is a general rule that agreement prevails over the law'.[99] This old sympathy was bolstered by the dual legal principle of equity, or *aequitas*, outlined by fourteenth-century jurists. At that time, Baker argues, equity became 'institutionally separated' from the common law, as judges in the latter courts became more rigid and less discretionary. As well as comprising the 'spirit' of law, equity later became, in the words of Jones, a 'criterion for interpreting written law according to the true meaning of the lawmaker, on the basis that words were an imperfect vehicle for expressing legislative intention in detail'. In the later middle ages the idea of 'fairness' became a principal sense of equity, and in the 1570s, according to Ibbetson, merchants' descriptions of courts as 'of equitie' meant simply that 'strict law would not be applied'; the courts were not 'hamstrung by Common law rules and processes', and it allowed them even to intervene 'against the rules of the Common law'.[100]

The absence of codification (or simple non-observation of the rules, as the Privy Council complained in relation to insurance regulation in 1601, stating that some merchants 'refuse to submytte and conforme them selves to the order of Commyssioners'), obviously eliminated the problem of inflexibility.[101] Thus, the Privy Council called regularly for merchant arbitrators to decide cases 'as to justice and equitie appertaineth'.[102] Sachs argues that 'the practice of mercantile law… was more flexible than the translation of "the law merchant," with its reifying definite article, would imply', but this is exactly its strength.[103]

The 'force and effect' clause

Van Niekirk argued that: 'The marine insurance policy was not merely a recognition of the legal relationship between the parties to the contract it embodied, but also the source and, because of its form, the bearer of an emerging body marine insurance customs'.[104] Customs emerged and evolved differently from place to place. One challenge hindering the acceptance of the Law Merchant as a set of governing rules (let alone a distinct body of law) is compounded by this, one of its key characteristics, despite the common assertion that the Law Merchant is universal. That it may be, but often it must defer to local custom. In practice, the Law Merchant too varied

---

[99] '*Quippe generaliter enim uerum est quod conuentio legem uincit.*' Hall, G. D. G. (ed.): *The treatise on the laws and customs of England commonly called Glanvill* (*c.*1187–1189), London: Selden Society and Thomas Nelson & Sons, 1965, p. 129.

[100] Baker, Sir John: *The Oxford history of the laws of England, vol. VI, 1483–1588*, Oxford: Oxford University Press, 2003, VI, pp. 40–41; Jones, W. J.: *The Elizabethan Court of Chancery*, Oxford: Clarendon Press, 1967, pp. 9–10; Ibbetson, David: 'A house built on sand: equity in early modern English law', in Koops, E. & Zwalve, W. J. (eds): *Law & Equity: Approaches in Roman Law and Common Law*, Leiden: Martinus Nijhoff Publishers, 2013, pp. 56–57, 76.

[101] Dasent, *Acts of the Privy Council*, XXXI, p. 252–253.

[102] See, for example, Dasent, *Acts of the Privy Council*, Vol. VIII, p. 167.

[103] Sachs, 'From St. Ives', p. 760.

[104] van Niekerk, *Principles of insurance law*, I, p. 248.

from place to place, often subtly, but sometimes dramatically. As the Ferrantyn case makes clear, those deciding insurance disputes in late medieval London were aware of such local inconsistencies, and respected contractual clauses which invoked the governance of a contract by one version of the Law Merchant or another. It is implied also in the decision of various Mediterranean insurance centres, and later Antwerp, to allow the members of different merchant nations resident there to adjudicate any insurance disputes arising within their own communities themselves, by the consuls of the relevant expatriate nation.[105]

In recognition of this, almost all extant English-language marine insurance policies from the middle of the sixteenth century forward carry a form of a clause which indirectly places the contract under the jurisdiction of the Law Merchant, and which specifies which body of rules – that is, which city's Law Merchant – is to be applied. This practice reduced ambiguities of interpretation, making the Law Merchant a more effective institution of contractual enforcement. The relevant body of Law Merchant custom appears almost always to have been stated explicitly in policies, within a clause which employed words such as 'this present writing of assurance shall have as much force and effect as any policy of assurance heretofore made in' (some specified location). The phrase is used in almost all policies issued in London from about 1600.

The Alexander Ferrantyn case, heard in the Guildhall in 1427, turned on such an expression of the locality of the Law Merchant to be applied. The insured, Ferrantyn, was refused a claim for a vessel, the '*Seint Anne of London*' (John Starling, master), which was carrying a cargo of wine to England from Bordeaux. Both vessel and cargo, insured for £250 by seventeen Italian merchants resident in London, had been seized by Spaniards, but Ferrantyn, through an agent, had repurchased the vessel and cargo, which the privateers had sold to Flemish merchants. The policy (referred to in the aldermen's court as a 'bill of contract') specified that the 'order, manner, and custom of the Florentines' was to govern the contract. The claimant requested indemnity 'by the law merchant and according to the manner, order and custom of the Florentines'. The disputing parties claimed respectively that Florentine custom required the indemnity to be paid despite the recovery, and that it did not. The case was to be decided based on a finding of settled Florentine Law Merchant. Both parties promised to produce notarised testimony from the Italian city, which stated the prevailing local custom in such situations. So confident were the defending insurers that they paid the disputed £250, plus £100 as surety, into the court. In the words of the editor of the relevant *Calendar of plea rolls*, 'the defendants appear to have pleaded that the words about the custom of the Florentines were qualifying words, and that payment was subject to certain exceptions and conditions customary among the Florentines, but not mentioned in the contract. The plaintiff stood on the plain terms of the contract.'[106] (The outcome of the case unfortunately is unknown.)

The modification of actual contractual terms by the application of specified local custom was to continue in London's insurance market for more than a century, but

---

[105] De ruysscher, 'Antwerp 1490–1590', p. 80.

[106] Thomas, *Calendar of plea & memoranda rolls*, pp. 208–210.

soon London practice was sufficiently established to provide a reference point for applicable custom. A contemporary English translation of the earliest policy in the Admiralty archives, written originally in Italian and dated 1547, states that 'it is to be understood this preasente writinge hathe as muche forse as the beste made or dicted byll of surance w'ch is used to be made in this lombarde streete of London'.[107] Thus, the Law Merchant which was to govern the policy was that reflected in the insurance practices of the merchants of Lombard Street, home to the concentration of north Italian merchants who succeeded those who had introduced insurance to London more than a century earlier. (The phrase 'dicted byll' further implies the importance and validity at this time of verbal contracts of insurance, and that they too operated under the Law Merchant.)

A second example, from 1557, shows how the language of policies was not fixed, but that the presence of a force and effect clause was conventional.[108] A cargo policy unknown until I identified it in the papers of the High Court of the Admiralty, now lodged in the National Archives, states:

> In the name of God the viii^th day of marche 1558 from the natyvyte

> John Mowse of Nedam in Suffolk confesse to be assured in his own^e name, and of eny other he will, to whome yt may apertain^e upon two shippes the one named the prymyrose of dertemouthe M[aste]^r _____ and the other named the Thomas of London Mr Pentirose Harrys, or howsoev they be named or called, upon Iron or Win^e, or eny other mchaundys^e whatsoev, laden or to be laden in the same Shippes in Bilbao or Saynte Sebastian, or eny other portes thire aboutes in Biscaye, by John Browneryk^e, and George Monnox, or eny other for them. The adventure and perill to begin from the day and howur that the said good[s] were or shalbe laden untill suche tym^e, as the same shalbe arryved here in the ryver of Thamys, and the good[s] dyscharged on land in good saveti^e. Understonding^e them the asseurers do bind them in the same force and forme wch the wrytinges of assurunce are used to be made in lombarde Strete of London, And in Testymony of truthe, the asseurers shall hereunder subscrib^e with ther proper hand. God send them in savetie.

> We Robert dowe and Robert Wells are content to assure in man well abovesaid for one hundreth Nobelles in the said two shipps the 8 of mche 1557 xxxiii^li vi^s viii^d

> I George barne am contented in to assure in the primros of dartmouth & in the Thoms of london the some of xxv^li 8 day of mche anno 1557   xxv^li

---

[107] TNA HCA 24/27 f. 199, policy underwritten for Giovanni Broke, 20 Sept. 1547.

[108] I am grateful for the assistance of Dr Guido Rossi in the initial transliteration of this document, here corrected. The policy header states the year as 1558, but the underwriters state it is 1557. Since under old-style dating the year advanced on Lady Day, 25 March, and since the policy was clearly drawn before the later signatures were signed and dated, this discrepancy is not easily explained. It seems more likely that a single error was made in the header by a clerk who was thinking ahead to Lady Day than that four underwriters made the same error more than eleven months into the year. TNA HCA 24/30 f. 233, policy underwritten for John Mowse, 8 Mar. 1557.

We Roger lighfor & John Robyns are content in man aforesaid for twelf pound x^s in the same ii shipps the ix day of mche 1557 I sa   xii^{li} x^s

I Rafe Greneway am contentid for xxix^{li} iii^s iiii^d in man & forme folowing that is two say upon the prymrose of dartmouth and in the Thoms of london the ix day of mche 1557 I say   xxix^{li} iii^s iiii^d

The legal historian Holdsworth states that such force and effect clauses, which appear in one form or another in all of the policies preserved in this series of Admiralty records, 'probably had the result of producing a uniformity in the legal effect' of all of them. They provided all parties to an insurance contract, and courts which may be called to adjudicate disputes, with a known – if uncodified – body of customary practice to govern proceedings.[109] Jones argues that, with the force and effect clause, 'the merchant attempted to bolster up his position by incorporating [into his policy] the entire body of the Law Merchant, in so far as it was worked out in relation to marine insurance'.[110] It had been 'worked out' to a considerable extent, as the work of Francesco Rocci, a jurist of Naples and judge of the *Magna Curia*, proves beyond doubt. His *Treatise on Insurance*, first published in Italian in 1655, presents one hundred 'notes' on insurance, many of which are not dissimilar to entries in London's draft 'Booke of Orders of Assurances' compiled in the 1570s, with 126 articles.[111] Where it was not worked out, merchant arbiters made decisions which added to the otherwise uncodified law.

Another document, comparable to a modern expert opinion, accompanies another surviving policy which had been brought under suit in the High Court of the Admiralty. It reinforces the assumption about the longstanding practice of insurance, and likens practice, and thus the Law Merchant which governs the business, to that of Antwerp, stating 'That the use and custome of makynge bylls of assuraunce in the place comonly called Lumbard Strete of London and likewyse in the Burse of Antwerpe, is and tyme oute of mynde hathe byn emonge m'chants usinge and frequentinge the sayde & severall places and assuraunces'.[112] Although the policy in question, which insures the Florentine merchant Robert Ridolphye (better known for his plot to assassinate the queen), mentions only Lombard Street, the accompanying legal opinion brings to bear the custom of both London and Antwerp.[113]

In this specific case, the point of custom in question is the ability for one man to insure, in his own name, the goods of another. Rossi argues that this practice was permitted in the Netherlands, following the practice of Antwerp, but was prohibited

---

[109] Holdsworth, W. S.: 'The early history of the contract of insurance', *Columbia Law Review*, Vol. 17, No. 2 (1917), p. 98.

[110] Jones, 'Elizabethan marine insurance', p. 55.

[111] Roccus (Rocci), Francesco: *A treatise on insurance* (first published in Latin, 1655), in Reed Ingersoll, Joseph (ed. and trans.), *A manual of maritime law*, Philadelphia: Hopkins and Earle, 1809; BL Add. Ms. 48,023, ff. 246–273, the 'Booke of Orders of Assurances' (1574?).

[112] TNA HCA 24/35 f. 46, legal opinion on the Ridolphye case, undated (1562?).

[113] TNA HCA 24/35 f. 283, policy underwritten for Robert Ridolphye (Roberto Ridolphi), 11 Mar. 1562.

under the Italian Law Merchant. London, by adopting this practice, experienced 'a major rupture with the consolidated practice of Lombard Street'. The decision is similar to that in a slightly earlier case under arbitration involving a policy under-written in 1558 and bearing the signature of fifteen merchant witnesses, which 'attests to the importance of the decision', according to Rossi. He argues that the finding approved a change from Italian to Dutch practice, apparently despite the legal opin-ion recorded just a few years later in the Ridolphye dispute, that the practice had been in use 'time out of mind' among the merchants of Lombard Street.[114] This change to prevailing custom shows flexibility on the part of London merchant-in-surers to accommodate the needs of their insurance-buying customers, and of the courts (or, at least, the Court of Admiralty), to follow changing merchant custom in their decision-making approach.

A further policy in the Admiralty series, drawn up in 1555 to insure the mer-chant Anthony de Salizar, makes the Antwerp connection directly, stating that 'thys assurauns shall be so stronge and good as the most ample writinge of assurauns wch is used to be maid in the strite of london [Lombard Street] or the burse of antwerp or in any other forme that shulde have more force.'[115] Rossi argues that the change in London merchant-insurers' preference for Dutch over Italian practice is reflected in this jurisdiction clause: a change from making reference only to the Italian-English Law Merchant of Lombard Street to include the insurance customs of the Dutch, which followed the precedents of Antwerp.[116] However, during this brief period London was sometimes the point of reference adopted in policies made in ports with which the city traded. A 1566 policy underwritten in Antwerp contained the clause 'according to the usage and custom of Lombard Street of London and this Bourse of Antwerp', apparently indicating that the full force of the Law Merchant of both cities was brought to bear upon the policy. At least four earlier Antwerp policies also referred to 'the street' in London.[117]

Van Niekerk states that 'it is not absolutely certain but at least highly proba-ble that the points on which the [de Salizar] policy contravened the *placcaat* [an Antwerp regulation of 1563 which a subsequent Amsterdam ordinance required to be observed in the latter city] were at the same time the points on which it agreed with London insurance practices and customs'.[118] However, this explanation does little to clarify why some Dutch policies issued before the 1563 regulations cited London's authority, which according to Rossi reflected Italian practice transmitted through the Ordinances of Bruges. These clauses serve to weaken slightly Rossi's implied argument that the change in the authority clause in mid-sixteenth-century English insurance policies reflected a shift from preference of the Law Merchant of Italy to that of Antwerp/Amsterdam, and strengthen Holdsworth's claim that the clauses

---

[114] Rossi, *Booke of Orders*, pp. 243–244.

[115] TNA HCA 24/29 f. 45, policy underwritten for Anthony de Salizar, 5 Sep. 1555.

[116] Rossi, *Booke of Orders*, p. 243, n. 6.

[117] '*a l'usance et coutume de las Strade de Londres et de ceste boursse d'Anvers*'. Quoted in French in van Niekerk, *Principles of insurance law*, I, p. 256, n. 256, 261–262.

[118] van Niekerk, *Principles of insurance law*, I, p. 256, n. 262.

were intended to produce a 'uniformity in the legal effect' under contracts prepared for merchants trading between commercial centres whose local Law Merchant, as it applied to insurance, was not itself entirely uniform.[119]

The locations cited to indicate the relevant Law Merchant authority for policies underwritten in London remained fluid, and seem in part to have followed practice. The London Corsini policies of the 1580s show this clearly.[120] Each states that 'Yt is to be understanded, that thys p[rese]'nte wrytinge is & shalbe of as muche force, strengthe, & effecte, as the beste & moste sureste pollecis or wrytinges of assurance wch hath byn ever heretofore used to be made in Lumbarde Streate, or *now* w^thin the Royall Exchange in London.'[121] The addition of reference to the Royal Exchange followed the establishment of an official policy registration office at that location, where Corsini's policies were drawn up.[122] However, reference to the Royal Exchange appeared earlier. A royal patent of 1575/6 referred to 'the auncient custome of merchauntes in Lomberd strete, and nowe the Ryall Exchaunge', indicating either that insurance underwriting was already commonplace there, even before the establishment of the Office of Assurance, or perhaps that it was about to be concentrated there, with the opening of the Office under patent.[123]

The customs of Lombard Street were to remain an important point of reference, just as those of the Royal Exchange had become. A policy issued in 1641 to George Warner of London cites 'Lumbardstreete or exc^e', the latter presumably a shorthand reference to the Royal Exchange.[124] The absence in London of a regulation specifying the regional Law Merchant to be applied, as the 1563 Dutch *placcaat* did for the Netherlands, and the fluidity of the Law Merchant selected, must have contributed to the flexibility of the insurance product offered in London. Given the variety of force and effect clauses which appear in London insurance documents before the widespread take-up of printed blank policy forms later in the seventeenth century, presumably insurance brokers, underwriters, or buyers – or more likely a combination of them – had, and actively made, choices about which body of Law Merchant was to apply to each contract drawn up and entered. This would have given London an advantage over its competitors, when the latter were more restricted in this choice, and especially when underwriting for foreign clients, who may have preferred a different, more familiar or appropriate, set of rules.

The authority of the Law Merchant specified by the force and effect clause could also be avoided directly, in favour of policy terms and conditions which suited the buyer and seller at the time of underwriting. For example, buyers may have preferred a narrower coverage than that typically offered according to the customs of Lombard

---

[119] Rossi, *Insurance in Elizabethan England*, p. 148; Rossi, *Booke of Orders*, p. 242 ff.

[120] CLC/B/062/MS 22,282, insurance policies underwritten for Bartholomew Corsini.

[121] Emphasis added. GHL 062/MS 22,281, policy underwritten for Bartholomew Corsini, 24 Sept. 1582.

[122] See pp. 76 ff.

[123] TNA C66/1131, 17, Eliz. Part 9, M 41, Patent granted to Richard Candeler, 21 Feb. 1575.

[124] TNA SP 46/84 f. 159, policy underwritten for George Warner, 25 Jan. 1641/2. I am grateful to Dr Richard Blakemore for bringing this policy to my attention.

Street, in exchange for a lower premium, or may have paid more for a broader cover. A policy of 1613, drawn up and underwritten in the Office of Assurance, illustrates this. Goods aboard the vessel *Tyger* for its voyage from London to the near Mediterranean were insured under a policy which, in roughly the usual form, was 'to be understood that this prsnt writinge of assurance beinge made & registred accordinge to the kings maj^te order & appoyntm^te shalbe of as much force strenghte & effect, as the best and most suerest pollacie or writinge of assurance wch hath binne or heretofore used to be made Lost or not Lost in the afors^d streete or Royall Exchange'. However, the policy also overrides the specified customs of Lombard Street and the Royal Exchange, stating that coverage will remain in place should the cargo not be unloaded at the ports specified, that 'any order custome or usage or any thing in this pollicie mentioned to the contrary notwithstandinge'. Further, with regards to the conventions of news of losses, it states 'any order custome or usauge heretofore had or made in Lumbard Street or nowe in the Royall exchange in London to the contrary notwithstandinge'.[125] With these additions to the usual wording, the drafters of the policy created a unique insurance product which met the specific needs of the insurance buyer, as well as acknowledging not only the authority of custom of the Royal Exchange, but also noting the authority of the Office of Assurance.

Policies issued to the estate of Thomas Brailsford between 1690 and 1692, after the closure of the state-sanctioned Office of Assurance, include a force and effect clause which refers only to 'Lombard-street, or elsewhere in London'.[126] As London insurance practice spread, so too did the use of London generally as a point of authority in such clauses. However, the authority of the custom of the Royal Exchange was permanently to return – even before the underwriters of Lloyd's began regularly to trade there in 1771 – but elsewhere. A policy underwritten in New York in 1760 states 'That this Writing, or Policy of Assurance, shall be of as much Force and Affect as the surest Writing or Policy of Assurance heretofore made in *Lombard-Street*, or in the *Royal Exchange*, or elsewhere in London', as do other US policies in this series issued to 1763.[127] This exact clause was included in policies issued by Lloyd's and other London marine insurers, save for the removal of the redundant words 'writing or policy of assurance', until the entire policy wording was revised through the Institute of London Underwriters in 1983.[128] It appears in the sample Form of Policy included as a schedule to the *1906 Marine Insurance Act*.

The clause was to change again over time and distance. An 1859 policy issued in Hong Kong to private merchants and covering a shipment of opium states the policy shall have as much force as any in, simply, 'London'.[129] Outside Britain and

---

[125] BOD MS Tanner 74, ff. 32–33, policy underwritten for Morris Abbot and Devereux Wogan, 15 Feb. 1613.

[126] TNA C 110/152, Policies underwritten for the executors of the estate of Thomas Brailsford, 19 Sept. 1690–21 May 1692.

[127] Emphasis in original. LMA 063/MS32992/1, Policy of Thomas Newton, 27 Oct. 1760.

[128] See, for example, ALC (uncatalogued), Policies underwritten for the Baltimore Steam Packet Co. at Lloyd's and the Institute of London Underwriters, 20 Feb. 1950.

[129] ALC (uncatalogued), Policy underwritten for Jaynaraen Lukhimchund, 23 Feb. 1859.

the British Empire, it seems clear that the preferred jurisdiction took some time to settle. A policy underwritten for 'Messers Wales and Field' by the broker Chardon Brooks in Boston, Massachusetts on 17 September 1794, following the independence of the United States, states only that the underwriters agree that 'this writing or policy of assurance shall be of legal effect'.[130] However, another policy, underwritten six months earlier in Rhode Island, states that it 'shall be of as much Force and Effect as the surest Writing, or Policy of Assurance, heretofore made in the United States of America'.[131] An 1806 policy, underwritten by the Merrimack Marine and Fire Insurance Company in Newburyport, Massachusetts (and thus not by private underwriters, as in the previous examples), states no Law Merchant authority.[132] This follows a precedent set for corporate insurance underwriting in London in the 1720s. A policy issued by the London Assurance in 1741 similarly includes no force and effect clause.[133] A policy issued in Halifax, Canada and underwritten by thirty-nine individuals (and subscribed on their behalf by their joint attorney, in 1836, prior to the incorporation in 1840 of the underwriters as the Halifax Marine Insurance Company) also contains no 'force and effect' clause, but refers disputes to 'referees mutually to be chosen', or else to 'His Majesty's Courts in Halifax'.[134]

Dispute resolution – arbitration

As might be expected, methods of enforcement in insurance, which spread from Italy across western Europe, followed a similar early geographical path to the practice of underwriting itself. De Roover states that judges in Bruges consulted prominent Italian merchants to learn the norms of contract interpretation, and gave 'much weight' to their mercantile custom when resolving disputes. Thus, the Bruges courts accepted the weight of Italian Law Merchant principles. These include that the underwriters gain ownership of salvaged goods after indemnities have been paid, that cover does not commence until the vessel sails, that cover is void if the insured fails to disclose loss information before underwriting, and that indemnities need not be paid on overdue vessels until the insured has assigned title to the insured goods to the underwriters.[135]

The Bruges courts also accepted the Italian Law Merchant tenet that an insurance contract was void if the insured vessel was actually lost at the time of underwriting. This, however, must have been a grave limitation on the practicality of insurance in a time of severely restricted information flow. A vessel easily could have foundered

---

[130] ALC (uncatalogued), Policy underwritten for Wales and Field, 17 Sept. 1794 (image only).

[131] ALC (uncatalogued), Policy underwritten for Charles D'Wolfe, 29 Mar. 1794.

[132] ALC (uncatalogued), Policy underwritten for John Davenport, 15 Nov. 1806 (image only).

[133] HALSC DE/R/B293/1, Business records of the Radcliffe family, policy underwritten for Edward and Arthur Radcliffe, 7 May 1741.

[134] ALC (uncatalogued), Policy underwritten for B. Almen [?], 12 May 1836.

[135] de Roover, 'Early examples', pp. 198–199.

months before news of the loss reached insurance buyers. Therefore, by the early seventeenth century, flexible London marine insurers had abandoned the custom that made void an insurance contract if the insured vessel was actually lost at the time of underwriting. This change was explicit. A contemporaneous copy of a policy underwritten in 1613 on the vessel *Tyger* includes the words 'lost or not lost', explicitly superseding the convention.[136] The 'lost or not lost' clause was to be included in all printed London policies issued thereafter until 1983.[137] This concession to buyers must have made the London insurance market more attractive than its competitors to most purchasers of insurance, in this respect at least, and especially to buyers of insurance for vessels which were overdue, which was a common but expensive practice. It was used, for example, when Waddell Cunningham, a merchant of New York, instructed a London correspondent to 'get £300 Sterling insured on [the *Diamond*] if she is not arrived when their [letter] comes to hand'.[138]

Another Italian custom accepted by the judges of Bruges, which was altered by adjudicators and practitioners in London, was that over-insurance makes void an insurance contract.[139] This provision, intended to prevent frauds perpetrated by purchasing cover of greater value than the actual goods insured, then making inflated claims, has an obvious drawback. If a merchant purchased insurance to cover the anticipated value of cargo to be loaded at a future date in a distant port, but ultimately his factors shipped goods of lower value (due, perhaps, to local market conditions), such a convention would leave the merchant uninsured. Instead, London merchants agreed that in such cases of over-insurance, the earliest policy underwritten, and the earliest merchant-insurers to subscribe their names, would be those that were 'on-risk'. As a 1622 commentator wrote, 'the Custom is, that those Assurors that have last subscribed to the Policy of Assurance, bear not any adventure at all, and must make restitution of the *Premium* by them received, abating one half in the hundred for their subscription'.[140] Despite the elegance of this solution, over-insurance was much abused by outsider-buyers, and was a frequent target of interventionists until the late eighteenth century, as shown below. It is a good example of a custom which functioned well only when all the participants chose to play by the rules of the game.

With London's rules residing outside statute, it was principally those individuals within the insurance market – the merchant-insurers and brokers – who knew them. Thus, the usual initial method of dispute resolution was arbitration within the merchant community, including in the Mayoral court.[141] Such recourse to arbitra-

---

[136] BOD MS Tanner 74, f. 32, Insurance policy on the *Tyger*, 15 Feb. 1613.

[137] At least, it is included in all that I have examined.

[138] Waddell Cunningham to Martin Kuyckvan Mierop, 13.09.2011. *Letterbook of Greg & Cunningham, 1756–57, Merchants of New York and Belfast*, Truxes, Thomas M. (ed.), Oxford: The British Academy, 2001, p. 202.

[139] de Roover, 'Early examples', p. 199.

[140] Malynes, *Lex mercatoria*, p. 112.

[141] Here 'arbitration' is used to refer to all non-judicial dispute resolution methodologies outside the formal courts. Arbitration remains a preferred system of dispute resolution

tion by panels of experts was common to all Tudor jurisdictions, and was especially pervasive in mercantile cases.[142] This had been the predominant practice in Italy, and continued in the succeeding insurance centres of Antwerp, Amsterdam, and Hamburg.[143] Merchants and insurers typically avoided formal courts where possible, preferring *en camera* arbitration, whether formal or informal, which preserved their trade secrets, and was both faster and cheaper.[144]

To favour non-judicial dispute resolution is not limited to insurance questions. Anthropologists have observed consistent patterns of disputants, unwilling to involve agents of the state in their conflicts, turning to chosen third parties, and of states choosing to encourage arbitration as a less-costly substitute for more formal procedures.[145] The pattern of internal resolution of disputes is evident in the 1499 Ordinances of Bristol's new City Charter, which states the masters and wardens of its merchant-dominated Common Council were to meet up to twice weekly 'to here complayntes and sett direccions accordyng to reason and good conscience bit-weene partees of the same company beyng atte variaunce or debate, or to send the said parties with their causes as they have founde theym certifyed unto the maire of Bristowe'.[146] As an anonymous English jurist wrote in 1694, arbitration could be adopted to 'prevent the great Trouble and frequent Expence of Law-Suits'.[147]

Merchants found the courts to be 'slow, expensive, and inasmuch as they raised the spectre of countersuits, vexatious'.[148] In the 1566 action *Barnes* v. *Paviot*, for-ty-eight underwriter-plaintiffs stated they were willing to have their case settled 'by the order of marchaunts for avoidinge of trowble, costs and expenses in lawe', a course apparently unacceptable to the Rouen merchant Charles Paviot, since the case was brought before the Chancery (after a parallel action had been launched by Paviot in the Court of Admiralty).[149] A century and a half later, John Barnard, a wine merchant, politician, and leading underwriter, testified before a parliamentary special committee in 1720 that 'in Disputes about Losses or Averages the Insurers are generally desirous to have them adjusted by Arbitration, it being in their Interest to

---

in London. For example, Lloyd's until about 2010 maintained an 'arbitration desk' at a central point on the floor of the Underwriting Room at its premises on Lime Street.

[142] Jones, *Court of Chancery*, pp. 266, 269, 271.

[143] van Niekerk, *Principles of insurance law*, I, p. 230, nn. 155–156.

[144] Price, J.: 'Transaction costs: a note on merchant credit and the organisation of private trade', in Tracy, J. (ed.): *The political economy of merchant empires*, Cambridge: Cambridge University Press, 1991, p. 296.

[145] Roberts, Simon: 'The study of dispute: anthropological perspectives', in Bossy, John (ed.): *Disputes and settlements: law and human relations in the West*, Cambridge: Cambridge University Press, 1983, p. 17.

[146] Quoted in Sacks, David Harris: *The widening gate: Bristol and the Atlantic economy, 1450–1700*, Berkeley: University of California Press, 1991, p. 89.

[147] *Arbitrium redivivum, or, the law of arbitration*, by the author of *Regula placitandi*, London, 1694 (unpaginated).

[148] Hancock, David: *Citizens of the world: London merchants and the integration of the British Atlantic community, 1735–1785*, Cambridge: Cambridge University Press, 1995, p. 249.

[149] TNA C 3/26/78, petition of John Barnes and forty-seven others, 1566.

do so, and that the Insurers very often pay unreasonable Demands, rather than suffer themselves to be sued'.[150] Evidence of the latter claim can be drawn from even the earliest extant policies. When an underwriter had paid a claim, it was customary to cross his name off the original policy document. A policy underwritten in 1555 shows that fifteen of twenty-two subscriptions are struck out, indicating the vast majority had made good a claim against them, but six names are not, including that of John Blackman, the underwriter who is named in the suit.[151]

A further reason to avoid the courts was that policies sometimes did not comply with regulation, for example when policies were not registered, as prescribed, with an authorised authority, when stamp duty had not been paid, or when an insurance agreement fell outside the jurisdiction of the otherwise-appropriate tribunal.[152] Although the number of litigation actions increased significantly during the sixteenth century – Ibbetson states that it was in the 1530s and 1540s that 'insurance disputes began to become "legalised" '[153] – the number of insurance-related cases which reached the courts and for which evidence survives are relatively few, since arbitration remained the preferred alternative for merchants and their insurers (and possibly since disputes were relatively unusual among the merchant-insurers).

Recourse to arbitration was often agreed at the time of underwriting. This is shown in the 1555 policy of de Salizar, cited above, which states that 'yf godes will be that the said shippe shall not well procede' the parties to the policy 'promys to remyt yt to honist m'chaunts and not to go to the lawe'.[154] While the arbitration clause was not present in all policies, it appears to have been common. Another extant policy, underwritten in March 1564, requires the parties, 'wheare upon myght growe any difference, to stande to the judgement of m'chaunts indifferently chosen w'thoute goying to any other lawe'.[155] Similar clauses appeared in policies issued in Antwerp, Amsterdam, and Rotterdam.[156] A piece of Elizabethan legislation attests to a long history of arbitration within the community. It declares that 'Assurers have used to stande so justlie and p'ciselie upon their credites, as fewe or no Controv'sies have risen thereupon, and if any have growen, the same have from tyme to tyme bene ended and ordered by certaine grave and discreete Merchantes, appointed by the Lorde Mayor of the Citie of London, as Men by reason of their experience fittest to

---

[150] 'Average' is a system under the Law Merchant used to calculate the share of discrete losses to be allocated to each of several insurance policies, when several policies are triggered by an individual loss event. *The special report of 1720*, testimony of John Barnard, p. 44.

[151] HCA 24/29 f. 45, policy underwritten for Anthony de Salizar, 5 Aug. 1555.

[152] van Niekerk, *Principles of insurance law*, I, p. 231.

[153] Ibbetson, 'Law and custom', p. 293.

[154] TNA HCA 24/29 f. 45, policy underwritten for Anthony de Salizar, 5 Aug. 1555.

[155] Although suits under this policy went to the courts. For a detailed discussion of the case, see Ibbetson, 'Law and custom', pp. 294–295. TNA HCA 24/35 f. 283, policy underwritten for Robert Ridolphye, 12 Mar. 1564.

[156] van Niekerk, *Principles of insurance law*, I, p. 232, n. 167.

understande, and speedilie to decide those Causes'.[157] London underwriters' preference for arbitration resulted in reduced transaction costs. Further, it maintained
commercial secrecy, granting insurance buyers a benefit not extended to those purchasing cover in cities where formal adjudication procedures were predominant or
prescribed. With these benefits, arbitration endures as a preferred route for the resolution of disputes. Examples of the practical use of arbitration in the eighteenth
century are commonplace, such as an incident described by the merchant-broker
Robert Plumstead in 1756.

> I mentioned the *Beaver* having gone a different Voyage then ordered to be insured,
> and now at thy request I have laid thy Letter before the Underwriters. They said
> there was no return [of premium] due, suspecting that if [the vessel] had been
> lost, a Demand would have been made upon them. But this not being satisfactory
> to me, we left it to reference. And the Opinion of the Referee was, in these Words,
> "The Assured must have no return of Premium".[158]

As far away as Calcutta, as the English marine insurance tradition spread, blank
insurance policies were advertised 'with the Arbitration Clause'.[159]

Marine insurance in the courts

As the above tends to illustrate, the merchant community in London was relatively small. The group transacting insurance must necessarily have been somewhat
smaller, as not every adventurer would choose to buy insurance. Thus, the community of merchant-insurers was also small, and likely close-knit, especially during
the earliest period, when insurance was primarily a club good traded within the
resident Italian community. However, as London's importance as a commercial
port increased, and her insurance market gained in breadth and sophistication, the
number of merchants, both local and foreign, purchasing insurance in London multiplied. This was caused in part by changing trade patterns, which brought increased
insurance demand, and a requirement for new insurance products. Until the last
quarter of the sixteenth century, most international trade from London was carried
only very short distances, to Antwerp or Hamburg. Thereafter, however, English
merchants and carriers began regularly to trade to much more distant ports. Vessels
were sometimes years at sea. London garnered a much greater share of national
exports, and commodities other than cloth became increasingly important trade
items.[160] The long-established methods of private dispute resolution among the
merchants would no longer suffice to resolve amicably or successfully all disputes
arising under insurance policies.

Meanwhile, litigation became generally more fashionable. The total number of
cases in the common law courts of King's Bench and Common Pleas numbered

---

[157] Elizabethæ C. 12, 'An Act Conc'ninge matters of Assurances, amongste Merchantes',
HeinOnline, 4 Statutes of the Realm, 1547–1624, pp. 978–979.

[158] Robert Plumstead to Captain William Blair, 18.03.1756, *Plumstead Letterbook*, p. 51.

[159] *India Gazette*, Vol. 2, Iss. 87, 13.07.1782.

[160] Davis, *English overseas trade*, pp. 9–10, 53.

2,100 in 1490. The total had risen to an annual average of 5,278 by 1560–1563, and to 23,147 by 1606. At the King's Bench the number of cases increased by eight times during the reign of Elizabeth. The numbers of suits *per capita* were much greater than in the present day.[161] Merchants' preference for arbitration had done little to advance judicial knowledge of the Law Merchant governing the business, which fuelled a loop of self-enforcement: cases brought to royal justice were often sent back to the merchant community for arbitration. For example, in December 1573 the Privy Council committed for resolution a resident foreign merchant's complaint about 'the assuraunce of a shippe' to 'Alderman Osburne, Hugh Offley, Wiliam Towrson, Blase Saunders, Barnard Field and Peter Perry, or any iiij of them, to make agreement if they can, orels to retorne in whom the fault is, and therewith their opinions what is to be donne, that thereupon furdur order may be taken as to justice and equitie appertaineth'.[162] Yet, although expertise in insurance matters was not rife within the judicial community, and not yet covered by the common law, final resort to the courts became more common.

The increase in disputes which reached the courts was widely recognised. The Insurance Act of 1601 makes specific reference to this mounting litigiousness, stating that 'of late yeeres that divers p'sons have withdrawen themselves from that arbitrarie course, and have soughte to drawe the parties assured to seeke their money... by Suites comenced in her Majesties Courtes, to their greate charges and delayes'.[163] However, the correct jurisdiction for such actions was not firmly established, such that by the 1570s, according to Ibbetson, the situation was 'thoroughly anarchic'.[164] Jones describes sixteenth-century insurance in London as existing 'only precariously and chaotically' (although the description seems intended to apply only to the legal standing of insurance).[165] With jurisdiction disputes ongoing, several courts continued to hear insurance cases. As the insufficiencies of the merchant-insurers' customary dispute-resolution institutions were revealed, multiple forms of law were brought to bear to fill the breach. King's Bench was a court of common law; Chancery of equity; the High Court of Admiralty an equity court which followed the international laws of the sea, part of the Law Merchant; London's Mayoral court applied custom under local Law Merchant. It is therefore unsurprising that legal historians describe the situation as chaotic: in these circumstances, buyers and sellers could not always be certain even which branch of law would be applied to a dispute, despite jurisdictional 'force and effect' clauses, let alone how it would respond.

From 1573 to 1590 the Privy Council was drawn into at least seventeen discrete insurance cases. Nine involved disputes brought by foreign merchants, often through the intervention of an ambassador.[166] By longstanding convention, alien traders were under the special protection of local monarchs. In England, their actions could be

[161] Williams, *The later Tudors*, p. 151.
[162] Dasent, *Acts of the Privy Council*, VIII, p. 167.
[163] Elizabethæ c. 12.
[164] Ibbetson, 'Law and custom', p. 296.
[165] Jones, 'Elizabethan marine insurance', p. 53.
[166] Dasent, *Acts of the Privy Council*, VII–XX.

heard by the chancellor, the Council, or by a special commission.[167] The latter approach was most typically favoured by the Privy Council when dealing with insurance matters. It usually first referred matters to arbitration by London's Lord Mayor and aldermen, or by a panel appointed by the Lord Mayor. It heard cases in person only when arbitration failed. Even then, councillors typically sought, as a guide to settlement, direction from the merchants of London as to the prevailing custom. In July 1574 their Lordships heard a complaint from the foreign merchant Peter Mertines against his London insurers, 'certein merchaunts', about an insurance issued for a ship sailing from Southampton to Bilbao. In the first instance the Privy Council instructed the Judge of the Admiralty 'to committe the cause to certein indifferent persons to whom it might be heard and determined acording to right and equitie'.[168] Five months later, the case having apparently gone unresolved, the Council instructed the Lord Mayor to *order* the insurers to appear before the appointed group of merchant arbitrators, which projected royal authority onto the case.[169]

Foreign merchants were buying regularly in London in the sixteenth century, apparently attracted by keen pricing. The Rouen merchant Paviot's multiple suits left his trace in the record. Ten years earlier, in 1552, Emmanuell Caldera and Benedicte Roderiges had purchased insurance in London, through a broker, to cover merchandise to be loaded at Calicut. Jones reports 'this was done "after the computacion of England" – there being marked differences in insurance rates between various countries.'[170] However, the price advantage was not always sufficient to appease buyers who deemed London practice to fall short. A 1592 letter from the London-based Italian merchant Bartholomew Corsini (a regular customer of London underwriters) to his Venetian counterpart, Stefano Patti, stated that 'to insure goods [in London] we assure you we would pay ten to twelve per cent, and we assure you there would be no lack of underwriters, but in case of damages it is painful to try to collect the claim… we advise you to insure there [in Venice] and spend rather one or two per cent more'.[171] It seems from the same Venetian archive sources consulted by Stefani, however, that local merchant-insurers were no less prone to dispute claims when outsider-buyers would not abide by Venetian custom (a fact perhaps lost on the distant Corsini). Stefani writes that 'insured parties accused [Venetian] insurers of being quarrelsome and failing to keep to terms. The latter blamed the insured parties of availing themselves of insurances to gain unlawful profits, instead of making use of insurances as a preventative measure against seafaring risks.'[172] It seems that the same pressures bearing down upon the London market were also being felt in Italy.

---

[167] Prichard, M. J. & Yale, D. E. C. (eds): *Hale and Fleetwood on Admiralty jurisdiction*, London, Selden Society, p. lxxx.

[168] Dasent, *Acts of the Privy Council*, VIII, p. 262.

[169] Ibid., pp. 262, 321, 326, 337, 349.

[170] Jones, 'Elizabethan marine insurance', p. 58.

[171] Quoted in Stefani, *Insurance in Venice*, p. 104.

[172] Ibid., p. 104.

Over the course of about two centuries, premium-based marine insurance had become firmly established in London. Based on a contemporaneous petition by an aspiring monopolist broker, Kepler describes the late sixteenth-century insurance market as 'unorganised', but the petitioner had probably exaggerated market dysfunction to further his cause.[173, 174] In contrast, Wright and Fayle found 'nothing to show that [the] system had proved inadequate to the requirements of commerce'.[175] Insurance was both purchased and underwritten by native merchant-insurers, who operated in cooperation with resident foreigners. Usually, the underwriters accepted risk as individual sole traders, but in some cases as partnerships, such as that of the de Salizar policy, under which John Blackman and John Watkins jointly assumed £25 worth of the risk, and very occasionally as special-purpose 'companies' of insurers.[176] For example, in 1552 merchants purchased – through their London broker Lewys Lobo – cover from the Company of Bonaventurers, comprising sixteen merchants, and the Company of Fifteen Assurers (who in fact numbered nineteen). Jones suggests the companies were *ad hoc* ventures, although the fact that nineteen individuals traded through the Company of Fifteen Assurers suggests not only longevity, but growth of the enterprise over time.[177] Multiple underwriters shared individual risks, promising severally to indemnify losses up to a specified maximum, under a remarkably mature policy document.

Very specific practices were known and agreed. In the 1570s, roughly thirty brokers and sixteen notaries operated in London. The former group facilitated the introduction and interaction between buyers and sellers of insurance, and managed financial relationships; the latter drew up policies, kept registers of their details, and managed client monies. However, merchants and their insurers sometimes dealt directly with one another, without the intermediation of third parties.[178] The activities of all were governed by a set of customs and principles based upon an inheritance from Italian merchants, and the modifications of merchant-insurers in Antwerp and Amsterdam. Disputes were resolved internally according to this inheritance, under the customs of the Law Merchant. However, as insuring became more common, and as more individuals who were unfamiliar with these practices entered London's insurance market – more outsiders – the initial institutional structures which had evolved to manage insurance disputes between merchant-insurers were shown to be inadequate. The need for authoritative intervention was recognised as necessary. Actions in the royal courts became more common, but this solution was slow, costly, and unpredictable due to the courts' paltry experience of insurance disputes, and their

---

[173] TNA SP 12/110/104, petition of Henry Roderigues (undated, marked 'prob. 1576').

[174] Kepler, J. S.: 'The operating potential of the London insurance market in the 1570s', *Business History* 17 (1975), p. 47.

[175] Wright, C. and Fayle, C. E.: *A history of Lloyd's*, London: Macmillan & Co., 1928, p. 35.

[176] TNA HCA 24/29 f. 45, policy underwritten for Anthony de Salizar, 5 Sep. 1555.

[177] TNA C 33/33/103–4, *Calderaand v. Company of Assurers* (1561); Jones, 'Elizabethan marine insurance', p. 58.

[178] BL Lansdowne MS 113/9, 'Some Merchants, Notaries, and Brokers petition Sir James Hawes, Lord Mayor of London, against Rich. Candley's grant for registering policies of assurance' (undated, 1574).

own divergent legal approaches and developing rivalries. Thus, by the close of the sixteenth century, it was clear to many merchant-insurers and royal administrators that new institutional measures were necessary to ensure the continued smooth and efficient operation of a growing market deemed critical to the nation's international trade. They turned to the state to develop structures to do so.

2.

1570–1688: Buyers and the first intervention

This chapter describes the first major intervention into the operations of the London insurance market, which was made in the years 1574 to 1601. It was a series of institution-building initiatives which were intended to answer challenges to the effectiveness of the incumbent system of the merchant-insurers. The system's shortcomings had been brought into sharp focus by the actions of outsider-buyers who wished to perpetrate fraud against underwriters, but the intervention was extended, perhaps beyond the wishes of the merchant-insurers, to measures which would both address the burden of outsiders who would not play by the merchant-insurers' rules of the game, and would set some restrictions on the operation of the market. The measures had the further aim of resolving the jurisdiction battle between different royal courts over the right to hear insurance disputes, and to ensure that merchants' customary practices and Law Merchant principles were brought to bear on those disputes which did arise. The intervention was sympathetic to merchant needs, and was structured such that it preserved much of the flexibility which characterised insurance practice in London. In this way it served further to formalise and entrench merchant practice in London. Ultimately, however, it was unsuccessful.

European trade and trade finance were expanding in the last decades of the sixteenth century, fuelled by a hundred years of economic recovery, urbanisation, and exploitation of new Atlantic trade. An initial engine was the international Bisenzone exchange fairs, which, at the orchestration of Genoese bankers, spread risk and credit in the European mercantile community.[1] It was also a period of increased state monitoring of, and intervention in, cross-border commerce. England, whose international trade had been dominated by foreign merchants, began the long reversal of its industrial backwardness relative to its Continental contemporaries. Merchants enhanced internal trade networks, and, as Hanse merchants were squeezed, then expelled, gained much-increased local control over international trade, despite later competition from Dutch carriers.

Internal and external trade alike were centred on London. The latter, dominated on the export side by cloth, was heavily focused on Europe, a situation not helped by Cockayne's disastrous project to establish a local wool-dyeing industry, but eased by the rise of the new draperies. Debasement of the currency in the 1540s was

---

[1] Braudel, *Afterthoughts*, pp. 24–25; Pezzolo, Luciano and Tattara, Giuseppe: ' "Una fiera senza luogo": was Bisenzone an international capital market in sixteenth-century Italy?', *Journal of Economic History*, Vol. 68, No. 4 (2008), pp. 1098–1099.

probably another driver of London merchants' extending reach. While the value of English international trade almost certainly was stagnant or declining from about 1550, it expanded geographically as English merchants' focus on the Low Countries declined. Especially after the fall of Antwerp, their interests extended north into the Baltic, south into the Mediterranean, and later to the Americas and the Far East. From the 1570s, English building of large merchant ships boomed. The Company of Merchant Adventurers lost their near strangle-hold on English exports, and a diversity of chartered monopoly companies – as well as of individual merchant adventurers – began to flourish. Regular trade began to extend beyond nearby ports in the Low Countries and on the German North Sea coast, first to Baltic and Mediterranean ports, then to destinations across the Atlantic and around the Cape.[2]

Braudel placed the arrival in England of higher-tiered capitalism in the era after 1688, but the elements of complexity, state involvement, diversification, and hierarchy were appearing in England during Elizabeth's reign.[3] These conditions created greater demand for more diverse provision of insurance, as trade was increasingly divided among more London merchants, and distributed to new markets. Old methods of governing marine insurance market practice began to prove insufficient in some situations. The system of informal dispute resolution and enforcement, based on the mutual interests of the merchant-insurers and the uncodified, flexible Law Merchant, was not always sufficient to ensure order in the market. The established judicial system was unable adequately to cope with insurance disputes which slipped out of the merchant-insurers' system, and was itself in turmoil. Merchants called for solutions; the Privy Council, and later parliament, chose to act. Both were, as always, interested in maintaining the efficacy of the insurance market, which was seen as essential to the support of trade, and thus to the continued flow of customs revenue.

The Privy Council emerged from the circle of royal councillors under Henry VIII, who drew a handful of men, primarily office-holders, into an inner advisory circle. They swiftly became a formal, separate, and permanent institution with a recording clerk, and formed, with the addition of the chief justices, the separate prerogative court of Star Chamber.[4] By the middle of the reign of Elizabeth, the Privy Council constituted a small, professional, active, and pragmatic ministry which excluded magnates, and was dominated by William Cecil, Lord Burghley. Its genuinely able men comprised the realm's leading forum for political discussion and influence; together they supplemented royal power, rather than diminishing it. Alongside the Privy Council's celebrated involvement in discouraging royal marriages, influencing international policy, and appointing provincial royal officials, the bulk of its

---

[2] Stone, Lawrence: 'Elizabethan overseas trade', *Economic History Review*, Vol. 2, No. 1 (1949), pp. 30, 48–52; Spufford, 'The places of insurance', p. 281; Smith, *Emergence of a nation state*, pp. 175–179; Davis, *English overseas trade*.

[3] Braudel, *Afterthoughts*, p. 64.

[4] Servini, Peter: 'Henry VIII: government and politics 1529–47', in Lotherington, John (ed.): *The Tudor years*, London: Hodder & Stoughton, 1994, pp. 121–124.

responsibilities lay in passing judgement on 'the minutia of everyday life', including the hearing of insurance disputes. For this, it met daily, often seven days a week.[5]

After insurance disputes had become part of its regular business, the Privy Council launched the first regulatory initiatives targeting the smooth operation of London's marine insurance market. Until the 1570s, the merchant-insurers who comprised this market had operated under their own rules, and with few exceptions resolved their own disputes. However, the number of disputes was increasing, confusion over the correct jurisdiction and form of law to govern them was mounting, and merchant complaints about the operation of the system became more formal and frequent. It seems, too, that a reputational impact was of concern. In February 1573/4 the Privy Council wrote to the Lord Mayor to complain that a sustained failure entirely to resolve a dispute between the merchant William Soninge and several of his insurers 'tendeth to the derogacion of so auncient a custome as assuraunce amongst merchauntes is, and breadeth grete discredit to the parties'.[6] In response to these problems, royal officers acted to implement institutional solutions to the difficulties which had arisen in part from the participation of a wider array of individuals in the expanding insurance market.

One result of the participation of a growing number of outsiders in a closely-knit market which traded in a club good was an increase in transaction costs arising from enforcement challenges, and, typically, increasing recourse to enforcement by third-party institutions. The rules of the game, known to the merchant-insurers trading in London, might not be known to new arrivals, and could be flouted by those who did not see adherence as important to their commercial future. Established dispute-resolution tools, comprising binding arbitration within the community, were no longer sufficient. Over the next several years the Council attempted to resolve the growing problem of insurance disputes with a three-pronged programme of action. It was to formalise the resolution of insurance disputes under the Law Merchant through the existing governing institutions of the city at the Guildhall; to codify that law to produce a more concrete set of regulations than the arcane 'custom of Lombard Street'; and to establish an information system which could help to counteract the involvement of individuals who did not know the rules, or were unwilling to play by them.[7] Through this programme, the Privy Council was to create new institutions of enforcement which were intended to cope with the arrival of newcomers, and with others who simply did not wish to play by the rules, whether they were outsider-buyers, -sellers, or both. The new institutions' focus on London insurance reinforced her merchant-insurers' custom, making practice elsewhere secondary.

---

5   Sloan, Roy: 'Elizabeth I: government of England', in Lotherington, John (ed.): *The Tudor years*, London: Hodder & Stoughton, 1994, pp. 212–221.

6   Dasent, *Acts of the Privy Council*, VIII, pp. 195–196.

7   In a different context, the legal historian Ibbetson identifies this three-part action. Ibbetson, 'Law and custom', p. 295.

The Office of Assurance

In February 1575/6 the Privy Council received a 'suit of the principal merchants of England' which complained that

> for wante of good and orderly kepynge in Register the Assurances made within this our Realme… the trade of merchaundize have bene and yet be oftentymes greately abused by evyll disposed people who for theyr private gayne and advantage have assured one thynge in sondrie places thereby intendynge if any losse should happen to recover in all the sayd places and so oftentymes have done to the great losse and hynderance of dyvers such honest merchauntes as did assure the same. And the auncient custome of merchauntes in Lomberd strete, and nowe the Ryall Exchaunge by that means almost growne out of estimation which here to fore as we are enformed hathe bene accompted the chief foundacion of all assurraunces.[8]

Unscrupulous merchants and sea captains – outsider-buyers – were attempting to maximise their returns from short-term plays in the insurance market by over-insuring, then making multiple, fraudulent claims. This, a gross breach of the rules of the game set out by the Law Merchant, amounted to fraud. Criminal law remedies existed to punish fraudsters, but for such prosecutions to succeed, the frauds necessarily had to be detected. Merchant-insurers preferred that they were avoided before they occurred, through an information-sharing institution.

In answer to the merchants' complaint, the Privy Council considered granting monopoly rights over the intermediation of the insurance business. Shortly afterwards, a patent was granted to Richard Candeler, a mercer, Treasury agent, and factor of Thomas Gresham (himself a regular insurance buyer, and his brother an underwriter). The patent gave Candeler the exclusive right to the 'making and registering of all assurances, policies and the like upon ships and goods going out of or into the realm made in the Royal Exchange or any other place in the city of London'.[9] Thus was erected the Office of Assurance. It was located in a ground-floor shop on the Royal Exchange, and was the only office accessible from the interior quadrangle of the iconic building.[10] Candeler's patent states that 'assurraunces not made with Candeler… shall be voyde', although this declaration appears to have carried no further legal weight.[11] No policy appears to have been argued at law to have been void because it was not made in Candeler's office, although non-registration may

---

8   TNA C66/1131/41, patent granted to Richard Candeler 21 Feb. 1575/6.

9   For Thomas Gresham's insurance buying and his relationship with Candeler [often 'Candler', although the patent and extant signatures include two letters 'e'], see Burgon, J. W.: *The life and times of Sir Thomas Gresham*, London: R. Jennings, 1839, pp. 329–330; also Lemon, John: *Calendar of State Papers, Domestic, Edward, Mary and Elizabeth, 1547–80*, Vol. XXXI, 1856, p. 232. Gresham's brother John appears as an underwriter on TNA HCA 24/30/151, a policy underwritten in London on 6 Dec. 1557. For a more detailed discussion of Candeler and his background, see Ibbetson, 'Law and Custom', p. 296.

10   Glaisyer, Natasha: *The culture of commerce in England, 1660–1720*, Woodbridge: Royal Historical Society & Boydell Press, 2006, p. 29.

11   TNA C66/1131/41, patent granted to Richard Candeler 21 Feb. 1575/6.

have meant that royal courts were completely inaccessible. This low level of illegality could have been comfortably ignored by merchant-insurers operating according to customary practice.

At roughly the same time, another market participant, Henrye Rodrigiz, made application to the Privy Council to be created sole broker of 'all the assuraunces that shalbe made w^{t}in the cyttye of London'. Two surviving documents, both undated, refer to his requests. A hastily written summary of his applications mentions his intention 'to keepe parfect registars of all pollisyes', which were intended to combat fraud.[12] However, in a second, more formal and detailed document Rodrigiz not only cited among the justifications for the grant of a monopoly patent the elimination of 'dubble enssuringe of adventurers'. He also added that buyers would know 'where to fynde the assurer and assuraunce', and 'the pollicyes and th^e dealinge touchinge the same assuraunce shallbe more orderlie, readie, and certen for all merchaunts', reasons reflecting provision of certainty for outsider-buyers.[13] He requested that all policies otherwise undertaken would be void. The application did not find favour. Because both the Rodrigiz petition and the summary of his request lack a contemporaneous date, it is not clear whether his requests competed with that of Candeler, were subsequent to it, or pre-dated it. Since Candeler's patent did not include the broking of insurance policies, it is possible that the Rodrigiz request came later, and was for a further function. In any case, the Privy Council chose not to grant to Rodrigiz a monopoly patent over the intermediation of insurance policies, which certainly would have limited the flexibility of London underwriting.

Creating the Office of Assurance under Richard Candeler was a genuine act of institution-building on the part of the Privy Council, made in response to a call for action by the community of merchants, as Candeler's patent clearly indicates. Candeler performed at least some of the responsibilities of his office personally; his own signature appears on nine extant insurance policies issued to the merchant Bartholomew Corsini in 1580–1583.[14] Upon the inception of the Office, the Privy Council took steps to ensure that the Office added only minimally to insurance transaction costs, by closely regulating the fees it was permitted to charge. The patent stated that Gresham, along with the Lord Mayor, the Mayor of the Staple, and the governor of the Merchant Adventurers could set the level of Candeler's fees.[15] The Privy Council suggested first that fees be set in line with those of other countries, but when it came to it, Candeler engaged in a protracted negotiation with Walsingham over this question, citing prevailing fees in Antwerp, and also registering concern that the appointed commissioners, through their fee schedule, were opening the door to the drawing of policies outside his Office, which Raynes has argued may have been their intention.[16] In support, the Privy Council solicited the

---

[12] BL Lansdowne MS 65 f. 104, summary of the petition of Henry Roderigues (undated).

[13] Also rendered Henry Roderigues. TNA SP 12/110/104, petition of Henry Roderigues.

[14] GHL CLC/B/062/MS22,281, CLC/B/062/MS22,282, the Corsini papers.

[15] TNA C66/1131, patent granted to Richard Candeler.

[16] For a detailed discussion of Candeler's negotiations with Walsingham over fees and the security of the monopoly, see Raynes, *British insurance*, pp. 43–46.

Lord Mayor 'to rate the prices for making and registringe of pollicies of assuraunces, wherein he shold do well to enquire and folowe the prices acustomablie paide in other count[r]ies adjoyninge'.[17] Candeler had to make do with much lower fees than he initially desired. Thus his actions, and those of Gresham, were not naked rent-seeking, and the position was not entirely a sinecure (although the office of Registrar of Assurances, as shown below, was to become a grant of privilege always awarded to court placemen).

Official registration of policies was not a new idea. In Venice, the *Avogaria di comun* had offered policy registration since the early fifteenth century, for example.[18] However, it was new to London, and it seems that the Office and office-holder had ambitions beyond simple registry. Candeler's role sometimes extended, whether or not according to the intention of the Privy Council, from simple registration and drawing-up of policies to the broking of insurance risk, or at least to the provision of a place for interested underwriters to make subscriptions. A policy insuring the *Tyger*, issued in 1613, states that 'wee the Assurers have hereunto sevally subscribed a^r names ... in the office of Assurance wthin the Royall exchange in London'.[19] However, the patent-holder did not always act as broker, nor was this the precedent upon the formation of the office. Some of the surviving policies drawn in Candeler's hand (or that of an amanuensis) in the 1580s name a third-party broker; others do not.[20] The Office of Assurance appears to have offered a flexible service.

The grant of a monopoly to Candeler resulted in petitions of protest to the Lord Mayor and aldermen from two key groups within London's insurance sector. These shed some light on the institutional structure of the market before the Privy Council's interventions. Brokers (at this time sometimes called *roggers*), who 'beinge thritie householders in nomber, and no more', claimed that they were likely to be ruined by the grant. Notaries, who numbered sixteen in 1574, also complained, stating the patent would mean the 'impovrishinge overthrowe and utter decaie of all the Notaryes publicke of this sitie w^{t}h their children servanntes apprentises and families to the number of one hundredth and twentie psones.'[21] The ruinous effects described were no doubt greatly exaggerated, since brokers and notaries almost certainly plied their trades in sectors other than marine insurance, but to be even remotely credible, the volume of marine insurance business transacted in London must have been substantial.

[17] Dasent, *Acts of the Privy Council*, VIII, p. 397.

[18] Stefani, *Insurance in Venice*, pp. 87–89.

[19] BOD MS Tanner 74, f. 32, contemporaneous copy of a policy underwritten for Morris Abbot and Devereux Wogan, 15 Feb. 1613.

[20] These policies refute van Niekerk's unwise contention that 'the earliest extant policy registered in the Office' was the *Tyger* policy of 1613. GHL CLC/B/062/MS22281–2, the Corsini papers, policies issued to Bartholomew Corsini; van Niekerk, *Principles of insurance law*, I, p. 225, n. 136.

[21] BL Lansdowne MS 113/36, 'Some Merchants, Notaries, and Brokers petition Sir James Hawes, Lord Mayor of London, against Rich. Candley's grant for registering policies of assurance' (undated, 1574?).

Notarial seals were not applied to insurance policies at this time, as was the practice in some Italian cities,[22] but notaries were often engaged to draw up policies, sometimes in Italian, French, Spanish, or Dutch, when their customers were merchant strangers and wished to send their policies abroad. In addition, they kept private registers of the policies which they penned. Their charge for drawing and registering a policy was two shillings, regardless of the sum insured under the policy. Sometimes too they acted as bankers for foreign clients, in that 'merchauntes straungers havinge assuraunces made in Englande beinge otherwise employed about their affayres have putte their Notaryes and Scrivenours to receave the same to large sommes, which hath ben honestly and trewlie repayed... and also some retornes of moneye when the assuraunce hath not taken place'. The brokers stated of themselves in their petition that they were 'bounde with sureties in diverse and sondry greate sommes of money for their honest and trewe dealinge in their facultie', indicating a bonding system among the broking community, and thus a significant level of sophistication.[23]

As well as arguing that the monopoly would infringe upon the freedom of individuals to prepare and place their own insurances, the notaries and brokers stated that all merchants would be disadvantaged by the loss of the swift, skilful, expedient, and confidential service offered by a diverse group of providers. They declared wryly that Candeler would become a 'notarye private', and suggested that the sums of clients' money that he might come to hold could be so great as to see him succumb to the temptation of theft. Further, the liberties of choice would be eliminated, and the practice of merchants garnering subscriptions to their insurances directly with underwriters (without the intervention of a third party, as seems to have occurred at least some of the time) would have been made impossible.[24] 'It would be a great Bondage to Merchants to be tied to one particular Person, who might either for Favour or Reward dispatch one Man, and for Displeasure or Ill Will delay another', a near-contemporary chronicler reported.[25] Green has speculated that the petitioning brokers, who were Freemen of the city, and the notaries, as members of the Scriveners' Company, may, through London's livery companies, have asserted some monopoly control over the business of intermediating various assurances, and even begun to specialise in the business.[26] The evidence in the petitions against Candeler's patent does not definitively confirm that theory, but it does indicate a highly structured and populous market.

The presence of thirty bonded brokers indicates a competitive and spirited market. Their testimony describes an established set of sophisticated practices which were followed within that market. Taken together, the Privy Council's actions and

---

[22] Jones, 'Elizabethan marine insurance', p. 55.

[23] BL Lansdowne MS 113/9.

[24] Ibid.

[25] Stow, John: *A survey of the cities of London and Westminster (Strype's edition)* (first published 1598), London: printed for A. Churchill and nine others, 1720, pp. 242–243.

[26] Green, Edwin: 'Brokers and marine insurance before 1574', *CIB Link: Monthly Bulletin of the Corporation of Insurance Brokers*, No. 50, Aug. 1973, pp. 1–2.

the market's response do not support the widespread historiographical belief that few English merchants purchased insurance in this period. Instead, it suggests that London's insurance market was, by the 1570s, large, vibrant, and widely used. Given the value of seaborne trade from London at this time, which although significant had not yet begun its long and marked rise, the evidence suggests that insurance was regularly purchased by at least a large proportion of London's mercantile community, covering an important share of trade goods.

London's merchants were not unanimously supportive of the Office, which had no power to compel insurance buyers to use its services. In July 1576 the Privy Council wrote to the Lord Mayor complaining that 'certain evill disposed persons do refuse to bring their assuraunces to be registred, so as the said Mr. Candeler cannot thereby receve the said commoditie of his office'.[27] Individual motivations for non-registration cannot be determined, but the desire for commercial secrecy in the time-sensitive arena of early modern trade is one more likely explanation for widespread avoidance than intent to defraud.[28] Registration threw open policies to public scrutiny, which could reveal to prying competitors competitively sensitive details about the timing and nature of merchants' voyages and cargoes. Braudel cites an unnamed Dutch merchant who, writing to a factor in Bordeaux, 'advised their plans be kept secret, otherwise "this affair will turn out like so many others in which, once competition comes into play, there is no chance to make a profit".'[29] Another motivation is the avoidance of fees, however regulated; a third is the simple preference of insider-merchants for their customary market practices. In his 1622 *Lex Mercatoria*, Malynes wrote that 'Assurances are made in the said Office [of Assurances] in the West end of the said Royal Exchange', which suggests exclusivity without a local alternative, but he was one of the architects of the Office, was close to members of the Privy Council including Walsingham and Cecil, and sometimes acted as consultant to them on mercantile matters.[30]

It does appear that use of the office became commonplace. Writing probably in the 1630s, Thomas Mun listed twelve 'qualities which are required in a perfect Merchant of Forraign Trade'. He enumerated as the seventh of these that a merchant 'ought to... ensure his adventures from one Country to another, and be well acquainted with the laws, orders and customs of the Ensurance office'.[31] However, it is impossible to know what share of insurance policies underwritten in London were prepared and/or registered by Candeler and his successors in the Office. One merchant who clearly did use the facility was Corsini, who wrote to a Venetian business partner that London's *in-faith* practice is not suitable to us', implying a preference for policies under official supervision or notarial seal (and perhaps indicating that

---

[27] Dasent, *Acts of the Privy Council*, IX, p. 177.

[28] Price, 'Transaction Costs', p. 296.

[29] Braudel, *Afterthoughts*, pp. 57–58.

[30] Malynes, *Lex Mercatoria*, pp. 106, 109; Gauci, Perry: 'Malynes, Gerard', *Oxford Dictionary of National Biography Online*, www.oxforddnb.com/view/article/17912 [Accessed 3 Dec. 2021].

[31] Mun T.: *England's treasure by forraign trade*, London: Macmillan & Co., 1895 (1664), p. 4.

transacting insurance outside the office remained commonplace in the early years of its existence).[32]

Regardless of its rate of penetration, it is clear that the institution was a feature of the London insurance market for over a century, surviving Civil War, Commonwealth, and Restoration, if not Revolution. In 1640 the Court of Committees of the East India Company noted the payment of £25 to 'Mr Pryor, of the Assurance-house' for writing up a policy covering pepper re-exported to Italy.[33] George Pryor, or Prior, had, with William Couper, purchased the right to operate the Office of Assurance from the third patent-holders, Giles and Walter Overbury.[34] The Office was clearly operating in 1641 with a staff of some size, since that year Edward Marckland, when giving testimony in the Court of Admiralty, identified himself as 'one of the clerks in the assurance office, London'.[35] The same year a policy issued to the merchant George Warner of London was signed 'Overberrie', who with his brother was granted the patent in 1609, and received a continuance of the office in 1634.[36] In 1645/6, in a deposition before the High Court of Admiralty, George Prior declared 'that hee hath bene an officer belongenge to the Assurance office in London for the space of twentye nyne years little more or lesse'. Prior had been called in to advise as an expert witness.[37]

The granting of the patent originally to Candeler seems to have been a partially pragmatic choice. Little is known of his life, but he was known to the Court through Gresham – his employer and a distant cousin – and appears to have been involved in the collection of crown revenues.[38] Upon his death in 1602, the patent passed by inheritance to Sir Ferdinando Richardson (alias Heyborne), Candeler's son-in-law. Richardson was a courtier and Groom of Elizabeth's Privy Chamber from 1586–1611, and a court musician.[39] Thus, unlike Candeler, he was neither a merchant nor involved in the mechanics of government. In 1604, a second Richard Candeler, also a London mercer, and the nephew of the original patent-holder, was granted the right

[32] Quoted in Stefani, *Insurance in Venice*, p. 104.

[33] Foster, William (ed.): *Court Minutes of the East India Company, 1640–1643*, Oxford: Clarendon Press, 1909, p. 40.

[34] Raynes, *British insurance*, p. 56.

[35] TNA HCA 13/57, Examinations, 1641–2, Deposition of Edward Marckland, 18 Dec. 1641. I am grateful to Dr Richard Blakemore for bringing this document to my attention.

[36] TNA SP 46/84/159 f. 145, policy underwritten for George Warner, 25 Jan. 1641/2. I am grateful to Dr Richard Blakemore for bringing this document to my attention.

[37] TNA HCA 12/60, Examinations in the High Court of Admiralty, 6 Feb. 1645/6.

[38] Candeler's death-date is according to his monument in Tottenham Church. Lysons, Daniel: 'Tottenham', *The environs of London: Vol. III: County of Middlesex* (1795), pp. 517–557; the year is confirmed in Burke, John: *A genealogical and heraldic history of the commoners of Great Britain*, London: Henry Colburn, 1833, p. 105; Chandler, John: 'The Candelers of London', *The Home Counties Magazine*, Vol. V (1903), pp. 231–234; Chandler, John: 'Richard Candeler of Tottenham', *The Home Counties Magazine*, Vol. II. (1903), pp. 301–304; for Candeler's role in state finance, Lemon, *Calendar of State Papers*, p. 232.

[39] Lysons, *Tottenham*, p. 537; Marlow, Richard: 'Sir Ferdinando Heyborne alias Richardson', *Musical Times*, Vol. 115, No. 1579 (1974), pp. 736–739.

of reversion of the patent upon the death of Sir Ferdinando, along with the latter's younger brother, Christopher Heyborne (reversion was used by the crown to raise revenue, and by the buyer to convert life tenures into 'semi-hereditary ones').[40]

Identifying incumbent patent-holders and active office-holders is complicated by the parallel existence of the office of the Registrar of Assurance, created by an act of parliament in 1601 and discussed below, which appears to have been separate to that which granted authority to operate the Office of Assurance, from whence the Registrar or his assignees worked. Various references to patents granted over the course of the seventeenth century make no distinction. In a 1610 note of a dispute over the payment of freight, Richard Candeler is named as Deputy Registrar of Assurances.[41] However, in December 1609 a lifetime grant of the patent to act as Registrar was made to Sir Giles Overbury and his brother Walter, despite the fact that Sir Ferdinando lived until 1618, and the junior Candeler was still active.[42] The Overburys were brothers of the murdered Sir Thomas Overbury, courtier, poet, and favourite of James I, and sons of the MP and judge Sir Nicholas Overbury.[43] They farmed the office to George Pryor and William Cowper for the significant annual sum of £400, which indicates a brisk business over its counter. Cowper, son of a London alderman and sometime sheriff, was created a baronet in 1641/2; jailed in 1642/3 as a royalist; and later knighted. His great-grandson was to become Earl Cowper and Lord Chancellor under George I.[44]

In 1628 the merchant Richard Bogan, a French resident of London whose sons were to be naturalised by the Long Parliament in 1640, petitioned for, and received, the grant of the reversion of the patent to him for thirty-one years after the death of Christopher Heyborne and the Overburys.[45] Thus, Heyborne and the Overbury brothers were holding the office concurrently. Later in the year Bogan was granted the office as 'Registrar of the Assurance Office',[46] but while the Overbury brothers were living; in 1634 the brothers petitioned for a continuance of their office, which was granted immediately. William Cowper petitioned for the office in 1639 with George Pryor, who had held it from the Overburys since early in the century; his son, also William (and later the second baronet), petitioned for the office, in reversion from Bogan in 1660 for a period of fifty-one years, and claimed the office was

40 See Williams, *The later Tudors*, p. 156. Green, Mary Anne Everett (ed.): *Calendar of State Papers domestic, James I, Vol. IX, 1603–1610, Aug.–Oct., 1604* (1857).

41 Harris, G. G.: *Trinity House of Deptford Transactions, 1609–35: Vol. 1, 1610*, London Record Society, No. 19 (1983).

42 Green, Mary Anne Everett (ed.): *Calendar of State Papers domestic: James I, Vol. L, Dec. 1609* (1857).

43 Considine, John: 'Overbury, Sir Thomas', *ODNB*, online edn, Jan. 2008, www.oxforddnb.com/view/article/20966 [Accessed 3 Dec. 2021].

44 Cokayne, G. E. (ed.): *Complete Baronetage, Vol. II, 1625–1649*, Exeter: Pollard & Co., 1902, p. 160.

45 Bruce, John (ed.): *Calendar of State Papers Domestic: Charles I, Vol. XCII, Feb. 1–11, 1628* (1858); *Vol. XCV, March 1–14, 1628* (1859).

46 Green, Mary Anne Everett (ed.): *Calendar of State Papers domestic: Charles I, Vol. XVII, Sept. 1660* (1860).

'void'.[47] Two years later Nicholas and Thomas Veel, son and grandson respectively of the royalist army officer and conspirator Colonel Thomas Veel, were granted the office in return for service – both had been imprisoned – and held its profits of £400 per year in trust for the colonel. This valuation is noted in the senior Veel's will, and appears to be based on the farm-price of the office realised by the Overburys fifty years earlier.[48] Before Veel's death, however, the office was granted to another loyalist conspirator, Sir Allen Broderick.[49] Broderick appears not to have operated the office himself, at least not as Candeler and Overbury had done. The *London Directory* of 1677 lists instead 'Cap. Nunssan *at the Insur. Office*',[50] and a 1684 petition to the Lord Chancellor reveals Thomas Hardwick as Broderick's assignee to carry out the office.[51] The final patent-holder was a relative, William Broderick.

In 1662, the same year that Broderick was awarded the patent to operate the Office of Assurance, the institution was given a royal boost through further legislative endorsement. *An Additional Act concerning matters of Assurance used amongst Merchants* reaffirmed that only those policies registered at the 'Office of Assurance of the City of London' were subject to dispute resolution through the Court of Assurance, described below.[52] The bill was carried up by Broderick himself. Both the Act and the appointment of Broderick suggest an effort to re-establish royal institutions following the Restoration. Charles Molloy hinted at this; in 1676 he distinguished between '*Publick*' and '*Private*' insurances, the former 'made and entered in a certain Office of Court... on the *Royal Exchange*'.[53] This distinction again suggests that the completion of insurance policies outside the formal channels was widespread.

By the 1680s, the practice of avoiding the Office of Assurance, and instead using alternatives, appears to have been increasing. The decade marked a time of commercial prosperity for London and England,[54] and competing broking offices apparently were established to meet increasing demand for the services supporting seaborne trade, even in the Royal Exchange itself. For example, a 1680/1 edition of the *City Mercury* carries an advertisement announcing that 'the Office at the Royal Exchange' offers merchants and ship masters a range of services, including insurance broking, as well as bottomry and charter-parties. The 'Office' may also have been the last gasp of the centenarian Office of Assurance, but the range of services on offer, including

47 Ibid.
48 Green, *Calendar of State Papers domestic: Charles I, Vol. LV, May 28–31, 1662* (1861); *Vol. LVI, June 1662* (1861); Warmington, Andrew: 'Veel, Thomas', *ODNB*, online edn, Jan. 2008, www.oxforddnb.com/view/article/28171 [Accessed 3 Dec. 2021].
49 Helms, M. W. and Watson, P.: 'Sir Allen Broderick'; *History of Parliament Online*, www.historyofparliamentonline.org/volume/1715-1754/member/williams-sir-john-167-1743 [Accessed 3 Dec. 2021].
50 *The little London directory of 1677*, reprinted London: J. C. Hotten, 1863.
51 Timings, E. K.: *Calendar of State Papers domestic: James II, Vol. II, Jan. 1686* (1964).
52 Car. 2 C. 23, *Statutes of the Realm 1625–1680*, Vol. 5, HeinOnline, p. 418.
53 Molloy, *De jure maritimo*, p. 282.
54 Harris, *Politics under the later Stuarts*, pp. 34–35.

shipping and freighting agency, implies a more entrepreneurial venture. An advertisement in the paper later the same year described an insurance policy 'made' in the office the previous September, which had since been lost, and implored the subscribers to the policy to 'come into the Insurance Office and subscribe the new policie, that it may be known who the insurers are'. The announcement named 'Tho. Astley in the Insurance Office on the Royal Exchange' as the contact.[55]

If this was the Office of Assurance, it was no longer acting satisfactorily as a public registry, as the lost policy proves. However, it may have been a competitor, as the patent-holder's rights were clearly under threat. In 1686 James II made a proclamation to condemn 'private Offices for making Policys of Assurances', in order to protect Broderick's patent rights. The action followed a petition to the Lord Chancellor by Thomas Hardwick, who operated the office as Broderick's assignee, and complained that 'several persons have set up private offices for making policies, etc., and make no entries of them in the office aforesaid', and requested that the king issue a proclamation 'commanding obedience to the said letters patent'.[56] Published the following year, the proclamation stated that the letters patent granted to Broderick would remain in force for thirty-one years after his death, or that of 'William Broderick, Merchant' (presumably a brother or nephew, as Broderick is believed to have died childless[57]). The proclamation threatened that 'no other Person or Persons do presume to erect any other Office or offices for Making or registering any Assurances or Policys contrary to the said letters patent, as they will answer the same at their Peril', although no specific sanction is described.[58] Condemnation from above was no longer over refusal to use the Office, but now was over organised usurpation of the patent-holders' rights. Competition must have been sufficient to erode the income of the patent. This would, of course, have been aggravated if the office had been 'void', as Bogan claimed, at the close of the Interregnum.

The Office's monopoly over policy registration appears to have expired over the next decade (perhaps, given its loyalist placeholder, it was a casualty of the Revolution). The institution of optional policy registration had reverted to its earlier form, with registers kept by private intermediaries; in effect, the functions of the Office of Assurance were privatised. The 1699 edition of Edward Hatton's *Comes Commercii* explains that 'Insurances for Merchants are either made in publick or in private. Publick insurances are such as are Registered in a Publick Office, as Mr. *Tucker's*, Mr. *Bevis's*, &c. on the East Side of the *Royal Exchange, London.*'[59] 'Private' insurances presumably comprised any which were unregistered, although the categorisation causes obfuscation when attempting to determine the end-date of the Office of Assurance. Brief reference was made in the *Manuscripts of the House of*

55　*City Mercury*, No. 204, 20 Jan. 1680; ibid. No. 255, cited in Martin, *History of Lloyd's*, p. 59.

56　Timings, *Calendar of State Papers domestic.*

57　Helms and Watson, *Sir Allen Broderick*, History of Parliament Online.

58　*By the King, A proclamation for the better execution of the office of making and registering policys of assurance in the City of London*, The King's Printers, 1687.

59　Hatton, Edward: *Comes Commercii, or the trader's Companion*, first edition, London: printed by 'J. H. for Chas. Coningsby' and three others, 1699, p. 289.

Lords in February 1693/4 to 'the public office of Assurance on the Royal Exchange, London'.[60] The nature of the authority of this office is, alas, unstated. If it was the office which operated under Broderick's patent, it had competitors again within the decade, as Hatton's description proves.

By creating the Office of Assurance, the Privy Council had begun, at the behest of at least some of the merchant-insurers, to overcome one of the problems caused by the entry of outsiders into the expanding London insurance market: that of information-sharing among a broader group of merchant-insurers. While the solution was not universal and did not survive indefinitely, it marked the first step in state intervention into London's marine insurance sector. However, one impact endured. The most lasting institutional impact of the intervention was the partial fixing of the wording of the marine insurance policy used in London, and later around the world. The policies in the archives of the High Court of Admiralty, all drawn before the Office was established, have many common elements, but they follow no standard wording. Those underwritten for Corsini in Candeler's office in the 1580s adopt a form of words which is a close match to successive London forms. The sample policy presented in West's 1615 reference manual *Simboleography* is different in only a few details from that of Candeler's precedent.[61]

Changes in future policies, until reform in the 1980s, are few. Although the Office standardised policies, it was not an institution of underwriting inflexibility. For example, extant sixteenth-century policies underwritten in London named the specific goods insured. A policy underwritten at the Office of Assurance for Bartholomew Corsini in 1582 states that it insures 'one case of silckes'.[62] However, soon after, specification became somewhat more lax. The 1613 *Tyger* policy, also underwritten in the Office of Assurance, covers 'woollen & lynnen cloth leade kersies Iron & any other goods & merchandize', showing that the formal institution of the Office was one agent of underwriters' increasing flexibility, allowing merchants to insure distant cargoes which might not yet even have been purchased.[63]

The 'Booke of Orders'

The second institutional development ordered by the Privy Council in the 1570s to accommodate the shift of insurance from a small community to a larger market which included outsider-buyers and -sellers was the codification of insurance regulation, as it was understood according to the Law Merchant. The councillors set out not to change the customary rules of the game, but instead to create certainty, and to give the rules regulatory teeth by defining formally the accepted practices of

[60] *Manuscripts of the House of Lords, 1693–1695, Vol. I, New Series*, London: HMSO, 1900, p. 359.

[61] West, William: *Simboleography, which may be termed the art, or description, of instruments and precedents*, two vols, London: Companie of Stationers, 1615, I, sec. 663 [unpaginated].

[62] GHL 062/MS22,282, f. 8, insurance policy underwritten for Bartholomew Corsini, 15 Jun. 1582.

[63] BOD MS Tanner 74, f. 32, contemporaneous copy of a policy underwritten for Morris Abbot and Devereux Wogan, 15 Feb. 1613.

Lombard Street, and the system of underwriting developed by the merchant-insurers. This is in keeping with an institutional development identified by North as reducing transaction costs: the blending of the Law Merchant into formal English law.[64]

Several major port cities had already promulgated insurance codes, ordinances, or other forms of written regulation. Although not comprehensive, the earliest was probably that of Barcelona, set out in 1435, which required parties to bring disputes to the city's maritime court, and was affirmed in 1458 and 1484. Nearly a century had passed before Florence codified its insurance regulations in 1523. Burgos established ordinances in 1538, and Antwerp in 1563.[65] London was late to the trend. In December 1574 their Lordships of the English Privy Council wrote to the Lord Mayor of London, requesting that he, 'by conference with suche as be moste skilfull in [insurance] cases, should certifie my Lordes what lawes, orders, and customes are used in those matters of assuraunce, to thend they may be put in use acordinglie'. The third-party enforcement required when outsiders chose to disavow insiders' rules could not be conducted adequately without consistent rules of the game. Codification would address this problem. By June 1575 the Orders must not have been transmitted, because the Privy Council again wrote to the Lord Mayor 'to certifie their Lordships what had been done for the setting downe of some orders for matters of assuraunce which their Lordships required to be donne long agoe'. Following the election of a new Lord Mayor, a further letter was despatched requiring that 'by sume learnid in the Civill Lawes and other skilful merchaunts certen orders might be set downe wherebye controversies arising out of matters of assuraunce might be decided'. A sharper, fourth missive requesting the orders was sent in July 1576, since 'the wante whereof doth dailie brede grete trobles', words which imply that insurance-market disputes were increasingly frequent, and out of hand.[66]

The *Booke of Orders of Assurances within the Royall Exchange*, c.1577, set out standard insurance customs as practised in London under the Law Merchant. Two manuscript copies, with slight differences, have survived, both unfinished.[67] They contain 126 and 128 provisions respectively, and set out the rules in a broad range of relevant areas ranging from the timing of the commencement of coverage to the making of insurances for vessels 'lost or not lost'. One version of the *Booke* contains a specific provision stating that all policies must be made by the Registrar of Assurance, and recorded by the patent-holder, and both contain multiple references to the Commissioners of Assurance described below. Things were moving relatively quickly during the first intervention, at least in terms of the typically very slow evolution of customary law; it appears almost as if the authors of the *Booke* struggled to 'keep up' with the structural changes which were being imposed on London's

---

[64] North's argument has been roundly refuted; see pp. 20–21. North, Douglass: 'Institutions, transaction costs, and the rise of empires', in Tracy, James (ed.): *The political economy of merchant empires*, Cambridge: Cambridge University Press, 1991, p. 30.

[65] van Niekerk, *Principles of insurance law*, I, p. 199; Magens, *An essay*, II, p. 1.

[66] Dasent, *Acts of the Privy Council*, VIII, pp. 321, 397; IX, pp. 43, 163.

[67] BL Add. Ms. 48,023, ff. 246–273, 'Booke of Orders of Assurance'; BL Harleian Ms. 5103, 'Booke of Orders of Assurance' (later version).

marine insurance market. The *Booke of Orders* is reproduced and analysed in detail in Rossi's masterful legal treatise, *Insurance in Elizabethan England: the London code*.

The code was never adopted by statute, although Kepler's scepticism that the rules 'were ever used by merchants' is odd, since by definition they comprised the merchants' established practice.[68] A 1572 petition by the London merchant Thomas Cure, related to a dispute over the insurance of a shipment of broadcloths from Spain, states that the policy was drawn 'according to the order of assurance used among merchaunts in the royall exchaunge in London', *before* the rules were codified at the request of the Privy Council.[69] Rossi argues that the written Orders comprise the 'earliest attempt to codify customs' in England, and discusses at length the question raised by Kepler as to whether or not the code was ever formally adopted. He concludes that it was, citing a 1601 letter from the Privy Council to a Judge of the Admiralty in which, in Rossi's words, the Orders are described as 'confirmed by the same Privy Council some years before'.[70] While this may seem scant confirmation that the Orders had been formally adopted, it is certain that the rules laid out in the Orders were never imposed under a parliamentary act or formal proclamation.

It may be that the orders never proceeded beyond draft stage. If any records of the Office of Assurance have survived, they have yet to be identified. Thus, if a *Booke of Orders* was kept by the Office, and regularly updated, it has been lost. However, Rossi argues, based on his interpretation of primary evidence, that the judges of the Admiralty 'considered the code as written evidence of the insurance customs of a given period, and so as a set of rules subjected to change over time', and that the merchants who sat as arbiters of insurance disputes did not see them as definitively authoritative. Thus, he concludes, the Orders reflect the fact that 'the inner flexibility of customs ultimately prevailed on the rigidity of law'.[71] The adaptability of the Law Merchant survived in London; her merchant-insurers' flexibility to provide the insurance product their customers desired remained unimpaired by this attempt at codification.

The Commissioners of Assurance

As discussed above, the Privy Council on several occasions had called for the formation of arbitration panels on an *ad hoc* basis to handle specific disputes. Their recognition of the insufficiency of the common law courts was recorded following a meeting held on 7 November 1576. A letter was drafted to Sir William Cordell, Master of the Rolls, and to the Justices Southcote, Harper, and Jeffries, 'touching the hearing and examyning of a metter in controversye' between a merchant and his insurers. 'Foreaasmuch as the matter is of some waighte, and therefore dowbtfull whether it may be tryed by the Common Lawe or not, the Lord Chief Justice and the Lord [Justice] Dyer are required to joyn with the abovenamyd, and to examyne

---

[68] Kepler, 'Operating potential', p. 47.

[69] Cited in Jones, 'Elizabethan marine insurance', pp. 58–59.

[70] Rossi, *Booke of orders*, pp. 260, 250–252.

[71] Ibid., pp. 251–252.

the said controversye a new, considering the circumstaunces requireth thadvice and opynion of such as are learnid in the Civill Lawe'.[72] Three months later they were to establish a more permanent solution than this *ad hoc* panel of justices of the common and civil law. In this, the Privy Council's third action to address the challenges of the changing institutions of London insurance, their Lordships instructed the Lord Mayor to formalise the arrangements for dispute resolution.

The details of the civil law solution are set out in the records of the city's Court of Aldermen. In January 1576/7 the Court did, for the term of one year, 'ellecte nomynate and chuse, for the desidinge and endinge of the causes [of assurance, seven men]... as indifferent p'sons to order, judge, and determyne all suche causes touchinge assurance made or hereafter to be made, wᵗhin the Royall Exchange, or the cittie of London'. The named men were to be 'after the seconde daye of the moneth of ffebruarye nexte, comynge two dayes in the weeke, that ye to be mundays and Thursdays, sitt in the office howse of assurance in the Royall Exchange'. Candeler – now styled Registrar of Assurances – or his designate was to act as recorder, incorporating new decisions into the *Book of Orders* to form an evolving, and thus flexible, body of insurance law.[73] This direction too indicates the flexibility of the rules governing insurance in London, and supports Rossi's contention that the rules were known contemporaneously to be 'subject to change'. Commissioners were not permitted to charge a fee for their services, so the creation of this permanent panel of arbitrators will have had a neutral or downward pressure on transaction costs.

Shortly afterwards, Admiralty Judge David Lewis was appointed by the Privy Council to sit as an additional commissioner. Almost concurrently, he received a Royal patent for the summary determination of maritime disputes, after his repeated complaints that his Admiralty post was insufficiently remunerative to supply a living wage.[74] Lewis, an outsider, was presumably appointed to lend the new body the Admiralty's procedural knowledge related to insurance disputes.[75] However, the Commission remained primarily an institution of the merchant-insurers. This did not suit everyone: foreign merchants – the most frequent appellants to the Privy Council on insurance matters – were not appeased. They complained, and in response their Lordships, meeting at Nonesuch on 15 June 1593, wrote to the Lord Mayor and aldermen. 'Marchant strangers, having occasion to deale in matters of assurance, remaine discontented that no strangers are admitted to joyne with suche Englishe Comissioners as you appoint in theis causes'. In appointing the commissioners, the aldermen had 'omytted to make chise of some two or three straungers, a matter very meet to have bene remembered in respect that many of sondrie nations within the cittie are dailie intressed in causes of assurance'.

---

[72] Dasent, *Acts of the Privy Council*, VIII, p. 230.

[73] LMA COL/AD/01/022 (MR X109/037), Letter Book Y, fos. 126–127.

[74] For a discussion of the circumstances surrounding Dr Lewis appending to the panel, and the jurisdictional battle between the prerogative, common law, and private courts over jurisdictions in marine insurance disputes, see Ibbetson, 'Law and custom'. Senior, William: *Doctors' Commons and the old Court of Admiralty: a short history of the civilians in England*, London: Longmans Green, 1922, pp. 79–80.

[75] Ibbetson, 'Law and custom', p. 298.

The aldermen were ordered to appoint 'yearlie unto the rest alreadie established or in liewe of some of them three strangers of forrein nations, being marchantes knowne to be of worthe, judgement and integritie'. These men were always to be called to participate when merchant strangers were involved in arbitrations, following a principle in Edward I's *Carta Mercatoria* of 1303, which allowed foreign merchants to request that juries include up to six merchant strangers.[76] Such compromises served to maintain the flexibility of the rules in London. As has been shown, insurance practice varied between major trading cities. It seems likely that a foreign merchant acting as a commissioner would have a different understanding of the local rules in at least some circumstances. By inviting foreigners to participate in arbitration panels, not only was a valid reference point provided to the possible understanding of foreigners involved in disputes (as with the consultation to Florentine custom in the Ferrantyn case), but also English merchants were exposed to alternative customs which may have been preferable to their own.

Malynes provided a contemporary account of the routine of the Commissioners of Assurance. An insured with a claim would gather testimonials, witnesses, letters, and other evidence of the loss, and bring it, along with any policies, charter-parties, bills of lading, invoices, and other relevant documents, to the Office of Assurance for examination by the commissioners on one of their appointed days of hearing. The insurers would be summoned to appear, and a record made of the proceedings. If foul play was suspected, the commissioners could examine the claimant under oath, 'then deal therein as they find cause, according to the Custom of Assurances'.[77]

With this third set of actions the Privy Council had made a concerted (if not consciously coordinated) attempt to resolve the issues raised by the increasing use by outsider-buyers and sellers of London's insurance market. It had established a system of information exchange, a codified body of rules of the game to aid enforcement, and a permanent tribunal to deal with disputes arising in the merchant-insurers' market after the arrival of outsiders; some foreign and therefore unfamiliar with the custom of Lombard Street, some genuinely unfamiliar with the local Law Merchant, and some simply unscrupulous. In so doing, the queen's policymakers had taken steps to keep flowing the contingent capital which allowed trade to proceed and expand, and had attempted to improve market institutions such that they could effectively reduce transaction costs by improving enforcement mechanisms.

Impacts of the acts

Several characteristics of this set of interventions were important to the long-term success of London's insurance market, since they did not stifle its institutional advantages as, for example, a fixed and statutory codification of the regulations governing insurance did elsewhere. The 1523 Ordinances of Florence, for example, required the intervention and approval of at least three of the city's 'insurance

---

[76] Dasent, *Acts of the Privy Council*, XXIV, p. 313; Oldham, James C.: 'The origins of the special jury', *University of Chicago Law Review*, Vol. 50, No. 1 (1983), p. 173.

[77] Malynes, *Lex Mercatoria*, p. 116.

deputies' before insurers could make indemnity for goods cast overboard in order to save a distressed vessel, or for ransoms paid to recover a ship or cargo that had been seized.[78] Both were common sources of claims, and were insured as a matter of course in London.

There, the continued but formalised employment of merchant arbitrators to resolve disputes in an inexpensive, swift, regular, and unbureaucratic manner made dispute-resolution facilities more accessible, especially for those outside the regular community of merchant-insurers (Malynes describes what today we would call 'counter service'), but did not change the character of the dispute-resolution mechanism, despite the addition of lawyers and foreign merchants to the panel. It remained predominantly an institution of self-enforcement. Continued flexible interpretation of the Law Merchant, which despite codification was to be regularly amended based on decisions arising from the commissioners' authority, allowed the regulations to remain flexible and reactive to market and merchant needs, while retaining the principle of equitable resolution, which was a key target of the state in resolving individual cases. Finally, the use of a new facility for the registration of policies was officially required, but was not enforced by any authority. Extant policy documents from London suggest its use was widespread, however, since many were made in the Office of Assurance. Marine insurance arrangements by established merchants could, however, have been made outside the facility, and almost certainly were.

The Privy Council's institutional intervention into the workings of London's market had international imitators. In 1577, one Francesco di Nasi, perhaps informed by Candeler's success in London, proposed the establishment of a similar registration office in Venice. Had the proposal been accepted, the erection of an office would have marked a reversal of a longstanding trend: the institutional development of the Italian insurance market would have begun to follow precedents set in London. Instead, development further diverged when Nasi's suggestion was rejected. A second proposal, advanced in 1580 by Zuan di Nasi, would have established a registry as an official civic office, much like that erected over Candeler's operation in London following the legislative act of 1601.[79] This proposal was also rejected. However, Venice did begin to follow London in 1596 when, in the face of disputes between insurance buyers and their underwriters, the *V Savi alla Mercanzia* (a standing committee with legislative powers appointed by the Venetian Senate in 1506 to investigate matters of trade) ruled that goods were to be valued for the purposes of insurance based upon their purchase price, rather than on anticipated sale values.[80] The convention of insuring a projected sale-value must surely have been complicated by the radical swings in commodity prices which were occurring in key Venetian markets, especially her Levantine sources of supply, as Hispano-Portuguese trade in pepper and other eastern

[78] Magens, *An essay*, II, p. 3. For more Florentine examples, see p. 43.

[79] See pp. 95 ff.

[80] Stefani, *Insurance in Venice*, pp. 104–106.

luxuries was threatened by north European interlopers, and the Venetian Levant trade entered the final years of its decline.[81]

The Office of Assurance, the formal panel of commissioners, and the codification of insurance law were not unique to London. There were many precedents, such as those adopted in Florence in 1523.[82] But London also set precedents. Shortly after the acts of the English Privy Council, in 1598, Amsterdam's city government formed a chamber of assurances which had 'first-instance jurisdiction' over all disputes related to policies underwritten in the city, and had additional duties in adjudicating averages and information dissemination, although it does not appear to have acted as an office of registration. Nor did merchant-insurers sit as commissioners.[83] A similar chamber was established in Rotterdam in 1604; others were appointed in Middleburg (1600) and Vlissingen (Flushing). In Dordrecht, a tribunal established in 1439 to hear maritime cases was, at some unknown date, granted jurisdiction over insurance disputes.[84] This fragmentation of judicial authorities, each of which operated under divergent regulations, must have complicated enforcement procedures in the Low Countries, especially for disputes over policies which had been underwritten by merchant-insurers from more than one city. In contrast to the state-sanctioned institutional developments to govern foreign insurance markets which were made both before and after the Privy Council's actions in the 1570s, developments in London were measured interventions made with sympathetic respect for the merchant-insurers' custom and practice.

Insiders and outsiders

Much of the analysis presented above, and much of what follows below, has turned on a distinction between market 'insiders' and others, 'outsiders', whether those others are simply strangers, or individuals with more nefarious designs. The approach to the historical analysis of trade relationships known as New Institutional Economics (NIE), which searches for the drivers of economic growth in the development of institutions, sometimes adopts a theoretical framework which distinguishes between 'individualists' and 'collectivists' in markets.[85] The framework is borrowed from sociology, and has been used by Ebert in his analysis of the development of insurance markets.[86] Ebert argues that 'colonial trade tended to lead to accelerated

---

[81] Braudel, Fernand: *The Mediterranean and the Mediterranean world of Philip II*, two volumes (Reynolds, Sian: trans.), London: Harper Colophon, 1976 (1949), I, pp. 556–565.

[82] See p. 43.

[83] See pp. 87 ff.

[84] The Chamber was called *Den Commissarissen vande Kamere van Asseurantie alheir*. van Niekerk, *Principles of insurance law*, I, pp. 207–217, 220, 223–224; Go, *Marine insurance in the Netherlands*, pp. 97–99.

[85] See, for example, Greif, Avner: *Institutions and the path to the modern economy: lessons from medieval trade*, Cambridge: Cambridge University Press, 2006.

[86] See, for example, Triandis, H. C., McCusker, C., and Hui, C. H.: 'Multimethod probes of individualism and collectivism', *Journal of Personality and Social Psychology*, Vol. 59, No. 5 (19902), pp. 1006–1020.

state involvement in the activities of the merchants involved, and consequently spawned an evolving institutional framework... one of which... was the development of maritime premium insurance practices situated partly in a state-supported institutional context mainly during the years 1550 to 1630.'[87] Note that this assertion specifies *colonial* trade as the catalyst, not the conventional European trade which formed the bulk of commerce, and which was changing in the period 1550 to 1630. Ebert goes on to specify further that the 'spread of state-supported premium insurance practices [occurred] in order to facilitate Atlantic trade'.[88] He employs Greif's distinction between collectivists and individualists to support this assertion, focusing on the diaspora of Portuguese merchants in western Europe and the carriage and import of Brazilian sugar (his main field of study).

Neither the balance of extant documents nor NIE theory supports Ebert's thesis. Evidence such as the London policies underwritten in this period shows that development of institutional structures supporting insurance responded primarily to disputes over policies which, in the vast majority, related to non-colonial trade to Europe and the Mediterranean. The balance is further tilted away from the Atlantic when disputes over policies covering the India trade are included. For example, de Salizar's insurance dispute, brought in London in 1555 by a Portuguese merchant, and discussed above, related to the India trade.[89] Nor was it the trade of this period specifically which 'spawned an evolving institutional framework'. As has been shown, by 1550 the framework of insurance markets, including state involvement, had been evolving for at least two centuries.

Ebert claims that 'Insurance was especially associated with "rich trades", that is, trade in overseas commodities.'[90] Regardless of whether or not this classification includes Brazilian sugar, the 'rich trades' – high-value goods ranging from silks to spices – comprise only a subset of 'overseas trade'. It has often been argued that higher-value trade goods were more likely to be insured, but much evidence shows that during the sixteenth century bulky, low-valued commodities were regularly insured. The Bristol merchant John Smythe insured his shipments of iron in 1539; by the 1570s, fishing vessels and their cargoes were also regularly insured: a tract about the Newfoundland fishery published in 1580 reports that 'A shippe of Excester is gone to the Warde house, to fishe for Codd and Lyng; the venture for the Shippe, Salte, and Victualls is three hundredth pounde; for eightene pownd [i.e. 6%] all is assured.'[91] Insurance was not limited to luxury items. Ebert shows that some changes in insurance institutions occurred concurrently with the rise of Atlantic trade, but provides no evidence of a causal link. The absolute growth of trade in the period Ebert examines, the entry of outsiders into local insurance markets, and the need

[87] Ebert, 'Early modern Atlantic trade', pp. 89–90.

[88] Ibid., p. 100.

[89] See pp. 61, 67. TNA HCA 24/29 f. 45, policy underwritten for Anthony de Salizar, 5 Aug. 1555.

[90] Ebert, 'Early modern Atlantic trade', p. 102.

[91] Hitchcock, Robert: *A Pollitique Platt for the Development of the Fisheries*, London: 1580, cited in Tawney and Power, *Tudor economic documents*, III, p. 253.

for merchants to develop more efficient, more effective instruments which separated capital provision from risk transfer were the key drivers of new imbalances which demanded institutional change, not Atlantic trade exclusively, or even particularly.

While the collectivist/individualist model provides a useful framework for analysing the London market, it is not without serious shortcomings. A fundamental weakness of the construct is the simple reality that people usually defy sweeping categorisation, as was the case in insurance markets. Consider, for example, the case of the Quaker merchant James Claypoole, who traded in a variety of commodities in Europe and the West Indies in the time of Charles II, before leaving England with William Penn as a founder of Philadelphia. His letterbook, which survives for the years 1681 to 1684, reveals him to be astute and successful, but also willing to cheat customs officers and correspondents, and when it suited him, to smuggle.[92] He was quick to go to law, even with family members, but also employed reputational remedies and, when called, would go to arbitration. As a member of the Society of Friends (and not a passing one; he was treasurer of the Society at a time when many were imprisoned for their faith, and often died in prison) and of the close-knit London merchant community, he was plainly a collectivist in the jargon of NIE.[93] However, as a cheater in business and a frequent litigant, he was an NIE individualist. In practice, though, he remained a market insider. This tension is apparent in his insurance dealings.

Claypoole regularly purchased cover in London for, among others, his Lisbon correspondent, Richard Gay. He dealt through brokers, and thus was a member of the merchant-insurers' secondary, international distribution force. He had purchased £400 of cover for goods belonging to Gay *en route* from Hull to Lisbon on the *Swallow*, which sailed in late December 1681. However, events coincided to complicate the routine. By early March the *Swallow* was overdue. Gay, already in financial difficulty, was to return to England, then at Claypoole's suggestion to head to Ireland to hide from his creditors. In order to pay off some of these associates, Claypoole endeavoured to collect quickly the insurance indemnity due for the loss of the *Swallow*. He wrote to the creditors that 'tomorrow I am to dine with the insurers in order to agree with them, and I shall, if I can possibly, secure this money for your account [with Gay]'.

Claypoole was planning an aggressive stance, and was willing to litigate. 'If no other way will do it, I intend to lay an attachment privately in your names.' The dinner was a partial success. Some of the insurers attended, and agreed to pay £78 per £100 insured, within two months. Claypoole agreed to return the money if the ship arrived in Lisbon before the end of the following February, but, apparently unsatisfied with the wait (probably fearing other of Gay's creditors would get their hands on the insurance money first), Claypoole offered to accept a further 2% reduction in exchange for immediate payment. The insurers, no doubt suspicious, refused this offer. Claypoole immediately sued. Soon after the Lord Mayor placed

---

92 A heavily edited selection has been published. Balderston, Marion (ed.): *James Claypoole's letter book, London and Philadelphia, 1681–1684*, San Marino, CA: Huntington Library, 1967.

93 Harris, *Politics under the later Stuarts*, p. 179.

an attachment of £1,000 on Gay's assets, potentially including the indemnity. By October Claypoole was satisfied that at least three of the insurers would pay him – one had done so – but four more had 'joined with the attacher... so I lately arrested them, all four, and we are now on a trial'. In January 1682, he wrote to Gay to explain: 'I have at length made a full conclusion... we see that the lawyers at last would get all if we went on, and we should have nothing to divide.'[94]

Despite these events, which cannot have endeared Claypoole to the underwriters in question, he continued successfully to arrange insurances for his clients and correspondents around the world, and was not excluded from the market; his value as an intermediary for overseas insurance buyers may well have preserved his place. Regardless, the incident shows the difficulty in categorising merchants active in the insurance market (as the NIE theorists sometimes attempt) as either collectivist, a group playing by the rules of the game, or individualist, playing every man for himself. Claypoole had all the characteristics of the former, but often behaved like the latter. Further, the market did not react according to Greif's framework. Claypoole was not roundly excluded from the community; he was neither ostracised nor black-listed, and thus continued to buy insurance.

A late seventeenth century commentator outlined the subtle difference between the parties described herein as insiders and outsiders, and illustrated how underwriters, as well as their customers, can count as outsiders. In roughly 1693, William Leybourn, the mathematician, surveyor, and printer, published his master work, entitled *Panarithmologia*. Primarily a ready reckoner comprising tables ranging from measurement conversions to annuity payments, it included an appendix, 'Containing Heads of Daily Use to all Traders', which covered topics including insurance. He advised insurance buyers suffering a loss to inform their underwriters swiftly,

> for if they are punctual Men, and value their Reputations, they will presently pay you; if not they will shuffle you off, and endeavour to find out flaws, and raise Scruples for a larger abatement [a withholding from the total value of the indemnity] than ordinary; and sometimes will keep you a Year or two out of your Mony, and many times never pay; but generally get, in case of Loss, 15 or 20 *per Cent.* abated. I have known 40 *per Cent.* abated, upon very small pretensions; which makes a common Proverb about such Insurers, *What is it worth to insure the Assurers?* Be careful therefore to deal with Honest Men; that value their Reputation when you have any thing to be Insured.[95]

The maintenance of one's reputation was critical. Reputation was the foundation of trust in early modern markets, and thus of commercial credit; it was the glue that held the insurance market together. According to Muldrew, 'These ethics meant that wealth was gained through reputation, not accumulation, individualism, or inward piety.'[96] The merchant-insurers' system operated successfully because individual participants correctly trusted each other to meet their obligations. When market participants did not interpret their obligations in a like way, the system had no measures

---

94 Balderston, *Claypoole's letter book*, p. 136 ff.

95 Leyborun, William: *Panarithmologia*, London: for John Dutton *et al.*, 1693, p. Ap. 33.

96 Muldrew, *Economy of obligation*, 1998, p. 2.

beyond exclusion, no remedies to encourage compliance. Such rules would have to be imposed from outside, by an authority with the ability to assess greater penalties.

The Insurance Act of 1601

Despite the Privy Council's success at the creation and shaping of a permanent panel of insurance arbitrators, which gained the name 'Commissioners of Assurance', the Council was still occasionally called upon to intervene in insurance disputes. Alterations to the composition of the panel were not sufficient to excuse the councillors from occasional adjudication duties related to insurance. Although the usual channels of dispute resolution remained extrajudicial, on the occasions when they proved insufficient, no clear path through the formal courts was apparent. Insurance-related cases in the High Court of Admiralty dwindled at about the time of the Privy Council's tripartite overhaul of the institutions of insurance-contract enforcement, but this is perhaps the result of the presence of Dr Lewis, who may have directed cases to the targeted tribunal of which he was a member.

The Admiralty Court was further pressured under the jurisdictional battles between the civil and common law communities which heightened at this time, under what Levack called a 'full-scale attack' launched by 'common law judges' against courts including Admiralty and Chancery.[97] Judges issued writs of prohibition against appeals to civil law, for example, which required plaintiffs to come before the issuing court and justify their choice of venue.[98] Levack argues, however, that too much may be made of the divisions between civil and common lawyers, who often acted together.[99] The example of the Court of Assurance supports this view. Although it was constituted at the height of the division between law and equity, which in the Privy Council was embodied in the royal law officers, some motivations (presumably pragmatism and a desire to make the court effective) led these legal rivals to require that lawyers of both stripes were involved as commissioners, along with the judge of the Admiralty, the senior legal figure involved.

The courts of King's Bench and Chancery, and the Privy Council itself, continued to hear insurance cases. This was in part a result of the lack of statutory power of enforcement on the part of the Commissioners of Assurance. In March 1601 the Privy Council wrote to the Lord Chief Justice of King's Bench and the Judge of the Admiralty – heads of institutions locked in an ongoing jurisdiction battle – enclosing a petition from merchant-insurers which complained that the system was not working. They complained that 'certaine orders devysed and sett downe some yeres sithence and confirmed by us touchinge assurances amonge merchantes uppon the Exchange are not put in execucion, but greatly impunged by willfullnes and forward disposicion of some whoe refuse to submytte and conforme them selves to the order of Commyssioners appointed to heare those causes'. They asked the judges to

---

[97] Levack, *Civil lawyers*, p. 73.

[98] Steckley, 'Merchants and the Admiralty Court', p. 143.

[99] Levack, *Civil lawyers*, pp. 73–78, 126.

consult with leading merchants and consider a way forward.[100] Here again the institution-building cooperation between merchants and the state was to be invoked in an attempt to create mutually efficacious and beneficial solutions.

One of the merchants involved in the consultations was Malynes, author of *Lex Mercatoria*. In it he recorded that 'I have sundry times attended the Committees of the said Parliament, by whose means the same was enacted'. Malynes reported that the discussions 'were not without some difficulty', and attested to a weakness in the authority of the Commissioners of Assurance. 'There were many suits in [common] Law by Action of *Assumpsit* [breach of promise] before that time, upon matters determined by the Commissioners for Assurances, who for want of Power and Authority could not compel contentious persons to perform their ordinances'.[101] The need was clear: insurance buyers and sellers who did not wish to play by the merchant-insurers' rules of the game were causing strife.

Proposed solutions were advanced in *An Act Concerning matters of assurances amongst merchants*. The 1601 law established formal dispute-resolution facilities for insurance, including the creation of a specialised court 'for the hearing and determining of causes arising and policies of assurances', and for an 'office of assurances within the city of London'. The Act stated specifically that one aim of the legislation was that 'no Suite shalbe depending… in any of her Majesties Courtes'. Provisions included the appointment of Court Commissioners, to include a Judge of the Admiralty, the Recorder of London, two doctors of civil law and two common lawyers, and eight merchants (any five of whom constitute a quorum); that the court should be summary, foregoing formalities of pleadings and proceedings; that the commissioners, who were to take an oath of office before the Lord Mayor and aldermen, could call witnesses, could imprison, without bail, those who did not adhere to their summons, but could not charge fees for their justice or hear cases in which they were a party; that the court should meet once per week at minimum in the Office of Assurance or elsewhere in public; and that appeals against its judgments could be made to the High Court of the Chancery, upon payment in the interim of awards into the Court, in order to avoid imprisonment, and which would be doubled if the appeal should fail.[102]

The new court created by the Act was a legislative afterthought. According to the address Sir Francis Bacon, presumed author of the bill, made to parliament when he tendered the proposed legislation, the Court was introduced following discussions of an earlier version by a committee including Bacon, Walter Raleigh, Dr Julius Caesar (a Judge of the Admiralty and protégé of Assurance-Office proponents Walsingham and Lewis[103]), the merchant and former Lord Mayor Stephen Soame, and others. Bacon told the House: 'The Committees have drawn a new bill far differing from the old. The first limited power to the Chancery, this to certain commissioners by way of Oyer and Terminer [roughly, to hear and determine]. The first that it should only be there, this that only upon appeal from the commissioners

100 TNA PC 2/26 f. 138, *Privy Council letterbook*, 29 Mar. 1601.

101 Malynes, *Lex Mercatoria*, p. 106.

102 Elizabethæ c. 12.

103 Levack, *Civil lawyers*, p. 28.

it should be there finally arbitrated.' The committee believed trials at Chancery would take too long, which merchants 'cannot endure', and that the appointment of commissioners would fill a knowledge gap, which existed 'because our Courts have not the knowledge of [insurers'] Terms, neither can they tell what to say upon their Causes which be secret in their Science'.[104]

The legislation was passed by a parliament called primarily to approve taxation to fund Elizabeth's war with Spain, a motive which sat uneasily with Bacon, but which also attempted to limit royal prerogative by curtailing patents, which were integral to its function, given its connection to the Office of Assurance.[105] Bacon opposed the action against patents, but the insurance law suited his interest in science and precision, and more directly, in legal certainty. Foreshadowing Lord Mansfield, who would re-make the common law governing marine insurance more than a century and a half later, Bacon wrote in *De Augmentis Scientiarium* (1623) that 'certainty is so essential to law, that law cannot even be just without it... It is well said also, "That that is the best law which leaves least to the discretion of the judge" [citing Aristotle]; and this comes from the certainty of it.' He went on to say that uncertainty in law arising from an absence of prescription can be solved in one of three ways: by cautious reference to precedent, by using examples which were not yet law (presumably custom), and through arbitration.[106] In its structure, the institution established by the Act, with the support of those established earlier by the Privy Council, went some distance towards providing all three solutions. The bill appears at this point to have been uncontroversial, as on 14 December 1601 only slight amendments to it were read, twice, and the legislation was ordered engrossed.[107]

The committee's changes were innovative. The tribunal they sketched out was not a common law court, but nor was it purely a prerogative court, given its parliamentary constitution, although it seems to have been a creation of the Privy Council (which was itself a prerogative court). Its operation alongside, but outside, the common law allows it best to be classified as a court of equity (as were Chancery and the Court of Requests, which heard cases brought by the poor), but its informal charge of enforcing the Law Merchant governing insurance contracts places it most closely with the prerogative High Court of Admiralty, which Aylmer described as 'in a category by itself'.[108] While the combination of civil and common lawyers was not uncommon in the English formal courts,[109] the odd constitution of the Commissioners of Assurance, neither jury nor panel of judges, *was* unusual. Yet by incorporating a group of merchant-insurers among its panel of commissioners,

---

[104] Bacon, Francis: 'Speech on bringing in a bill concerning assurances amongst merchants' (1601), in Spedding, James (ed.): *The letters and life of Francis Bacon, Vol. III*, London: Longmans, Green, Reader and Dyer, 1868, pp. 34–35.

[105] Jardine, Lisa and Stewart, Alan: *Hostage to fortune: the troubled life of Francis Bacon*, London: Victor Gollancz, 1998, p. 255; Williams, *The later Tudors*, p. 378.

[106] Robertson, John M. (ed.): *The philosophical works of Francis Bacon*, Abingdon: Routledge 2013, pp. 614–615.

[107] d'Ewes, *Journal of the House of Commons*, 1682.

[108] Aylmer, *King's servants*, p. 44.

[109] Levack, *Civil lawyers*, p. 126.

as well as lawyers from both legal schools, the design of the Court of Assurance cleverly circumvented the twin problems of the common law jury's usual lack of legal knowledge, and the civil judge's sometimes arbitrary approach, while retaining familiar dispute-resolution practice in London. The court was also able to act much more quickly than its competitors. It extended the merchant-state cooperation to the nation's judicial institutions.

The Court of Assurance was, in effect, an extension of the dispute-resolution system established by the Privy Council in the 1570s, and the commissioners an expansion of the permanent panel of Commissioners of Assurance they created, and who were appointed by Guildhall. The significant difference was the inclusion of lawyers, whom Bacon described as having little knowledge of the Law Merchant. The civil lawyers at least would have been comfortable with the notion of equity, the humanist ideal of law which permeated the civil law, and the universities' curricula. 'Equity,' Baker writes, 'involved the relaxation of known but unwritten general rules of law to meet the exigencies of justice or conscience in particular cases.'[110] Lieberman states that the 'elusive identity of English equity was simply a reflection of the ambiguous status of precedents in common law'.[111] Thus a certain flexibility of legal interpretation was to guide the commissioners' decisions: when the Judge of the Admiralty is included in the equation, civil lawyers, governed by notions of equity, held the balance of power on the Commission. Fourteen of the 200 civil lawyers active between 1603 and 1641 and catalogued by Levack are listed as having acted as a commissioner for at least a year; Edmund Pope sat in the Court of Assurance for ten years from 1619. Many commissioners were senior legal academics, including John Cowell, who sat in 1603 and 1605, while he was Regius Professor of Civil Law at Cambridge, and Master of Trinity Hall.[112]

As for the common lawyers, presumably they were to learn on the job. Additional notes added to the extant contemporaneous copy of the *Tyger* policy hint at their thought process (although no direct evidence affirms that the notes were added by Commissioners of the Court). Beneath the contract wording reproduced in the copy, an extracted clause outlining permissions for putting-in of the vessel has been repeated, with the following added:

> The Question is: 1. whether it be Lawfull or not for the said Shipp to Touch twise at one porte in this prsnt voyadge wthin the Scope lymitted if the M[aste]r. & ffactors doe thinke it soe ffitt / And .2. though ther were noe expresse covenant that had relacon to the ffactors discretion yett in case the shipp (haveing discharged her goods) should in the intercime of tyme while monys were pvidinge goe 24 howrs saylinge thence & retourne in saffety wthout losse of tyme or priudize proved (not more than if the shipp had stayed soe longe toegether in porte) whether the assurance ought in conscience to be made voyde or noe.[113]

---

[110] Baker, *History of the laws*, VI, pp. 40–41.

[111] Lieberman, David: *The Province of legislation determined: legal theory in eighteenth-century Britain*, Cambridge: Cambridge University Press, 1989, p. 85.

[112] Levack, *Civil lawyers*, pp. 203–282.

[113] BOD MS Tanner 74, f. 32, contemporaneous copy of a policy underwritten for Morris Abbot and Devereux Wogan, 15 Feb. 1613.

Table 3: Some civil lawyers acting as Commissioners of policies of Assurance

Name	Year(s) active
Pope, John	1602–05
Cowell, John	1603, 1605
Ferrand, William	1608
Hone, John	1609
Amye, Sir John	1609
Dunn Sir Daniel	1609–11
Amye, Sir John	1611
Hone, John	1613
Hayward, Sir John	1613
Bird, Sir William	1615
Amye, Sir John	1616
Wood, Basil	1618–19
Pope, Edmund	1619–29
Clarke, Richard	1621
Merrick, Sir William	1629, 1634–37
Wood, Basil	1634–38
Exton, John	1639–40
Wiseman, Sir Robert	1645

Source: Compiled from Levack, *Civil lawyers*, pp. 203–282.

The principles of equity seem here of utmost importance, as the adjudicators attempt to determine what 'in good conscience' ought to be their verdict.

In any case, given that only five members of the panel of commissioners needed to be present, no change at all was required to the actual constitution of any panel of commissioners from that directed by the Privy Council a generation earlier. Despite this, it evidently became difficult to achieve a quorum in a timely way. This shortcoming was addressed following the Restoration, when *An Additional Act concerning matters of Assurance used amongst Merchants*, adopted in 1662, changed the requirement slightly: only three, including at least one lawyer, could comprise a quorate panel of commissioners. Their appointment remained the responsibility of the Mayor and aldermen at the Guildhall. Their powers were extended to include the calling of witnesses 'beyond the Seas', and to make judgements not just against the person of the defendant, but also against his goods and chattels (although not both simultaneously).[114]

The commissioners sometimes acted as arbiters of non-insurance disputes. For example, in December 1610 the Chancery ordered the Master and two others of

---

[114] Caroline c. 23, HeinOnline, 5 *Statutes of the Realm, 1625–1680*, pp. 418–419.

Trinity House, which under an Elizabethan order had jurisdiction over certain maritime disputes (for example, over monies owed by masters to seafarers), and 'Ralph Freeman, Humphry Basse and Robert Bell, commissioners for insurance policies' to hear a dispute over non-payment of a charter party and the resulting wage liability to crew members.[115]

Some insight into the popularity and functioning of the Court can be gleaned from a letter of the Canaries merchant John Paige. In March 1652 he met with underwriters about a claim related to the vessel *Susan*. 'I was fain to put them to suit in the Insurance Court before I could bring them to any reason', he wrote to an agent. In a later dispute, Paige predicted victory because 'there's several precedents of the very same nature upon record in the Insurance Court'.[116] Still, older methods of dispute resolution were preferred. In a third dispute over a claim, Paige brought underwriters around to settlement having 'given the insurers upon the *Swan* a dinner at tavern, where I found them inclining to reason'.[117]

Certain prerogative courts, notably the Star Chamber and the High Commission, had been dismantled under the Commonwealth, and were not revived after the Restoration.[118] However, judicial evidence and merchant records suggest the Court of Assurance – a parliamentary foundation – continued to operate throughout the interregnum. The survival of the Court shows that equity and prerogative were not always tied. Equity courts had a broader and more widely regarded function. Commissioners were sworn at Guildhall regularly until 1662, when this requirement was dropped under the *Additional Act*. The continuity of the Office of Assurance, and of the position of Registrar, a royal placeman, seems less certain. William Cowper's 1660 petition states that the office was 'void', indicating an interruption.[119] Although the Court could hear only cases arising under policies registered at the Office, it is possible that this requirement had been overlooked during the period of the Commonwealth. It is further possible that the office of Registrar was suspended, but that the clerks of the Office of Assurance continued to carry out its functions. It seems to have been a going concern during the later years of the Protectorate, when Captain John Lymbrey proposed that, to reduce its cost, insurance should be underwritten by the state. Under his scheme, premium rates would be fixed (and one per cent higher for foreigners), profits would be diverted to trade protection through convoys, and the business conducted from the 'Office of Assurance'.[120]

---

[115] Dec. 1610: Westminster. Order in Chancery to Hugh Merricke, Master of Trinity House. Harris, *Trinity House of Deptford Transactions*, p. 6.

[116] John Paige to William Clerke, 5 Mar. 1652, 18 Nov. 1653, Steckley, G. F. (ed.): *The letters of John Paige, London merchant, 1648–1658*, London: London Record Society, 1984, pp. 64, 97–98.

[117] Paige to Clerke, 1 Mar. 1653. Steckley, *Letters of John Paige*, p. 86.

[118] Harris, *Politics under the later Stuarts*, p. 34.

[119] Green, Mary Anne Everett (ed.): *Calendar of State Papers domestic: Charles I, Vol. XVII, Sept. 1660* (1860).

[120] BL Egerton Ms. 2395, ff. 149–151, 'Proposalls to bee presented to his Highness the Lord Protector and his Councell, for the greater encouragement of Merchants in their Navigations' (1657?).

The system established through the first intervention survived these and several further proposals for radical change. For example, a group of individuals led by Colonel John Russell, with William Brereton and Sir William Killegrew, in 1662 applied for letters patent to incorporate a Society for Sea Insurance Office, backed by a joint stock of £100,000 (later £500,000). Russell argued that an insuring corporation would offer greater security to merchants, thereby prompting an increase in trade.[121]

> tis hoped and may be rationally concluded yt (when the Office shall be thoroughly established and Merchants perceive the certaine benefitt) scarce a Cargo will be sent to Sea without first Insuring and many Cargo more then now will be yearely adventured to Sea... Ant it may in time be hoped to become ye Generall Insurance Office of Europe, especially if encouraged by Act of Parliament.[122]

The petitioners' 'Rationall Guess' of the Society's income was £175,000 per annum, based on their assumptions that the whole trade of England was £7 million (based on 'the Customes'), and that the Society would insure the 'moyety' (half) of this trade at an average rate of 5%.[123] 'Noblemen Gentlemen and Marchants' were to support the venture through a subscription to create a reserve fund, and also for investment.

> Joynt stock of 500,000 li or more if it bee necessary... deposited in the hands of the East India Companie upon a moderate interest, or bee disposed of in some publique, secure and profitable way... And soe become an incouragment to all Marchants Owners of shipps or goods, and others as well Aliens as Natives... outeward or inward and to and from all parts and places whatsoever.[124]

The Council of Trade required amendments to the proposal, including requirements to limit speculative investment by the Society and to prevent a monopoly from evolving, but the venture appears to have made no further progress, perhaps because these conditions rendered the scheme less attractive to its projectors. In any case, it provided a hint of what was to come during the second intervention.

Erosion of the Office and Court

The Court of Assurances appears to have become a landmark institution. Samuel Lambe, a merchant who offered his suggestions for the advance of trade to the Lord Protector in 1657, proposed the establishment of a 'Court of Merchants' which could be accomplished by broadening the jurisdiction of 'the Court of Insurance sitting in the Insurance Office, who are yearly chosen, [that it] may have power to determine

---

[121] I am indebted to Anastasia Bogatyreva, whose unpublished undergraduate dissertation informs the following paragraphs.

[122] TNA, *State Papers Domestic*, Car. II., Vol. LXVI, No. 53: *Projected Corporation of Ensurers, 1660.*

[123] Ibid.

[124] TNA, *State Papers Domestic*, 13 Ca. R. Rawlinson MSS, A. 478. Folio 81: *Report 23 January.*

all such matters as they do causes of Insurance'.[125] But despite its prominence, and Charles II's *Additional Act*, which increased its powers, this institution of dispute resolution continued to suffer shortcomings, largely because competing courts progressively eroded its jurisdiction during a period when the courts, and particularly the common lawyers, were staking further claims in other areas of jurisdiction.

When Privy Councillor Sir Edward Coke became Chief Justice of King's Bench in 1613, the common law assault upon civil law jurisdictions was renewed with vigour. In 1614 Coke prohibited the interference by courts of equity into the findings of common law courts, and claimed mercantile law as the province solely of the King's Bench, insisting especially that the Admiralty had no jurisdiction over any contracts made on land, in England or overseas. Even the London Sherriff's Court encroached upon Admiralty. It used a legal fiction to claim jurisdiction over trade-related disputes by arguing that contracts which had been signed abroad were in effect signed in London. Common law judges issued prohibitions against Chancery, preventing it from hearing cases. Coke clashed with Lord Chancellor Baron Ellesmere, held the constant enmity of Bacon, and later fell out with James I, who was a natural proponent of the civil law. Coke's fall was delayed by his role as judge in the 1615 trial of the murder of Sir Thomas Overbury, brother of the holder of the patent for the Office of Assurance, and despite his setbacks, he proved both a political and literal survivor, returning to relative favour before retiring aged 74.[126]

Civil lawyers gained ground during the reign of Charles I. In 1633, with his intervention, an agreement was reached which restored or underlined Admiralty jurisdiction in several areas. Efforts by the common law judges to remove from the Admiralty any jurisdiction over commercial disputes were more concretely reversed under an ordinance of the Long Parliament in 1648. A restatement of the agreement of 1633 returned responsibility for resolving disputes over merchant contracts, charter-parties, and seamen's wages to the Admiralty. This was the same parliament that had abolished the Star Chamber and Court of High Commission, but complaints about the adequacy of common law to handle merchant disputes, which arose from a broad spectrum of the London merchant community including Trinity House, seem to have led to Admiralty's preservation, despite opposition in the Commons with support in the Lords, until 1659, when the Ordinance was not renewed. Upon the Restoration, all bills presented to the Commons to support the Admiralty failed to pass. Steckley has used this episode effectively to demolish the New Institutional Economics claim of North and Thomas that the ultimate shift away from equity to common law was the inevitable result of institutional improvement and cost saving, and was driven by merchants who preferred a cheaper and more efficient common law. Throughout the interregnum, when merchant voices were heard, they rallied behind the civil courts.[127]

---

[125] Lambe, Samuel: *Seasonable observations humbly offered to his highness the Lord Protector*, London: Printed at the authors charge, 1657, p. 13.

[126] Senior, *Old Court of Admiralty*, pp. 66–67, 84; Steckley, 'Merchants and the Admiralty Court', pp. 143–145; Boyer, Allen D.: 'Coke, Sir Edward', *ODNB*, online edn, www.oxforddnb.com/view/article/5826 [Accessed 3 Dec. 2021].

[127] Steckley, 'Merchants and the Admiralty Court', pp. 137–140, 146–150.

In 1663, the year after the *Additional Act* was passed, a book by Richard Zouch, an Admiralty Judge from 1641, was published posthumously under the title *The jurisdiction of the Admiralty asserted*. Zouch stated, 'As to the instances of Policies of Assurance held tryable at the Common Law', and Coke argued in *Dowdales Case* that common law trials can occur only in the place where the *assumpsit* occurred, even when the primary question at issue took place elsewhere (in *Dowdales*, the arrest of a ship in France). When no alternative venue is possible this makes sense, Zouch conceded, but the precedent had been invoked 'to the prejudice of the Admiralty jurisdiction'. Even in the example Coke cited in *Dowdales*, heard in 1588/9, 'the Cause being Maritime, and amongst Merchants, it might more properly have been tryed in the Admiralty or in the Assurance-Court, without a Jury or Tryal of Twelve Men, by Witnesses'.[128] Zouch was in error in his final point; the Court of Assurance was not yet founded in 1589 (a fact of which he was aware, since he stated, in the same paragraph, that 'by the Statute of the 43. of *Elizabeth*, it has been shewed, that the Proceedings in those [insurance] Causes at the Common Law, were altogether inconvenient to the Kingdom').[129]

Nonetheless, Chancery, and the civil courts in general, were threatened in the seventeenth century. At issue was the balance between the desirability of equity and the need for stability in legal rules. The question turned upon a perceived connection between strict rules and English liberty. Equity could appear not only as 'an institutional jurisdiction distinct from common law, but as a system of adjudication essentially antithetic to the genius of English jurisprudence'. The overriding concern appears to have been a constitutional issue – the fear that decisions at Chancery might overrule the common law.[130]

The Court of Assurance was unable to settle the turf wars, and was soon to be affected directly by them. In the 1658 case *Came* v. *Moye*, an insured had sued his insurer in the Court, where his claim had been dismissed. At the Court of King's Bench the insurer-defendant's barrister, Sir Thomas Twisden (later a judge of the regicides) agreed to jurisdiction, since the Admiralty had overlapping jurisdiction in many matters over which the common law courts also held sway, but declared it was not correct for one to overrule the judgment of another. He argued further that the plaintiff had made his choice of venue and, in the common interest, there was no need to hear the case again, and, finally, that the statute which established the Court of Assurance specifically allowed for appeal to Chancery, not King's Bench. However, Lord Chief Justice John Glynne found that the Court of Assurance, as a court of equity, held jurisdiction *in personam* (where action is against an individual), rather than *in rem* (where action relates to property), and that Equity Court decisions *in personam* did not remove the remedy of common law, and thus that the case could lie before him.[131] The decision was a clear victory of the common law

---

[128] Zouch, *Jurisdiction of the Admiralty*, p. 108.

[129] *Dowdale's Case*, 1589, 6 Co. Rep. 46 b; Zouch, *Jurisdiction of the Admiralty*, p. 108.

[130] Lieberman, *Province of legislation determined*, p. 78.

[131] I am extremely grateful to Dr Neil Jones of Magdalene College, Cambridge for his translation from English legal French of *Came* v. *Moye*, K.B., 1658, 2 Siderfin 121 (82 E.R. 1290).

over the civil courts, and perhaps prompted the inclusion, in the *Additional Act* of 1662, of powers to act against property, and of the restatement of the Chancery as the designated court of appeal.

Merchants remained discontented. Writing about merchant disputes at law in the 1660s, Josiah Child said suits over trade issues are

> commonly first commenced in the *Admiralty Court*, where, after tedious Attendance and vast Expences, probably just before the Cause should come to determination, it is either removed to the [Court of] *Delegates* [an *ad hoc* appellate court of both civilian and common law judges], 'where it may hang in suspence until the *Plantiff* and *Defendant* have empty purses and gray Heads, or else because most Contracts for Maritim Affairs, are made upon Land (and most Accidents happen in some Rivers or Harbours here, or beyond Sea, and not *alto mari*,) the *Defendant* brings his Writ of *Prohibition*, and removes his Cause into his *Majesties Court of King's Bench*, where, after great Expences of Time and Money, it is well if we can make our own *Council* (being *common Lawyers*) understand one half of our Case, we being amongst them as in a Foreign Country, our Language strange to them, and theirs as strange to us; after all, no Attestations of foreign *Notaries*, nor other public Instruments from beyond Sea, being Evidences at Law, and the Accounts depending, consisting perhaps of an hundred or more several Articles, which are as so many Issues at Law; the Casue must come into the *Chancery*, where after many Years tedious Travels to *Westminster*, with black Boxes and green Bags, when the *Plantiff* and *Defendant* have tired their Bodies, distracted their Minds, and consumed their Estates, the Cause, if ever it be ended, is commonly by order of that Court referred to *Merchants*, ending miserably, where it might have had at first a happy issue if it had begun right.

More important, perhaps, than this colourful picture of merchant frustration with the courts after a century of jurisdictional battles, Child goes on to call for the establishment of a 'standing Court Merchant' in the City of London, comprising twelve elected merchant arbiters, to adjudicate mercantile disputes as a Court of Record. Appeal would be to a further group of merchants. Although insurance is not specifically mentioned in Child's list of matters in the proposed court's jurisdiction, it includes bills of bottomry, and 'any other thing related to trade or shipping'.[132]

Decisions in the common law courts continued to erode the authority of the Court of Assurance. In *Delbye* v. *Proudfoot and Others*, some thirty-five years after *Came* v. *Moye*, Bartholomew Shower, the lawyer for the defending insurers (who was also the reporter of the case) argued successfully that 'the court of Commissioners of policies of insurance only extends to suits by the insured against the underwriters', and that 'any other construction would make a clashing of jurisdictions'.[133] The insurers had wished to sue their clients as having acted fraudulently. Shower argued that this made void the policy, and therefore removed the case from a court

---

[132] The passage was written between 1668 and 1670, according to Letwin; indeed, Child opens the chapter cited with reference to 'the late Fire in London'. Child, Josiah, *A new discourse of trade*, London: T. Sowel, 1698 (1692), pp. 132–138.

[133] *Delbye* v. *Proudfoot and Others*, 1692, 1 Shower. K.B. 396 (89 E.R. 662).

established to make rulings under insurance policies. 'It was never intended further than the relief of the insured against the insurers, and being such a law, was not to be extended further than the words', he argued (without any particular evidence), claiming that the intention of the policy was to limit litigation by providing a venue in which the insured could sue all underwriters at once under a policy, rather than pursuing each individually (notwithstanding the convention that the outcome of a suit against one subscriber to an insurance policy was, according to custom, followed by – if not binding upon – all the others).[134]

Nothing concrete has been found in the record showing that the Court of Assurance was active after 1692, when Shower showed that its jurisdiction was limited to suits brought by policyholders. Thus an important indirect implication of the case, which did not involve honest merchants sharing risks among themselves (Shower reported that the defendants had no interests in the vessel or goods they were insuring), was the removal of a whole category of actions from the dedicated insurance court. But already the weight of insurance cases had left the civil law court in favour of the common law, especially when criminal fraud may be shown. Such a case was witnessed by Samuel Pepys in 1663, at the Guildhall before the King's Bench. According to Pepys's diary entry for 1 December that year, Lord Chief Justice Hyde, with 'all the great counsel in the kingdom in the case', heard how an unnamed ship's master over-insured a ship laden with bogus cargo worth at most £500 ('vessels of tallow daubed over with butter, instead of all butter'), then abandoned it to flounder on the rocks at low tide, refusing the help of pilots who came to his aid. The judge found in favour of the insurers, one of whom had salvaged the ship, uncovered the fraud, and later repaired the vessel for just six pounds.[135]

Another case before the King's Bench, described in 1682 by the London press as a 'great Tryal between some Merchants, and those of the Insurance-Office' (presumably the underwriters, not the Registrar, since the defendant was the leading insurer), turned on the question of verbal amendments to an insurance contract which had not been recorded in the policy document.[136] The case shows how the traditions of the Law Merchant were incorporated into legal precedent. Chief Justice Pemberton (himself the son of a merchant) found that 'policies were sacred things, and that a merchant should no more be allowed to go from what he had subscribed in them, than he that subscribes a bill of exchange, payable at such a day, shall be allowed to go from it'.[137, 138] In recording the case, Skinner emphasised the importance of accepted community practice. 'The custom of merchants ought to be proved by those that have had frequent experience, and have known cases so ruled,' he wrote.

---

[134] See pp. 96–97.

[135] Latham and Matthews, *Diary of Samuel Pepys*, IV, pp. 401–404.

[136] *Loyal Protestant and Domestick Intelligence, on NEWS both CITY and Countrey*, No. 174, 29 Jun. 1682, p. 1.

[137] Halliday, Paul D.: 'Pemberton, Sir Francis', *ODNB*, Oxford University Press; online edn, Jan. 2008, www.oxforddnb.com/view/article/21821 [Accessed 3 Dec. 2021].

[138] *Kaines v. Sir Robert Knightly*, 1 Jan. 1681; Skinner 54; 90 E.R. 26.

The case appears to have been heard three times: first the insurer, Sir Robert Knightley (former Sheriff of Sussex), argued that while the policy stated the voyage to be insured was from Archangel to Leghorn, a verbal side agreement revised the cover to be only from the Downs, off the Kent coast. The jury initially found, against Pemberton's instruction, for the insurer. Later the case was heard a second time, and this time was resolved in favour of the insured merchants. The final hearing – that described in the pages of the *Loyal Protestant* – supported the decision of the appellate court. This ultimate airing of the case was of some import, as the leading barristers of the city were involved, including, for the underwriters, serjeant-at-law John Maynard, Henry Pollexfen (later Attorney General), Edmund Saunders (later knighted), and John Holt (later Chief Justice), and for the merchants, Sir George Jeffreys (later Lord Chief Justice and Lord Chancellor), and his colleague in the Monmouth trials, Sir Francis Wythens. According to the newspaper, 'many Eminent Merchants [were] produced as Witnesses on either side'.[139]

Yet merchant-insurers appear still to have preferred the course of arbitration. Blackstone, in his *Commentaries on the Laws of England*, wrote of the Court of Assurance that

> The jurisdiction being somewhat defective, as extending only to London, and to no other assurances but those on merchandize, and to suits brought by the assured only and not by the insurers, no such commission has of late years issued: but insurance causes are now usually determined by the verdict of a jury of merchants, and the opinion of the judges in case of any legal doubts; whereby the decision is more speedy, satisfactory, and final.[140]

Despite the sympathetic intervention of the Privy Council and the House of Commons to establish new enforcement mechanisms to ensure the continued smooth operation of a market now comprising both outsiders and merchant-insurers exploiting a club good, London's merchant community effectively wound back the clock and returned to a system of internal dispute resolution and enforcement. This return to the status quo was aided by jurisdictional battles between the English courts, which eroded the new structures founded to support the insurance market, and by the absence of a mechanism to compel merchants to use the Office of Assurance. Merchant preference obviously drove the return: use of the Office was never universal, as illustrated by the protests of the Privy Council just after its inception, and of James II just before its collapse.

One reason that this return to insider practice was possible must be that London's community of merchant-insurer-insiders remained relatively close-knit. Extant documents can be used to illustrate this. Over forty-seven months from 1664, Charles Marescoe purchased 108 policies underwritten by just thirty-one discrete individuals, ten of whom accounted for almost 84% of the total value of the policies. The underwriters John Berry, Peter Lupart, and Nicolas Skinner each participated in

139 *Loyal Protestant*, No. 174, 29.06.1682, p. 1.

140 Blackstone, William: *Commentaries on the Laws of England*, IV vols, Oxford: Clarendon Press, 1765–1769, III, pp. 74–75.

thirty-eight or more of the policies (Berry in fifty-three).[141] This extremely cooperative market was also highly horizontally integrated. Many underwriters, perhaps
most, were also active merchants. Both Marescoe and his commercial successor,
Jacob David, were merchants trading between London, Baltic, French, and Spanish
ports in the post-Restoration period. Each was a regular buyer of insurance, and an
underwriter of other merchants' cargoes and vessels.[142]

Additionally, London's insurance market was physically small. A record of insurance transactions made in 1654 and 1655 survived until the late nineteenth century
in the Rawlinson manuscripts. Before it was lost, a transcription was published by
Martin in his *History of Lloyd's*, in 1876. Described by Martin as 'perhaps representing the accounts of some insurance broker', the lost document is instead almost
certainly the record of an underwriter, since it records the same details recorded by
underwriters in extant eighteenth-century risk-books. It shows that insurance policies were underwritten at addresses including Bartholomew Lane, Crutched Friars,
Mark Lane, St Helens, and Threadneedle Street, all within an easy walk (and all of
which, incidentally, are insurance office addresses in the twenty-first century).[143]

Because of these factors, information was widely known within the insurance
community. Thus, importantly, in most instances it would have been difficult for
individuals to gain an information advantage over colleagues, given their closeness
and interconnection. Samuel Pepys once thought he had such an advantage, which
could be used to profit from underwriting. In November 1663 he learned 'at the
Coffee-house... by great accident' that a vessel carrying naval stores from Archangel
had arrived safely in Newcastle. 'Now, what an opportunity I had to have concealed
this, and seemed to have made insurance and got 100*l*, with the least trouble and
danger in the whole world.'[144] It seems unlikely, however, given the nature of information exchange within London's merchant community, that Pepys (who was an
occasional, although by no means frequent, speculator in insurance) could have kept
his deception secret for long.[145]

Enforcement of the rules of the game poses only minor challenges when it is in
the interests of the other party to live up to agreements, North argues, and indeed
this is usually the case in the insurance market.[146] It is likewise eased when it is in the
interests of all players of the game to see that all the others play honestly. Milgrom,
North, and Weingast describe the institution comprising the Law Merchant, along
with the systems of judges used to enforce it, as having the five-fold effect of successfully encouraging merchants to behave honestly, of imposing sanctions on violators,

---

[141] Roseveare, Henry (ed.): *Markets and merchants of the late seventeenth century: the Marescoe-David letters, 1668–1680*, Oxford: Oxford University Press, 1987. See especially Appendix E, p. 582.

[142] Ibid., pp. 583–588.

[143] I learned, after two days of searching at the Bodleian, that this fascinating source has been missing since the 1890s. Martin, *History of Lloyd's*, pp. 53–54.

[144] Latham and Matthews, *Diary of Samuel Pepys*, IV, pp. 395–396.

[145] For the culture of commercial gossip and commercial information-sharing in seventeenth-century London, see Glaisyer, *Culture of commerce*, 2006.

[146] North: *Institutions, institutional change*, p. 33.

of securing information about the behaviour of others, and of compelling merchants both to provide evidence against cheaters, and to pay any judgements assessed against them.[147] In other words, it is very likely that another merchant-insurer would also have heard the story of the arrival in Newcastle, and prevented or uncovered the deception which Mr Pepys considered. In any case, the hearing of the case at King's Bench shows the ineffectualness of the reforms of the Privy Council and parliament. An insurance dispute had arisen despite the registration facilities established, and was being heard neither at the Court of Assurance, nor under appeal at Chancery. The challenges of dealing with outsiders active in the London insurance market had not been resolved.

[147] Milgrom, P. R., North, D. C., & Weingast, B. R.: 'The role of institutions in the revival of trade: the Law Merchant, private judges, and the Champagne fairs', *Economics and Politics*, Vol. 2, No. 1 (1990), pp. 1, 6–7.

3.

1688–1720: The sellers' intervention

By the end of the seventeenth century, the new institutions which had been introduced in the sixteenth to govern the insurance market had been overturned. The Law Merchant governing practice had not been formally codified, the royalist Office of Assurance had been replaced by private brokerages, and, following the Glorious Revolution, the Court of Assurance appears to have fallen into abeyance, a victim of its tenuous jurisdiction and the merchants' preference for arbitration. These direct interventions into the functioning of the London market did not endure, even though they had been implemented sympathetically, at the request and with the cooperation of market practitioners, the merchant-insurers themselves, in order to ease the impact of abuses of the system perpetrated by outsiders, and to strengthen the mechanisms of enforcement which could be applied to those who would not play by the rules of the game. The market returned to its self-regulatory practice under custom and the Law Merchant, and the state to the hands-off approach under which the market had originally been formed and had grown, without imposed limitations which restricted its flexibility.

England's international trading system had become part of Braudel's higher capitalist tier in the later sixteenth century, and its insurance market quickly followed. It became, in the early decades of the eighteenth century, a Braudellian 'world-economy'.[1] London was at the pole of an insurance world-economy which increasingly supplied international buyers within a large, multinational space. The city's network radiated out to subordinate zones where agents and merchant-buyers performed distant transactions against the underwriting capital of merchant-insurers in London. For example, during the English Civil War Dutch merchants were insuring in London, as the merchant Samuel Lambe revealed. In 1657 he wrote 'it is the Hollanders custom… that when they send any single ship to the southward for their own accounts, oftentimes to insure them in England'.[2]

London's market was already thriving when William III filled the vacant English throne. As war raged against France, and the risks faced by merchants and assumed by their insurers multiplied in the face of an emboldened belligerent threat, the insurance market was to prove that its institutional structures were sufficiently robust to enable it to withstand a catastrophic loss, although not without suffering significant

---

[1] For definitions, see above, or Braudel, *Afterthoughts*, pp. 80–83.

[2] Lambe, S.: 'Seasonal observations humbly offered to his Highness the Lord Protector' (London: 1657). Reprinted in Scott, W. (ed.): *A collection of scarce and valuable tracts of the most interesting and entertaining nature, vol. sixth*, London: Printed for T. Cadell and six others, 1811, p. 448.

damage. At a time when English trade descended to a nadir, when parliamentary politics reached new heights of partisan division, and when war at sea was frequent and devastating for vessels and merchants, the solvency of some merchant-insurers was stretched beyond its limits. Despite the ultimate denial of proposed relief for underwriters and their customers, the insurance market was to survive. Renewed parliamentary interest in the regulation of insurance emerged in the first years of the eighteenth century, again at the behest of merchants and underwriters, and again to address their concerns over fraud by some outsider-buyers. Legislative initiatives of 1700–1703 echoed those of the Privy Council in the 1570s and of parliament in 1601, but rather than resulting in sympathetic institution-building, this time parliamentary interventions came to nought.

Less than two decades later a dramatic change was to be made to the institutional structures of underwriting in London, following an intervention by outsider-sellers comprising financial capitalists underwriting only for profit, without mutual benefit. From 1717, joint-stock, corporate underwriters joined the market, and commenced accepting insurance risk. They operated on a much-different basis from the traditional, private merchant-insurers, and possessed potentially large capital stocks comprising pools of cash which could be invested for profit. Against the backdrop of the financial revolution, which involved many or most of London's wealthy and prominent merchants, the launch of joint-stock insurance companies must have been predictable: such proposals had been made before, in England and elsewhere.[3] However, in the eighteenth century they were to be successful for the first time.

In 1720, two of the nascent joint-stock marine insurers, the London Assurance and the Royal Exchange Assurance, received royal charters which granted them a statutory duopoly over marine insurance underwriting by companies. All existing and potential corporate competitors were swept away, and remained prohibited until liberalisation in 1824. Individuals previously underwriting through partnerships were required henceforth to assume risk as individuals only. However, more than one motivation lay behind the erection of the corporate duopoly. That of improving the foundations of the London insurance market was present, but at best was only secondary. In the heated debate which surrounded the granting of the companies' charters, no arguments were advanced about protecting the market from outsiders who did not wish to play by the customary rules. This had been the key motivation of the failed legislative interventions twenty years earlier, and of the successful initiatives of the late sixteenth century. Some proponents of joint-stock insurance genuinely sought systemic improvement, but others wished primarily to create a new security for stock-jobbing. Janeway's financial capitalists were to mount an intervention, at the height of Dickson's financial revolution.

The advance of political interests was another extremely important motivation. As with the failed legislation of 1693/4, partisan advance was a key driver, as the joint-stock insurers' increasing momentum, driven by diverse ambitions, was hijacked by key actors of state. Their motivations were to secure direct rents for the crown,

---

3   See p. 101.

rather than indirectly to improve royal customs income by fostering trade through insurance. Their involvement sealed the establishment of long-lasting duopolistic control of corporate marine insurance in London and Great Britain. Some hoped, and others feared, that the duopoly would assume control over the entire London market, by driving out the private merchant-insurers. The intervention was an immediate success, but had an unintended effect: by limiting the competition faced by the merchant-insurers, who were permitted (as individual venturers only) to continue in their business, the duopoly ultimately succeeded only in strengthening the position of the private insurance market, and bolstering the importance of its established, flexible customs. The intervention introduced a new institutional model, but strengthened the merchant-insurers' existing institutions. They were to endure and flourish, and ultimately propel London and Lloyd's, the city's primary insurance marketplace, to the forefront of global marine insurance.

The post-revolutionary structure of the London marine insurance market

Newspaper announcements show that Lloyd's Coffee-house, predecessor of the world-famous insurance market, had been launched by 1689.[4] Many historians of Lloyd's have set this date a year earlier, and Lloyd's itself continues to recognise major anniversaries counting from 1688, but this is based upon confusion over the old-style dating of the *Gazette*, and more recently, no doubt, upon Lloyd's own erroneous claims. No reference to the Coffee-house has come to light which predates February 1688/9.[5] In terms of the development of insurance, however, the difference is trivial. It was at least two generations before Lloyd's Coffee-house became the leading centre for London's underwriting activity. Zahedieh asserts that 'by the 1680s, marine insurers had established a regular meeting place at Lloyd's coffee house near the Exchange[,] where they reaped cost savings through pooling information, greater specialisation, more careful loss assessment (gaining from contemporary interest in mathematics and probability), and the development of a market in second-hand policies. All served to reduce the costs of collection and the risks of providing cover, and underpinned London's rise as a major insurance centre.'[6]

While the second part of this analysis describes accurately the later achievements of individual underwriters, the institutions of their market, and developments at Lloyd's in the years to come, and while the genesis of the Coffee-house in the 1680s has been much heralded by chroniclers of the Lloyd's market, it is unlikely that merchant-insurers showed particular favour for Lloyd's at this early date. Wright and Fayle, in their 1928 *History*, state that 'there is nothing to suggest that Lloyd's was more closely associated with underwriting [during the lifetime of the founding

---

4   *London Gazette*, No. 2429, 21 Feb. 1688/9, p. 2; ibid. No. 2482, 26. Aug. 1689/10, p. 2.

5   In their histories of the market, both Gibb and Wright and Fayle point out the error. Gibb, D. E. W.: *Lloyd's of London, a study in individualism*, London: Macmillan & Co., 1957.

6   Zahedieh, Nuala: *The capital and the colonies: London and the Atlantic economy 1660–1700*, Cambridge: Cambridge University Press, 2010, p. 86.

proprietor, to 1713] than with any other branch of foreign trade'.[7] Indeed, there is no evidence of underwriting occurring there until much later. A comprehensive parliamentary report on the state of insurance in London, published in 1720, makes no mention of Lloyd's Coffee-house, although several references are made to underwriting at the Royal Exchange.[8] As Wright and Fayle assert, 'there can be little doubt that, even during the lifetime of Edward Lloyd, many policies were subscribed or discussed' at his coffee shop,[9] as they would have been at any gathering-place frequented by merchants, especially following the closure of the Office of Assurance, but it was not yet the centre of London marine insurance.

Very early in his career as a self-described 'coffee-man', Lloyd had begun to cater for a clientele of merchants, ship owners, and sea captains. By 1692 he was publishing for this community a two-part news sheet which reported the arrivals and departures of vessels in London and elsewhere. The first section was entitled *Ships Arrived at, and Departed from several Ports of England, as I have Account of them in London*, and the second *An Account of what English Shipping, and Foreign Ships for England, I hear of in Foreign Ports*.[10] The newspaper was the predecessor to *Lloyd's List*, which is still published today. The earliest copy of the publication discovered by McCusker, a historian of the business press, is number 257, dated 22 December 1696. He calculated that the newspaper had appeared, at latest, by January 1692.[11] At about that time, Lloyd had moved his business to the corner of Lombard Street and Abchurch Lane, at the heart of London's mercantile district. Other publications by Lloyd followed, or ran alongside this predecessor to *Lloyd's List*, including *Lloyd's News*, a single-page information sheet which contained general news about European military and naval action, and news about ship movements (including warships). It was first published some time in 1696,[12] and provided merchants with information which could inform them in a timely way of potential dangers to shipping, including threats of belligerents.

Lloyd's in the late seventeenth and early eighteenth centuries was not yet the important centre of underwriting which it was to become, but the business was already widely practised in London, as indicated by parliamentary interest and the volume of the extant documentary record. Conventional historical opinion has been that during this period the purchase of insurance moved from being an instrument used only in exceptional circumstances or by the extremely cautious, to become a routine hedge by merchants. Brewer, for example, restates the received wisdom that

7   Wright and Fayle, *History of Lloyd's*, p. 34.

8   *The special report of 1720*.

9   Wright and Fayle, *History of Lloyd's*, p. 34.

10 'Ships Arrived…' states 'Printed for *Edward Lloyd* (Coffee-man) in *Lombard-Street*'. SHL, Special Collections, GL Box 2, broadsides, *Ships Arrived at, and Departed from several Ports of England*, No. 257, 22 Dec. 1696.

11 McCusker, John: 'The early history of Lloyd's List', *Historical Research, the Bulletin of the Institute of Historical Research*, Vol. 64, No. 155 (1991), p. 428; McCusker, John J.: *European bills of entry and marine lists: early commercial publications and the origins of the business press*, Cambridge, MA: Harvard University Library, 1985, pp. 52–53.

12 ALC, uncatalogued, *Lloyd's News*, 'Numb. 20, October 15, 1696'.

'In the late seventeenth century the majority of trading vessels were uninsured.'[13] As has been shown, the wars of William III's era encouraged wider uptake of insurance. However, awareness of insurance, its importance in public debate, its mention in almost every extensive extant collection of merchant records or correspondence since the mid seventeenth century (and even earlier), and the significant government interventions from the end of the sixteenth, suggest that the assertion that insurance was only a minority option until the early eighteenth century must, at least, be called into question. An example where insurance was not purchased may illustrate: in March 1679, Charles Hedges, a civil lawyer who would later become a Judge of the Admiralty and secretary of state,[14] wrote a disappointed letter to an unidentified business associate discussing a loss of money, which would, the letter implies, routinely have been insured.

> Sr Wm Hedges [the writer's cousin, a Turkey merchant] paid ye money to ye Captain, and tooke a Bill of Lading as advised, and ye next day after this was done ye ship was burnt in ye River, ye money was paid on Thursday last, and the ship burnt on ye Friday... we shall use all possible means to retrieve ye loss, but I am afraidd it will be ye more difficult because ye ship and all gods in her were burnt... It was a most unfortunate accident and so suddain after ye money was paid that there was no time to ensure it, as was resolved to be done.'[15]

Surviving documents shed much light on underwriting practice in the immediate post-revolutionary period. One, headed 'Ensurance made on ship and goods of ye Velez Merch^t Capt Christopher Kebll from Malaga to London for acc^t of Mr Cha. Peers [future chairman of the East India Company] and part for acc^t of ye Executors of Mr Tho. Braylford [Brailsford]', and dated December 1691, shows that the vessel was insured by Brailsford's executors and Peers in Amsterdam for the amount of ƒ. 11,450, roughly £1,030.10.0.[16] However, much of the deceased merchant's insurance was underwritten in London. Ten London policies insured, in total, £3,950,[17] indicating, alongside the Amsterdam cover, a pragmatic choice of markets, and the ability at the turn of the century of those in either city to insure large sums. All of the London policies were made on identical printed policy forms, which name no intermediary or office-keeper (although this does not indicate that none was involved), and were completed between July 1690 and July 1692. The policies bear no evidence of registration or making at the Office of Assurance. The policy wording includes a

[13] Brewer, *Sinews*, p. 194.

[14] Handley, Stuart: 'Hedges, Sir Charles', www.historyofparliamentonline.org/volume/1690–1715/member/hedges-sir-charles-1650-1714 [Accessed 3 Dec. 2021].

[15] BL Add. MS 24,107, fo. 149, *Doctors Commons Library*, correspondence and papers, 1694–1702, of Sir C. Hedges, letter to unidentified, 1 Mar. 1679; de Krey, Gary: 'Hedges, Sir William', *ODNB, online edn*, www.oxforddnb.com/view/article/12860 [Accessed 3 Dec. 2021].

[16] Exchange calculated using www.pierre-marteau.com/currency/converter.html [Accessed 3 Dec. 2021]. TNA C 110/152, *Brailsford* v. *Peers*, 'Ensurance made on ship and goods...', 4–16 Aug. 1692.

[17] TNA C 110/152, *Brailsford* v. *Peers*, various insurance policies, 1690–1693.

force and effect clause which cites 'Lombard-street, *or elsewhere in* London' as the governing body of Law Merchant, the phrase 'Royal Exchange' having been dropped (presumably following the decline in importance of the Office of Assurance). In each case a handwritten addition to the policy states that the insurance buyer is to bear a deductible of one tenth of the policy value, with words such as 'in Case of loss to abate ten Pounds p Cent', or 'in Case of Loss to pay Ninety pounds pcent'.[18] Abatement is discussed in detail below.

In total, forty-six different underwriters subscribed the ten policies. Each of them, varying in number from three on a policy granting cover of £100, to sixteen underwriting £1,050 on a single form, subscribed in person, as the varied penmanship shows. Only two of the forty-six, George Sitwell and Charles Torriano, subscribed to Brailsford's policies in each of the three years for which they survive. Many underwrote only one policy, and only Torriano assumed risk on five of them, the maximum signings on this set of policies by a single underwriter. All of this implies considerable risk-sharing among the underwriting community. John Berry, who underwrote three lines on Brailsford's policies, is the lead underwriter among twelve who granted cover of £800 to Peter Joy in 1692, to insure cargo aboard the vessel *Maria* from Stockholm to London, at the rate of 3%.[19] Shortly afterwards, he was to face bankruptcy due to overwhelming claims, as were Sitwell and Torriano.[20]

One policy in the Brailsford series illustrates the routine payment of a loss. It states in a handwritten addition that 'Whereas a losse hath hapned to ye goods assured by ye w^thin written pollicy of ye truth whereof wee ye assurers are fully staisfied wee therefore whose names are hereunder written doe each one for himselfe and & not one for another promise and oblige our selves to pay or cause to be paid unto [the] as[sure]^d within named... or their assignes after ye rate of Eighty five pounds p cent for an in full payment of our severall subscriptions & that on demand Wittness our hands...'.[21] This note of loss, relating to cargo aboard the *Lisbon Merchant* while en route from Jamaica to London, further illustrates the several liability of underwriters, according to the clause 'we the Assurers are contented, and do hereby promise and bind our selves, each one for his own part'. In contrast, a 1582 policy drawn up in the Office of Assurance makes the note of several liability less clearly, stating, 'And so the assurers are contented, and doe promys & bynde them selves, & any of them... for the trewe pformance of the promisses', but includes a further clause stating that 'in testymonie of the trowthe, the assurers have hereunto sevallie subscrybed their

---

18 Note that a modern deductible is often 'horizontal', and expressed as an amount, rather than a percentage. For example, the first £100 of a claim of £700 may be deducted from a claim. In the case of an abatement, the deduction was 'vertical': a 10% abatement of a £700 claim would be £70.

19 TNA C 110/152, *Brailsford* v. *Peers*, various loose policies (unpaginated); Burrell, William and Marsden, R. G.: *Reports of cases determined by the High Court of Admiralty*, London: W. Clowes and Sons, 1885, pp. 267–268.

20 See p. 125.

21 TNA C 110/152, *Brailsford* v. *Peers*, policy underwritten for Charles Peers and Edmond Tooke executor of Thomas Brailsford, 26 Nov. 1690.

names, & sumes of money assured'[22], indicating that liability is not joint. The *Tyger* policy of 1613, which was completed at the Office of Assurance, contains an identical additional clause.[23]

A contemporary description of the methodology of purchasing insurance was included in William Leybourn's 1693 book *Panarithmologia*. Aimed at instructing those unfamiliar with the workings of the London insurance market, the section *On insurances* suggests

> Suppose you ship 300 *l.* of Goods for *Jamaica*, you being unwilling to run so great a hazard your self; you go to the *Assurance-Office*, behind the *Royal Exchange* in *London*, and there acquaint the Clerk you would ensure 200 *l.* 250. or if you will the whole 300 *l.* (for you may ensure the whole, or any part) upon such a Ship for so much Goods you have on board. The Clerk presently speaks to other Men and Merchants, that make it their trade to ensure, and you agree with them at a price for so much in the Hundred, and this is called *Primo*: In consideration of this *Primo*, the Man that is your Insurer, runs all the hazard that can be imagined, until your Goods arrive safe at *Jamaica*. Before you pay the *Primo*, you have a Policy of Insurance sign'd by the Man or Men you agree withal; for you may deal with two, three, or four to underwrite for you several Sums: This Policy of Insurance ought to be copied in the Office of Assurance, in a Book kept there for that purpose, and for which you pay a certain Sum unto the Clerk or Clerks, sitting at that time. In the Policy is exprest the name of the Person that causeth himself to be ensured, the place he ensures for, the Masters name, the Sum of Mony, the dangers you are Ensured from, and how long that lasteth, with the name of the Party or Parties, that ensure or underwrite the Policy for you... as soon as you hear that a certain Loss is happened, you must inquire at the Office for the Insurers (if you know them not) and acquaint them of the Loss, and how you come to know of it, and desire them to inform themselves of the Truth if they please, and are not satisfied with your report. When they are satisfied there is a real loss, there is generally an abatement of 10 *per Cent.* for prompt Payment.[24]

Leybourn's description of the purchase of insurance would provide strong evidence of the continued existence of the Office of Assurance in 1693, the year of publication, but for the possibility that it was published a long time after it was written. A sample policy reproduced in the description is dated 1683, suggesting that the descriptive passage was written in that year. Much of *Panarithmologia* was borrowed by Leybourn from earlier writings by others, which he had held for many years before publication.[25] Thus, the source is not a reliable one for dating the cessation of the Office of Assurance. (In contrast, the parenthetical phrase

---

[22] Ibid.; GHL CLC/B/062/MS22281, CLC/B/062/MS22282, the Corsini papers, policy issued to Bartholomew Corsini, 15 Jun. 1582.

[23] BOD MS Tanner 74/ ff. 32–33, policy underwritten for Morris Abbot and Devereux Wogan, 15 Feb. 1613.

[24] Leybourn, *Panarithmologia*, pp. 35–38.

[25] Kenny, C. E.: 'William Leybourn, 1626–1716', *The Library*, Fifth Series, Vol. V, No. 3 (1950), p. 159.

'if you know them not' provides strong evidence of the division of the market between insiders and outsiders.)

All of this evidence suggests a mature and well-functioning insurance market in London in the years immediately after the Glorious Revolution, one where the first hints of its future institutional development – in the form of the publishing of shipping intelligence by Edward Lloyd – had already begun. Even in the absence of war-related losses, the need was clear. Acts of God provided a powerful incentive to insure, and very often caused ships and cargoes to be damaged or destroyed. For example, Defoe recorded a massive loss to coastal shipping in 1692. 'A fleet of 200 sail of light colliers... were taken short with a storm of wind at north-east... above 140 sail were all driven on shore, and dashed to pieces, and very few of the people on board were saved. At the very same unhappy juncture [other coasters]... also met with the same misfortune, so that, in the whole, above 200 sail of ships, and above a thousand people, were lost in the disaster of that one miserable night'.[26] No record of insured losses arising from this event has come to light, but the insurance of coastal shipping was widespread in later years.[27]

The losses of 1693

Three of the Brailsford policies include another handwritten clause of considerable interest, a warranty which required the insured vessel to travel in convoy. A September 1690 policy insuring goods *en route* from Cadiz to London is 'Warranted to depart with convoy'. Another, insuring the vessel *Peter Me'cht* for a voyage from London to Malaga in December 1691, includes the words 'Warranted to depart with the Convoy'. A third, covering the *Good Fortune* from Bilbao to London in March 1691, is 'Warranted to depart with English Dutch or Spanish convoy'. In this series, only insurances provided on voyages to the south are so warranted; the remainder, covering shipments to the Baltic or the West Indies, carry no such additional clause.[28] At this time the waters off Spain were indeed dangerous, with a large French fleet patrolling the Straits of Gibraltar from the autumn of 1690. Several skirmishes are recorded, such as the taking, after several hours of battle, of a homeward-bound Dutch merchantman by French privateers in April, 1690.[29]

It is unclear precisely when underwriters began to offer reduced rates or premium rebates to vessels which travelled through dangerous waters in convoy during wartime, but the conditions probably predate insurance in London. The effect of doing so on underwriters' assessment of risk is made clear in the correspondence of London wine factor John Paige, an interregnum 'new merchant' and associate

---

[26] Defoe, D.: *A tour through the island of Great Britain divided into circuits or journeys, Volume I, eighth edition* (first published 1724), London: W. Strahan *et al.*, 1778, pp. 59–60.

[27] As shown, for example, in various underwriters' risk books. See bibliography for details.

[28] TNA C 110/152, *Brailsford v. Peers*, policy underwritten for Charles Peers and Edmond Tooke executor of Thomas Brailsford, 11 Sept. 1690, 25 Mar. 1691, 16 Dec. 1691.

[29] Luttrell, Narcissus: *A brief historical relation of state affairs from September 1678 to April 1714*, Vol. II, Cambridge: Cambridge University Press, 2011 (reprint of OUP edition, 1857), pp. 32, 128.

of Maurice Thomson.[30] In January 1653, at the height of the First Dutch War, Paige wrote to an associate in Tenerife that

> above 20 sail of gallant ships now in the river [Thames] laden for several ports in the Straits which durst not adventure thither but stay for convoy. And whereas you desire to have insurance made upon ditto design [the same route, but not in convoy], I went yesterday to the [insurance] office purposefully and proposed the voyage from Tenerife to Genoa, or any port thereabouts, and back to Canaries. Many would not write at any rate; the rest asked no less than 60 per cent.[31]

Without the protection of convoy, this adventure through the Straits was economically uninsurable, and thus untenable.

Sea captains and the merchants they answered to were sometimes reckless in their eagerness to arrive first to a foreign port, when prices would be highest, causing them to break from convoys, which necessarily travelled at only the maximum speed of the slowest vessel in the group. Rebate was therefore the preferred method of premium reduction, because overpaid premiums would be returned only after the voyage was completed and the insured merchant's decision to remain with the convoy throughout the voyage could be confirmed. Still, insurance was sometimes blamed for merchants' cavalier approach to remaining in convoy. The MP Sir Robert Cotton told the Commons in 1693 that he believed 'having insured, [merchants] ran for Markets, and saved themselves well enough in the whole, though often they miscarried; and they might often have had Convoys, but would not stay for the above said reason.' Cotton acknowledged, however, that convoy provision was insufficient, stating in the same breath that 'There is not a sufficient number of proper cruising Ships for Convoys.'[32] It was not long before this tense situation led to significant losses.

Although invaluable to the protection of trade, neither convoys nor insurance were infallible, as a maritime military disaster in 1693 illustrates. It brought unprecedented claims against London's merchant-insurers, some of whom were unable to withstand a sustained and concentrated loss. That year the combined Anglo-Dutch Mediterranean trading fleet, comprising roughly 260 ships, plus a few from allied nations, was much larger than usual because both England and the Netherlands had failed to despatch such a fleet in 1692,[33] which according to a contemporary was due to the unavailability of convoy vessels.[34] The Levant Company had described the convoy as 'the richest that ever went for Turkey'. The fleet was travelling in convoy, and under the protection of the Royal Navy and the command of Sir George Rooke. On 27 June, at the First Battle of Lagos, near Cape St. Vincent at the south-western tip of Portugal, the convoy was overwhelmed by French privateers and men-of-war,

---

[30] George F. (editor): 'Introduction', *Letters of John Paige*, p. x.

[31] Paige to William Clerke, 15.11.1650, 04.01.1653. Steckley, *Letters of John Paige*, pp. 28, 63.

[32] Grey, A. (ed.): *Grey's debates of the House of Commons*, X, 1 Oct. 1693, p. 294.

[33] For an account of the loss, see West, David: *Admiral Edward Russell and the rise of British naval supremacy*, Kinloss, Scotland: Librario, 2005, pp. 301–312.

[34] Anderton, William: *Remarks upon the present confederacy, and late revolution in England, &c.*, London: 1693, p. 44. The author was executed for sedition the same year.

despite the assignment to its protection of twenty-one Anglo-Dutch escorts. Roughly three-quarters of the vessels escaped, but ninety-two or more merchant ships, valued with their cargoes at as much as £1,800,000, were captured or destroyed.[35] The Dutch bore the brunt of the captures – roughly two-thirds – and Dutch and Baltic merchants the preponderance of the direct losses. The English Levant Company and its members lost five of nine ships chartered at common expense, with total tonnage of 1,750 tons, and one private ship licensed to carry English cloth. The Company later declared that in total it had lost goods worth £600,000, including the substantial (and perhaps greater) losses incurred when salvaged goods resumed their voyage after the event (in 1694, another twelve vessels were lost in a hurricane beyond the Straits).[36]

Known as the Smyrna catastrophe (named after Smyrna, an important coastal trading city in Anatolia, Turkey, located within modern İzmir), a very large share of the losses fell to London underwriters. An active market existed in the trading of this risk, no doubt driven not only by merchants with goods and vessels at sea, but also by underwriters who wished to reinsure their exposures, as well as speculators who hoped to profit from frequent fluctuations in the prevailing cost of offloading Smyrna sea risk. Rates for vessels and cargoes in the Smyrna convoy had been high, at 25% the day before the loss. Ironically, the price had fallen to 20% on the day of the battle, and to 10% by 1 July, but that was before the event was known to any but those on the scene. That day the chronicler Luttrell recorded 'no news of the Turkey fleet, which encourages us to think they are safe'. Prices remained at 10% until at least the end of the week; definitive news of the misadventure did not reach London until 15 July.[37]

Luttrell's record of these rates illustrates two characteristics of the London insurance market at this time. First, a market price was prevalent. The chronicler does not suggest that some underwriters offered these prices, but that they were 'going rates'. Second, the price decline indicates idle capital in London's merchant community. The period is acknowledged as one of slumping trade, following the boom of the 1680s. While it is true that insurance capital can and usually is employed

---

35 Palmer, M.: *Command at sea*, Harvard University Press, 2005, pp. 78–79.

36 The number of vessels in the convoy is uncertain. Peters and Vaughn, who were aboard the *Asia* throughout, stated in their log account that 'we judge the whole fleet together consisted of juxta 500 sail' (MSS of the HoL, vol. 1 N.S., 1693–1695, p. 224), but the normal estimate given for the size of the fleet is about 400. About a third of the vessels arrived safely in the Atlantic ports of Spain and Portugal before the French struck, leaving two thirds of the later estimate as the working figure used here. Anderson, Sonia P.: 'The Anglo-Dutch Smyrna fleet of 1693', in Hamilton, Alastair *et al.* (eds): *Friends and rivals in the East*, London: Brill, 2000, pp. 95–116; Luttrell, *A brief historical relation*, III, p. 161; *History and the Proceedings of the House of Commons, Vol. II, 1680–1695* (1742), p. 416; Palmer, M.: *Command at sea*, Harvard University Press, 2005, pp. 78–79; Anderton, William: *Remarks upon the present confederacy, and late revolution in England, &c.*, London: 1693, p. 44. Anderton was executed for sedition the same year.

37 Luttrell records very few insurance prices. It is superb coincidence that this is one of the handful which he set down in his daily chronicle. Luttrell, *A brief historical relation*, III, pp. 126–128, 131, 136.

elsewhere even as it supports underwriting, the eagerness with which merchant-insurers offered contingent capital to Turkey merchants, or speculated in the secondary market for Turkey-fleet risk, implies a surplus of resources. It should be noted that the crowding-out effect sometimes attributed to government fundraising in the post-revolutionary period probably did not affect insurance underwriting. Given the liquidity of national debt instruments in secondary markets, merchant-insurers' capital could be held in the form of state debt, and sold if necessary to raise cash to meet claims.[38]

A large proportion at least of the vessels and cargoes of the Smyrna convoy were insured, so the event was to prove costly to the merchant-insurer community. Some relief could have been provided to insurers through salvage. Under insurers' ancient customary rights, upon the payment of insurance indemnities the title to insured goods and vessels is transferred to the insurers. Salved goods and vessels may therefore be used to recoup claims paid. A report from the port city of Corunna dated 2 September stated that 'the four English Turkey Ships lately sunk at *Gibraltar*, were weighted, and the Goods unladen, Washed, Dried, and Housed, with little Damage'. However, in this case, according to Anderson's research, the Levant Company paid the salvage costs, and recovered them through a levy on the affected merchants. This suggests that insurance indemnities were not initially offered against the cargoes of the four common-chartered ships. However, since the goods were the property of private member-merchants, each member would have insured his cargo (or his share of joint cargoes held with others) under separate insurance policies. Similarly, chartered vessels would have been insured by their owners under separate policies to cover each owned fraction. In any case, Anderson's research has found that no Levant Company member was made bankrupt by the losses of 1693 and 1694. The same cannot be said of the London merchant-insurers who had taken a share of the risk, including under insurance policies issued to the many Dutch and Baltic merchants who purchased cover in the city.[39]

Despite the high rates – even 20% was much more than the peacetime norm – at least nineteen underwriters were unable to meet all of their commitments.[40] In a market where each underwriter assumed risk under a policy with several liability, the assets of some were insufficient to meet the claims filed against them, and fourteen such underwriters petitioned the state for aid. A precedent-setting intervention was mounted in answer.

A parliamentary relief scheme for the beleaguered merchant-insurers was read to the Commons on 9 December 1693.[41] Its intent was to preserve value by distributing the underwriters' available assets equitably between affected policyholders, without driving the insurers into bankruptcy. If a qualified majority of creditors agreed to

---

[38] Neal, *Rise of financial capitalism*.

[39] Bensa, Enrico: *Il contratto di assicurazione nel medio evo: studi e recerche*, 1884, translated to French as Valéry, Jules (trans.), *Histoire du contrat d'assurance au moyen âge*, Paris: Anciemme Librairie Thorin et Fis, 1897, p. 28; *The Gazette*, 11 Sept. 1693, p. 1; Anderson, *Fleet of 1693*, pp. 111, 113–114.

[40] See pp. 117 ff.

[41] *Journal of the House of Commons: Vol. 11: 1693–1697* (1803), 9 Dec. 1693, pp. 25–27.

individual underwriters' offers, the minority would be bound to it. In this respect, the special case of the merchant-insurers proposed a return to England's pre-1621 bankruptcy regime, the longstanding Law Merchant approach to insolvency, and indeed to statutory practice elsewhere in western Europe, under which an enforceable pro rata payment scheme could be adopted and enforced. It was also intended to keep alive the growing London insurance industry.

On 21 December, after hearing a petition 'of sundry Merchants, residing in London [who were] Creditors of the said Insurers for very great Sums', a committee of MPs was struck to consider the petition and amend the legislation. It included the Whig notable Sir Samuel Barnardiston Bt., who had been the Levant Company's agent in Smyrna (and was fined for possible involvement in the Rye House Plot),[42] and Tory supporter of parliamentary trade issues Sir Thomas Vernon.[43] Both were prominent Levant merchants, and almost certainly suffered losses.[44] Other merchant-MPs were called to the committee, to help to settle the detail of the question, including Robert Waller and Thomas Blofield, the mayors of York and Norwich respectively; the tobacco merchant Jeffrey Jeffreys; George England, a merchant of Great Yarmouth; both of Bristol's Merchant-Adventurer MPs; brewing magnate and joint-stock investor John Perry; plantation owner Samuel Swift; and 'all the Members of the House who are Merchants'. In this, parliament was following long-established practice: privy councillors, judges, and others often called upon merchants to determine optimal courses of action in matters of dispute concerning merchants, although like the range of commissioners appointed by the 1601 Act, the parliamentary committee included outsiders with different interests.

The resulting *Bill to enable divers Merchants-Insurers, that have sustained great Losses by the present War with France, the better to satisfy their several Creditors* stated that the underwriters 'have sustained such losses as tend to their utter ruin, having paid since the war with France very great sums of money for losses by Assurance... by which the greater part of their capital is exhausted'. However, the insurers had made offers of settlement, and most of their creditors had agreed to accept partial payments. According to the Bill, 'the far greater part of the... creditors have agreed by signing and sealing'. The legislation would have made an agreement between a distressed merchant-insurer and two-thirds of his creditors binding upon the remaining third, whether the latter group liked it or not. Under the Bill, affected policies would have to be registered at a designated office.[45] Further, a single creditor would not be able to drive a debtor into bankruptcy, with the attendant attachments and costs that such actions inevitably brought to bear on all creditors, the debtor,

[42] Hart, James S. Jr, 'Barnardiston, Sir Samuel', *ODNB*, online edn, www.oxforddnb.com/view/article/1461 [Accessed 3 Dec. 2021].

[43] Gauci, Perry: 'Vernon, Sir Thomas', www.historyofparliamentonline.org/volume/1690–1715/member/vernon-sir-thomas-1631-1711 [Accessed 3 Dec. 2021].

[44] *Journal of the House of Commons: Vol. 11: 1693–1697* (1803), 9–21 Dec. 1693, pp. 25–39; Cruickshanks *et al., House of Commons, 1690–1715*, Vols. *III–V*, pp. III 138–139, 247, 976; IV 289, 447–449, 574–575; V 129–130, 747, 765.

[45] *Manuscripts of the House of Lords*, Vol. I (New Series), 1693–1695, London, HMSO, 1900, pp. 358–360.

and the state. Instead, debtors' assets would be relatively swiftly and efficiently distributed *pro rata* among creditors.[46] The intervention, if successful, would have created a new, statutory mechanism which would have eased disputes arising from underwriting at times of extreme circumstances, when traditional practices under custom and the Law Merchant had proved insufficient.

The Bill attracted significant debate both inside the House of Commons and in the City, such that on 15 January 1693/4 five additional members were appointed to the committee, including Edward Clark, the Auditor General, and Sir Robert Clayton, Commissioner of the Customs and leader of the City Whigs. On 6 February its amendments were reported to the House. Additional creditors wished to be heard, and the bill was returned to committee.[47]

Around the same time an undated broadside appeared, entitled *REASONS Humbly offered for the Passing of a BILL...*[48] Its anonymous authors argued that the scheme would benefit all insurance buyers, because there was a real danger that the few underwriters who had failed would also bring down agreements with apparently solvent insurers. Fear of a systemic collapse appears to have been genuine: the pamphlet also stated that the 'Practice and Custom of Assurance in the Kingdom is both Antient and Creditable', and would be damaged if underwriters were allowed to fail. Registration of the affected policies, the pamphlet stated, would be the only way for insurers to 'accommodate their affairs with their respective Creditors, which are very Numerous, many of them unknown; because the Assurances are made in Trust for divers Persons in remote Parts of the Kingdom, and Places beyond the Seas'. This was not just a local issue: London underwriters must have had captured sufficient overseas business for these policyholders to be deserving of representation. The pamphlet goes on to highlight an important underpinning of the institution of London insurance. Posing the question: 'Why may there not be some Design of Fraud, by the Persons desiring this BILL?', its authors went on to answer: 'There [*sic*] Reputations are so generally known, they humbly presume, there is no ground for such Objection, having been known Merchants and Traders beyond the Seas for many Years past, and have paid great Sums of Money for Customs, and always honestly and truly discharged their several Debts, as well in England as elsewhere'. The broadside also argued that it was only a small group of insurers that was unable to reach settlement.

On 22 February the name of merchant-insurer Daniel Foe (later Defoe) was inserted into the Bill (perhaps he was the author of the eloquent pamphlet published

---

[46] Provisions for such distributions are possible today under English law through a process called a 'scheme of arrangement', which is widely used by distressed insurers. 'Schemes' were not introduced into law until the passage of the *Companies Act 1985*, some 292 years after the debate over the merchant-insurers bill. Section 425 of the Act outlines the rules for effecting a scheme of arrangement. *FSA process guide to decision making on Schemes of Arrangement for insurance firms*, UK Financial Services Authority, July 2007.

[47] *Journal of the House of Commons: Vol. 11: 1693–1697* (1803), 11 Jan.–8 Feb. 1693/4, pp. 59–87.

[48] BL GRC 816.m.12, 16, *Reasons humbly offered for the passing of a bill to enable divers Merchants that have been great Sufferers by the present War with France, the better to satisfy their Creditors*, undated, 1693/4.

just before). The presence of Defoe as a petitioner is not without interest. Rogers has shown that the writer had been in Fleet Prison for debts in 1692, before the Smyrna underwriting loss occurred. He states: 'In later years, Defoe liked to give the impression that his bankruptcy was occasioned by his dabbling in marine insurance during the war.' Rogers then goes on to suggest that this may have been an enlargement of the truth, since Defoe's troubles arrived earlier, and since his business connections did not extend to international merchants beyond those trading to Lisbon. However, several factors bear against denial of Defoe's war-related underwriting losses as at least a compounding factor in his financial woes. First, he could have insured familiar Lisbon merchants whose vessels were participating in the Smyrna convoy, since it called into port there. Second, through a broker he could have underwritten policies purchased by any insured, great or minor, without knowing them personally (the pamphlet published in favour of the bill states that 'many Creditors are unknown to the Debtors'). Third, underwriting – wisely or otherwise – was one of the common 'high-risk strategies of gambling for resurrection' which Sgard describes as a route out of insolvency for those in financial trouble. Finally, Defoe had been an owner of a vessel, the *Desire*, which makes it very likely that he would have had the connections to enter the world of underwriting.[49]

Five days after Defoe's name was appended to the Bill, it passed its third reading in the Commons and was ordered carried to the Lords.[50] The hearing of multiple creditors by the Commons committee, and its passage of the Bill, suggests that the merchant-insurers and their creditors favoured the proposed legislation. Creditors no doubt believed that accepting a 'haircut' on their insurance claims was better than no payment at all. Further, they must have been aware that many prominent and longstanding underwriters would be forced into bankruptcy, should the hold-outs fail to agree partial payment, and the legislation fail to pass. Thus, it was in their mutual interest to accept what money they could, and to allow the underwriters to stave off bankruptcy. Sadly, neither a record of the House of Lords' debate over the bill nor a newspaper account seems to have survived, but the *Journal of the House of Lords* states that the peers rejected the bill upon its second reading in March.[51] Narcissus Luttrell recorded, with characteristic terseness, that 'The Lords have flung out the bill for merchants ensurers.'[52]

The legislation was caught in one of the gravest political issues of the day. The Smyrna disaster was widely blamed (to use the language of the Bill) on 'miscarriages of the sea affairs'. These in turn were the product of what was described in

---

49 *Journal of the House of Commons: Vol. 11: 1693–1697* (1803), 22–27 Feb. 1693/4, pp. 102–111; Rogers, Pat: 'Defoe in the Fleet Prison', *Review of English Studies*, Vol. 22, No. 88 (Nov. 1971), pp. 453–455; *Reasons humbly offered…*, 1693/4; Sgard, Jérôme: 'Bankruptcy law, majority rule, and private ordering in England and France (seventeenth–nineteenth century)', OXPO Working Papers, OXPO_09–10b, Oxford Sciences Po Research Group, p. 5.

50 *Journal of the House of Commons: Vol. 11: 1693–1697* (1803), 22–27 Feb. 1693/4, pp. 102–111.

51 *Journal of the House of Lords*, Vol. 15: 1691–1696 (1767–1830), pp. 389–390.

52 Luttrell, *A brief historical relation*, III, p. 281.

the Commons as the 'notorious and treacherous mismanagement' of the navy.[53] The issue drove a wedge into the Anglo-Dutch alliance, and led William III first to fire his joint naval commanders, and then to dismiss the Earl of Nottingham, his Tory secretary of state. These actions were taken both to satisfy the Whigs, and to create greater party balance in his ministry at a time of increasing party polarisation.[54] The bill had been brought by the York MP Robert Waller, a former Lord Mayor of the city and a locally prominent Whig, who from 1690 was Keeper of the King's manor there (although his political allegiances in this time of party shifts seem to have been somewhat fluid; Harris notes that 'political reality was not quite as simple' as a straight bipartisan structure[55]). The MP Robert Harley in 1691 saw Waller as a Country supporter, which is in keeping with his support of several merchant bills.[56] Meanwhile, the destruction of the Levant fleet led to the collapse of government credit in the City, as Lord Treasurer Sidney Godolphin had warned the king in July.[57]

In addition, the relief bill was brought to the Lords at almost exactly the same moment that the new land tax, which fell most heavily on landed Tories, who dominated the upper chamber at this time, was beginning to bite.[58] Robert Harley, as Commissioner of Public Accounts, was connected to the Levant trade through his brother Nathaniel, one of its leading merchants, and was rising to be the leader of the parliamentary opposition to the Court contingent.[59] This may have been a source of backlash, but in the absence of more information from the House of Lords, explanations of the peers' motivations can amount to no more than speculation. In any case, the Merchant-Insurers Act was caught up in tumultuous politics. A partisan battle between nascent political constituencies was more important to this post-revolutionary parliament than strengthening creditors' confidence in their counterparties' ability to pay. In contrast to the acts of the monarch's Privy Council more than a century earlier, parliament failed to authorise an initiative costless to the state which would both have allowed debts partially to be met, according to right and equity, and would have strengthened the state's commitment to the important income stream arising from international trade. It seems likely that, given the Whigs' political victory in securing Nottingham's resignation, the Tory Lords were unprepared to allow further concessions. It may too

---

53 *History and the Proceedings of the House of Commons, Vol. II, 1680–1695* (1742), p. 418.

54 Rodger, *Command of the ocean*, pp. 153–154; West, *Admiral Edward Russell*, p. 307.

55 Harris, *Politics under the late Stuarts*, p. 161.

56 Cruickshanks, Eveline and Hayton, D. W., 'Waller, Robert', www.historyofparliamentonline. org/volume/1690–1715/member/waller-robert-1698 [Accessed 3 Dec. 2021].

57 Horwitz, Henry: *Parliament, policy and politics in the reign of William III*, Manchester: Manchester University Press, 1977, p. 116.

58 Harris, *Politics under the late Stuarts*, p. 102; Holmes, Geoffrey: *The making of a great power: late Stuart and early Georgian Britain, 1660–1722*, London: Longman, 1993, pp. 289, 336.

59 Carswell, John: The South Sea Bubble, London: Cresset Press, 1961, p. 45; Speck, W. A.: 'Harley, Robert, first earl of Oxford and Mortimer', *ODNB*, online edn, www.oxforddnb. com/view/article/12344 [Accessed 3 Dec. 2021].

have been that the preponderance of Tories who dominated the Levant Company refused to accept anything more than full payment of their indemnities, and preferred instead to bankrupt recalcitrant underwriters.

Insurers thus bore the losses, some to the exhaustion of their fortunes. Defoe, at least, left the business of trade and insurance. Most of the affected underwriters have proved impossible to trace. Extant insurance policies issued in London in the 1690s and examined by the author show that of forty-six London underwriters known to have been active before the Smyrna loss, only one was still insuring marine risk afterwards, although the sample is far too small to draw any conclusions more concrete than the obvious deduction that many insurers got out of the business after the market-wrenching losses of 1693. However, the failed *Bill to enable divers Merchants-Insurers, that have sustained great Losses by the present War with France, the better to satisfy their several Creditors* was a key step towards England's return to an efficient bankruptcy regime which was, from 1706, to help prevent insolvent merchants from being pushed across the threshold from insolvency to ruin by the demands of their creditors.

A widely recognised shortfall in naval strength had contributed to the loss; the Lord High Admiral's Council subsequently received a stream of representations from merchants about defence. In 1702, for example, Maryland merchant Tobias Bowles presented a detailed deployment plan for trade protection vessels 'to bring Monsieur down'.[60] Later that year the Lords warned the queen that 'the Sea Preparations of Your Majesty's Enemies seem such as intended not for encountering and fighting your Royal Navy, but rather for making a Piratical War, to the Interruption of Commerce'.[61] The Council recommended allocating 110 of 167 naval vessels in service to trade protection, but admitted such a large allocation could endanger national defence.[62] The actual allocation still did not reach fifty, however, as the navy was too small adequately to defend both Britain's growing trade and her coastline. Trade and the navy were growing at roughly similar rates, and thus the latter remained too small to meet its dual responsibility. Table 5 compares merchant tonnage with the total number of naval vessels in roughly similar years. An index-number problem means the growth rates must be considered with caution – small changes in the earliest year make a big difference in the total change over time – and merchant tonnage figures are fraught with difficulty.[63] Nonetheless, the clear picture is one of a merchant navy growing faster than its military counterpart.

---

[60] *Calendar of State Papers, Domestic Series, Anne vol. I, 1702–1703*, London: HMSO, 1916, pp. 196–197.

[61] *Journal of the House of Lords*, Vol. 17: 1701–1705, p. 147.

[62] *Calendar of State Papers, Domestic Series, Anne vol. I, 1702–1703*, London: HMSO, 1916, p. 326.

[63] See Davis, *Rise of the English shipping industry*, pp. 395–406.

Table 4: Underwriters named in the Merchant-Insurers' Bill of 1693

John Ashby	Daniel Foe	Gilbert Nelson *
John Baker *	Henry Harrington *	Mark Praedfott
John Berry *	John Hodges	John Prince *
Charles Blackhall	John Jurin	George Sitwell *
George Burrish	Henry Mansfield *	Charles Torriano *
Edward Callender *	Nathaniel Molyneux	
James Cretchtown	Samuel Nash *	

Note: * These ten men have been identified as among the underwriters of policies issued in the years 1690–1692 and examined by the author. They are among forty-six underwriters identified by examining extant policies of the period.

Table 5: British merchant tonnage v. navy fleet, 1629–1786

Merchants / Navy	Merchant tonnage	Change	Navy vessels	Change
1629/1633	115,000		50	
1686/1685	340,000	196%	118	64%
1702/1705	323,000	-5%	188	59%
1755/1755	473,000	46%	191	2%
1786/1785	752,000	59%	270	41%
Total growth		**554%**		**275%**

Source: Tonnage data from Davis, *Rise of the English shipping industry*, p. 27. Navy numbers from Rodger, *Command of the ocean*, pp. 607–608.

Recovery and calls for change

As England's economic fortunes revived in the later 1690s, so too did the insurance market resume its path of growth. Ongoing war with France bolstered demand, and trade voyages increased in frequency and value with the improving economy. The foundation of the Bank of England in 1694 and the recoinage of 1696 together did much to restore the financial stability of the nation, and underpinned merchant trade. Marine insurance flourished. In 1697, in his *Essay on Projects*, Defoe wrote that 'Assurances among merchants... have been of use time out of mind in trade, though perhaps never so much a trade as now.'[64] Only one underwriter of the Brailsford policies, Richard Alie, appears as a subscriber to any of the many policies examined which were underwritten in the decades after 1693, but new men replaced those

---

[64] Defoe, *An essay on projects*, 1697.

ruined by the Smyrna loss and the subsequent failure of the relief bill. The large loss borne by underwriters did not bring the market to a halt, nor was London's reputation ruined, as some had feared.

The swift recovery of the private underwriting market was essential, as alternatives were proposed. In early February 1693/4, before the final nail was driven into the coffin of the merchant-insurers bill, James Whiston, the London broker and publisher of the *Merchants Remembrancer*, proposed that the king should become the insurer of all ships 'at a moderate rate, which should lye in bank at the custome house to answer the merchants losses, whereby they would save considerably, they now paying 20*l*. per cent., which his majesty might doe for 3 or 4; and then the king would be obliged to provide good convoys, otherwise he would receive a losse'. Luttrell recorded that the proposition was to be considered.[65] A similar proposal was made by William Sydenham (grandson of the Cromwellian commissioner of the Treasury) in 1696. Under his 'PROPOSALS for the Security of Trade', the king would 'undertake the *Sole Ensuring*' during the war of all English merchant vessels, both out and home, 'according to the Method of Common Ensurances'. The House of Commons was to set rates, all vessels would be required to sail with convoy or face a fine and lose their insurance, and claims would be based on the invoice value of goods at the point of lading. The rest of the details were to be left to the Commons.[66] In this instance the state did not intervene to insure the nation's shipping, although the idea is far from fanciful. Such a plan was developed more than two centuries later, and put into effect in 1914.[67]

Shortly after, Defoe, in his *Essay on projects*, was to propose a state insurance scheme almost identical to Whiston's, which was to be part of the state control of all shipping – roughly the complete blending of the navy and the merchant marine under state control. A new 'court or office' would be established to control shipping, to be funded by advances for seamen's wages, plus forty shillings per ton of goods imported to cover freight. The fund accrued would act as a security fund for a mandatory state insurance scheme, requiring that

> The merchants shall further pay upon all goods shipped out, and shipped on board from abroad, for and from any port of this kingdom, four pounds per cent. on the real value, *bona fide*; to be sworn to if demanded. In consideration whereof the said office shall be obliged to pay and make good all losses, damages, averages, and casualties whatsoever, as fully as by the custom of assurances now is done, without any discounts, rebates, or delays whatsoever; the said four pounds per

---

[65] Luttrell, *A brief historical relation*, III, p. 264; Glaisyer, Natasha: 'Whiston, James', Oxford Dictionary of National Biography, Oxford: Oxford University Press, 2004, www.oxforddnb.com/view/article/65789 [Accessed 3 Dec. 2021].

[66] Sydenham, William: '*PROPOSALS of William Sydenham, Esq; for the Security of Trade; and the Raising of a very considerable Sum of Mony towards the Carrying on the Present WAR with France, Humbly offered*', London: 1696.

[67] Leonard, A. B.: 'Wartime marine insurance and the state: insuring British shipping during WW1', unpublished conference paper, presented at *The First World War at Sea, 1914–19*, National Maritime Museum, Greenwich, 4 Jun. 2018.

cent. to be stated on the voyage to the Barbadoes, and enlarged or taken off, in proportion to the voyage, by rules and laws to be printed and publicly known.[68]

Coastal and fishing vessels were to be excluded. The scheme was intended to reduce the cost of wages, freight, and insurance. Defoe, no doubt still smarting from his bankruptcy in 1693, resulting from his own over-extension as an underwriter, saw the latter as providing exceptional profits to merchant-insurers. 'I myself have paid 100 pounds insurances in those small premiums on a voyage I have not gotten 50 pounds by; and I suppose I am not the first that has done so either.'[69]

None of the plans was adopted. By leaving the state responsible for losses which exceeded the premiums paid by merchants, each would have removed a character-istic of insurance which contributed to British divergence: the channelling of private funds to public projects (for example through the purchase of state debt, explored below). Instead, the only successful state intervention into insurance at this time was the launch of an indirect tax upon policies, under a parliamentary act of 1694 which levied stamp duty upon documents. The *Act for granting to theire Majesties severall Dutyes upon Velum Parchment and Paper for Four Yeares towarde carryyng on the warr against France* levied six pence 'For every Skinn or Piece of Velum or Parchment or Sheete of Paper upon which any Charter-party Policy of Assureance Passport Bond Release Contract or other Obligatory Instrument or any Protest Procuracin Letter of Attorney or any other Notariall Act whatsoever shall be ingrossed or written'.[70]

Innovations

The post-revolutionary period was one of innovation in English finance, character-ised by the growth of expertise and participation in financial markets (especially secondary markets), and the rise of joint-stock companies. However, the new insti-tutions of the Financial Revolution were not yet embedded, and were the cause of much public and political strife. The conflicts – and the practices – which arose appear occasionally to have extended to marine insurance. John Cary, in his 1695 *Essay on the state of England in relation to its trade, its poor, and its taxes, for carrying on the present war against France*, referred to jobbing in insurance itself. He complained of the 'irregular Practices of some Men (especially since this War)', stating that they chose to ignore the true purpose of insurance, and instead,

> without any Interest [in the vessels they insured] have put in early Policies, and gotten large Subscriptions on Ships, only to make advantage by selling them to others, and therefore have industriously promoted false Reports, and spread Rumours on the *Exchange* to the Prejudice of the Ship or Master, filling all Mens Minds with Doubts, whereby the fair Trading Merchant when he comes to insure his Interest either can get no one to underwrite, or at such high Rates that he finds it better to buy the others Policies at great advance; by this means

[68] Defoe, *An essay on projects*, 1697.

[69] Ibid.

[70] & 6 Will. & Mary c. 21, *Act for granting to theire Majesties severall Dutyes upon Velum Parchment and Paper for Four Yeares towarde carryyng on the warr against France.*

these *Stockjobbers of Insurance* have as it were turned it into a Wager, to the great Prejudice of Trade.

Some of these 'stockjobbers of insurance' (the spreading of false rumours notwithstanding) would today be described as reinsurers, those who legitimately insure the insurers; the practice of trading in insurance risk is probably as old as insurance itself. However, those active in trading insurance but not in merchant trade were an important category of outsiders, one which was to grow, despite the widespread public opprobrium towards stock-jobbing during this period, which led to pamphleteering and parliamentary action. Cary also complained of outright frauds, stating that

> Likewise many ill designing Men their Policies being over-valued have it's to be feared to the Disparagement of honest Traders contrived the loss of their Ships; on the other side the Underwriters when a Loss is ever so fairly proved boggle [sic] in their Payments, and force the Insured to be content with less than their Agreements, only for fear of engaging themselves in long and chargeable Sutes.

Cary called upon parliament to return insurance to 'its first design… to encourage the Merchant to export more of our Product and Manufactures, when he knew how to ease himself in his Adventure, and to bear only such a proportion thereof as he was willing', by requiring the buyer 'to run a proportionable part of his Adventure the Premio included, and the Insurers to pay their full Subscriptions without abatement'.[71]

This call came during a period which Hoppit described as including a 'growing torrent of legislation between 1660 and 1800'. Most acts were neither amended by the Lords nor subject to a division of the House of Commons. Under Hoppit's definitions, more than half of this parliamentary activity, including failed bills which did not become law, related to economic matters, and of that share nearly 70% related to the public finances or overseas trade. These experienced a 'surge' in the 1690s, in part due to the exigencies of sustained warfare.[72] It is unsurprising, in these circumstances, that marine insurance began again to reach the parliamentary agenda.

The 1697 Act 'to restrain the Number and ill Pratice of Brokers and Stock-Jobbers' does not appear to have been applied to insurance brokers, or at least it was not observed by them. In any case, the 1697 Act was, in the words of Bowen, a 'dead letter'.[73] An act under Anne, requiring 'all Persons that shall act as Brokers' in London to be admitted by the Mayor and aldermen, and to pay an entrance fine

71　Cary, John: *An essay on the state of England in relation to its trade, its poor, and its taxes, for carrying on the present war against France by John Cary, merchant in Bristoll*, Bristol: W. Bonny, printer, 1695, pp. 141–143.

72　Hoppit, Julian: *Britain's political economies: parliament and economic life, 1660–1800*, Cambridge: Cambridge University Press, 2017, pp. 39, 52, 69, 73, 76.

73　Will. III, Cap. 32, *An Act to restraine the Number and ill Practice of Brokers and Stock-Jobbers*; Bowen, H. V.: ' "The pests of human society": Stockbrokers, jobbers and speculators in mid-eighteenth-century Britain', *History*, Vol. 78 (1993), p. 51.

and annual fee of forty shillings,[74] seems also to have been ignored by insurance bro-kers.[75] Similarly, bills to combat insurance fraud, brought to parliament in the open-ing years of the eighteenth century, were to fail. They represent a further attempt to impose a new institutional structure on London's insurance market, and like the Act of 1601 which followed merchant complaints, legislative cures proposed between 1699 and 1702 were intended to remedy the problem of outsider-buyers who refused to play by the rules of the game, which increased the cost of insurance for all players.

The first bill was brought in February 1699/1700 by Edward Harley MP, brother of the more famous MP of the same name. The problem of 'fraudulent insurances' was introduced to the House in response to a petition 'of several merchants and others, in the City of *London*', and was intended to address the problem that 'the fair Trade of Insurance of Ships is a great help to Trade in general; but of late Years many Frauds and Deceits have been acted therein, to the great Discouragement of the fair Traders, and Navigation'.[76] The bill was prepared by Harley and read twice, then sent to a committee of parliamentarians including Bartholomew Shower, a lawyer who had acted in insurance disputes, twenty-three others, plus 'all the merchants of the House'.[77] Amendments were made, read, and discussed; the debate was adjourned and later taken up again, when more amendments were made; a clause was added that allowed insurers to reinsure their exposures under specific policies; following still further amendments, on 5 April 1700, the bill 'passed in the negative' – failed – on its third reading.[78]

The proposed legislation attracted pamphleteering. The broadsheet *The CASE of Assurances as they now Stand: And the Evil Consequences thereof to the Nation*, prob-ably published during debate over the bill of 1700, provides clues as to the content of the proposed legislation.[79] The pamphlet called for regulations which could have helped to prevent fraud (as registration of policies in 1601 was intended to do), but which would also have restricted the flexibility of insurance underwriting. The first of these proposed that it be 'Enacted, That all Merchants and others, should run the 10 *per Cent.* of their Adventure, the Sum not exceeding 1000 *l.* and 5 *per Cent.* on greater Sums', in order to prevent over-insurance and the insurance of vessels already lost, such that shipping would be 'well set to Sea, and Trading Encouraged'. Further proscriptions proposed would ensure that the insurance buyer's name, or that of his client if the buyer is an agent, was always inserted in the policy, along with the details of the vessel; that no vessel may change its name during a voyage; that no shared claims should be paid for leakage of liquids, or for the loss of perishable

---

74　Anne c. 68, *An Act... for granting an Equivalent to the City of London by admitting Brokers*, HeinOnline, 8 Statutes of the Realm, 1702–1707, p. 817.

75　Weskett, *Complete digest*, p. xxiii.

76　*History and the Proceedings of the House of Commons, Vol. III, 1695–1706* (1742), p. 223.

77　Ibid., p. 304.

78　Hoppit, Julian (ed.): *Failed legislation, 1660–1800, extracted from the Commons and Lords Journals*, London: Hambledon Press, 1997, pp. 234, 236, 240.

79　*The CASE of Assurances as they now Stand: And the Evil Consequences thereof to the Nation* (1700?), BL 816.m.10.(116).

goods, unless by storm damage certified through 'a Legal Survey... by the *Trinity-House* at Home, [or] Authentick Certificates from our Consuls or Agents abroad'; that the specific goods insured under a policy be named, and the vessel always identified by name; that insurers should not be held liable for ships damaged by hull-worm or simple deterioration as a result of lingering in African waters for long periods (a risk later managed by sheathing hulls in copper); and that salvaged goods should be retained by the insured, and any salvage income be deducted from the amount of the claim. In short, these were very practical proposals, which had the clear design of limiting the amount of damage which could be done to the underwriting market by outsider-buyers who did not wish to play by the rules.

With the possible exception of jobbing in insurance policies, none of these concerns were new in 1700. All had been addressed for centuries under the Law Merchant. However, London underwriters had sometimes diverged from the customary practice of other insurance centres, presumably to make their product more flexible, and thus more attractive to merchants, such as the easing of the requirement to name goods insured.[80] These relaxations of policy terms and conditions were perhaps driven by competition between underwriters in a thriving market, as occurs today. Ultimately, cargoes insured were almost never described. A policy issued to Peter Joy in June 1692 covers 'any kind of goods and merchandizes whatsoever loaden or to be loaden'.[81] The transfer of salvage rights to underwriters was long established under the Law Merchant.[82] The advantages of the beneficiary of salvage proceeds managing the sale of such goods seem obvious.

It was not uncommon for underwriters to insure goods being transported on unnamed vessels, usually specifying on the policy 'ship or ships' in place of a vessel name, a practice which was of great benefit to merchants trading over great distances, especially to the East Indies, where exports and imports were insured under a single policy, but the vessel of return carriage was unknown at the time of underwriting. Magens, in his *Essay on insurances*, stated in 1755 that 'When Merchandizes are sent to distant Parts, from whence no Letters can regularly come, and it cannot therefore be certainly known, in what Species, or in what Ships, the Returns will be made; it is customary to insure on Goods, in any Ship, or Ships expected, or that may come from thence'.[83] Eden stated in 1806 that 'it became necessary to insure such [privately traded India] Goods, "on any Ship or Ships," with a view to cover a whole Fleet, or even a whole Season; the individual not knowing in what particular Ships he would be allowed to send his Property... This Kind of Accommodation, and some other Alterations tending to benefit the Assured, and operating against the Underwriter... This new Mode of Insurance "on Ship or Ships," was not much coveted by Insurers'.[84]

[80] See above, pp. 60–61.

[81] Burrell and Marsden, *Cases determined by the High Court of Admiralty*, p. 267.

[82] See p. 37.

[83] Magens, *An essay*, I, p. 13.

[84] Eden, Sir Frederick Morton: *On the policy and expediency of granting insurance charters*, London: Burton (printer), 1806, p. 32.

As has been discussed above, 'abatement', the practice of requiring the insurance buyer to retain a proportion of the risk, was commonplace. A policy underwritten for 'Joseph Paice of London, Merchant' in October 1703 carries the handwritten endorsement 'In case of Loss to abate ten pounds p Cent'.[85] Charles Marescoe, writing to Jacob Momma, a Swedish trading partner in November 1656, stated that 'we do not find it advisable to have the insurance done here [in London] as most of our insurers are not to our liking. In case of a loss one has to wait, 3, 4, or 6 months, and then they deduct 15 or at least 10 percent, as well as the premium, before they pay up'.[86] Roseveare, editor of the Marescoe letters, states, based on this, that 'London's speciously cheaper premiums disguised the convention that the insured was expected to bear' this percentage, but his observation grossly misstates the situation.[87] The abatement was clearly disclosed in the policy, which was plainly cheaper as a result, and was a negotiable condition. Then, as now, insurance buyers could pay more to reduce the abatement. Legislating abatement at a statutory level of £10 per cent on all policies would have been an obvious deterrent from the London market for Marescoe, who later came to use it regularly, including to participate as an underwriter.

As for policies which do not carry the name of the insured, these under the conventions of the Law Merchant are void, and it seems extremely unlikely that any court would assign liability under a contract in which one party was not identified. While this may have been the custom, however, longstanding practice was different. As Roccus, a judge of the *Magna Curia* of Naples, wrote in his 1655 *Treatise on insurance*,

> If any one effect insurance on the goods of A. by name, *or of any other person whatever*, but does not name that other person; not only the person named is comprehended in that insurance, but also any other person though not named: for in liberal contracts such as insurance, all persons interested in the goods insured, are included in the contract. It is asserted by some authors that no one is comprehended [as insured], even if the owner of the goods, unless expressly named, but the contrary is observed in practice.[88]

Policy wordings evolved in this respect, too. The 1582 policy cited above stated that Corsini 'causeth hym selfe to be assured'. The two buyers of the *Tyger* policy in 1613 'caused them selves and every one of them to be assured'. By 1641/2, describing the identity of the party insured under a contract had become much more complicated. One policy covering a ship owned by the London Merchant George Warner, and underwritten at the Office of Assurance, stated that he 'aswell in his owne name as for or in yᵉ name or names of any other person or persons to whom yᵉ same doth may or shall appertaine in part or in all doth make assurance and causeth himselfe

---

[85] LMA CLC/427/MS24,176/548, The Bowrey Papers, policy issued to Joseph Paice, 28 Oct. 1703.

[86] Marescoe to Momma, 14 Nov. 1566, cited in Roseveare, *Marescoe-David letters*, p. 569.

[87] Ibid., p. 382.

[88] Roccus, *A treatise on insurance*, p. 113.

or them or any of them to bee assured'.[89] Once again, the Office of Assurance had standardised policy wordings, but had not set them in stone, as they responded to merchant needs. Printed contracts, which began to appear later in the century, stated the name of the insured (which was inserted by hand), and that the insurance was made by him 'as well in his own Name, as for and in the Name and Names of all and every other Person or Persons to whom the same doth, may, or shall appertain, in part or in all, doth make assurance'.[90]

Further attempts to legislate against fraud were brought in 1701 and 1702, but failed upon their first readings.[91] It appears that, after much consideration, under-writing flexibility was chosen over statutory intervention, despite the obvious desire of some merchants to codify formally the rules governing some aspects of the oper-ation of insurance contracts. This flurry of failed legislation must reflect a measure of dissatisfaction with institutions in the London market, similar to that experienced a century earlier, which resulted in the establishment of the Court of Assurance. However, on this occasion legislation was not to interfere with the market. In its absence, disputes were to be dealt with in the traditional, internal manner, and fraud was to be avoided through prudent underwriting and the employment of expanding knowledge networks.

Only one piece of legislation targeting fraud, plus a modification, actually made it to the statute books. A law of 1702/3 prescribed death for any 'Captain Master Mariner or other Officer' guilty of the 'wilful casting away burning or otherwise destroying… of Ships under their Charge… to the prejudice of the Owner or Owners thereof or of any Merchant or Merchants that shall load Goods there-on'.[92] The law imposed the greatest possible legal sanction for fraud, but by focus-ing on appointees and employees who might damage ships or goods, it missed its key intended target: principals plotting to destroy insured assets and defraud their insurers, thus to the *benefit* of the owners.[93] The deficiency was repaired in an act of 1724/5, entitled in part *For explaining and amending a late act for more effectual pun-ishment of such as shall wilfully burn or destroy ships*. Since 'some doubts have arisen touching the nature of the offence provided against', the word 'owner' was added to the list of those targeted by the Act.[94] According to Martin, underwriters attempted to bring actions against suspected fraudulent claimants under both the original and revised acts, but none succeeded.[95]

---

[89] TNA SP 46/84/159 f. 145, policy issued to George Warner, 31 Jan. 1641/2.

[90] LMA CLC/427/MS24176/548, The Bowrey Papers, policy issued to Joseph Paice, 28 Oct. 1703.

[91] Hoppit, *Failed legislation*, pp. 236, 240.

[92] Ann. Stat. 2, c. 10, *An act for punishing of Accessories to Feloneys and Receivers of stolen Goods and to prevent the wilful burning and destroying of Ships*, 8 Statutes of the Realm 168, 1702–1707, p. 169.

[93] Martin, *History of Lloyd's*, p. 257.

[94] Pickering, Danby: *The Statutes at large*, Vol. XV, Cambridge: Joseph Bentham, 1765, pp. 260–261.

[95] Martin, *History of Lloyd's*, p. 270.

Notwithstanding proposals to take insurance underwriting completely into the hands of the state, which proponents hoped would reduce its cost, none of the interventions into the market suggested since 1601 envisioned changes to the basic methodology of underwriting in London. The legislation advanced in 1700, for example, would have left intact the basic structure of the market, in which each policy was subscribed by multiple individuals for specified sums with several liability against their own resources. The overall security of the individual merchant-insurer system was not questioned, despite the insurer insolvencies which followed the Smyrna catastrophe, but it was to become a major point of debate during the next major intervention into the structure of the market: the outsider-sellers' introduction of joint-stock insurers. As will be shown, despite the market's recovery after the losses of 1693, underwriter failures in the wake of the Smyrna catastrophe were to become a focal point of discussions about market reform some twenty-five years later.

The marine insurance market during the financial revolution

In 1720, a parliamentary enquiry was held to determine the state of London's marine insurance market, in response to the launch of several joint-stock insurance companies in the city. The enquiry is of immediate interest because the resulting report provides an invaluable source for understanding the London insurance market in the period following the regime change of 1688/9. Testimony within it proffers a fairly complete picture of the insurance market at this time, although the evidence must be used with care, since it contains contradictory observations presented by opposing parties, one of which hoped to change the structure of the London insurance market and another that wished to preserve it.

For example, the report cites an affidavit of the Africa merchant Humphrey Morice, a supporter and eventually a major customer of one of the companies petitioning for a charter, who stated that private merchant-insurers 'will run the Danger and Hazard of an Adventure from four or five hundred Pounds Value in a Vessel, when they will not adventure so many thousand Pounds'.[96] This simply was not true. Several extant policies from the period show that private insurers in London would and did make insurances to these higher values. One such policy, underwritten for Ralph Radcliffe in 1715, provided cover totalling £5,050.[97] Gaining such cover was not necessarily easy, however, especially when the subject adventure was perilous or uncertain. To attract £2,100 in cover for a voyage to and from any point beyond the Cape of Good Hope on the vessel *Morris Frigate*, John Fletcher had to increase the rate he would pay from six pounds to six guineas, and to return to at least one underwriter, Rochdale, to seek a second line on the risk.[98] A group of brokers, in answer to the affidavit of Morice, declared that 'they could have procured Insurances to be

---

[96] *The special report of 1720*, p. 42; BOE 10A61/7, Humphrey Morice Papers, 1709–1731, f. 2; BOE 6A49/1, 'Royall Exchange Insurance Company account with Humphrey Morice'.

[97] HALSC DE/R/B293/24, Business records of the Radcliffe family, policy underwritten for Edward and Arthur Radcliffe, 7 May 1741.

[98] BL Add. Ms. 43,731 f. 60, policy issued to John Fletcher (transcription).

made by private Insurers on Mr *Morrice's* Ships... if Mr *Morrice* would have given the *Præmium* other Merchants thought fitting to give the Private Insurers'.[99]

Despite the inherent bias of the testimonials it contains, the report reveals concretely the nature of the market at the turn of the eighteenth century. Individual underwriters remained the driving force, and perhaps the whole source of cover. 'Insurance is now in the Hands of private Persons, called Office-Keepers, carried on by Brokers', wrote Nicholas Lechemere, the Attorney General to whom petitions against the companies had been referred. Their 'Employment is to procure for the Merchant, as his Occasions require, Persons to subscribe the Policies of Insurance on such Terms as shall be agreed on'. The Office of Assurance was not mentioned in the report in this or any other regard. Eight brokers submitted to Lechemere a list of 163 individuals who 'had subscribed Policies of Insurance on Ships and Merchandizes' which they had arranged. Overlap between brokers and underwriters continued; the same John Fletcher, one of the eight brokers, subscribed to at least one of Radcliffe's policies. This model merchant-insurer is named as the insured party in a policy issued in 1716, insuring goods to the value of £1,000 on a voyage from London to China and back.[100] However, it can be assumed that specialist brokers who did not underwrite were active in London, since seven of the eight did not subscribe to any of approximately one hundred policies underwritten in London between 1690 and 1717, extant in various archives, and examined by the author.[101]

Several underwriters cited in the report attested that arbitration remained the preferred method of dispute resolution. John Barnard, a wine merchant, leading underwriter, and future MP, stated that 'Insurers are generally desirous to have Disputes about Losses or Averages adjusted by Arbitration, it being in their Interest to do so, and that the Insurers very often pay unreasonable Demands, rather than suffer themselves to be Sued'. John Bourne, a broker of twenty-five years' experience, said that, when facing a customer suit, underwriters offer 'That if he will bring his action against one Insurer, they will abide the Judgement that shall be given', and this is 'the Method practised', except 'when the Assured is Disposed to multiply Actions, rather than attain an amicable Satisfaction'.[102]

Bourne, along with Fletcher, was a signatory of the broadside entitled *The Office-Keepers ANSWER to a Scandalous Reflection on them by the Societies of the Mines-Royal &c.*, which revealed an insider-outsider breach within the broking community. The brokers as a homogenous group (which they were not) were charged with inserting the names of non-existent underwriters into their policies, based on the example of an insurance of the vessel *Vansittart*. In their 'Answer', the brokers denied the 'foul, false, and malicious Charge', invited 'all the merchants of England' to produce evidence that they have so falsified an insurance policy, and stated that the man

---

[99] *The special report of 1720*, affidavit of John Bull, John Gregory, and John Wilson, p. 45.

[100] BL Add. Ms. 43,731 f. 58, policy issued to John Fletcher, 5 Dec. 1716 (transcription).

[101] *The special report of 1720*, Lechemere's report to the King, various affidavits, pp. 40, 44–45; HALSC DE/R/B293/1–47, Business records of the Radcliffe family, policies underwritten for Radcliffe and others. For other policies underwritten 1690–1717, see the manuscripts section of the bibliography.

[102] *The special report of 1720*, various affidavits, pp. 40, 44–45.

responsible for the swindle on the *Vansittart* policy was 'a Person since dead, who was not an Office-Keeper, but one who acted as a Broker for discounting Notes, and did sometimes make Policies'. He was, therefore, an outsider.[103]

The number of underwriters appears to have continued to grow since the Smyrna loss, and new leading underwriters to have emerged. Between 1709 and 1717 Ralph Radcliffe purchased policies underwritten by eighty-six discrete underwriters, although in 1716, from when eighteen Radcliffe policies survive, only forty-four discrete individuals underwrote a share of his risks. Of these, twenty-eight participated in only one of the eighteen policies, but John Barnard, Richard Cambridge, and William Hayton took a share of the risk under five or more policies (and Cambridge twelve).[104] Selection of favourites or the preferences of a broker probably limited the number of underwriters involved in these examples, while higher wartime rates certainly encouraged more dabblers into underwriting. Still, the core of underwriters remained small. Barnard, who had been 'conversant in the Business of Insuring Ships and Merchandizes at Sea for fifteen Years and upwards, both as Insured and Insurer', testified that 'there are about one hundred Persons of very Good Repute, who Insure Ships and merchandizes at Sea'.[105] Presumably there were others of lesser reputation.

The report reveals that by 1720 London was attracting considerable foreign insurance custom, in part due to the competitiveness of rates in the city. Barnard stated that 'Foreigners from almost all parts of *Europe* have continual Recourse to the Insurers of *London*, to be insured for very large Sums of Money'. This, he believed, was because 'in Time of Peace... the *Præmiums* for Insurances were lower in *London*, than in any other Part of *Europe*'. He stated that 'at *Cadiz*... the *Præmiums* on *English* and *Spanish* ships during the last Peace was frequently Double the *Præmium* given here in *London* on the same Ships'. A group of four testifiers gave an account 'of many Foreign Insurances made here in *England*; Foreigners being, as they believe, encouraged to Insure here from the Lowness of the *Præmiums* and the Goodness of the Security'. Further, by 1720, the London underwriters had established an international agency network to obtain this business. Barnard's agent in Cadiz, for example, would accept risks in the Spanish port on his behalf, at the high rates cited. An early form of reinsurance had developed, which gave London merchant-insurers another source of geographical risk diversification. Barnard noted that 'Foreigners have allowed their Correspondents here a *Premium* to Insure the Insurers'.[106]

Merchants of other nations were paying more for the same insurance, creating an advantage for English commerce. This international spread of London's underwriting business was long established, according to evidence of 1693, which reveals that it was commonplace that 'Assurances are made in Trust for divers Persons in

---

[103] Praed, Peter and ten others: *The Office-Keepers ANSWER to a Scandalous Reflection on them by the Societies of the Mines-Royal &c.*, London: 1719?, BL SPR 357.b.3.73.

[104] Business records of the Radcliffe family. *Hertfordshire Archives and Local Studies Centre*, DE/R/B293/1–47.

[105] *The special report of 1720*, affidavit of John Barnard, p. 44.

[106] Ibid, affidavits of John Barnard and of James Mendes, George Tobias Guissuen, and Robert Aston, p. 44

remote Parts of the Kingdom, and Places beyond the Seas'.[107] This testimony shows that, shortly after the Glorious Revolution of 1688/9 during London's financial revolution, London became an important international centre of marine insurance, as underwriting began to shift from multi-local supply to a service provided from a leading international centre.

The Bubble Act and a corporate duopoly

This smoothly operating market was to face its second major intervention during the height of the financial revolution, at the end of the second decade of the eighteenth century. The previous intervention had responded to complaints about fraud, but managing outsider impacts did not motivate the second intervention. Some merchants and pundits professed to be unhappy with the security of the merchant-insurers, and asserted their inadequacy. Others wanted to erect new institutions for reasons which had nothing to do with insurance or trade. Among them were personal gain and the advancement of corporate interests. As will be shown, the second intervention was largely a product of London's evolving financial capitalism, the developing role of the king-in-parliament and the state following the Glorious Revolution, of emerging party politics, and of a rising class of 'monied men' within the nation's social order. By becoming international, London's merchant-insurers had risen to Braudel's second tier of capitalism, and the financial capitalists of Janeway's three-player game were attempting a hostile takeover.

A key backdrop to these events was a peak in the formation of new joint-stock companies in London. This form of business, characterised by the issue of transferable shares which gave the owner a stake in the company's assets and its financial fortunes, was extremely controversial in the early eighteenth century. In London the creation of joint-stock companies expanded through a 'boom' in 1692–1695, when shares were traded in at least 150 companies with total paid-up capital of £4.35 million.[108] By the beginning of the eighteenth century, 'all of the requisite institutions of a functioning market' in shares were present in London.[109] The promotion of joint-stock companies assumed breakneck pace: between September 1719 and August 1720, around 190 discrete joint-stock company promotions were underway.[110] From the latter date, new launches were halted for over a century by provisions of the well-known *Bubble Act*.

From late in 1717, even before this apparent frenzy of public offerings, several subscriptions were opened for the funding of joint-stock corporations to underwrite marine insurance. The timing of their launch probably had more to do with the state

---

[107] BL GRC 816.m.12, 16, *Reasons humbly offered for the passing of a bill…* undated, 1693/4.

[108] Scott, William Robert: *The constitution and finance of English, Scottish, and Irish joint-stock companies to 1720, three volumes*, Gloucester, MA: Peter Smith, 1968 (first published 1912), I, p. 327; Neal, *Rise of financial capitalism*, pp. 45–46.

[109] Mirowski, Philip: 'The rise (and retreat) of a market: English joint stock shares in the eighteenth century', *Journal of Economic History*, Vol. 41, No. 3 (Sep. 1981), pp. 564, 566.

[110] Scott identified this number, although he overestimated the number of insurance promotions by one. Scott, *Joint-stock companies*, I, p. 327; III, pp. 445–458.

of the market for shares in joint-stock companies than any broad need for such a venture. No specific trigger-event such as a market loss or swathe of underwriter failures is apparent, and, as shown above, the unsuccessful interventions into the market after 1693 focused on management of the consequences of a very large loss event, and the resolution of disputes which followed, rather than on dissatisfaction with the basic structure of the market, which was expanding, and particularly capturing foreign customers. The absence of more than a handful of recorded suits in the formal courts indicates that the market was operating smoothly. Meanwhile 1719 and 1720 proffered 'several conditions, which were likely to result in considerable speculative activity in the stock-markets', including apparently plentiful capital, low interest rates, and the pervasive 'ideal of the indefinite expansibility of a [notional] fund of credit' which could be tapped through joint-stock companies.[111] Such a pool of credit would be attractive to insurance buyers, since the sole primary purpose of the instrument itself is the provision of contingent capital.

Alongside adequate conditions, some contemporary testimony suggests that merchant support existed for the formation of corporate marine insurers with a fixed stock of dedicated capital. However, alongside it existed widespread support for the established system of individual underwriting by private merchant-insurers operating under the Law Merchant. Spanning these two divergent views about the best market structure for insurance was the commonplace consensus that the provision of insurance was essential for trade. Those objecting to the new subscriptions argued that introducing insurance companies would destroy the economics of a working system, in the interests only of stock-jobbing. Those in favour argued that the credit of private insurers was unsecure, and subject to failures, and therefore that joint-stock structures were preferable.

The so-called *Bubble Act* was actually entitled *An Act for better securing certain Powers and Privileges, intended to be granted by His Majesty by Two Charters, for Assurance of Ships and Merchandize at Sea, and for lending Money upon Bottomry; and for restraining several extravagant and unwarrantable Practices therein mentioned.*[112] Both of the Act's dual functions are thus evident in the name of the legislation: it banned the formation of new joint-stock companies, and approved the formation, under royal charter, of two new JSCs to underwrite marine insurance (the London Assurance and the Royal Exchange Assurance). Thus, a tension lay at the heart of the legislation, which simultaneously curtailed the use of the joint-stock structures, and allowed an immediate and near-final exception.

Historians writing about the Act have acknowledged this tension, and have chosen to accept it. However, upon close observation it is clear that the apparent contradiction constitutes no such tension. The alignment of interests is distinct between the individuals involved in projecting the London and Royal Exchange

---

[111] Ibid., I, pp. 396–397.

[112] Geo I c. 18. Denial of the actual name of the act continues, as, for instance, in Patterson, M. and Reiffen, D.: 'The effect of the Bubble Act on the market for joint stock shares,' *Journal of Economic History*, 51 (Mar. 1990), n. 1, p. 163, which states incorrectly that the name of the act 'was, more precisely, "An Act to Restrain the Extravagant and Unwarrantable…",' thereby misleadingly ignoring the marine insurance connection.

Assurance companies, and those behind the proscriptive sections of the *Bubble Act*. In many cases, they were the same people. Thus, the balance of motivations which led to the second major intervention was skewed. Not all of the actors promoting the new companies were doing so in the interests of improving the market. Some did so to create a further opportunity for personal gain through stock-jobbing, and others to advance the interests of the South Sea Company, as shown below. For this reason, because of its long-term impact on the development of London marine insurance, and because the episode has not heretofore been considered from this perspective by historians, it is analysed in detail here.

Harris has described the argument that the *Bubble Act* 'was an attempt to hinder alternative investment opportunities and to divert more capital to South Sea shares' as 'viable from all perspectives'.[113] His work and findings put to rest earlier historiographical explanations of the motivations which drove the famous, joint-stock-limiting component of the legislation, but in late May 1720 the pending law framed to curb joint-stock company formations – the future *Bubble Act* – was amended to include the incorporation of the two marine insurers.

Harris acknowledges that the two matters then covered by the Act were 'somewhat contradictory'. He notes that its first seventeen clauses relate entirely to the marine insurers, and that 'out of a total of 29 clauses, only 6, if any, deserve the moniker "Bubble Act".'[114] Yet in practice, the two matters were indeed combined in one legislative instrument. It cannot be that the motivation of diverting more capital to one company's shares is 'viable from all perspectives' when the same legislation established legitimacy for two new joint-stock companies which indeed competed, successfully, for investors' cash. Harris is not wrong in relation to the clauses of the *Bubble Act* related to the limitation of joint-stock companies.[115] Indeed, his revisionist explanation of the motivations for limiting the formation of JSCs appears sound. However, a more complete picture of the odd juxtaposition of actions within the Act may be gained by examining the motivations for the passage of legislation in direct contradiction to the intended effects of the pre-marine-insurer version of the Act, so adeptly outlined by Harris. It finds that the launch of the insurers was in fact wholly beneficial to the South Sea Company and the financial capitalists of the City of London, and that the entire affair was an extension of the political rivalries of the age.

The era of joint-stock marine insurance companies in England began in 1717, when the first steps were taken to create what would become the Royal Exchange Assurance. Early that year Mr Case Billingsley, whom Scott describes as 'a solicitor interested in financial ventures, who had an office in the Royal Exchange',[116] and his business partner James Bradley presented to the Solicitor General, Sir

---

[113] Harris, Ron: 'The Bubble Act: its passage and its effects on business', *Journal of Economic History*, Vol. 54, No. 3 (Sept. 1994), p. 612.

[114] Harris, 'Bubble Act', pp. 613–614.

[115] Later in his article Harris moderates his view, presenting evidence which he says shows 'that the South Sea Company was behind the Bubble Act, or at least substantial parts of it'. Harris, 'Bubble Act', p. 615.

[116] Scott, *Joint-stock companies*, III, p. 397.

William Thompson, their plan for a subscription to fund a marine insurance company. A Whig lawyer and parliamentarian, Thompson initially described the plan as an 'Excellent Scheme'. He informally approved the proposal 'without altering one Word', and was assumed by Billingsley to be 'not only a Friend to us, but to the Undertaking', since he offered guidance on answers to objections raised to the project. On 2 February 1717/18 the matter was referred to the Lords Commissioners for Trade and Plantations, and to 'Mr Attorney and Sollicitor Generals' for assessment (an outcome discouraged by Thompson, who had hoped the question could be addressed to one or the other, such that, in Billingsley's words, 'it might be in our power to bring it to him [Thompson], and he assured us he would do it justice').[117] Billingsley and Thompson had perhaps cooperated on another venture, involving the chartered York Buildings Company.[118]

Billingsley, Bradley, and their partners sought formal, royal approval for their project, but meanwhile, on 12 August 1717, they opened a subscription at the Mercer's Hall in London 'for Raising the Summe of ONE MILLION Sterling, as a FUND for Insuring Ships and Merchandize at Sea'. Their fundraising target was reached by 16 January 1717/18,[119] well before the deadline of Lady Day, 25 March.[120] A lead promoter emerged: Sir Justus Beck. 'An eminent Merchant of London', Beck was the first baronet created by George I.[121] An occasional insurance broker and share dealer of Dutch descent, he did much business in Amsterdam, and in 1710 became a director of the Bank of England as a member of the Tory slate of usurping candidates. Next a noble patron was recruited, Baron Thomas Onslow, a member of a prominent trading and political family. His cousin Sir Richard Onslow 3rd Bt. was a governor of the Levant Company; his younger cousin Arthur Onslow had held several government posts from 1714. Both had been Speakers of the House.[122] Lord Onslow's prominence in the promotion gave the planned insurer its temporary name, 'Onslow's Insurance' (notwithstanding Onslow's relatively passive involvement).[123] On 25 January 1717/18, the projectors presented to the Privy Council a

[117] *The special report of 1720*, affidavit of Case Billingsley, pp. 32–33.

[118] Ibid., pp. 69–70.

[119] BL Add MS 8225.a.38, *A list of the names of the subscribers…*, p. 1.

[120] *Abstract of a scheme for an office: and raising one or two millions sterling by a voluntary subscription, for a fund to insure ships and merchandize at sea, &c.*, London: 1717, SHL GL 1717 f. 5361, p. 1.

[121] Cokayne, G. E. (ed.): *Complete Baronetage, Vol. V, 1707–1800*, Exeter: Pollard & Co., 1906, p. 8.

[122] Ellis, Kathryn: 'Onslow, Richard, first Baron Onslow', *Oxford dictionary of national biography online*, www.oxforddnb.com/view/article/20794 [Accessed 3 Dec. 2021]; Sedgwick, Romney R.: 'Onslow, Sir Richard, 3rd Bt.' *History of Parliament*, www.historyofparliamentonline.org/volume/1715-1754/member/onslow-sir-richard-1654-1717 [Accessed 3 Dec. 2021]; Sedgwick, Romney R.: 'Onslow, Arthur (1691–1768)', *History of Parliament*, www.historyofparliamentonline.org/volume/1715-1754/member/onslow-arthur-1691-1768 [Accessed 3 Dec. 2021].

[123] Onslow, despite being appointed the company's first governor, was not much involved in its operations. Supple, Barry: *The Royal Exchange Assurance, A history of British insurance 1720–1970*, Cambridge: University Press, 1979, n. 1, p. 13.

petition carrying 287 signatures, requesting the issue of 'Royal Letters-Patents' to incorporate the venture as a 'Joint-Stock'.[124] With only a handful of exceptions, the names on the petition were those of the subscribers.

The key projectors of the scheme included a number of high-placed Levant merchants, some of them notable Tory politicians. Sir John Williams, a future Master of the Mercers' Company, was a prominent City Tory and future MP for Aldeburgh. In addition, he was an Assistant of the Levant Company, and a director of the South Sea Company from 1711 to 1715, and he became a deputy governor of the insurer in 1720. He has been described as resting 'at the head of the Turkey trade' and 'the greatest exporter of cloth in England'.[125] Another wealthy Levant merchant and insurance company subscriber, Sir Richard Lockwood, was to become a director of the proposed marine insurer, and later its deputy governor. He sat as Tory MP for Hindon from 1713 to 1715, and was later an Assistant of the Royal Africa Company.[126] With Charles Goodfellow, another future director of the insurer, Sir Richard was a business associate of the South Sea Company directors William Astell and Edward Gibbon, the latter a subscriber to Onslow's, the former a named petitioner in its favour before Lechmere in 1719.[127] One prominent Whig, Sir Randolph Knipe, was also among the key subscribers. Knipe was an assistant of the Levant Company, later an Eastland Company trader, and from 1712 a director of the Bank of England. He was a member of the City Whig Club in 1717, where, as at the Bank, he associated with the Bank's former governor, Sir Gilbert Heathcote.[128] Supple notes that 'many lesser subscribers were also Levant traders'.[129] The Smyrna catastrophe was obviously an extremely costly loss event for merchants trading to the Levant, who therefore suffered the concentration of losses arising from the underwriter failures which followed. Serial joint-stock promoters were also among the lead subscribers. Alongside Billingsley, these included the Irish MP Sir Alexander Cairnes, Bt., a City of London banker and promoter of a scheme for colonising Nova Scotia, a Liverpool waterworks company floated in London, and an unsuccessful joint-stock company for trading to Germany.[130]

---

[124] *The special report of 1720*, pp. 17–20.

[125] Cruickshanks, Eveline: 'Sir John Williams', *History of Parliament*, www. historyofparliamentonline.org/volume/1715-1754/member/williams-sir-john-1676-1743 [Accessed 3 Dec. 2021].

[126] Hayton, D.W.: 'Richard Lockwood', *History of Parliament*, www.historyofparliamentonline. org/volume/1690–1715/member/lockwood-richard-1676-1756 [Accessed 3 Dec. 2021].

[127] Dickson, *Financial revolution*, p. 117 n; *The special report of 1720*, p. 49.

[128] Francis, John: *History of the Bank of England, its times and traditions*, London: Willoughby & Co., 1847, pp. 262–263; Horwitz, H., Speck, W. A., and Gray, W. A. (eds): *London Politics 1713–1717: Minutes of a Whig club 1714–1717*, 1981, www.british-history.ac.uk/report.aspx?compid=38804 [Accessed 3 Dec. 2021].

[129] Supple, *The Royal Exchange Assurance*, p. 14.

[130] Wadsworth, Alfred P. and Mann, J.: *The cotton trade and industrial Lancashire, 1600–1780*, Manchester: Manchester University Press, 1965, p. 216; Carswell, 'South Sea Bubble', pp. 166–167.

Onslow, Beck, Bradley, Billingsley, Williams, and Cairnes were the core subscrib-ers who appeared before the Commissioners of Trade and Plantations when their petition was discussed.[131] Judging, then, by this cast of characters, Onslow's was a ven-ture projected primarily by Tory Levant merchants and serial joint-stock promot-ers. The partisanship of the preponderance of the promoters is unquestionable. It is not clear when this balance of interests developed, although the memory of insurer failures following the Smyrna catastrophe may have provided impetus. The men who framed the company, financial capitalists including Billingsley, Bradley, Beck, Onslow, and perhaps Thompson, seem to have done so for personal gain through a new joint-stock venture during the period of subscription frenzy. Political interest was brought to bear shortly afterwards, however, perhaps based on Beck's connec-tions. It is notable that the Whig Thompson, an early enthusiast for Billingsley's corporate marine insurer, did not endorse the project as Solicitor General. Instead, his report advised the king to take the opposite course.

Before that recommendation was made, the petition for Onslow's elicited a pair of counter-petitions from the 'merchants and traders' of London and Bristol. Together they carried an even larger number of signatories. The former group was led by Sir Gilbert Heathcote, a staunch Whig and a founder and early governor of the Bank of England. Heathcote was later to lead a delegation before the Commissioners for Trade and Plantations to oppose the insurer.[132] Other Whig leaders of the Bank sign-ing the counter-petition from London included Sir Theodore Janssen, a promoter of the Bank in its earliest days and one of the richest men in the City; Peter Godfrey, son of Michael, who launched the Bank with Heathcote; and Samuel Houblon, another son of a Bank founder. Former Bank governors James Bateman and George Boddington also signed, alongside members of the Sedgwick and Lordell families, which also produced governors of the iconic Whig financial institution.[133]

Another high-profile contingent of Whig petitioners against Onslow's was made up of those who were the lead actors in the establishment of the New East India Company, including the leading subscribers Heathcote, Janssen, and Bateman, plus its fourth-largest subscriber, Joseph Martin, directors Thomas Vernon and John Ward, and its parliamentary hopeful Samuel Shepherd.[134] Not surprisingly, many active individual underwriters also signed the petition. At least forty-five counter-pe-titioners' names match those of subscribers to extant policies underwritten in the five years to 1717.[135] Thirty-eight known underwriters did not sign; of them, during the period twenty-three subscribed to only one policy among those examined (com-pared to a mean of 2.44 and a maximum of 22), while the names of six can be found on the list of investors in Onslow's, including Knipe.

---

[131] *Journal of the Commissioners for Trade and Plantations, Vol. III: March 1714–5 to October 1718*, London: HMSO, 1924, pp. 335–397.

[132] *Journal of the Commissioners, Vol. III*, p. 339.

[133] *The special report of 1720*, pp. 17–25; biographical details from various sources cited elsewhere in this thesis.

[134] Walcott, Robert: 'The East India interest in the general election of 1700–1701', *English Historical Review*, Vol. 71, No. 279 (1956), pp. 223–239.

[135] Viz., all policies of the period 1712–1717 cited in this book.

Sir Edward Northey, the moderate Tory Attorney General, advised the petitioners for the company that a charter would be required. At a subsequent meeting, the project's opponents complained that 'by the Terms of the Subscription, every Subscriber till he paid in some Money was at Liberty, whether he would pay in any thing or not'.[136] Contemporaries were well aware, it appears from this intervention, that subscription had to be structured as a commitment, rather than as an option.[137] One or perhaps both of the crown's legal officers thus advised that the subscription be redrafted to close the loophole. A revised subscription was drawn up; the books were opened on 14 March 1717/18, and completed 'in about fourteen Days; into which most of the former Subscribers came, and were bound absolutely to pay in their Money'.[138] (Scott had argued that this second subscription was for a discrete venture, but, as Supple states, this finding was mistaken.)[139]

Some structural aspects of the new company are noteworthy. First, it was launched as a '*Copartnership*' in which 'every Member shall be answerable for his *own particular Part* of the *Capital Stock* and no more'. This attempted to limit the liability of shareholders to the amount of their subscriptions: each subscriber was to 'pay upon any *Loss*, what shall be call'd for by a Majority of the *Managers*; but not pay more than he has *subscribed*. The *Summes* call'd for are to be in Proportion to the *Losses*, the *Subscription* of each Member, the *Stock* in hand, and the *Expence* of the Office', while 'every *Policy* and *Arbitration-Bond*, shall be *valid* and binding on the whole COMPANY *jointly*'.[140]

Second, one quarter of the subscribed capital was seen as sufficient resources for the operations of the company; any surplus could be returned as dividends. Assets not invested in land, specified as a 'Security to the Insured', could be 'lent his MAJESTY from Time to Time on such *Funds* as are or shall be *settled*; where *Provision* is made by *Parliament* for *Borrowing* Money of the Subject; And if no such *Occasions* present; the Money shall be put out on *Parliamentary* Securitys to support the *Honour* and *Credit* of the *Government*; But on no other *Securitys* but such as the *Company* at a GENERAL COURT shall judge proper, the better to support the *Credit* of the *Office*... and the *Profits* of such *Securitys*... shall be divided among the

---

[136] *The special report of 1720*, p. 33.

[137] Much academic ink has been deployed in debating whether or not a subscription in this period represented a commitment or an option to pay future calls. See, for example, Shea, Gary S.: 'Understanding financial derivatives during the South Sea Bubble: the case of the South Sea subscription shares', *Oxford Economic Papers*, No. 59 (2007), pp. 73–104; Dale, R. S. *et al.*: 'Financial markets can go mad: evidence of irrational behaviour during the South Sea Bubble', *Economic History Review*, Vol. 58, No. 2 (2005), pp. 233–271; and Shea's rejoinder, 'Financial market analysis can go mad (in the search for irrational behaviour during the South Sea Bubble)', *Economic History Review*, Vol. 60, No. 4 (2007), pp. 742–765.

[138] *The special report of 1720*, p. 33.

[139] Supple notes that Scott's interpretation was based on a misinterpretation of old- and new-style dating conventions. Supple, *The Royal Exchange Assurance*, pp. 396–397.

[140] *Abstract of a scheme for an office*, 1717, pp. 2, 3, 4.

Members'.[141] The document, akin to a modern corporate prospectus, stated that each subscriber was to pay half a per cent on top of his subscription towards the costs of obtaining a charter.[142] Thus the maximum cost of this pursuit was to be £5,000, but, as will be shown, vastly greater sums were expended in this quest, exceeding the initial paid-up capital.

The law officers were offered substantial rewards for securing a charter. Thompson was promised, in a written note from Billingsley, a 'fee' of 'one thousand Guineas, which we will never either directly or indirectly mention to any Soul living'. Both men were told, again in writing, that the projectors 'have reserv'd Room in the Subscription for ten thousand Pounds for you, which if you think fit may be subscribed by any one that you can trust, which we doubt not will be a good Estate to you'.[143] However, Northey and Thompson were not corrupted. They advised the king on 12 March 1717/18 that

> the making an Experiment in a thing of this Nature, if it should prove amiss, would be of utmost Consequence to the trade of this Nation, and that it so highly concerns trade and commerce, That it will be proper for the Consideration of Parliament, and therefore we cannot advise the erecting a Corporation, for the insuring Ships and Goods at Sea… And we are not able to determine of what Consequence, the erecting of another Corporation in *London*, with a stock of a Million of Money, may be to the Publick.[144]

Thus, both the novel approach to insurance and the creation of another large joint-stock company were rejected, since the king's law officers feared that too great an intervention would upset what they believed was an adequately functioning and nationally important market. The merchant-insurers' traditional market structure must have appeared to them to be satisfactory.

The projectors pressed on, buying controlling shares in the Elizabethan-charter-holding company the Mines Royal and Mineral and Battery Works, for £2,904.14.0.[145] They planned to use its charter to legitimise Onslow's. A new subscription was organised to reflect the changed venture and increase its capital; the entire issue of £1.152 million was taken up very swiftly, but the paid-up capital was just £60,480, or 5.25% of the authorised capital.[146] On 3 March 1718/19, after more than six months' delay, Onslow's announced that, 'on Monday next the 9th of March, they will begin to assure Ships and Merchandize, at their Offices in the Royal Exchange of London'.

The announcement noted that disputes arising 'with respect to the Proof of any Loss, or the Allowance of any Average claimed by the Assureds' would, with the customer's consent, be referred to arbitration. If the customer instead would 'chuse to

[141] Ibid., p. 2.

[142] Ibid., p. 3.

[143] *The special report of 1720*, letters of Billingsley and Bradley to Thompson and Northey, 6 and 10 Mar. 1717/18, pp. 25–31.

[144] Ibid., p. 28.

[145] Scott, *Joint-stock companies*, III, p. 397.

[146] Ibid., p. 398.

try it at Law', no 'expensive or unnecessary Delay' would result from procrastination by the company.[147] This promise constituted an attempt to allay potential customers' possible concerns about plaintiffs' ability to bring suit against a corporation, a concern often expressed by those opposed to the companies.[148] In this respect, the new approach to underwriting appeared to offer an advantage. Since only a single underwriter was involved in each policy, disputes which could not be resolved through arbitration could be settled through a single suit in the formal courts. However, this perceived advantage ignored the practice, described above, whereby following underwriters would respect court decisions made against a single or leading underwriter.[149] Nor did it deal with the courts' lack of knowledge of the customs of insurance under the Law Merchant.

The new insurer met with early success, reportedly insuring ships and cargoes to the value of £1,259,604 within its first nine months of operations. One reason it attracted this business may have been its undercutting of the private market. Ostend traders, according to one account, were underwritten 'two Guineas per Cent. cheaper than was done by private Insurers', as the company 'very considerably reduced the Premiums of Insurance'.[150]

Yet it continued to meet with controversy. A petition of 189 London and Bristol merchants condemned the re-tasking of an obsolete charter for the purpose of underwriting insurance, 'in open Defiance of Royal Prerogative'.[151] A pamphlet campaign was launched. The fledgling insurer published *REASONS Humbly Offer'd By the SOCIETIES of the Mines Royal, &c. who Insure Ships and Merchandize, with the Security of a Deposited Joint-Stock.* As well as arguing that its charters were 'not obsolete', the pamphlet rehearsed the arguments in favour of incorporation, stated that seventy-three merchants who had petitioned against the company were now 'endeavouring to be incorporated', and that many were insuring with the corporation. It argued too that claims had been paid, and that the insurer had 'not been concerned or ventured one Shilling in the perilous Mystery of Stock-jobbing'.[152] Opponents published rejoinders and letters, both supportive and opposed, such as the published and circulated *LETTER to a Member of Parliament by a Merchant*.[153]

The project attracted imitators. Soon the joint-stock insurer which was to become the London Assurance was under way. According to Drew, historian of the company, the promotion was the brainchild of Sir John Lambert Bt.,[154] a London France merchant who was granted his baronetage by Harley after loaning £400,000 to

---

[147] *Daily Courant*, No. 5417, 3 March 1719.

[148] See, for example, *The special report of 1720*, p. 44.

[149] See pp. 96–97.

[150] Eden, *Insurance charters*, p. 15.

[151] *The special report of 1720*, pp. 35–37.

[152] BM 816.m.10/117 f. 297. See also *Reasons humbly offered against*, BM 357.b.3 f. 76.

[153] T.S.: *A LETTER to a Member of Parliament by a Merchant*, London: 1720, BL SPR 357.b.3.62.

[154] Drew, Bernard: *The London Assurance: a second chronicle*, Plaistow: Printed for the London Assurance at the Curwen Press, 1949.

the state in 1710, and who in 1720 was a director of the South Sea Company.[155] Drew reports that Lambert recruited Philip Helbut, 'a certain Jewish broker in Change Alley', late in 1719. He proposed that Helbut approach the goldsmith banker Stephen Ram (who had been a first-round subscriber to the South Sea Company, for £9,188, in 1711) about opening a subscription for a marine insurer.[156,] [157] Two million pounds were subscribed, without deposit, by early November, but subscribing merchants seeking a functional company, rather than a jobbing play, apparently objected to the number of brokers included. Ram was asked to prepare a list which excluded speculators.[158]

On 18 November a notice was placed in the *Daily Courant* explaining that 'whereas much more was subscribed than is thought necessary to carry on the said Business... in order to admit all the Subscribers and reduce the whole to 1,200,000 l... the Subscribers who desire to continue their Subscription, are... to pay the said Mr. Ram 2 s. 6 d. on every 100 L. of their Stock... at Garraway's Coffee-house in Exchange-Alley'.[159] Some 365 followed the instructions.[160] In December 1719, the fledgling company merged with a third marine insurance joint-stock, 'Colebrook's Insurance', which had raised subscriptions of £800,000 under the leadership of James Colebrook, a London scrivener who, like Ram, was among the first subscribers to South Sea shares, having taken £16,344 in 1711.[161] The combined subscription of £2,000,000 was supported by 512 investors.[162] After a call for an additional payment towards the subscription of £17.6.0, in early 1720 the company had taken in £20,000 towards its capital, of which £18,060 was 'deposited in *South Sea* bonds'.[163]

First to subscribe had been Walter Lord Chetwynd, for £15,000. The viscount, a Sunderland Whig, acted as front-man for the Company during its formation; it became known as 'Chetwynd's Insurance'. He eventually became its first governor, but like Onslow, neither involved himself in day-to-day operations, nor remained as governor beyond his first term. Nor was the insurance company his only City interest. Chetwynd was later criticised in parliament for accepting gifts of stock from the South Sea Company, and is dubbed by Carswell 'one of [that] Company's purchased friends'.[164] His brother, the future Second Viscount, was the MP John [Jack] Chetwynd, who at George I's accession in 1715 was appointed to the Board

---

[155] Cokayne, G. E.: *Complete Baronetage, Vol. V*, Exeter: W. Pollard & Co., 1906, p. 10.

[156] Dickson, *Financial Revolution*, p. 449n.

[157] Drew, *The London Assurance*, p. 6.

[158] Ibid., pp. 6–7.

[159] *Daily Courant*, No. 5640, 18 November 1719.

[160] Drew, *The London Assurance*, p. 7.

[161] Ibid, p. 11; Dickson, *Financial Revolution*, p. 449n.

[162] *The special report of 1720*, p. 34.

[163] *Journals of the House of Commons, Vol. 19*, London: 1803, p. 346.

[164] Cruickshanks, Eveline: 'Chetwynd, Walter'; *History of Parliament Online*, volume/1715-1754/member/chetwynd-walter-1677-1736 [Accessed 3 Dec. 2021]; Carswell, 'South Sea Bubble', p. 224.

of Trade.[165] Balancing Chetwynd's moderate Whiggism was the second subscriber, Lord Guilford, a former President of the Board of Trade (1713–1714) and a prominent Tory. Third to subscribe, for £10,000, was Horatio Townshend, a wealthy London merchant and former director of the South Sea Company (1715–1718), Walpole's brother-in-law, and brother of the more renowned Viscount Townshend.[166]

Other notables among the projectors of the insurer were several South Sea Company men. Sir William Chapman Bt. was a Spain merchant, a friend of Walpole, and a director of the Company since 1712. He was to become a sub-governor of the London Assurance. Sir Jacob Jacobsen, a merchant born in Hamburg, had been a Company director since 1715, and was also made sub-governor of the insurer. Militia officer and Indiaman captain Colonel Hugh Raymond, also a director since 1715, held a like position at the insurer. Other current South Sea directors signed-up to the project included Robert Chester (later a director of the insurer), Richard Houlditch, William Morley, and Thomas Reynolds. Subscriber Daniel Hayes' South Sea Company directorship had lapsed. In addition, subscriber John Caswell's son George had been a South Sea director, as had James Dolliffe's father Sir James, and Sir Joseph Eyle's cousin Francis. Perhaps the clearest indication of a connection is the signature of John Blunt, architect of the South Sea Scheme itself, and a man unlikely to have made any financial decision without placing the interests of his major joint stock adventure foremost.[167]

Onslow's had only a smattering of South Sea Company directors among its sub-scribers and opponents, but a subset of the South Sea Company executive was the driving force behind Chetwynd's. It has not been presented as such, though, neither contemporaneously, nor by historians. Drew states that 'it cannot be too strongly insisted that both these corporations [Onslow's and Chetwynd's] had their origin in the recognition of a real need for such institutions'.[168] One piece of evidence sup-ports this assertion (the preponderance of South Sea Company management not-withstanding): the presence, on the petition for Chetwynd's Insurance, of the names of sixty-three individuals who objected to Onslow's, including eight who were active underwriters, including Sir William Chapman (Lambert, who subscribed to at least one insurance policy as an underwriter in 1714, was also a subscriber to Onslow's venture). A contemporary pamphlet, with the cumbersome title *Reasons assigned by several Members of the Subscription for 2,000,000 l. for Insuring Ships and Merchandize, who formerly with others, signed a Petition to your Majesty against a Corporation for Insurance Ships and Merchandize*, stated that the initial 'Petition for a Charter being

---

[165] Cruickshanks, Eveline: 'Chetwynd, John'; *History of Parliament*, www.historyofparliamentonline.org/volume/1715-1754/member/chetwynd-john-1680-1767 [Accessed 3 Dec. 2021].

[166] For subscribers Guilford and Townshend, see the photo facing page six of Drew, *The London Assurance*. Lea, R. S.: 'Townshend, Hon. Horatio', *History of Parliament*, www.historyofparliamentonline.org/volume/1715-1754/member/townshend-hon-horatio-1683-1751 [Accessed 3 Dec. 2021]; Carswell, 'South Sea Bubble', p. 284.

[167] *The special report of 1720*, pp. 51–53; Carswell, 'South Sea Bubble', pp. 139, 273–285; Dickson, *Financial Revolution*, pp. 112–117.

[168] Drew, *The London Assurance*, p. 7.

subscribed by a large number of Persons, of which very few were Merchants, it was rational to fear a Monopoly, or some other difficulty on trade might be intended or arise thereby... which induced them to sign a Petition against a Charter'. The pamphlet went on to call for 'two Societies for [the] Purpose' of marine insurance.[169]

Some private insurers continued to protest against all corporate underwriting, and argued that two corporations would eventually unite to monopolise – and that the petitioners had colluded to such an end. They further claimed that 'the only Design was that of Stock-jobbing', since the insurance market functioned perfectly well without joint-stock incorporations.[170] However, sixty-three petitioners against Onslow's venture opted to subscribe to Chetwynd's, perhaps prompted in part by the support it received from the prominent merchant-insurer Chapman, and from Sir Theodore Janssen, an extremely high profile City figure, who petitioned in the Company's favour with Charles Joye and the financier Sir Lambert Blackwell Bt. Like Chapman, all three, additionally, were directors of the South Sea Company. Joye was its deputy governor.[171] Alongside eighty merchants, these three directors argued that, 'provided [charters for the company] do not exclude private Insurers [from underwriting, the company] will be for the Security, Advantage, and Encrease of the Trade and Navigation of *Great Britain*'.[172]

A fourth project had been launched by the broker Helbut. He aligned with another goldsmith banker, Charles Shales, to organise a marine insurance company subscription. 'Shales Insurance' was subscribed for £1,000,000, but in the words of Eden, the project 'fell to the ground'.[173] Meanwhile, the rivals charged ahead. In January 1719/20 a new petition was sent to the king on behalf of the subscribers to Chetwynd's, now merged with Colebrooks, styled *The Merchants Society for Insuring Ships and Merchandize*. The petitioners, self-described as 'a very considerable part of the Body of Merchants on the Exchange of *London*', stated that they had entered into a voluntary subscription to raise a joint stock of £2 million for their venture. It too was referred to Lechmere, who now held petitions from three competing societies of subscribers seeking charters to underwrite insurance through joint-stock corporations. On 17 November 1719 Humphrey Morice wrote to Lechmere to express his support for Onslow's venture. Earlier he had signed the petition opposing Onslow's, and had appeared in person before the Board of Trade and Plantations to argue his opposition, but as he attested to the Attorney General, he was opposed only to the formation of a single, potentially monopolistic marine insurer.[174] He had been insuring with the companies, and told the Attorney General

[169] Quoted in *The special report of 1720*, pp. 54–55.

[170] Ibid., p. 55.

[171] Speck, W. A. and Kilburn, Matthew: 'Promoters of the South Sea Bubble', *Oxford Dictionary of National Biography*, online edn, www.oxforddnb.com/view/theme/92793 [Accessed 3 Dec. 2021].

[172] *The special report of 1720*, p. 54.

[173] Eden, *Insurance charters*, p. 13.

[174] *Journals of the Board of Trade and Plantations*, Vol. 3, March 1715–October 1718 (1924), 'Journal Book T, February 1718', ff. 110, 132; *The special report of 1720*, p. 42.

I can assure you that when Private Gentlemen have refused to insure any thing for mee upon Shipps that I have sent abroad, that this Company, have readily insured for mee on such Adventures to my Satisfaction at moderate Terms, and had they refused to Insure for mee as Private Insurers had Done, I should not have exported five hundred pounds of the Manufactures of this Kingdom, where I have sent abroad Six & Seven thousand pounds in a shipp… give me Leave to Say I think this Insurance Company very usefull & Beneficiall to Trade & Navigation, that they deserve the protection & encouragement of the Governem^t that to Supress or Restraine them from Insuring will be to discourage Commerce, to diminish and Lessen the Revenue of the Crown, and give an occasion to our Neigbour Nations, the French & Dutch, that are our Rivalls & Competitors at forreigne Markets to undermine & Supplant us in trade, and according to the Degree of Trade Great Brittaine enjoys, she will be more or Less powerfull in Europe & make a Figure in the World.[175]

His letter was, in modern parlance, very much on-message. An extant record from Morice's ledgers shows that he insured extensively with Chetwynd's in the 1720s, expending premiums of £11,390.3.0 between 23 February 1724 and 3 October 1727, received cash rebates of £5,000, and collected claims for two losses totalling £1,651.4.0.[176]

On 3 March 1719/20, after completing his enquiry and hearing witnesses, Lechmere reported his opinions to the king. He declared the use of obsolete charters 'Illegal and Unwarrantable'. On the question of joint stock insurers in general, he opined 'that such a Corporation, not being made in any Manner exclusive of Others… may be of great Advantage to Trade; but whether it is advisable to erect such a Corporation with so large a Joint Stock, as is mentioned in the Petition, may deserve particularly to be considered'. Four days later he wrote yet another opinion, reiterating his favour for a 'far less Joint Stock than… proposed', and adding the guidance that 'if your Majesty shall be graciously pleased to Erect such a Corporation… that it is by no Means advisable to create two or more Corporations of that Nature'.[177]

The documents related to the application process survive only due to an intrigue that surrounded the chartering process – the 'devious ways' of obtaining charters referred to by Scott.[178] On 12 March 1719/20 one W. Clarke wrote to the Archbishop of York, Sir William Dawes Bt. (a Privy Councillor who had been permanent pastor to William III and Queen Anne), at his Palace in Lambeth, that:

This morning at a very crowded Comittee the Solicitor [General William Thompson] alleged that the Attorney Genirall [Lechmere]… had taken money for makeing a report in favour of a petition about Insurance of ships, wch the Solicitor [Thompson] & A[ttorney] G[eneral Edward] Northey reported against, when referrd to them, tho' each of them was offered a thousand pounds

---

[175] BOE 10A61/7, Humphrey Morice Papers, 1709–1731, f. 2.

[176] BOE 6A49/1, 'Royall Exchange Insurance Company account with Humphrey Morice'.

[177] *The special report of 1720*, pp. 47–48, 57.

[178] Scott, *Joint-stock companies*, III, p. 396.

in money, & 10000^{lt} stock in that project... You may be sure that this is a matter of great xpectation.[179]

The committee referred to by the correspondent was a parliamentary one established to 'inquire into, and examine several Subscriptions for Fisheries, Insurances, Annuities for Lives, and all other Projects carried on by Subscriptions, in and about the Cities of *London* and *Westminster*', which had been struck on 22 February 1719/20. On 1 March the petitions and other documents related to the various insurance promotions were handed over to the committee.[180] Against this backdrop, on 18 March the committee's chairman, John Hungerford, reported to the House of Commons. Hungerford, a barrister of Lincoln's Inn, was a Tory MP of long standing, and former standing council to the East India Company. He had spent seven years in the political wilderness after being expelled from the House in 1695 for bribe-taking.[181] His report included Thompson's bombshell: 'Large Sums of Money have been received by His Majesty's Attorney General [Lechmere], contrary to his Duty... on Account of some of the Matters referred to him... from some of the Persons concerned, and who did solicit the same before him'.[182] The resulting investigation, which called witnesses including Billingsley and many others associated with the insurance company launches, found the accusations against Lechmere to be 'Malicious, False, Scandalous, and utterly Groundless'.[183] The findings were ordered to be published, and the *Special Report* of Hungerford's committee, including otherwise private documents related to the insurance company subscriptions, thus survived.

The Hungerford Committee's findings were reported to parliament on 27 April 1720. As well as detailing the committee's findings in relation to the insurance companies, a long list of other public subscriptions for joint-stock companies was presented, along with Lechmere's recommendations. It was twice resolved 'That the House do agree with the Committee... that the Subscribers having acted as Corporate Bodies, without any legal Authority for their so doing, and thereby drawn in several unwary Persons into unwarrantable Undertakings; the said Practices manifestly tend to the Prejudices of the publick Trade and Commerce of the Kingdom.' The House then ordered 'to bring a Bill to restrain the extravagant and unwarrantable Practice of raising money by voluntary Subscriptions, for carrying on projects dangerous to the Trade and Subjects of this Kingdom: and that Mr Secretary *Craggs*,

---

[179] BOD MS Ballard 20 f. 141, Clarke to Dawes, 12 Mar. 1719/20; Handley, Stuart: 'Dawes, Sir William (1671–1724)', *Oxford Dictionary of National Biography*, Oxford University Press, 2004, www.oxforddnb.com/view/article/7336 [Accessed 3 Dec. 2021].

[180] *The special report of 1720*, p. 3.

[181] Ibid.; Sedgwick, Romney R.: 'Hungerford, John', *History of Parliament*, www. historyofparliamentonline. org/volume/1715-1754/member/hungerford-john-1658-1729 [Accessed 3 Dec. 2021].

[182] *Journals of the House of Commons*, Vol. 19, London: 1803, p. 305.

[183] *The special report of 1720*, p. 13.

Mr. *Walpole…* and Mr. *Hungerford*, do prepare, and bring in, the same'.[184] It was the genesis of the *Bubble Act*.

It looked like Lechmere's recommendations might be followed, but he was embroiled in a controversy. The Attorney General has been remembered by at least one historian to have 'only just survived an investigation for alleged corruption'. A Sunderland Whig, he was removed from his post shortly after the Whig reunion, and was no friend of Walpole.[185] He was replaced by Sir Robert Raymond, the moderate Tory who reportedly had advised Billingsley and Bradley to use obsolete charters as an experiment to legitimise their marine insurance company. The false accusation was more directly painful for Thompson, whose patent as Solicitor General was revoked the day after the finding. One biographer stated that the key reason for Thompson's removal 'seems to have been his association with the ousted Walpole-Townshend group of Whigs', a political group connected by blood to the project through Horatio Townshend's subscription to Chetwynd's Insurance, and one which was to become intimately involved in the end-game of the launch of the joint-stock marine insurers.[186]

Thompson was replaced by Macclesfield's protégé, Philip Yorke, who was aged just twenty-nine. The story, however, did not end with Lechmere's report. As has been shown above, powerful political and partisan corporate forces were backing the two main projections. They were not to fail. According to Plumb, Walpole himself was the architect of a plan to raise £600,000 as a gift for the king to cover the accrued debts of the Civil List, and in so doing to reconcile a rift between the king and his heir, while restoring Walpole's own political fortunes, along with those of Townshend.[187] In this account the source of the funds –parallel gifts of £300,000 from Onslow's and Chetwynd's, in exchange for which they were both to receive charters and carte blanche to raise a joint stock of the size of their choosing, despite Lechmere's advice – is immaterial. Plumb does deliver evidence that shows Walpole himself purchased, on 26 April, shares in each of the companies with a total nominal value of £24,000, for a price of £2,550, and sold them on 12 May for £5,162.10.0, thereby doubling his money in roughly two weeks.[188] Walpole was no doubt regularly informed of the course and development of the companies by his friend William Chapman, and by his brother-in-law Horatio Townshend, whose involvement as a leading investor in Chetwynd's has heretofore gone unnoticed by historians.

On 4 May John Aislabie, the Chancellor of the Exchequer under Sunderland, and so strong an advocate of the South Sea Company that he was later sent to the

---

[184] *Journals of the House of Commons*, Vol. 19, London: 1803, p. 351.

[185] Hanham, A. A.: 'Lechmere, Nicholas, Baron Lechmere (1675–1727)', *Oxford Dictionary of National Biography*, Oxford University Press, 2004, www.oxforddnb.com/view/article/16262 [Accessed 3 Dec. 2021]; Plumb, J. H.: *Sir Robert Walpole: the making of a statesman*, London: Crescent Press, 1956, p. 304.

[186] Lemmings, David: 'Thomson, Sir William (1678–1739)', *Oxford Dictionary of National Biography*, Oxford University Press, 2004; online edn, Jan. 2008, www.oxforddnb.com/view/article/27281 [Accessed 3 Dec. 2021].

[187] Plumb, *Walpole*, pp. 285–292.

[188] Plumb, *Walpole*, p. 291.

Tower over his 'most notorious, dangerous, and infamous corruption' in relation to the affair, brought a message to the Commons from the king. It stated that the charter-seeking insurers had 'offered to advance a considerable Sum of Money, for His Majesty's Use... to enable him to discharge the Debts of His Civil Government without burdening His People with any new Aid or Supply', should they receive the *exclusive* right of incorporation to underwrite marine insurance. The House divided, with 186 in favour of taking the money, and only 72 against. On 12 May (the day Walpole sold his shares) members agreed to combine the bills for restraining joint-stock subscriptions and for chartering the insurers; on 31 May it was passed by a vote of 123 to 22.[189] The Royal Exchange Assurance (Onslow's) and the London Assurance (Chetwynd's) were confirmed as a corporate duopoly in the field of marine insurance, with only private underwriters to compete against them. Alongside their £600,000 gift to the Exchequer, the companies each agreed to loan to the government £156,000, some of which both companies borrowed from the Bank of England, which Supple finds might 'seem to indicate that the loan was a more or less formal condition of incorporation'.[190] Royal assent was granted on 10 June, and on the following day the king, addressing the Commons, said 'it is a particular Satisfaction to me, that a Method has been found out for making good the Deficiencies of my Civil List, without laying any new Burden upon my Subjects'.[191]

Insurance companies possess a secondary speciality in the business of investment. Consequently, control of an insurance company provides control of a stream of investment funds. The favoured investment instrument of the new insurance companies in England in the period before the Bubble burst was South Sea Company securities, particularly their annuities.[192] These activities were enthusiastically pursued as the Bubble – in the shares of the South Sea Company but also in those of the new marine insurers – advanced to dizzying new heights. On 13 July, as South Sea stock was nearing its peak of £980 per share, the Royal Exchange Assurance made application to subscribe £74,300 of the South Sea Company's redeemable debt, in anticipation of the opening of the lists the following month, while of £20,000 of the paid-up capital of the London Assurance, £18,060 was already invested in the South Sea Company's investment instruments.[193, 194] The Royal Exchange also invested heavily in South Sea stock. Even before it was chartered, it was selling East India Company shares to speculate in South Sea paper: shares with a nominal value of £4,500 were sold on 6 October 1719; £200 more on the 15 December; and £2,400 on 11 February 1720, yielding in total £13,050. Scott observes: 'It may be conjectured that

[189] *Journals of the House of Commons*, Vol. 19, London: 1803, pp. 355–356, 361.

[190] Supple, *The Royal Exchange Assurance*, pp. 35, n. 35.

[191] *History and Proceedings of the House of Commons*, Vol. 6: 1714–1727, London: History of Parliament Trust, 1742, pp. 198–218.

[192] John, A. H.: 'Insurance investment and the London money market of the 18th century', *Economica*, New Series, Vol. 20, No. 78 (1953), p. 145; Wright and Fayle, *History of Lloyd's*, p. 63; Scott, *Joint-stock companies*, III, p. 404.

[193] Scott, *Joint-stock companies*, III, p. 404.

[194] *Journals of the House of Commons*, Vol. 19, London: 1803, p. 346.

this realisation was not to pay losses, but for the purpose of purchasing South Sea stock, which was just beginning to advance.'[195]

The South Sea Company itself operated primarily as a vehicle for financial capitalists. Its merchant trade to South America, which the Company's name suggests was its primary corporate function, in practice ranked a very distant second to debt conversion on behalf of the state, and the inflation of share prices to support that enterprise (and enrich the directors and their supporters). Recent attempts to re-evaluate the importance of the Company's commerce, and especially its slave-trading activities, have proved unconvincing.[196] The insurers also seem to have had a secondary activity as a primary interest: creating an investment vehicle for the South Sea Company.

The tactic is commonly employed today, for example by the renowned investor Warren Buffet, whose company National Indemnity is one of the largest insurers in the world. Buffet has explained that it serves to provide investment capital for his other businesses.[197] The key difference is that Buffet's pool of capital is the accumulated insurance premiums held to meet future claims, not cash advanced by speculative investors to purchase shares in the insurance company.

In the wake of the collapse in the value of the companies' South Sea shareholdings, each insurer planned a new subscription to raise the funds required to meet their commitments to the king and the government. Walpole wrote to his friend Chapman, now sub-governor of the London, to reserve a block of shares. Chapman replied that he had included the names of Walpole's 'friends' in his list of those to receive shares, and further that Francis Hawes, another South Sea director and sometimes commercial agent of both Walpole and Chancellor Aislabie, would handle any personal investment.[198] However, the subscriptions were stifled when an official warning was issued to the companies to stick to the terms of their charters, rather than break them by increasing their capital beyond the £1 million ceiling imposed.[199] A news item in the *Gazetteer* revealed that 'Last Tuesday there was a General Council at Whitehall... the Directors of the two assurances attended likewise, to whom, we hear, their Excellencies the Lords Justices were pleas'd to caution them to keep Expressly to the Limitations of their Charter, that no Complaints might lye against them to His Majesty.'[200] This prompted the Royal to announce that 'Whereas the Court of Directors of the Royal Exchange Assurance Company gave Notice, That the Transfer books would be Open on Tuesday next the 30th Instant; they, for several weighty Reasons, have ordered them to continue shut for some

---

[195] Scott, *Joint-stock companies*, III, p. 399.

[196] See, for example, Paul, H. J.: *The South Sea bubble: an economic history of its origins and consequences*, London: Routledge, 2011.

[197] See, for example, Ng, Serena and Holm, Eric: 'Buffett's Berkshire Hathaway buoyed by insurance "float" ', *Wall Street Journal*, 24 Feb. 2011, online edition, http://online.wsj.com/article/SB10001424052748704520504576162782244276342.html [Accessed 3 Dec. 2021].

[198] Plumb, *Walpole*, pp. 314–315; Carswell, *South Sea bubble*, p. 74.

[199] Supple, *The Royal Exchange Assurance*, p. 36.

[200] *Weekly Journal* or *British Gazetteer*, 27 August 1720, p. 1695.

Days longer'. The London, scrambling for cash, announced that 'The Governour and Company of the Corporation of the London Assurance give Notice, that Attendance will be given... in Order to take in the remaining Part of the Receipts commonly called Ram and Colebrook'.[201]

An anonymous pamphleteer, in his 1721 epistle addressed to 'Sir B----n J----n' and entitled *A New-Year's-Gift for the DIRECTORS* [of the South Sea Company] *With some Account of their Plot against The Two Assurances*, contended that the caution was the work of the South Sea Company, 'which was to have render'd those two Assurances (especially the *Royal Exchange*) insolvent, and by that Means to have forced them to forfeit their Charter'.[202] However, this assertion is the only apparent evidence of such a 'plot'. Similarly, the testimony of the embattled John Aislabie, in his second, defensive speech to the House of Lords, is neither corroborated nor specific. The disgraced chancellor told the Lords that 'the *S. Sea Scheme* was becoming *ungovernable*; and some of the wisest of the *Directors*, were so sensible to it, that to do them Justice, I must declare they came to the *Treasury*, and offr'd to advance the Money for the *Civil List* upon sure and easy Terms, rather than that those *Bubbles* [the insurers] should take place. But... those *Projects* and Others, had taken such deep Root in the *House of Commons*, and elsewhere, as made it impossible to oppose them'.[203]

Plumb's assertion that 'the South Sea Directors were bitterly opposed' to the insurance companies was perhaps based on these surviving testaments, but the presence of so many current and past South Sea Company directors among the projectors and investors of the London Assurance must show that if any genuine opposition was coming from the South Sea Company, it was from a faction which excluded Blunt. The directors may have been divided over the question of the insurers and their 'crowding out' of capital which otherwise could fuel continued bubbling of South Sea shares. Perhaps the impassioned statements of Aislabie and the anonymous author of *New Year's Gift* were exaggerations, or were intended to mask from merchant-insurers and others the South Sea Company's involvement in the insurance plays. Certainly Chapman, as both sub-governor of the London and a director of the South Sea, was not bitterly opposed to his own insurer. His correspondence with Walpole indicates a problem; he wrote in August 1720 that 'it is our misfortune (of the Insurances) always to incur from some gentlemen of the South Sea Company a censure', adding that 'I cannot say the Court of Directors [of the South Sea] has as yet done anything to us'.[204] Had a South Sea Company plot existed, Chapman was well placed to see it, but he espied none. Given the timing of this letter and its recipient, however, Chapman may have been writing to distance the insurers from the imploding South Sea Company. It is equally feasible that a plan to create an investment vehicle to fund the South Sea Company's ascent simply spun out of

[201] *Daily Courant*, 27 August 1720, Issue 5882, p. 1.

[202] Anonymous, *A new year's gift for the directors*, London: Printed for T. Bickerton, 1721, p. 24.

[203] Aislebie, John: *Mr. Aislebie's second speech on his defence in the House of Lords on Thursday July 20 1721*, London: printed for J. Roberts, p. 14.

[204] Quoted in Plumb, *Walpole*, p. 314.

control when the insurers' shares rose proportionally even higher. If the South Sea Company directors had such a plan, which the preponderance of evidence tends to suggest, ultimately it backfired.

This research explains the anomaly of the incorporation of two new joint-stock companies alongside an enactment which banned them. The initial impetus to launch the future Royal Exchange Assurance seems to have come from Billingsley, with the support of Thompson. At this point the project appears to have been pure promotion – just as had been the pair's 'York Buildings' scheme for an annuities company, backed by the seized landed assets of Jacobite rebels.[205] No mention is made in the Company's Abstract, a contemporaneous prospectus, of benefitting the nation through improving trade. Instead, it declares that

> EVERY ONE that *subscribes* to this FUND, will have an Opportunity of making a much greater *Improvement* of his *Money*, than he can any other *Way*, And yet will always have it at his own Command by a *Transfer*, Which cannot be done by any *private* Way of *Insurance*. The first *Subscribers* will have considerable *Advantages* before others... And may possibly make above *twice* as much as those that shall come in at *Last*, Because they will pay but *Ten Per Cent.* (unless any-thing extraordinary should require more), And it will be in their Power to direct *Twenty* or *Thirty Per Cent.* to be pay'd by those that come in upon a *second* or *third Subscription*, Whose Share of the *Profits* will not be in proportion to what they *pay*, but to what they *subscribe*.[206]

The addition of the Tory Justus Beck to the promotional team perhaps added the first political leanings, and moved the project in a direction which appears not to have been to the Solicitor General's liking: he did not officially endorse the marine insurer, which he had earlier praised. The promoters, and subsequently the directors of the company, were dominated by Tory merchants in the Levant trade, many with South Sea Company connections. John Williams, Richard Lockwood, Charles Goodfellow, William Astell, and Edward Gibbon all fit this pattern. Of the lead men involved, only Knipe does not; although a senior member of the Levant Company, he was assuredly a Whig, and a director of the Bank. Seeking political influence and limitations on interloping in their trade, the Tory Levant merchants formed an obvious group to support the development of the South Sea Company through an insurer, both to extend the leverage against unauthorised trade with a partner company trading to the west, and to support that company through investment drawn from the wider mercantile community through the insurance premiums paid in support of all trade.[207] Further, this group included surviving merchants who had suffered most by the insolvency of underwriters following the Smyrna convoy loss in 1693. That the initial opposition to the venture was led by Gilbert Heathcote, the staunch Whig who was an early governor of the Bank of England, reinforces the partisan positioning of the future Royal Exchange Assurance.

---

[205] Dickson, *Financial Revolution*, p. 137.

[206] *Abstract of a scheme for an office*, 1717, p. 4.

[207] Defoe, Daniel: *The case fairly stated between the Turky Company and the Italian merchants. By a merchant*, London: J. Roberts, 1720, p. 6.

This motivation seems even more clear in the case of the future London Assurance, a projection of John Lambert. Like the Royal, the London had a peer at its head (motivated no doubt primarily by the opportunity for gain), although ultimately Chetwynd's South Sea Company connections were widely publicised and condemned. Subscriber Horatio Townshend was another South Sea Company man, and brought political connections at the highest level. William Chapman, Jacob Jacobsen, Hugh Raymond, Robert Chester, Richard Houlditch, William Morley, Thomas Reynolds, Theodore Janssen, Charles Joye, Lambert Blackwell, and John Blunt were current directors of the South Sea Company – making eleven of thirty-four active promoters of the marine insurer. Thus, if the limitations on the formation of joint-stock companies passed with the *Bubble Act* were made in the interests of the South Sea Company, it is no anomaly that the chartering of two new joint-stock marine insurers occurred concurrently. As Malachy Postlethwayt wrote in his article entry entitled simply 'Bubble', in his 1774 *Universal Dictionary of trade and commerce*, 'The surprizing rise of the South Sea stock in the city of London, in the year 1720, gave birth to these [bubble] projects: for the first designers of them gave out these proposals, with the hopes of raising a sum, which they intended privately to be laid out in South Sea stock, expecting by the rise thereof to refund the subscribers money, with a great gain to themselves.'[208] The political endorsement of Walpole, whose interests were both financial and political, and were supported through ties of kinship and friendship, sealed the deal. A group of financial capitalists, a subset of the outsider-sellers, had completed the second significant intervention into the operations of London's insurance market.

The intervention did not move to address the complaints about abuses levelled in the decades which preceded the Act. During the debate, the arguments advanced in favour of the chartering of joint-stock insurers were primarily attacks on the existing market institutions of the merchant-insurers. None were made to address the long-standing challenges arising from outsiders' participation in the market. The debating points were new. Proponents of the joint-stock companies argued that the solvency of individual underwriters was dubious, and less secure than would be a corporation with a fixed joint-stock. One witness, the Levant merchant and former MP Joseph Paice, testified that thirty-three London 'Assurers and Office-Keepers had failed to his knowledge, by whom he and his Principals have lost very considerable Sums of Money'.[209] The number includes brokers as well as underwriters, and, in the latter group, at least nineteen who were made bankrupt twenty-six years earlier by the Smyrna disaster. A further complaint, described above, argued that individual underwriters could not provide adequate levels of cover to meet merchant demands. On the one hand, extant policies prove this complaint to be spurious.[210] On the other,

---

[208] Postlethwayt, Malachy: *Universal Dictionary of trade and commerce*, fourth edition, Vol. I, London: printed for W. Strahan and twenty-six others, 1774 (first published 1755, unpaginated).

[209] *The special report of 1720*, certificate of Joseph Paice, p. 43; Watson, Paula: 'Paice, Joseph', *History of Parliament Online*, www.historyofparliamentonline.org/volume/1690-1715/member/paice-joseph-1658-1735 [Accessed 3 Dec. 2021].

[210] See p. 163.

competing testimony also denied that insurance supply was restricted. The merchant-insurer John Barnard stated that 'five, ten, and twenty thousand Pounds and upwards have been Insured in one Policy'.[211] The third major argument advanced was that of the need for multiple lawsuits to resolve disputes. This complaint has also been discussed above; according to Barnard's testimony, common practice was for all underwriters to follow the outcome of a suit against one.[212]

Very few individuals, including the Attorney General, Nicholas Lechmere, objected in principle to the creation of a joint-stock company to underwrite marine insurance. However, concerns that such a company or companies could be granted, or could assume through market manipulation, a monopoly over marine insurance underwriting were widespread and genuine. The joint opinion of the king's law officers was to advise against them. They were concerned that a functioning market, with its supporting institutional infrastructure, could be displaced by one which had not been tested, and which might not operate as efficiently in its role as a catalyst of trade.[213] Because, as has been shown, the balance of motivations for creating a duopoly over corporate underwriting lay outside the desire to improve the functioning of the market, the arguments supporting their receipt of royal sanction were at best minor ones, and at worst, simply spurious.

Unlike the initiatives of 1570–1601, the impact of the intervention of 1720 was to create an entirely new structural basis for underwriting. However, since the incumbent approach to underwriting by individuals according to custom and the Law Merchant was not proscribed, the new system became only a parallel structure. Further, it did not address the challenges posed to the market by outsiders who did not wish to play by the rules of the merchant-insurers. This remained a challenge to be solved over the course of the eighteenth century, through the developments of the third major intervention into the institutions of the London marine insurance market. Meanwhile, by preventing further competition from joint-stock companies or any other entities, including even private partnerships, and because, as will be shown, the Royal Exchange Assurance and the London Assurance did not gain significant market shares in marine insurance, the *Bubble Act* of 1720 became, in effect, an incubator which allowed the customs and practices of London's merchant-insurers to survive and thrive.

Insurance and the intervention in the Americas

After the restrictive provisions of the *Bubble Act* were extended in 1741 to cover Britain's North American colonies, the 1720 intervention had a significant impact on underwriting in the Americas, where they remained in effect to prohibit corporate underwriting until independence and the resulting revocation of British legal jurisdiction.[214] Extant correspondence shows clearly and repeatedly that merchants

---

[211] *The special report of 1720*, testimony of John Barnard, p. 44.

[212] See pp. 96–97.

[213] *The special report of 1720*, p. 28.

[214] Index, *House of Commons Sessional Papers of the Eighteenth Century 1715–1800*, p. 90.

resident in America purchased insurance from their London suppliers and agents, despite the evolution of a local market of private underwriters which emerged to compete. For example, in the years 1664 to 1667 the English merchant Charles Marescoe underwrote insurance in London, through brokers, for voyages from Virginia and New England to English ports.[215] Insurance was often purchased in London by local merchants exporting to the Americas, sometimes following clients' instructions, and with the cost sometimes borne by their clients. When Joseph Cruttenden, a London suppler of apothecaries' materials, wrote in 1710 to his Boston-based client Habijah Savage, he stated that 'I have complyd with your desire and charged but $6^{lt}5$ pCent advance on all the things now sent... allowing for insurance which may be high'. Later Cruttenden wrote to another Boston client, John Nichols, 'You see by the invoice I have charged you with the Ensurance which was done with your ffriends consent, for it was noe way reasonable for me to run the risque.'[216]

As transatlantic trade increased, the American colonies became an increasingly important insurance market for London underwriters. Meanwhile, many American merchants began underwriting local risks, in line with the growth of American trade to other British colonies and elsewhere. They followed the marine insurance practices that prevailed in London. In Philadelphia in 1721 demand for local insurance was sufficient to encourage one John Copson to launch an insurance brokerage office. His advertisement of May 25 that year in the *American Weekly Mercury* announced the opening by him of an 'Office of Publick Insurance on Vessels, Goods and Merchandizes'. It has been widely regarded as marking the advent of local insurance in the British American colonies. The announcement stated that 'the merchants of this City of Philadelphia and other ports have been obliged to send to London for such insurance, which has not only been tedious and troublesome, but ever precarious, and for the remedying of which this office is opened'. Copson promised that the underwriters would 'be Persons of undoubted Worth and Reputation', but no other record of the venture has survived. By mid century insurance brokers were recorded in Philadelphia and Boston.[217]

Among British North America's fledging merchant-insurer community was Obadiah Brown, a prominent merchant, ship owner, and manufacturer active in Rhode Island. His *Risk Book* records 161 marine insurances he underwrote between 1753 and 1762, nearly half of which covered voyages to or from Surinam, Jamaica, or Hispaniola, and shows that Brown achieved a pure underwriting profit of £1,045

[215] Roseveare, *Markets and merchants*, Appendix E, pp. 582–588.

[216] Letterbook of Joseph Cruttenden, letter 17 June 1710, to Habijah Savage, Boston; letter 28 July 1714, to John Nichols, Boston, Bodleian Library, MS Rawl. Lett. 66, pp. 17–18, 158–159.

[217] Huebner, Solomon: 'The development and present status of marine insurance in the United States', *Annals of the American Academy of Political and Social Science*, Vol. 26, (Sept. 1905), p. 423; Crothers, A. Glenn: 'Commercial risk and capital formation in early America: Virginia merchants and the rise of American marine insurance, 1750–1815', *Business History Review*, Vol. 78, No. 4 (Winter, 2004), p. 611.

during his recorded experience as a marine insurer.[218] Local underwriters had competitive advantages over the London underwriters they emulated. They possessed clear information for risks in their hemisphere, paid losses locally, and eliminated both a level of agency cost and significant problems of delay. However, insurance was generally cheaper in London, and its underwriters were perceived to be more creditworthy. 'Our Premium are about 70 per Cent more then are paid in London', New York merchant Waddell Cunningham reported to his business partner in 1756.[219] Further, the colonial insurance market was divided between its major commercial ports, was unable to match the concentration or organisation achieved at Lloyd's, and had no international diversification.[220] Therefore, a significant proportion of American risks added to the London risk pool, and the city remained the colonies' chief source of coverage.

Pares noted, based on his examination of contemporary correspondence by American merchants in the Caribbean trade, that 'London underwriters disliked policies for vessels whose condition they could not judge because they had never seen them, on cross voyages [those which do not touch at the underwriter's home port] whose risks they could not estimate, stuffed with all sorts of contingent additions or returns of premium according that the vessel might touch at this island or not touch at that. They would protect themselves by charging higher premiums than an American underwriter, and they might not touch the policy at all.'[221] Some evidence supports Pares's assertion, although underwriters' records from the era show plainly that London merchant-insurers did insure the distant trade between British North America and the Caribbean.

For example, on 7 February 1759 the London wine merchant and prominent marine insurance underwriter William Braund insured the vessel *Sally* on her voyage from New York to the Leeward Islands at the rate of 15%. The following day, however, he insured the slaver *Chesterfield* from Liverpool to Guinea and the West Indies for just 12%. The insurance of the latter culminated in a claim; the vessel was captured by the French. The failed voyage was a Liverpool venture, but American slaving vessels were also sometimes insured in London for the triangular voyage. For example, a few months later the owners of the Charleston-registered, New England-built, 16-gun *Bance Island* bought cover from Braund through a broker, William Oswald, for its voyage from London to Africa and the West Indies (Braund was unlucky; this

---

[218] Brown, Obadiah: 'Marine insurance book, 1753–1762'. Rhode Island Historical Society (RIHS), MSS 315/SS4/2/32; for a detailed discussion of Brown's underwriting, see Leonard, A. B.: 'From local to transatlantic: insuring trade in the Caribbean', in Leonard, A. B. and Pretel, D.: *The Caribbean and the Atlantic World Economy: Circuits of trade, money and knowledge, 1650–1914*, Basingstoke: Palgrave Macmillan, 2015, pp. 137–159.

[219] Cunningham to Thomas Greg, 10.05.1756 *Letterbook of Greg & Cunningham*, p. 114.

[220] Kingston, C.: 'Marine insurance in Britain and America, 1720–1844: a comparative institutional analysis', *Journal of Economic History*, Vol. 67, No. 2 (June 2007), pp. 391–393.

[221] For the overall dominance of London in the insurance of Atlantic commerce, see, for example, Huebner, *Development and present status*, p. 433. Crothers, *Commercial risk and capital*, p. 612. Pares, Richard: *Yankees and Creoles: the trade between North America and the West Indies before the American Revolution*, London: Longmans, Green & Co., 1956, pp. 4, 23.

vessel too was seized by the French). European voyages dominate Braund's under-writing record, and reflect the continued great importance of European markets throughout the long eighteenth century, but voyages to or from the western Atlantic were also very commonly insured by Braund, as were East India and slave voyages. Cross-risks in the Americas are far less numerous in the record, but could not be considered unusual. In August 1759, to offer one more example of many, the London merchant-insurer put a line of £100 on the *Mary* for a trading voyage from Boston to the Leeward Islands and Jamaica, for a premium of eight guineas per cent. Even in wartime, the rates Braund charged for these distant voyages were strikingly compet-itive with those charged by Brown for what were, for the Rhode Island underwriter, relatively local voyages. His underwriting terms offered scope for the insured to ply the British Caribbean without breaching his cover, or requiring 'all sorts of contin-gent additions or returns of premium'.[222]

London's marine insurance market was thus engaged seriously and directly in the provision of cover for merchants on both the eastern and western borders of the Atlantic World, for their transatlantic voyages and their regional trade. Few extant bundles of merchant correspondence do not include references to transat-lantic insurance-buying. For example, the Boston merchant Henry Lloyd, writing to London clients in November 1765, requested that they 'make insurance to the value of the cargo' which was to be shipped westwards to England.[223] Agents repre-senting underwriters at Lloyd's were present in Virginia, Alexandria, Baltimore, and Norfolk at least as early as the 1780s.[224] American merchants therefore must have at least sometimes preferred the inconveniences of using London underwriters to the alternative of insuring at home, despite the challenges of time and distance that accompanied the use of an overseas financial services market.

Nonetheless, the private insurance market in Rhode Island appears to have been operational in 1794. That year Charles DeWolf (rendered in the policy D'Wolfe), who was a member of a prominent Rhode Island merchant family and brother of the better-known merchant, slaver, and later senator James DeWolf, insured his vessel *Sally* and its cargo with private underwriters for £600 'Lawful Money' to cover a voyage from Havana to his home port of Bristol, Rhode Island. The risk was divided between four underwriters, including the partnership Gibbs & Channing, a Rhode Island merchant firm headed by Walter Channing and George Gibbs. One element of continuity is recourse to arbitration: a clause in the printed policy states 'in Case of any Dispute arising hereupon, the Matter in Controversy shall be submitted to, and decided by Referees, chosen by each party'. The DeWolf policy bears the name of no intermediary, but another, issued in Boston the same year, was 'Underwritten in the Office kept by *Peter Chardon Brooks*', a Boston merchant and insurer who

---

[222] ECRO D/DRu B7, William Braund's *Journal of Risks, 1759–1765; Trans-Atlantic Slave Trade Database*, www.slavevoyages.org [Accessed 3 Dec. 2021]. For the life and business interests of Braund, see Sutherland, Lucy: *A London merchant, 1695–1744*, London: Oxford University Press, 1933.

[223] Cole, Arthur H.: 'Tempo of mercantile life in colonial America', *Business History Review*, Autumn 1959, 33, p. 287.

[224] Crothers, *Commercial risk and capital*, p. 611.

in 1789 reportedly 'engaged in the business of marine insurance, and accumulated a large fortune'. Brooks went on in 1806 to become president of the New England Insurance Company. The 1794 policy grants cover of £900 on the schooner *Nancy* and her cargo for a voyage from Boston to Baltimore and back, and was underwritten by five private individuals.[225]

American independence released the nascent United States from the prohibition of corporate underwriting set out in the *Bubble Act* of 1720, and a number of marine insurance companies were formed shortly afterwards, as US merchants 'energetically developed domestic sources of marine insurance', according to Crothers. The first was the Insurance Company of North America, established by Philadelphia merchants in 1792 with authorised capital of $600,000, although it began operations with just $40,000 in subscriptions. Many others soon followed. The corporate structure of the new US insurers was not standard; some underwrote with a limitation of shareholders' liability, while others underwrote with explicitly unlimited shareholder liability. Most had explicit protections against joint liability among the shareholders. Other underwriting associations were unincorporated groups of merchant-insurers, constituting simply a syndicate of private underwriters (often referred to as a 'Lloyds'), although they could raise and hold mutual capital. Most companies were launched by merchants, who simply took the traditions of the merchant-insurers of old into a new corporate structure (such as the thirty-nine individuals underwriting in Canada as the 'Halifax Marine Insurance Company').[226] Absent the limitation of a restriction of the number of corporate underwriting entities permitted, in the United States their formation proved a successful intervention.

[225] ALC, uncatalogued: policy underwritten for Charles D'Wolfe, 29 Mar. 1794; policy underwritten for Wales and Field, 17 Sept. 1794; Wilson, J. G. and Fiske, John (eds): 'BROOKS, Peter Chardon', in *Appleton's cyclopaedia of American biography*, Vol. 1, New York: Appleton & Co., 1887, p. 389.

[226] Crothers, *Commercial risk and capital*, pp. 615–616; Testimony of Jones, Jenkin: '*Report from the Select Committee on Marine Insurance (Sess. 1810), 5 March 1810*', House of Commons, BPP (226) 1810 IV 247, reprinted 11.5.1824, pp. 36–39; Leonard, *From local to transatlantic*, p. 154; see above, p. 64.

4.

To 1824: Lloyd's and the common law

The effect of the second intervention

The Royal Exchange Assurance and the London Assurance had the potential to change the structure of the London insurance market beyond recognition. This did not happen; their marine insurance business did not flourish. The new companies did well at the outset: John Williams, deputy governor of the future Royal, told the Hungerford Committee that the insurer, in its first nine months of operation, had insured ships and goods to the value of £1,259,604.[1] In 1810, a pamphleteer identifying himself only as a subscriber to Lloyd's estimated credibly, based on this figure, that both companies together had underwritten a tenth of the country's marine insurance.[2] Eight merchants sent a petition to the committee stating that 'they had assured their Adventures at Sea, to a considerable Value, with [the Royal], some of which having been Losses or Averages, [were] Adjusted and paid… according to their Contract, without Delay, to entire Satisfaction'. Further, Sir Justus Beck certified that he and 'several other Merchants of *London*… have for this present Year received very considerable Commissions from Merchants in Foreign Parts, to make Assurances in *London*', and that those orders were to be filled with the companies.[3]

Still, the companies' immediate fortunes were not good. Both 'had invested largely in South Sea Stock', and 'had sustained a heavy loss on twelve Jamaica ships'. These bad investments caused their share prices to collapse.[4] They were unable to meet the payments owed to the government under the conditions of their charters, and sought relief. Further subscriptions, which would have raised their nominal capital (if not their paid-up capital) beyond the limits specified in their charters, were halted by government intervention. They did not make significant additional calls upon their existing shareholders to increase their paid-up capital; presumably this constituency was reeling under other Bubble-era losses. In order to survive,

---

[1] *Journals of the House of Commons*, Vol. XIX (1803), p. 344.

[2] A subscriber to Lloyd's: *A letter to Jasper Vaux*, London: Printed for J. M. Richardson, 1810, p. 47.

[3] *The special report of 1720*, affidavit of eight merchants, pp. 41–42.

[4] A subscriber, *A letter*, p. 44, cites Malachy Postlethwayt for the loss of a dozen Jamaicamen. The claim is repeated in Relton, Francis Boyer: *An account of the fire insurance companies*, London: Swan Sonnenschein & Co., 1893, p. 156.

both companies sought, and were granted, charters to underwrite fire and life assurance.[5] In the words of Wright and Fayle, 'the companies' difficulty was the [private] underwriters' opportunity'.[6] Thereafter the companies were unable ever to obtain a position of significance in London's marine insurance marketplace (although both remained active in this class of insurance, as do their descendants). By 1809, their share of the national market had fallen from about 10% to slightly more than 4%. Private underwriters, by one reckoning based on stamp duties, insured goods and vessels in the amount of £140 million, the companies about £5.2 million.[7]

Asymmetry in the insurance market has been proposed as the main challenge which the companies could not overcome, since private insurers' superior information gave them a significant advantage over corporate rivals in the post-1720 environment.[8] An information advantage may have existed, although this was unlikely to have been significant. At least one of the companies had equal access to the same information networks as private underwriters, as a member of the Society of Lloyd's. Further, brokers – who worked both with the companies and the private insurers – were another, perhaps leading source of knowledge equalisation. Similarly, information asymmetries surely existed among the private underwriters, some of whom were thoroughly embedded in the business from day to day, while others were mere dabblers. The London insurance market, dispersed at the Royal Exchange proper, at Lloyd's Coffee-house, on Lombard Street, in Change Alley, and elsewhere, was a market of individuals, and as such it was fiercely competitive.

Even if an information deficit did disadvantage the companies, other relevant factors were more important to the limitation of their success in marine insurance. Among these is the fundamental desirability of employing multiple underwriting bodies to spread large risks as widely as possible. This reality of insurance underwriting was the reason underlying the chief factor which limited the scope of the companies' marine insurance underwriting: the actual risk appetites of the London and the Royal Exchange Assurance companies. Despite hopes and fears that they could assume all of Britain's marine business, their risk appetites were limited, perhaps because the loss of the dozen Jamaica vessels which they had insured in their first year as chartered companies showed starkly how a large, concentrated loss could deal a costly and considerable blow to underwriting entities which held significant shares of all of the risks involved in such a loss. Soon after, the companies limited the types and values of risks that they would underwrite, and maintained such limitations for the balance of the period under review. For example, of £148,100 insured on the Indiaman *Scaleby Castle* in 1799, one of the companies underwrote only £10,000,

---

5   For an account of these very early difficulties of the duopoly companies, see Supple, *Royal Exchange Assurance*, pp. 34–44.

6   Wright and Fayle, *History of Lloyd's*, p. 63.

7   *Report from the Select Committee on Marine Insurance, Sess. 1810*, London: House of Commons, 1824, committee report, p. 3, testimony of J. J. Angerstein, p. 68.

8   Kingston, Christopher: 'Marine insurance in Britain and America, 1720–1844: a comparative institutional analysis', *Journal of Economic History*, Vol. 67, No. 2 (2007), pp. 379–409.

the other nothing, despite the vessel owners' desire for even greater coverage than was achieved. Private underwriters did the rest.[9]

However, pricing was the companies' most obvious disadvantage in competition with the individual underwriters. Their standard rates were higher than those of private underwriters, even for the same risks, as they sought to limit their exposures. The Royal Exchange Assurance charged 20% more than every other underwriter involved in the *Scaleby Castle* policy.[10] By the later eighteenth century, unlike the practice among private underwriters, both companies regularly charged more to insure vessels considered inferior, which does not imply reduced access to information, but a greater willingness to employ that which they possessed in the process of active underwriting.[11] According to Supple, 'the two chartered corporations approached the expanding demand for insurance with such caution as to retain only a very small proportion', approximately 4% between them.[12]

The second intervention was, however, to have an indirect, entirely unintended, but particularly important impact on marine insurance underwriting in London. Prior to the Act, subscribers to insurance policies sometimes included individuals underwriting in the name of a commercial partnership, or on behalf of a special-purpose insuring venture.[13] Under the Act of 1720, such underwriting was prohibited. An important impact of this limitation was explained in 1810 by Joseph Marryat, a merchant, broker-underwriter, and Lloyd's parliamentary spokesman.[14] In his pamphlet *Observations on the report of the committee on marine insurance* he stated that the limitation meant that the funds accumulated to pay insurance claims were not intermingled with those invested through commercial partnerships' other 'mercantile speculations'. He argued that failed partnerships typically pay 'little or nothing' of their debts, while a failed individual 'very typically pays in full'.[15]

While an elegant argument, in practice the strict limitation of underwriting to individuals seems not always to have been observed. For example, the merchant-insurer Peter Du Cane, who commenced extant records of his underwriting activity in 1737, headed the relevant ledger entries 'D^r to Insurances on the Joint of Edmund Boehm & myself for Policys underwrote by me', indicating that Du Cane's individual underwriting was indeed carried out on behalf of a partnership, in violation of the law.[16] A prosecution for breaking this prohibition does not appear to have occurred until 1789, in *Sullivan* v. *Greaves*. The plaintiff, and underwriter, had written a line on

---

[9]   *Report from the Select Committee*, p. 21, testimony of George Simson.

[10]   Ibid.

[11]   Eden, *Insurance charters*, p. 31.

[12]   Supple, *Royal Exchange Assurance*, p. 53.

[13]   See, for example, p. 71.

[14]   Taylor, Lawrence and Fisher, David: 'Marryat, Joseph', *History of Parliament Online*, www. historyofparliamentonline.org/volume/1790-1820/member/marryat-joseph-1757-1824 [Accessed Dec. 2021].

[15]   Marryat, Joseph: *Observations on the report of the committee on marine insurance*, London: Printed by W. Hughes, 1810, p. 50.

[16]   ECRO D/DDc A16, Journals of Peter Du Cane, 1735–1744, 31 Dec. 1837.

behalf of himself and a third party, Mr Bristow, who had paid his share of a loss to the defendant, the broker of the policy. Sullivan sought to recover Bristow's share of the claim paid from Greaves, the broker. Lord Chief Justice Kenyon supported the non-payment, describing the arrangement as 'clearly a partnership within the Act', and the contract between Sullivan and Greaves to share in the underwriting proportionately as 'founded on a breach of the law'.[17] The case highlights a particular truism about marine insurance (and indeed any other sort of non-life insurance protection). As a contract based on trust, it may be illegal *per se*, but the impact of this breach is limited to its unenforceability in the courts.

Perhaps more concretely, Marryat explained how the customs of the London insurance market which determined cash-flows meant that 'the holders of policies of assurance' underwritten at Lloyd's were granted 'so much [more] security' than that 'given by law to any other description of merchant creditors'. In the case of debts arising from insurance claims, he wrote, an underwriter 'cannot but have funds sufficient, or nearly sufficient, to pay his losses'. By convention, claims were at this time paid within one month. However, premiums were not collected until 'after the expiration of the year... thus the underwriter, from one year to another, has always a capital advanced, which it is out of his power to dispose of in any possible way. This capital, so locked up, serves as a deposit made for the security of the assured.'[18]

Given the limited role of the duopoly companies, the second intervention could be looked upon as a failure. It provided an alternative underwriting structure for some of London's customers, but it did not change the underlying structure of the market. Instead, since competition of all types was prohibited, and was to remain so for more than a century, it allowed the merchant-insurers, who continued to operate according to custom and under the Law Merchant, to flourish. The problem which earlier interventions had attempted to solve – that of outsiders trading in the market, and sometimes refusing to do so by the rules – was not addressed. By returning, in effect, to governance under the institutional structures introduced by Lombard merchants in the fifteenth century, London's insurance market continued to face the problem of outsiders who did not wish to play by the rules of the game, which had first arisen in the later sixteenth century.

The challenge was at last answered over about four decades, through an intervention beginning in the 1740s. It had three major strands. First, parliament grappled with draft legislation which was intended to deal with the transgressions of some outsider-buyers, and with activity by outsider-sellers which was deemed either inconsistent with custom, or with the national interest. Second, a body of legal principles covering insurance issues was incorporated into the common law through decisions at the King's Bench, which had emerged as the leading formal jurisdiction for insurance disputes. Third, after several decades of trading in an institutional vacuum, a group of merchant-insurers created their own, self-governing institutions to regulate

---

[17] Raynes's recounting of this case is entirely incorrect; he has the underwriter accepting risk on behalf of the broker. Park, J. A.: *A system of the law of marine insurances*, sixth edition, London: Butterworths, 1809 (first published 1787), p. 8; Raynes, *British insurance*, p. 160.

[18] Marryat, *Observations*, pp. 50–52.

practice in the market. The understanding of the rules of the game based on the longstanding practices of Lombard Street and the Royal Exchange, and resolution of disputes through agreement and arbitration, continued to govern market practice within their new institutional structure, through cooperation with state institutions.

Jones describes the second process as 'the engulfment of the Law Merchant by the common law of England'.[19] The project was championed by Lord Justice Mansfield. Like the Privy Council two hundred years earlier, Mansfield worked to ensure that prevailing merchant practice was the source of the key principles underlying the new common law. The Law Merchant, as it applied to insurance, was concertedly incorporated into the precedents of common law, in sympathetic response to and in cooperation with evolving merchant practice. The formal courts were at last equipped to handle outsiders' disputes according to insider custom, despite the ultimate victory of the common law over the more flexible and better-suited civil law, after 200 years of rivalry.

The third intervention created a dual solution to the outsider problem which incorporated increasingly sophisticated self-organisation on the part of the merchant-insurers and the exogenous but sympathetic intervention of the state's formal institutions to create an aligned operational and dispute-resolution environment which could operate harmoniously with that of the merchant-insurers. The dual structure established through this parallel effort of market and state was to create the system which allowed London's market of private underwriters successfully to continue its dominance of British and international insurance. It infused certainty by aligning the merchant-insurers' old rules of the game with the external mechanisms which governed insurance disputes outside the customary system. As Britain's trade continued to expand (due in part to eighteenth-century government stimulus), each component of the intervention made the system increasingly able to cope. Ultimately, London insurance practice was exported and adopted elsewhere, cementing London's position at the centre of a world-economy in insurance, and forming the basis for insurance underwriting around the world.[20]

Parliamentary interventions of the 1740s

If war characterised the period between William's accession in 1689 and the Peace of Utrecht in 1713, a growing sense of national optimism, confidence, and pride did so for the twenty-five years that followed.[21] Commerce and finance grew in importance and in volume; with some fluctuation, British overseas trade was roughly stagnant between 1700 and 1720, but grew steadily thereafter. Exports of British produce and manufactures increased by roughly two and a half times between 1700 and 1750. The nation's merchant marine began to grow with them.[22] It is impossible to say

---

[19] Jones, 'Elizabethan marine insurance', p. 57.

[20] For example, see Leonard, *Underwriting British trade*, 2012.

[21] Porter, Roy: *English society in the 18th century*, London: Penguin, 1982, pp. 7–11.

[22] Wilson, Charles: *England's apprenticeship 1603–1763*, second edition, Harlow: Longman 1984 (first published 1965), pp. 264, 268–269, 276.

how common was the insurance of cargoes in peacetime during the mid century, but the absolute number of vessels and the volume of goods which could be insured was rising significantly. Unfortunately no comprehensive example of an English underwriter's records, which provide the most complete picture of insurance purchasing for any period, has been discovered for any time before December 1737, when the ledgers of Peter Du Cane begin to include his record of 'Policys underwrote by me'.[23] This was peacetime, and Du Cane accepted a very broad range of risks on vessels and cargoes travelling the world over, but already political tensions were high, especially in South Atlantic waters. Many merchants bought insurance. Following the outbreak of war Du Cane underwrote many more risks than in earlier years, almost always at rates higher than during the preceding peace, although this alone does not indicate a greater uptake of insurance. Du Cane could have increased his subscriptions to take advantage of the higher market prices.

Even decades before, many foreign risks had been insured in London because its prices were lower than those offered in other underwriting centres, or had been reinsured in the city to arbitrage the differential.[24] By the 1740s London had become the leading European centre of insurance, as John Barnard testified to parliament in 1741/2, describing as 'incontestible' his assertion that insurance was 'now carried on, chiefly by this nation, though not solely'.[25] A significant proportion of the insurances for international trade purchased by the merchants of France, Spain, Portugal, Sweden, and the United States was underwritten in London.[26] It is not possible to identify the precise moment when insurance-buying went from being a multi-local activity to one in which a 'world-economy' with a single city at its epicentre came to dominate. Certainly, this process took many decades. This shift had taken place by the outset of the 1740s, after more than a century of international insurance-buying in London.

The combination of this international breadth and Britain's frequent wars meant that some insurance buyers became enemy traders. In 1746, for example, the London Assurance paid claims of £18,000 to Spanish and French policyholders for losses arising from British captures during the War of the Austrian Succession.[27] Unlike the situation in 'Holland, France, Sweden, and most other countries', where insuring enemy vessels and property was prohibited, in Britain it was tacitly permitted, and had become common practice.[28] Insuring the enemy was not typically an accidental happenstance. Rather, it was a minor but important part of the business, partly no doubt because it was lucrative, but also because it had a significant positive impact

---

[23] ECRO D/DDc A16, Journals of Peter Du Cane, 1735–1744, 31 Dec. 1837.

[24] *The special report of 1720*, testimony of John Barnard, p. 44.

[25] *Cobbett's Parliamentary History of England*, Vol. XII, A.D. 1741–1743, London: T.C. Hansard, 1812, col. 9.

[26] *Parliamentary History*, Vol. XIV, A.D. 1747–1753, London: T.C. Hansard, 1813, cols 108–133.

[27] John, A. H.: 'The London Assurance Company and the marine insurance market of the eighteenth century', *Economica* 25 (1958), pp. 126–141.

[28] Weskett, *Complete digest*, p. 292.

on underwriters' expanding portfolios of insured risks. If one insured only British shipping, and a Smyrna-style military event were to occur, claims against an individual insurer or the market as a whole could have been unbearable. If, however, the goods and vessels of the victorious side were also insured, allied losses could more easily be met, and perhaps a profit secured, as the claims were correlated negatively with those made by enemy insureds.

However, even before wars commenced, as the clouds gathered London underwriters would exclude coverage of losses arising from capture by British naval forces. Du Cane did so in May 1738, when, through a broker who no doubt set the policy's terms and conditions, he wrote an extraordinary line of £150 on

> the Ship Nª Sⁿ Delas Augustias Sᵗ Antonia de Padua, alias El Canaries, Capt. Gonzales Travitso, from Grand Canaries to Guaira [in modern Venezuela], to Porta Cabello on the Coast of Carracas, and back to Guaira, and during her stay in each Port, & back to Sᵗᵃ Crixa in the Grand Canaries with Liberty to touch at Puerto Rico, @ £7½ PCᵗ 98, *Warranted free from English Capture* _ _ _ _ _ _ 11:5:0.[29]

The policy was issued when the forthcoming trade war with Spain was easily predictable. The Spanish *Guarda-Costa* was harassing British shipping in the West Indies, and parliament had already petitioned the king to seek redress, which was soon to come in the form of the War of Jenkins' Ear.[30] The same month, Du Cane wrote a policy for an English vessel 'Warranted free from Spanish Capture in any Port or road of Spain'.[31]

In the early 1740s, when the 'armed contest for empire between Britain and France was about to begin', insuring the enemy became a public and political issue.[32] This occurred at a time when lawmaking was a booming activity in England: the number of acts of Parliament rose from an average per session of fifty-eight under George I to 254 under his grandson.[33] Hoppit calculated that of 2,442 acts of parliament related to 'economic' issues passed between 1660 and 1800, which applied nationally or internationally, 1,490, or 61%, were passed during the final 40 years of the period, and 520 general economic acts were passed by the parliaments which sat between 1714 and 1760, compared to just 432 during the 54 years following the Restoration.[34]

Insurance did not escape the legislative tide. The debate over insuring the enemy advanced to parliament in 1741/2, with a *Bill to prevent the Inconveniences arising from the Insurance of Ships*. It included, among other provisions, the prohibition of

---

[29] This entry relates the vessel's full name, its common name, the master's name, the voyage, the rate, the deductible (2%), any conditions, and the premium paid. Emphasis added. Journals of Peter Du Cane, 1735–1744, 31.04.1738. ECRO, D/DDc A16.

[30] Pares, *Yankees and Creoles*, pp. 30–32.

[31] Journals of Peter Du Cane, 1735–1744, 31.04.1738. ECRO, D/DDc A16.

[32] Holmes, G. & Szechi, D.: *Age of oligarchy: pre-industrial Britain 1722–1783*, London: Longman, 1993, p. 63.

[33] Langford, Paul: *A polite and commercial people: England 1727–1783*, Oxford: Oxford University Press, 1989, p. 298; Lieberman, *Province of legislation determined*, p. 13.

[34] Hoppit, *Britain's political economies*, Table 3.2, p. 71.

underwriting insurance or reinsurance upon 'Ships or Effects of the Subjects of any Prince or State, not in Amity with the Crown of *Great Britain*'.[35] The bill's proposer was the Bristol MP Edward Southwell, who was an agent of the city's merchant community.[36] Although some private insurance was underwritten in the outports, the vast majority of the business was transacted in London. Provincial traders, especially West India merchants, would not lose business through a ban, but potentially would gain through damage to competitors' commerce. The opposition was led by the underwriter Sir John Barnard, elected to represent London in 1722 based on popularity he garnered opposing the chartered companies, and through his work in 1721 to represent merchants' opposition to a bill detrimental to the wine trade, his chief merchant interest outside marine insurance.[37] Barnard argued that the business affected would simply move to another country, at the expense of London's underwriters, since there were 'offices of insurance along the whole coast of the Midland Sea, among the Belgians and even among the French... That this trade is now carried on, chiefly by this Nation, tho' not solely, is incontestable; but what can be inferred from that, but that we ought not to obstruct our own gain'. Even if the insurance business was not profitable, Barnard argued, 'there is a certain Advantage to the nation by the Money paid for Commission, Brokerage, Stamps [duties] and the Credit of Premium deposited here [that is, investment income]', and even a benefit to the Post Office.

Robert Walpole argued that the interests of the wider public, and not a select group of merchants, should be considered. 'Men unacquainted with the secret practices of our Merchants, do not suspect us of being stupid enough to secure our Enemies against ourselves... but it is often discovered... that the loss of the Spanish is to be repaid, and perhaps sometimes with interest, by the British insurers... the Insurance of Spanish ships ought to be prohibited, we shall indeed lose the Profit of the Insurance, but we shall be re-imburs'd by the Captures [of Spanish vessels]'.[38] In a ringing endorsement of the blue-water approach to British foreign policy, he argued that even superior enemies could be defeated through naval warfare, because their armies could 'only stand upon the Shore, to defend what their Enemies have no Intention of invading, and see those Ships seized in which their Pay is treasured, or their Provisions are stored'. To insure those vessels amounted to folly, Walpole contended.

---

[35] *Parliamentary History, Vol. XXII, A.D. 1741–1743*, London: T.C. Hansard, 1812, citing 'Dr Johnson'; Johnson, 'Debate in the House of Clinabs', pp. 3–15, 18–19.

[36] McGrath, Patrick: *The merchant venturers of Bristol: A history of the Society of Merchant Venturers of the City of Bristol from its origin to the present day*, Bristol: Society of Merchant Venturers of the City of Bristol, 1975, p. 32.

[37] Cruickshanks, Eveline: 'Barnard, John', www.historyofparliamentonline.org/volume/1715-1754/member/barnard-john-1685-1764 [Accessed 3 Dec. 2021]; Fox Bourne, H. R.: *English merchants, memoires in illustration of the progress of British commerce*, Second Edition, Vol. I, London: Richard Bentley, 1866, pp. 282–297.

[38] Hansard's record of the debate includes amendments, such as the substitution of 'the Dutch' for 'the Belgians'. Thus, the contemporary source is cited hereafter.

The publication of Dr Johnson's record of the debate in the *Gentleman's Magazine* indicates an unusually wide public interest in an insurance issue. No doubt many saw insurance of the enemy as scandalous. However, it seems that the main proponents of the bill were primarily interested in a technical underwriting issue, and the fraud which they said it caused. Their goal was the prohibition of the use of interest or no interest policies. Including the phrase in a policy meant that the buyer need not possess any beneficial ownership, financial interest, or other connection to the vessel or cargo insured (anachronistically, an 'insurable interest'), beyond the insurance policy itself. Practical applications of this policy condition were several in an era of uncertainty in trade. Used correctly, such coverage was a practical hedge in a precarious environment, and thus it became commonplace in the eighteenth century. For example, in 1744 underwriters issued a £200 'interest or no interest' policy to the merchant Thomas Hall for the vessel *Cæsar*, for its voyage...

> ... at or from London to all Ports or Places in whatsoever & wheresoever in Europe, Asia, Africa and America, all & every and any and either of them, with liberty to go backwards and forwards from port to port & place to place & cruize and stay on the High Seas or at any anchor at any grounds or at any Havens, Roads, Rivers or Elsewhere at and from all and every of the said ports, Grounds, Havens, Roads, & Rivers and back again to the same as often as there shall be occasion and also back again and into London.[39]

This broad cover cost just £3.7.16 for six months, plus £0.4s.6d for drawing-up the policy, or less than 2% of the sum insured. However, such cover could sometimes be very expensive. In 1738 Peter Du Cane wrote £100 'interest or no interest' on the vessel *Pelham* for a voyage from London to China and back at the staggering rate of £63 per cent.[40]

The interest or no interest clause is included in four policies issued to John Fletcher in 1715 and 1716, and in six policies issued to the merchant Thomas Hall or his agents between 1740 and 1744.[41] Perhaps most often the clause was inserted when the value of a distant cargo was unknown. 'An imaginary value is put upon the ship or cargo, often much above its real worth', Barnard explained to the Commons. He had participated as an underwriter on Fletcher's interest or no interest policies twenty-five years earlier, and on Radcliffe's policies, which did not carry the clause. He asked the House 'how can the value of a cargo [be] estimated, which is to be collected in a long voyage, at different ports?... An imaginary value must therefore be fixed upon, when the ship leaves port'.[42]

Despite this practical application, interest or no interest policies often were, in reality, simply wagers. Insurance was increasingly used explicitly in this way in the eighteenth century. It was this practice which the bill's proponents were targeting.

[39] Insurance policy, 03.04.1744, Business Papers of Thomas Hall, NA, C 103/132.

[40] Journals of Peter Du Cane, 1735–1744, 30.06.1738. ECRO, D/DDc A16.

[41] BL Add. Ms. 43,731 ff. 58–62, policies issued to John Fletcher, 10 Dec. 1715–6 Dec. 1716 (transcriptions); TNA C 103/132, Business papers of Thomas Hall, insurance policies issued 25 May 1740–18 Jun. 1744.

[42] Johnson, 'Debate in the House of Clinabs', p. 4. For policy references, see above.

Gambling was popular during the period, as concerns about betting against God's will abated, at a time when His 'plan for the world seemed more inscrutable.'[43] Wagers flourished against a wider sense of moral outrage over the betting, which was the target of four legislative restrictions between 1739 and 1745.[44] Mortimer described the 'cruel pastime' of taking life insurance policies on those on trial for cowardice and treason, on the gravely ill, and on property in cities under siege:

> Another manner of spending the vacation is, in insuring on the lives of such unfortunate gentlemen, as may happen to stand accountable to their country for misconduct. I am not willing to disturb the ashes of the dead, or I could give an instance of this cruel pastime, the parallel of which is not to be met with in the history of any civilised nation; and therefore, as a scene of this kind, fully laid open, might astonish, but could not convey instruction, humanity bids me draw the veil, and not render any set of men unnecessarily odious. … Of sham insurances, (that is to say, insurances, without property on the spot) made on places besieged in time of war, foreign ministers, residing with us, have made considerable advantages; it was a well-known fact that a certain ambassador insured 30,000*l*. on Minorca, in the war of 1755, with advice in his pocket at the time, that it was taken – our government did not get the intelligence till two days after this transaction, it was the third, before it was made public, and thus, the ambassador duped our people, who continued to accept premiums till the third day.[45]

The policies, as Mortimer suggests in this passage (first published 1761), were seen by many as incitement to fraud. Park, author of the *System of the law of marine insurances*, believed that unchecked, interest or no interest policies threatened 'the speedy annihilation of that most lucrative and beneficial branch of trade'. He noted that the practice was forbidden in England under the seventeenth-century Law Merchant, and does not appear to have been used at all there before the turn of the century.[46] Magens, despite expressing an inclination to let merchants do as they wished, thought it best to ban interest or no interest underwriting, and reported its prohibition in Amsterdam, Genoa, Konigsberg, Rotterdam, and Stockholm.[47]

In London, the practice had drifted into use. An anonymous merchant wrote in 1747 that interest or no interest policies first appeared there 'about the time my Lord Somers held the Great Seal'; between 1693 and 1697. He wrote that insurance for 'Gamesters, Wagerers, and cunning Fellows who pretended to deal in a speculation began to be almost as much concerned as the Merchants; so that a Policy of Insurance in a short Time acquired rather the effect of a Box of Dice, than a Contract

---

[43] Clark, Geoffrey: *Betting on lives: the culture of life insurance in England, 1695–1775*, Manchester: Manchester University Press, 1995, p. 36.

[44] Langford, *A polite and commercial people*, pp. 296–297.

[45] Mortimer, T.: *Every man his own broker, or a guide to Exchange-Alley*; tenth edition, London: G. G. J. and J. Robinson, 1785, pp. 119–122.

[46] Park, *Law of marine insurances*, pp. 346–347.

[47] Magens, *An essay*, p. 29.

to Secure Trade: and as Gamesters seldom play fair after a few of the first Games, it was not long before foul Play in Assurances began to appear'.[48]

Defoe, contemporaneously, also complained of the rise of betting in the insurance market.

> Wagering, as now practised by politics and contracts, is become a branch of assurances; it was before more properly a part of gaming, and as it deserved, had but a very low esteem; but shifting sides, and the war providing proper subjects, as the contingencies of sieges, battles, treaties, and campaigns, it increased to an extraordinary reputation, and offices were erected on purpose which managed it to a strange degree and with great advantage, especially to the office-keepers [the brokers]; so that, as has been computed, there was not less gaged on one side and other, upon the second siege of Limerick, than two hundred thousand pounds.[49]

Thus, for half a century, London's insurance market had been blurred into another, comprising now outsider-sellers of ill repute, which was damaging to the whole. Confusing any possible distinction was the occasional participation of otherwise upstanding merchant-insurers in such business, such as when the prolific underwriter Abraham Clibborn accepted the 'risk' of 'Peace till 14th May 1772'.[50]

A 1747 pamphlet, entitled *An Essay to prove that all Insurances on Ships and Goods at Sea, beyond the interest of the assured, ought to be prohibited*, reveals another dimension of the problem: the return of 'valued policies' which stated the value of the goods or share of a vessel insured. The problem was this: 'Valuing Goods at ten Times their Worth, nothing can happen so much to the Disadvantage of the Insured, as the Arrival of the Ship and Cargo, a Circumstance affording small Hopes of Safety in such Adventures, but it is the State in to which the Business of Insurance is brought, by leaving the Door to Fraud wide open'. War made the situation worse, claimed the writer, who believed that fraud was as large a line of insurance business as any other.[51] Much of the debate over interest or no interest policies was focused on fraud arising from excessive valuations, rather than from insurance of risks in which the buyer had no interest whatsoever.

Restriction of interest or no interest policies appears to have been the main goal of the initiators of the legislation of 1741/2, with the provisions to curtail the insurance of enemies tacked on to increase its chances. Barnard stated that he was not convinced that the legislation 'would remove the grievances' of the merchants of Bristol, which were not directly stated in parliament by Southwell, their representative. The MPs Richard Lockwood and Peter Burrell, Levant Company members and directors of the Royal Exchange Assurance, argued in favour of the bill more openly on the basis of its ban on interest or no interest policies, citing specific examples of fraud. Barnard replied to the accusations simply by declaring 'I know not of any fraudulent Practices openly carried on, or any established by Custom', and

---

[48] A merchant: *An Essay to prove that all Insurances on Ships and Goods at Sea, beyond the interest of the assured, ought to be prohibited*, London: 1747, SHL GL-Kress, 8301.3, pp. 4–5.

[49] Defoe, *Essay on projects*, 1697.

[50] TNA C 107/11, Risk books of Abraham Clibborn & Co., Vol. II (1771), f. 10.

[51] A merchant: *An Essay to prove*, p. 6.

suggested that to forbid any practice open to abuse would 'contract Trade into a narrow Compass'. The Tory MP Robert Willmott, an underwriter and former Lord Mayor of London, noted that trade should not be restrained, arguing that 'trade is so fugitive and variable... that no constant course can be prescribed to it', and thus 'regulations which were proper when they were made, may in a few months become difficulties and obstructions'.[52] Merchants, he said, should be left to operate as their experience dictates (a clear endorsement of governance under the Law Merchant).[53] Thus, a clear breach between the merchants of London and Bristol is exposed by the debate, unlike the unity they showed twenty years earlier when opposing the chartering of Chetwynd's Insurance.

Parliamentary opinion about the bill was further divided by its proposed restriction of the provision of insurance upon any foreign vessels, friend or foe, trading to the East Indies. The clause, in plain support of the East India Company's monopoly, was inserted to win the backing of MPs with EIC links. This created further divisions and rivalries; in 1730 Barnard had petitioned against the renewal of the Company's charter.[54] Sir William Yonge, the Whig Secretary of War and an ally of Walpole, said that because the bill's 'several clauses have relations and consequences so different, that scarce any one man can approve them all'.[55] Southwell called for his bill to be sent to committee for amendment. It was dropped when the number of Members sitting in the House fell below the minimum of forty required for a quorum.[56] This may, however, reflect the opposite of a lack of political interest in the issue. It was an occasional tactic of Members opposing a bill to block it by leaving the chamber to spoil the quorum.[57] No intervention was achieved.

The Bristol merchants' goal of banning interest or no interest policies was revisited by parliament in 1746, when brought to the House by Alexander Hume, a victualler, East India Company director, and consistent government supporter.[58] Wisely, Hume and other proponents of a ban chose to separate the issue from that of insuring the enemy, which, although still a concern, was distinct from the technical questions about underwriting. Unsurprisingly, the related debates attracted much less public interest, and are therefore unrecorded. However, the resulting legislation survives, and shows plainly the problems which were rife in the London insurance market in the middle of the eighteenth century, arising from its use by outsiders. In fact, it was increasingly obvious that, in a rapidly growing market which

[52] Cruikshanks, Eveline: 'Willmott, Robert', www.historyofparliamentonline.org/volume/1715-1754/member/willimot-robert-1746 [Accessed 3 Dec. 2021].

[53] Johnson, 'Debate in the House of Clinabs', pp. 8–9.

[54] Cruickshanks, 'Barnard, John', History of Parliament Online.

[55] Dickinson, H. T.: 'Yonge, Sir William', *Oxford dictionary of national biography online*, www.oxforddnb.com/view/article/30232 [Accessed 3 Dec. 2021].

[56] *Parliamentary History*, Vol. XXII, cols 25–26.

[57] Lieberman, *Province of legislation determined*, p. 21.

[58] Cruickshanks, Eveline: 'Hume, Alexander', *History of Parliament Online*, www. historyofparliamentonline.org/volume/1715-1754/member/hume-alexander-1693-1765 [Accessed 3 Dec. 2021].

was becoming increasingly complex, the original rules of the game – underpinned by custom and the Law Merchant – were far from adequate.

This is apparent in the preamble to the 1746 *Act to regulate Insurances on Ships belonging to the Subjects of Great Britain, and on Merchandizes or Effects laden thereon.* It states that 'the making of Assurances, Interest or no Interest... hath been productive of many pernicious practices' including the fraudulent destruction of many ships and cargoes, but also 'the carrying on many other prohibited and clandestine Trades, which by means of such Assurances, have been concealed... and by introducing a mischievous kind of Gaming or Wagering, under the Pretence of assuring the Risque of Shipping, and fair Trade, the Institution and laudable Design of making Assurances, hath been perverted'.[59] Thus, insuring ships belonging to the king or his subjects, or any goods aboard British vessels, 'Interest or no Interest, or without further Proof of Interest than the Policy, or by way of Gaming or Wagering, or without benefit of Salvage to the Insurer' was prohibited under the Act. Further, reinsurance was prohibited, except in situations of the insolvency or death of the original insurer. It was presumably seen as a tool for masking the details of the underlying risks and policy conditions, and for jobbing in insurance risk. Its use as a legitimate risk-sharing mechanism was sacrificed.

The legislation included two significant exceptions which recognised the value of interest or no interest policies in certain situations. Owners of British privateers could insure their vessels interest or no interest. Goods from Spain, Portugal, or their dependent countries in Europe or America, could be insured in the same way. The political arithmetician Corbyn Morris declared, in a contemporaneous pamphlet which argued against the insurance of enemy vessels, that 'for some imaginary Reasons the Prohibition was not extended to the *Ships* of *Foreigners*; which seems, as though it was of Concern, to prevent our being *defrauded* by *each other*, but that our being *defrauded* by *Foreigners*, was not to be interrupted'.[60] It is obvious, however, that both exclusions were offensive acts of trade war (as Morris surely realised). The decision to exclude foreign vessels was intended to increase the instances of fraud against enemy vessel owners, as an insurance claim was an additional reward for barratry, or of capture by privateers, who could claim a double-win. The exclusion for owners of privateers allowed them to insure such vessels for more than their value, including normally uninsurable investments in fitting-out, potentially making a risky venture more appealing. It also allowed them to insure cargoes not yet possessed, in anticipation of their capture. The explicit exclusion of Spanish and Portuguese vessels allowed merchants to continue to evade Spanish restrictions on foreign trade to Brazil and Spanish America through the connivance of Iberian masters. In effect, it allowed the continued insurance of smuggling enterprises. It also permitted continued insurance of the annual *flota*, the Spanish South America convoy, typically

[59] George II, c. 37, 1746.

[60] Morris, C.: *An essay towards deciding the question, whether Britain be permitted by right policy to insure the ships of her enemies?*, London: A. Millar, 1748, p. 25.

comprising about fifteen richly laden merchant vessels and their escorts, on which 'Insurances to a very large amount [were] every year made, in London'.[61]

An anonymous pamphlet, *REASONS Humbly Offer'd against the Bill, intituled A Bill to prevent some Inconveniences…*, explained why underwriters may prefer interest or no interest policies. 'Insurers know the Risque, and choose to have policies made so… were the Assured to [have to] prove Interest [in case of loss], they'd have in their Power to defraud the Insurers, by pretending their Effects were left behind; in which case the Premio's must be returned'. Among buyers, Spaniards trading from Spain to the West Indies could not declare an interest when that interest had not been registered, and English merchants were prohibited from any participation in trade to the Spanish Americas. Similarly, many countries had disallowed the export of bullion; if such cargoes were shipped in breach of such a restriction, they could prudently be insured only interest or no interest.[62]

Two further provisions of the Act dealt with procedural details in insurance disputes. When suing his insurers, a policyholder was to be required to state in writing within fifteen days the total sum insured on the property in question, presumably to uncover acts of fraudulent over-insurance. Underwriters (individual or corporate) who were sued under insurance policies were permitted to bring to court a sum of money, on offer as settlement of the dispute. Should the plaintiff refuse the offer, the suit would proceed to trial. If the jury found that the defendant was liable to pay no more than the offer, the plaintiff was to pay the defendants' costs. This provision is clearly designed to reduce frivolous suits, and uniquely included in the language of the Act was the phrase 'any Law, Custom, or Usage to the contrary notwithstanding', indicating a modification of the Law Merchant.

The Act of 1746 was significant as the first piece of legislation which dealt with the mechanics of insurance contracts. Heretofore London underwriters, unlike their counterparts in almost all other major insurance centres, had been free to use or develop policy wordings and underwriting conditions without statutory interference. Only custom and the Law Merchant defined conventions, which, as has been shown, were flexible. They could and did evolve over the years, in order that underwriters could provide a more attractive and more flexible product to their customers. The intervention of 1746 thus marked a significant break. The provisions of the Act which relate to disputes were framed in the interests of underwriters. They were significant in that they introduced a requirement, under law, for buyers of insurance policies to possess an insurable interest in the objects of their insurance. This principle was extended to life insurance policies in the *Life Assurance Act 1774*, which was intended to curtail wagering on the lives of others under policies of insurance.[63] Between the passage of these two pieces of legislation, the practice of underwriting wager policies was to prompt an important rift within the underwriters of London, described below.

---

[61] Weskett, *Complete digest*, p. 223.

[62] *REASONS Humbly Offer'd against the Bill, intituled A Bill to prevent some Inconveniences…* London: 1741/2, SHL GL Case II. 6. 7793.1.

[63] Geo. 3 c. 48.

Insurance of any type on French vessels or cargo was prohibited in 1747/8, after six years of the Seven Years War. The *Act to prohibit Assurance on Ships belonging to France, and on Merchandizes and Effects laden thereon, during the present War with France* received Royal Assent on 25 March, after another long debate which again attracted public interest and support due to its patriotic nature. It was brought by Stephen Janssen, an alderman and future Lord Mayor whose father, a Bank of England founder, was forced from parliament over the South Sea Company scandal.[64] The future Bristol MP and trade champion Robert Nugent, a regular speaker in favour of outports' interests (for which, in 1754, he was offered £10,000 by the Bristol merchants – as a campaign expense indemnification – to contest their constituency, which he held for two decades), opened the discussion with a declaration that to insure enemy vessels was surely high treason.[65] He suggested (without presenting any evidence) that some insurers had given their French clients intelligence about the stations and course of British cruisers and privateers, which would indeed have been a treasonous act. He also restated the main argument in favour of a ban: 'Without a cheap, easy, and secure Access to Insurance, no Nation can ever acquire, or long preserve, an extensive Commerce.'[66] The same interests of Bristol merchants which had driven them to support a ban on insuring the Spanish in 1741 no doubt drove their interest in 1747.

Nugent was answered by William Murray, who later became Lord Justice Mansfield, the judge credited with developing England's common law of insurance.[67] Murray argued that supporting the bill would 'make a Regulation under popular Pretences, which, in my Opinion, will ruin a very beneficial Branch of trade we are now in Possession of, I may say without a Rival, and will transfer it to our greatest Rival and most dangerous Enemy'. Janssen feared the ban on insuring the enemy would 'extinguish' insurance in England. The argument about the potential permanent loss of a foreign market had precedent. During the War of the League of Augsburg, French exports to England of the linens *dowlas* and *lockram*, valued at £200,000, had ceased. The void was filled, at English commission, by Hamburg, and the French export market was so badly damaged that the names of these fabrics fell from the English language.[68]

Mansfield suggested instead that naval action should make the seas so dangerous for enemy vessels that insuring them would become unaffordable for French merchants, and claimed that some of the richest vessels captured recently were encountered based on intelligence communicated by 'those employed to get Insurances upon them'.[69] Pamphleteering by Morris attempted to prove through equations that

[64] Veale, E.: 'Janssen, Sir Theodore', *Oxford dictionary of national biography online*, www. oxforddnb.com/view/article/14656 [Accessed 3 Dec. 2021].

[65] Woodland, P.: 'Nugent, Robert Craggs, Earl Nugent (1709–1788)', *ONDB*, 2004.

[66] 'Journal of the proceedings and debates in the political club', *London Magazine, or Gentleman's Monthly Intelligencer, for March 1748*, London: R. Baldwin, 1748, pp. 105–107.

[67] See pp. 215–216.

[68] John, 'War and the English economy', p. 338.

[69] 'Journal of the proceedings', *London Magazine*, pp. 107–112.

the economics of insuring the enemy could not be of benefit to the nation, although he ignored the benefits of risk diversification.[70] Ultimately his and the patriotic arguments superseded the business case, and insuring the French was banned without a division of the House. The restriction was automatically repealed by the cessation of hostilities seven months later, so neither the various theories about the efficacy of insurance as an offensive weapon nor the potential for France to unseat London as the leading insurance centre of Europe were properly tested on this occasion. Nor was the issue settled. The group that voted with the government to end the practice of insuring the enemy had won the day, but despite two additional, sustained naval wars over the next three decades, the prohibition was not reintroduced until 1793.[71]

A further legislative restriction was passed in 1751/2, when parliament agreed to protect, for a period of seven years, the interests of the East India Company under *An Act to restrain the making of Insurances on Foreign Ships bound to or from the East Indies*. Such actions had some precedent. In 1723 an act had been passed to prevent British investment in any new East India company established in the Austrian Netherlands.[72] In that case, the law may have been targeting the increasingly aggressive old French East India Company. No similar future law, however, was to protect the EIC against competitors. After the repeal of the prohibitive Act under legislation in 1758, French merchants established the New French East India Company in 1785.[73] From 1787 to 1789 the French engaged their London agents, Charles Harris & Co., to place in London 8.75 million *livres* of the total of 19.75 million worth of insurance they purchased for their ventures.[74]

The debate over the legislation to prevent the insurance of enemy vessels and cargoes illustrates several aspects of insurance in London at roughly the mid-point of the long eighteenth century. Nugent, no friend to London underwriters, stated that 'an opinion prevails generally among the merchants in France, that they cannot depend upon any insurances but those they meet with in England', as the London market was both less expensive and more secure. Mansfield, in opposition to the bill, described insurance as 'the only brand of trade we now enjoy without rival', advancing his belief that 'there is a great deal more of the insurance business done now in England, than in all of Europe besides… Even our enemies the French and Spaniards, transact most of their business of insurance here at London'. Janssen estimated that the French alone insured in London vessels and cargoes to a value of roughly one million pounds.

Speaking in opposition to the ban, Sir Dudley Ryder, who had been appointed Attorney General by Walpole, offered some details of the mechanics of the market.

---

[70] Morris, C.: *An essay towards deciding the important question*, London: 1747; Morris, C.: *An essay towards illustrating the science of insurance*, London: 1747.

[71] The *Traitorous Correspondence Act* made it illegal to insure French vessels or cargoes. 33 Geo. III c 27 v. Runnington, Charles (ed.): *The statutes at large: from the thirtieth year of the reign of King George III to the thirty-fourth year*, Vol. XII, London, 1794, pp. 308–309.

[72] According to the act 25 Geo. II. c. 2.

[73] Geo. II, c. 27.

[74] Harlow, Vincent: *The founding of the Second British Empire, 1763–1793*, Vol. II, London: Longmans Green & Co., 1963, p. 493.

British West India voyages were insured at rates of 25% to 30% when travelling without convoy; French vessels on the same route paid 30% to 35%. Merchants and insurance buyers 'pin their faith blindly on a few leaders' who set rates, 'without being themselves at the pains to make any calculations on the chances'. Brokers (still referred to as office-keepers) were paid 4s 6d for preparing each policy, and charged the underwriter a commission of 5%, and collected 10s per cent from claims paid. Local factors of foreign merchants were paid another 10s per cent for arranging policies, and 'one, sometimes two per cent on every sum he pays or remits'. Foreign-exchange dealers took another 10s per cent.[75]

The incentive pricing granted to insurance buyers who travelled with convoys under naval escort had been introduced by London underwriters at the latest in the 1690s.[76] The discount or rebate was substantial, as reported by Malachy Postlethwayt in his 1755 *Universal dictionary of trade and commerce*. For a wartime 'treble voyage... from England to Africa, from thence to America, and then home', the total premium with convoy was 23%, against 58% without. However, to recover all expenditures in case of a total loss, including insurance premiums, abatements, and commissions, the buyer must over-insure. To make full recovery of each £100 invested in cargo on this 'treble voyage', the merchant shipping on a vessel with convoy would spend £27.15.0 in premiums, and without, a probably prohibitive £94.3.5.[77] Thus, insurance was a critical driver of state trade protection efforts. It constituted an important part of the nation's 'sinews of power' supporting the blue-water strategy of defence through private institutions and capital.

An attempt to enact more comprehensive regulations for the insurance market, again to combat fraud, was being made at roughly the same time. In January 1747/8 a Commons committee was formed 'to consider Heads of a Bill for better regu-lating Assurances on Ships and Goods laden thereon, and for preventing Frauds therein'.[78] The committee was led by Alexander Hume, who had advanced the Act banning policies interest or no interest. Its members included Barnard, Southwell, Burrell, Stephen Janssen, Nugent, and Samuel Child, who would become head of his father's eponymous bank, and was an important EIC investor.[79] The EIC inter-est included Henry Gough, its former chairman, alongside director and Hamburg merchant John Bance, his brother-in-law John Frederick, son of the former gov-ernor of Fort St. George and a South Sea Company director, and the Fonnereau brothers, who were Hamburg merchants with large government victualling con-tracts and EIC ties. Atlantic traders included the West Indies merchant and future Lord Mayor William Beckford, who in 1752 would speak against a bill prohibiting the insurance of foreign ships (describing it as intended solely to protect the interests of the EIC), Slingsby Bethel, an Antigua planter turned wealthy Africa merchant, and

75 *Cobbett's Parliamentary History of England*, Vol. XII, A.D. 1741–1743, London: T.C. Hansard, 1812, cols 108–133.

76 See pp. 116–117.

77 Postlethwayt, *Universal dictionary*, unpaginated.

78 *Journals of the House of Commons*, Vol. XXV, 1745–1750 (1803), p. 493.

79 Wright & Fayle, *History of Lloyd's*, p. 81.

the West Indies merchant Robert Webb. As well as Frederick, South Sea Company directors on the committee included Hamburg merchant and army financier John Gore, comptroller of victuals Francis Gashry, and the financier-victualler Sir George Amyand. Also included was Lord Mayor Sir William Calvert, the largest brewer in London.[80] Despite all this expertise in marine commerce, the Commons could not draft an acceptable marine insurance law. Britain, unlike most maritime nations, continued without one until 1906.[81]

Despite the legislative failure, the committee's proposals are of great interest. Ten resolutions were brought to the House, and were expected to form the basis of a bill and subsequent law to govern marine insurance. Unlike the earlier proposals which were relatively simple, the committee's resolutions were detailed and technical. The ten were designed to swing the balance of favour in underwriting towards the underwriter. They shed light on the kinds of deceptions that some outsider-buyers were perpetrating, and leave the impression that the London insurance market of the mid-eighteenth century included many buyers who were unscrupulous, and many sellers who were incautious: too willing to trust that outsider-buyers would play by the rules of the uncodified Law Merchant.

First, regardless of the sum insured or the valuation of goods specified in a policy, in case of loss the insured would be able to recover only the actual value of the goods at the time and place of shipping, plus the cost of the premium (although, the committee suggested, this would not prevent the fixing, in the policy, of the value of a stated unit of goods).

Second, before executing any policy on ships, the buyer would be required to declare the ship's burthen, whether it was British or foreign-built, what share of the ship was to be insured, and the value of that share. Despite the latter, in case of loss underwriters would be free to dispute that value, and even at law the assured would be able to recover only, at maximum, that true value.

Third, insurance policies covering the wages of ships' masters or crew would be required to state the rate of pay per month or for the voyage, and in case of a claim, only an unspecified percentage would be recoverable.

Fourth, claims of barratry would be paid only when the master or mariners actually absconded with the vessel or cargo, or 'stole, pilfered, or imbezzled the same', and then only at the true value of the lost vessel or goods.

Fifth, any policies covering goods shipped from Europe, and any policies covering ships or goods from Asia, Africa, or America, would have to include, at the time of underwriting, a declaration signed by all the underwriters stating the identities of the beneficiaries of the policy. If no such declaration was included, then only the individual named on the face of the policy would be entitled to claim.

Sixth, any representations made by the buyer, broker, or agent which 'may materially affect the Terms of the Assurance' was to be stated in the policy, and no other information could later be claimed by the insured to have been communicated,

---

[80] House of Commons, *Journals of the House of Commons*, Vol. 25, p. 493; Sedgwick, *House of Commons*, Vol. I, pp. 431–432, 451, 460, 509, 519, 549, Vol. II, pp. 41–42, 52, 60, 71, 142, 158, 171, 293, 472, 485, 527.

[81] *Act to codify the Law relating to Marine Insurance*, 21.12.1906.

although the insurer would be permitted later to challenge the veracity of any information so noted, or to argue that information had been withheld.

Seventh, if the actual value of goods insured was less than the sum insured, the buyer of the policy would be entitled to a *pro rata* return of premium, less a handling charge, unless the policy had been made void due to fraud, when nothing could be recovered.

Eighth, if actions were to be brought under insurance policies by individuals living abroad, or out of the reach of the relevant court, the defendants would be allowed to request that funds be paid into court to cover costs, should the plaintiff discontinue, be 'Nonsuited', or lose the case.

Tenth, the insured would not be permitted, in cases of partial loss, to abandon to the underwriters their interest in the insured objects, and could claim only the actual value of the partial loss.

The ninth provision was clearly difficult, even for the highly knowledgeable committee: it states only that 'All Assurances Interest or no Interest, without the Benefit of Salvage, shall be _____.'[82]

The blank in the ninth resolution is significant. Although interest or no interest policies had been prohibited the year before, parliamentarians clearly remained unsure if this had been the correct course. Further, the legislation prohibiting such insurance had proved ineffectual. One writer stated that 'it is conceived that Statute is not sufficient effectually to answer the End proposed, though it has gone a good way towards it.'[83]

The MPs appointed to draft the bill included Alexander Hume; Solicitor General Hume-Campbell; East India Company director (and later governor) Alderman William Baker; plantation owner, Africa merchant, and future alderman and Lord Mayor of London Slingsby Bethell; and Stephen Janssen, who later went into the herring fishing business with Bethell.[84] This group of senior City insiders prepared their bill within the week, making very few changes to the language of the committee report, although inserting an extrajudiciality clause which would have made the legislation binding; first in Europe, then everywhere else in the world (presumably to prevent jurisdictional arbitrage by underwriters and buyers).[85]

Hume read the bill on 29 March. It was read a second time, ordered to be printed, and committed to a committee comprising the whole House, but is never again

---

[82] *Journals of the House of Commons*, Vol. XXV, 1745–1750 (1803), pp. 597–599.

[83] A merchant: *An Essay to prove*, p. 7.

[84] Matthews, Shirley: 'Baker, William', *History of Parliament Online*, www. historyofparliamentonline.org/volume/1715-1754/member/baker-william-1705-70 [Accessed 3 Dec. 2021]; Sedgwick, Romney R.: 'Hume Campbell, Alexander', ibid., / volume/1715-1754/member/hume-campbell-hon-alexander-1708-60 [Accessed 3 Dec. 2021]; Cruickshanks, Eveline: 'Bethell, Slingsby', ibid., /volume/1715-1754/member/ bethell-slingsby-1695-1758 [Accessed 3 Dec. 2021]; Cruickshanks, Eveline: 'Janssen, Sir Theodore', ibid., /volume/1715-1754/member/janssen-stephen-theodore-1777 [Accessed 3 Dec. 2021].

[85] *A Bill for the better Regulating of Assurances upon Ships, and Goods laden thereon, and for preventing Frauds therein*.

mentioned in the record.[86] No clue has survived as to why the bill failed, but it is clear from the committee's ten resolutions that the enlarged insurance market continued to face problems with fraud and unscrupulous practice. Just a year after the passage of the Act prohibiting interest or no interest policies, market regulation had returned to the agenda. A further bill was introduced in 1788; it would have repealed the 1746 *Act to regulate Insurances*. The bill stated that 'great Mischiefs and Inconveniences have arisen to Persons interested in Ships and Vessels, and also to Persons using Trade or Commerce, from the Effect' of the Act. Instead the Act would require that the name or names of the insured person, people, firms, or agents be stated in the policy, as was the traditional practice of the merchant-insurers.[87] The bill failed, but makes clear that new solutions were needed. Ultimately, part of the solution was self-regulation and institution-building by the merchant-insurers operating under the name of Lloyd's.

Institutions for information-sharing

In the decade or so after the formation of the corporate duopoly of the Royal Exchange Assurance and the London Assurance, Lloyd's Coffee-house, under a series of proprietors, continued to focus on the provision of current shipping information, and seems to have become a leading London actor in this field.[88] Some evidence suggests that, in 1697, Lloyd's intelligence network provided the government with the first news that the Virginia fleet had arrived in Ireland;[89] more concrete evidence shows that Richard Baker, owner of Lloyd's from 1738, was the first to inform Walpole of the navy's taking of Portobello in 1739/40, during the War of the Austrian Succession.[90] More uncertain is the date of the re-launch of Edward Lloyd's list of shipping arrivals as *Lloyd's List*, since the earliest numbers are lost, but March 1734/5 seems likely.[91] McCusker argues plausibly that it was a direct continuation of the earlier publication *Ships arrived*.[92] This publication of shipping information does not, however, indicate any significant concentration of London's insurance business at the Coffee-house at this stage, or at least it does not show that underwriting was more commonplace in Lloyd's than elsewhere.

For example, Peter Du Cane subscribed policies at office-keepers' premises. In 1737 he recorded risks 'Insured by me at [Thomas] Hayse's Office'. Similar entries show that risks brokered by John Praed and Stephen Peter Godin were 'signed by

[86] *Journals of the House of Commons*, Vol. XXV, 1745–1750 (1803), pp. 605, 614.

[87] *A Bill intituled, An Act to repeal an Act, made in the Twenty-fifth Year of the Reign of the present Majesty, intituled, An Act for regulating Insurances on Ships, and on Goods, Merchandizes, or Effects, and substituting other Provisions, for the like purpose, in lieu thereof*, 1788.

[88] For accounts of the early years of Lloyd's Coffee-house, see Wright and Fayle, *History of Lloyd's*; Gibb, *Lloyd's of London*.

[89] Gibb, *Lloyd's of London*, p. 13.

[90] Wright and Fayle, *History of Lloyd's*, p. 79.

[91] Wright and Fayle, *History of Lloyd's*, pp. 72–73, n. 73.

[92] McCusker, 'Early history of Lloyd's List', p. 430.

me at his Office'.[93] This evidence shows at least that not all insurance was routinely underwritten at the Coffee-house at this time. Instead, underwriting on the premises of brokers remained an important way of transacting business in the lead-up to the War of the Austrian Succession. The lengthy parliamentary discussions of insurance in 1741/2 and 1747/8 make no mention of Lloyd's; the practice of brokers coming there to meet waiting merchant-insurers had probably not yet come to dominate the business.

While the Coffee-shop may not yet have been the primary place for underwriting in London, it had retained its position of importance in the auction of vessels. For example, a 1757 edition of the *Public Advertiser* carries twenty notices of upcoming sales of ships by candle at Lloyd's Coffee-house (the candle acting as a count-down timer; when it expires, no more bids accepted).[94] More important for insurance underwriting, Lloyd's information services were useful and expanding. *Lloyd's List* had garnered an important place in Britain's commerce. For example, Glasgow tobacco merchants Buchanan & Simson, writing to Messers Fraser & Wharton in November 1759, reported that 'We find by this days Lloyds List that the [vessel] Maxwell foundered at Sea, as we have insurance made at Philadelphia, we desire you may by first Paquet to New York, send to Mr George Maxwell Merchant in Potuxant [Patuxent] Maryland a proper certificate of the ship being lost that our insurance may be received'.[95] As the correspondence shows, the shipping information in *Lloyd's List* was not only timely and widely distributed, but was of benefit to merchants and underwriters outside of London, and even outside England: in this case, in Scotland and the American colonies.

By this time the successive masters of the Coffee-house, rather than the underwriters, were responsible for the shipping list. In roughly 1760, however, London's underwriters themselves launched a joint information tool.[96] They formed a subscription-based society to produce a bound list of surveyed vessels, with detailed information about each of them. The content of the volumes was based upon the reports of professional surveyors engaged for the purpose. This marked a significant advance from the private registers which some underwriters are believed to have maintained. Lloyd's Register, the extant organisation which continues to compile the *Register of Ships* for use by underwriters and others, possesses what is believed to be the oldest surviving register of ships, dated '1764–65–66'. Its singed edges hint that it was at Lloyd's during the Royal Exchange fire of 1834. This book lists, for each vessel surveyed, its current and any former names, the names of its owner and master, its usual route of trade, its burthen and number of crew, armaments, age, port of origin, and classification of its quality, using the scale A, E, I, O, or U to rate its hull, and G, M, or B (good, middling, or bad) to rate its equipment. It has space

93 ECRO D/DDc A16, *Journals of Peter Du Cane, 1735–1744*, 31 Dec. 1837, 30 Apr. 1738.

94 *Public Advertiser*, No. 7,155, 30 Sep. 1757, p. 2.

95 NAS CS96/507 f. 16, *Letterbook of Buchanan & Simson*, letter to Fraser & Wharton, 30 Nov. 1759.

96 1760 is the genesis year claimed by Lloyd's Registry, based on the organisation's own statement of 1829. Wright and Fayle, *History of Lloyd's*, p. 85.

to record new information. Only a few registers from this era survive, but differences between them suggest that competing registers were published.[97]

Initially the book was for use only by the members of the original Register Society, who numbered 130 in 1778. The rule that outdated books had to be handed in before new editions were issued was soon dropped, as the value of the innovation was maximised by allowing non-members to participate, thereby incorporating the greatest possible amount of intelligence into the compendium. These included the two corporate insurers, and others from around the world.[98] Such print-based sharing of information should have allowed significantly improved underwriting decision-making, and reduced the incidence of successful fraud against insurers by making its discovery more likely. By 1798 the subscribers to the Registry had formed a committee, which included many Lloyd's members, and which met at Lloyd's Coffee-house, but the Registry and the underwriting organisation were separate. The first time the register or the society is known as Lloyd's Register is 1829, but even then it was a separate entity. As the organisation states today, 'Contrary to popular belief, Lloyd's Register and Lloyd's of London are two completely separate organisations, sharing only the origin of their names.'[99]

As the joint register developed, so too did underwriting at the Coffee-house, which its historians state grew in significance during Britain's mid-century wars. In 1771 the merchant Joshua Johnson wrote that he avoided buying insurance from 'a public office', that is, the Royal Exchange Assurance or the London Assurance, because of 'their particularity; they must know who you are and a deal of that; then again you are plagued more than little enough before you can get the money after a loss, and everybody prefers making theirs at Lloyds for that reason'.[100] However, private underwriting continued to be carried out elsewhere in London. Even in 1810, long after Lloyd's had become a formal institution for merchant-insurers, insurance policies were underwritten at the Jamaica and Jerusalem coffee-houses, at the Coal Exchange (presumably primarily on coastal colliers), and at underwriters' own 'counting houses'.[101]

Marine insurance and common law reform

Following the seventeenth-century decline of the Court of Assurance and the prerogative courts, the resolution of insurance disputes at law returned to non-specialist forums. Zouch argued that 'Policies of Assurance are grounded upon the Civil

---

97   *Annals of Lloyd's Register, being a sketch of the Origins, Constitution, and Progress of Lloyd's Register of British & Foreign Shipping*, London: Lloyd's Register, Wyman & Sons, Printers, 1884, pp. 6–9, 12.

98   Ibid., pp. 10–12, 38.

99   Ibid., pp. 13, 43; website of Lloyd's Registry, www.lr.org/documents/173508-lloyds-marine-collection.aspx [Accessed 3 Dec. 2021].

100 Johnson to his business partners, 26 Jul. 1771, Price, J. M. (ed.): *Joshua Johnson's letterbook, 1771–1774: letters from a merchant in London to his partners in Maryland*, London: London Record Society, 1979, p. 8.

101 *The special report of 1720*, testimony of J. J. Angerstein, p. 58.

Law', and civil lawyers, themselves grounded in equity, had long recognised the role of the Law Merchant in insurance.[102] Malynes wrote in 1622 that 'the Civilians have noted, that in Assurances the customs of the Sea-Laws, and use amongst Merchants, is chiefly to be regarded and observed'.[103] Little in the way of common law principles had been established for insurance.[104] Thus, an equity jurisdiction would have best matched the tenets of the Law Merchant and the customs of underwriting. Primary among the institutions of the law of equity was the Court of Chancery, which had specific jurisdiction over the law of contracts, and which had heard some insurance cases during the great jurisdictional battles of the sixteenth century.[105] It was Chancery which, under statute, had been designated to hear appeals against decisions of the Court of Assurance, and the chancellor who made judicial appointments to that short-lived court. For these reasons Chancery was perhaps the most logical venue for mercantile suits, but it was not to resume responsibility for insurance cases. This may have been due in part to the disrepute brought upon the equity courts in general, and Chancery specifically, following the trial and impeachment of Lord Chancellor Macclesfield in 1725. According to Rudolph, 'In light of crisis and scandal common law came to be especially valued, because it was seen to promote the kind of security of property rights necessary for lasting economic prosperity and positive commercial growth'.[106]

Malynes had stated that losses should be declared 'in the Office of Assurances, or the Court of Admiralty', but Admiralty also failed to regain its former position as the main forum for insurance cases.[107] Its long erosion is described above. Marsden observes that insurance law owes 'little' to Admiralty judges, whose court 'does not seem to have given satisfaction to underwriters or merchants'. He notes that until the mid-eighteenth century, most insurance cases were resolved through arbitration, broadly defined.[108] Steckley, citing Hill's revisionist view, states that the Ordinance of 1648 which appears to confirm Admiralty jurisdiction was actually intended to limit it, by specifying narrow areas of responsibility, and thereby curbing prerogative power.[109]

In any case, after the collapse of the Court of Assurance, insurance disputes which reached the courts were 'chiefly the subject of common law jurisdiction'.[110] The majority of recorded cases were heard at King's Bench, even though common lawyers had no significant body of legislation or common law precedent to guide

---

[102] Zouch, *Jurisdiction of the Admiralty*, p. 102.

[103] Malynes, *Lex Mercatoria*, p. 118.

[104] See p. 69.

[105] Lieberman, *Province of legislation determined*, pp. 75, 77.

[106] Rudolph, Julia: 'Jurisdictional controversy and the credibility of common law', in Coffman, D., Leonard, A., and Neal, L.: *Questioning credible commitment: perspectives on the rise of financial capitalism*, Cambridge: Cambridge University Press, 2013, p. 105.

[107] Malynes, *Lex Mercatoria*, p. 116.

[108] Marsden, *Select pleas*, II, p. ixxx.

[109] Steckley, 'Merchants and the Admiralty Court', p. 139.

[110] Park, *A system of the law*, pp. xli–xlii.

relevant decision-making. The Law Merchant remained, but courts of common law had tended to ignore it, even as knowledge of these quasi-official rules was increasingly shared among merchants through a proliferation of printed Law Merchant guides such as Gerard Malynes' 1622 *Consuetudo, vel, Lex Mercatoria: or, The Ancient Law-Merchant*. Common law judges instead tended to determine commercial cases 'by directing a common jury to decide the issue according to the individual circumstances of each case'. In commercial disputes, this process could result in decisions which were at odds with standard merchant practice, and which rarely established principles of law on which future, similar disputes could be decided.[111] Decisions in insurance cases were left 'entirely to the jury,' Park reported, 'without any minute statement from the bench of the principles of the law.' Points of law were often argued in private chambers, and no clue was left for future jurists as to the argumentative basis upon which preceding cases had been decided.[112]

The commentator Wooddeson argued that 'Where the positive laws are silent, all courts must determine on maxims of natural justice, dictated by reason; that is, according to the law of nature.'[113] In other words, in the absence of precedent, even the common law jurisdictions must adopt an equitable approach. In the case of mercantile disputes, Wooddeson wrote, 'especially since the great extension of commerce, and intercourse with foreign traders, [natural justice] is called the law of merchants', and has been 'admitted' to decide insurance cases. Such law depends on custom, is voluntary, and 'merely positive'.[114] Thus, the Law Merchant did exist as positive (if uncodified) law. However, Wooddeson was writing at the end of the eighteenth century, after a major intervention along this line into the operation of the common law governing commercial, and especially marine insurance, disputes. Until that reform had run its course, common law judges were hesitant to apply the Law Merchant. For example, Sir John Holt, Lord Chief Justice from 1689 to 1710, stated famously in a case over a disputed bill of exchange that such actions were 'innovations upon the rules of the common law; and that it amounted to the setting up a new sort of specialty, unknown to the common law, and invented in Lombard-Street, which attempted in these matters of bills of exchange to give laws to Westminster-Hall'.[115]

Lieberman describes Holt's statement as the '*locus classicus* on the common law's insularity and incompetence in dealing with mercantile affairs' before reform.[116] Rogers states that Holt, who was a key maker of the common law related to bills of exchange, was referring 'only to suits on notes being brought against the original maker *as actions founded on the custom of merchants*': under common law, the plaintiff would 'have to prove the facts that gave rise to the debt [under the

---

[111] Lieberman, *Province of legislation determined*, pp. 102, 114.

[112] Park, *A system of the law*, p. xlv.

[113] Wooddeson, Richard: *Elements of Jurisprudence, treated of in the preliminary part of a course of lectures on the laws of England*, Dublin: J. Moore, 1792, p. 134.

[114] Ibid., pp. 158–159.

[115] *Clerke* v. *Martin*, 2 Ld. Raym. 758.

[116] Lieberman, *Province of legislation determined*, p. 100.

disputed bill]. By contrast, in an action on the custom of merchants, the plaintiff could obtain judgment merely by proving that the instrument had been signed by the defendant'.[117] This would, apparently, be too great a usurpation of common law principles for Holt to stomach. His view, and the prevailing common law opinion, was perhaps understandable in an era when the fundamentals of English common law were seen to comprise 'a body of legal practices which had originated in the Saxon era and which had been preserved without break through the vicissitudes of the kingdom's history'.[118]

The debate suggests how confounding insurance disputes must have been to non-specialists. Conditions for proof under the Law Merchant were not only different in such cases, but they were, according to custom, incredibly complex, and flexible based on perceived intent. The two most common questions to reach the courts – 'is the loss covered by the policy' and 'is the policy void' – are painfully more complicated than 'did he sign the bill'. Only the extensive experience of customary practice is sufficient to answer such questions, given the obfuscating language of the London insurance policy, settled in Candeler's office while Elizabeth was on the throne.

Despite a general impression among historians that the period was characterised by the generally arbitrary application of the law, a further component of the challenge facing civil courts was a reluctance among common law jurists to allow any scope to judges.[119] Judicial discretion distinguished civil from common law. Francis, in his 1727 monograph *Maxims of equity* (regarded as the earliest book on the principles of equity jurisprudence), stated that

> the great difference between a court of law and a court of equity is this: the court of [common] law rigidly adheres to its own established rules, be the injustice arising from thence ever so apparent; whereas the court of equity will not adhere to its own most established rules if the least injustice arises from thence; for the same reason that enforces it to supersede the rules of law, will enforce it to supersede its own rules also.[120]

Equity judges' discretionary powers seemed 'contrary to the objectives and character of English law' in preserving 'legal "certainty" against possible judicial disruption'. Thus, eighteenth-century Chancery judges exercised their discretionary powers only cautiously, so as not to be seen as overruling common law. In many other nations, equity was part of any judge's authority. In England, uniquely, it was

[117] Emphasis added. Rogers, James Steven: *The early history of the law of bills and notes: a study of the origins of Anglo-American commercial law*, Cambridge: Cambridge University Press, 1995, pp. 180–181.

[118] Lieberman, *Province of legislation determined*, p. 41.

[119] Langford, *A polite and commercial people*, p. 297.

[120] Francis, Richard: *Maxims of Equity*, London: Lintot, 1727, unpaginated; Bryson, W. H.: 'Francis, Richard', *Oxford Dictionary of National Biography Online*, www.oxforddnb.com/view/article/47165 [Accessed 3 Dec. 2021].

the preserve of distinct, and historically competing, courts, where judges 'preserved the just application of legal rules in all cases'.[121]

With this separation, common law courts understood the prescriptiveness of law to be primary. At mid century it was not yet the norm to develop new prescriptive law under the guidance of the discretion of judges, whose precedents established general legal principles. Thus, Park had little positive to say about the two centuries of insurance litigation which occurred 'from the reign of Queen *Elizabeth* to the year 1756', because the common law judges had not settled principles to govern contracts. During that time, some 'sixty cases upon matters of insurance' had been heard at common law. Each of the reported cases yielded no more than 'a short opinion of a single judge, and very often no opinion at all, but merely a general verdict... it must necessarily follow, that as there have been but few positive regulations upon insurance, the principles, upon which they were founded, could never have been widely diffused, nor very generally known'.[122] Taken in combination, these factors created a further challenge for the application of common law to mercantile cases. It was not always clear whether the law was, or should be, guided by principles, or by the simple direction of precedent alone.

In the adjudication of insurance disputes, common law analogies and categories were often introduced. This blurred the distinction between English common law and the international Law Merchant, leading sometimes to judicial decisions which did not match merchant practice, as three branches of English law – common, civil, and merchant – were brought into conflict. Lieberman sets out the quandary as follows:

> Rival understandings of principles and precedents affected what lawyers made of the place of equity in English common law. If common law was principle, then the law resembled equity, and the common law judge enjoyed considerable flexibility in applying and modifying the rules of law. If common law was precedent, then law was opposed to equity, and the equitable authority of the judge needed to be constrained to prevent its undermining the law itself.[123]

The quandary was to be settled in the second half of the eighteenth century, in a process which established a set of common law principles overtly guided by the Law Merchant, under which insurance could operate. The door to judges' discretion was forced open, and the making of new common law principles followed. The eighteenth century encompassed a period of legal reform, a fashion which gained traction as the century progressed.[124] The geographical reach, volume, and diversity of England's mercantile activity expanded, one result of which was that commercial law especially required an upgrade. As Edmund Burke once declared

> As commerce, with its advantages and necessities opened a communication more largely with other countries; as the law of nature and nations (always part of the

---

[121] Lieberman, *Province of legislation determined*, pp. 74, 78–79.

[122] Park, *A system of the law*, pp. xli–xlii.

[123] Lieberman, *Province of legislation determined*, p. 87.

[124] Langford, *A polite and commercial people*, pp. 303–304.

law of England) came to be cultivated… as new views and combinations of things were opened, this antique rigour and overdone severity [of the common law] gave way to the accommodation of human concerns, for which the rules were made, and not human concerns to bend to them.[125]

Lieberman outlines two ways in which the understanding of the common law as 'a set of customary practices ultimately founded on rational precepts' could be mobilised to support its own reform. First, its historical character could be seen to be prone to obsolescence (the opposite of Holt's response to the legal 'innovations' of Lombard Street). Second, aggressive invocation of the foundational principles of nature and reason, fundamental to English law and required in the absence of case law, and even at the expense of precedent, could urge a new approach. These arguments were deployed to demand, at common law, increased judicial flexibility, new legal remedies, and innovative forms for new purposes. Simply matching established rules to immediate questions was not seen by reformers as sufficient.[126]

The remedy to the overall shortfall of English jurisprudence satisfactorily to govern insurance disputes which were not to be resolved internally by the insider merchant-insurer community was to focus on this blurring of the laws, and to favour the authority of the Law Merchant.[127] The task was embraced by Lord Justice Mansfield, the well-known reformer of English commercial law who had spoken in parliament against the prohibition of interest or no interest policies in 1741/2.[128] When Mansfield came to King's Bench he was familiar with merchant custom through his earlier legal practice, during which he had brought many cases before the Court of Chancery. As a judge, he maintained his City contacts, and served on the Commission of Appeals for prize cases brought up from the Court of Admiralty, with its unique take on the law which blended equity and the international Law Merchant. Oldham reveals that Mansfield, 'though a common law judge, [strove] to reach equitable solutions… as long as he could do so without upsetting established legal principles', an approach which 'anticipated the eventual merger of law and equity'.[129]

Mansfield's aims were clear. 'The great object in every branch of the law, but especially in mercantile law, is certainty, and that the grounds of decision should be precisely known,' he stated in the case *Milles* v. *Fletcher*. 'Whenever a question of law arises at Nisi Prius [King's Bench]… I avoid as much as possible blending fact and law together.'[130] The case was one of Mansfield's defining decisions regarding underwriters' liability in cases of capture and ransom. In the absence of guidance as to the current, local rules of the game, Mansfield regularly referred both to earlier English

---

[125] Cited in Lieberman, *Province of legislation determined*, p. 93.

[126] Lieberman, *Province of legislation determined*, pp. 73, 89.

[127] Ibid., p. 106.

[128] See p. 165.

[129] Oldham, James: 'Murray, William, first earl of Mansfield', *Oxford dictionary of national biography online*, www.oxforddnb.com/view/article/19655 [Accessed 3 Dec. 2021]; Lieberman, *Province of legislation determined*, pp. 111–112.

[130] *Milles* v. *Fletcher*, 1 Dougl. 233.

commentators, and, more unusually for a judge in England, to foreign jurists. He said that the question in *Goss* v. *Withers* – whether the insured loss of a vessel was partial or total – was 'a question of general law, not of any particular and local law… [and] must be determined by the Law of War, and by the Law of Nature, that is, of Right Reason', and in the courtroom cited Rhodian and Roman law, and the Laws of Oleron, among others.[131] He cited the Continental use of the Law Merchant as the governing body of law for commercial disputes, and looked to foreign legal authorities for rules, all of which reveals his sympathetic understanding of the Law Merchant as a legitimate source of legal principles. Principles were the 'essence of common law Precedents', which were themselves 'the illustrations of such rational principles'.[132] Through this circular relationship, the quandary was resolved.

One of the techniques which Mansfield employed in order to ensure that the principles of law which were created by his findings amounted to an equitable match to the intentions of the parties to a dispute, and to the tenets of the Law Merchant, was to appoint juries comprising members of the merchant community. The appointment of such 'special juries' was given statutory approval by the 1729 *Jury Act*, an early component of eighteenth-century legal reform (followed in 1731 by making English the language of the law). It was not uncontroversial, but merchant juries were not new.[133] Edward I's *Carta Mercatoria* of 1303 had allowed foreign merchants to request that juries include up to six merchant strangers, just as the Privy Council in 1593 had required the Lord Mayor and aldermen to appoint some Commissioners of Assurance who were foreign merchants.[134, 135] According to Matthew Hale, a seventeenth-century Chief Justice of the King's Bench, from the sixteenth century merchants were commonly brought into juries in the royal courts at the request of the litigating parties. Hale wrote that when cases in common law touched upon the Law Merchant, 'if it be a question touching the custom of merchants, merchants are usually jurors'.[136] However, despite these earlier precedents, Mansfield's approach was not always welcomed. In the words of Langford, 'among common lawyers he provoked predictable alarm', especially as he was willing to overturn longstanding common law principles.[137]

Practitioners were also called in as expert witnesses to custom, and to outline principles, rather than precedents. In the 1763 case *Camden* v. *Cowley*, for example, Mansfield stated that 'insurance-brokers and others might be examined, as to the general opinion and understanding of the persons concerned in the trade; though they knew no particular instance, in fact, upon which such opinion was founded'.[138] In another case the same year, Mansfield reached his decision in part 'by talking with

131 *Goss* v. *Withers*, 1758, 2 Bur. 683, 97 Eng. Rep. 511.

132 Lieberman, *Province of legislation determined*, pp. 86, 106.

133 Langford, *A polite and commercial people*, p. 300.

134 Oldham, 'Origins of the special jury', p. 173.

135 See p. 89.

136 Quoted in Oldham, 'Origins of the special jury', p. 173.

137 Langford, *A polite and commercial people*, p. 300.

138 *Camden* v. *Cowley*, 1 Black. w. 417.

intelligent persons very conversant in the knowledge and practice of insurances', who explained customary practice.[139] At least once, he reviewed a decision based on merchant feedback. On a question of the meaning of the warranty 'with convoy', Mansfield laid down a preliminary rule based largely on the testimony in court of a merchant-expert as to practice. However, when he learned that 'people in the city are dissatisfied with the verdict, and think the evidence of the plaintiffs' witnesses might be founded on a mistake', he changed his ruling.[140]

One of Mansfield's City insiders was the prominent underwriter Edward Vaux. Campbell, a contemporary, reported in his *Lives of the Chief Justices* that Mansfield 'did much for the improvement of commercial law... by rearing a body of special jurymen at Guildhall' which he involved in all mercantile cases there. Campbell stated that 'from them he learned the usages of trade, and took great pains in explaining to them the principles of jurisprudence by which they were to be guided'. He named Vaux as one of these men, revealing something about the predominance of Lloyd's.[141] Vaux was a member of the Committee of Lloyd's, having been elected in 1796 to replace the retiring John Julius Angerstein (on whom more below).[142] Campbell described Vaux, his contemporary, as having 'had almost as much authority as the Lord Chief Justice himself'. According to the *Roll of Lloyd's*, Edward Vaux Senior (one of four Vaux men to join New Lloyd's between 1796 and 1837) subscribed to the Coffee-house only in 1796, the year of his appointment to the committee.[143] Mansfield had effectively retired from the Bench ten years earlier, in 1786. If Vaux was one of his expert jurymen, he must have been an important London underwriter for many years before he subscribed to Lloyd's. Even during the first years of the French Revolutionary Wars, when the insurance business was booming in London, not all leading underwriters were part of the institution.

Through Mansfield's contextually astonishing, cooperative approach to setting down a set of legal principles under the common law to govern insurance practice, the Lord Chief Justice made an intervention that has endured. For buyers and sellers of insurance who operated outside of the community of merchant-insurers, an effective dispute-resolution alternative with royal authority now existed. Most importantly, it followed merchant custom, which meant that it was both flexible and in concert with merchant-insurers' practice. Mansfield's achievement in the area of insurance law is difficult to overstate. As Oldham observes, 'The sheer volume of insurance litigation that arose – accelerating as the years went by because of Mansfield's evident aptitude for and interest in the subject – facilitated the articulation of principles of indemnity

---

[139] *Glover v. Black*, 3 Burr. 1394.

[140] *Lilly v. Ewer*, 1779, 1 Dougl. 72, 99 Eng. Rep. 50.

[141] Campbell, John: *The lives of the chief justices of England*, first edition of two volumes, London: John Murray, 1849, II, p. 407*n*.

[142] Martin is in error at p. 232 of his *History of Lloyd's* in stating that it was Jasper, not Edward Vaux, who was elected at this time. According to the *Roll of Lloyd's*, Jasper Vaux subscribed only in 1800. LL Uncatalogued, Dawson, Warren R. (Honorary Librarian to Lloyd's): *Roll of Lloyd's, 1771–1930*, London: Lloyd's of London, 1931. See also Edward's unanimous election to the Committee, GHL CLC/B/148/A/001, f. 95.

[143] Jasper, 1800; Edward Junior, 1799; Ernest, 1837.

and the perception of relationships between insurance rules that had never before been accomplished.'[144] In 1908, Vance wrote that Mansfield's system of insurance laws 'has been much extended in modern times, but it has been little changed'.[145]

On insurance rates

It is impossible to say with certainty whether interventions into the London marine insurance market made between the late sixteenth and the mid eighteenth century had a direct impact on insurance prices. However, it is clear from extant data that prices declined, in some cases dramatically, and that rates in peacetime were significantly lower than those levied during times of war, as would be expected. Causation in the wartime price discrepancy may be plain, but it is much less difficult to determine with confidence for the period of notable decline between the winding-down of the Office of Assurance and the time of the various eighteenth-century interventions.

'Every voyage required its special conditions', Sutherland noted of marine underwriting.[146] Many had an impact on prices, as did market factors such as the level of competition. These factors are known from qualitative sources to include risk type (ship, goods, or bullion); the voyage and the quality of vessel and the competence of her master; recent political events local to the voyage; coverage details such as warranties, abatements, and limitations on average; broker involvement; the volume of insurance purchased by the buyer over time; the weather; and, from a different perspective, the reputation (that is, credit-worthiness) and experience of the underwriter. Unfortunately, no single source of marine insurance pricing data reveals all of these details. For example, surviving underwriting journals kept by the prolific underwriter William Braund record details of risks he insured between 1759 and 1773. They show, for example, that in 1759 he covered cargoes to Jamaica at prices ranging from 3% to 20%. The mean price was 9.2%. In March he once charged the unusually low price of 5%, but a few days later he charged the equally unusual rate of 20%. Late news or rumours of Caribbean naval action could have caused the spike, but it is equally feasible that Braund was reluctantly insuring a leaky vessel commanded by a drunkard, or that the ship was already months overdue. It is impossible to know the entire basis of his pricing decisions.

Very occasionally some clarity intervenes. On 26 January 1760 Braund underwrote £200 on a vessel for its voyage from New York to London at a rate of eight guineas, and another line of £100 for the same voyage, the latter warranted '/wth Convoy/', at four guineas.[147] This shows unambiguously that the cost of insuring the voyage from America to Britain was double the cost when sailing unescorted. It

---

[144] Oldham, James: 'Murray, William, first earl of Mansfield', *Oxford dictionary of national biography online*, www.oxforddnb.com/view/article/19655 [Accessed 3 Dec. 2021].

[145] Vance, William Reynolds: 'The early history of insurance law', *Columbia Law Review*, Vol. 8. No. 1 (1908), p. 17.

[146] Sutherland, *London merchant*, p. 52.

[147] Braund, William: *Journal of Risks*, 1759–1765. ECRO, D/DRu B7, p. 14.

does not, however, explain why the broker, Thomas Bell of Mark Lane, acquired one tranche of cover with the convoy warranty, and another without, on the same vessel and voyage. It may have been a hedging strategy. Neither does sight of a policy reveal all pricing factors, as one written on the *Frances* for a voyage from Quebec illustrates. The broker, Sanderson, Brothers, regularly used the blank second recto page of policies for correspondence. The extant letter states, 'We found it impossible to get it effected at a lower rate, as we have today [received] from our house at Quebec dated 20th August [a] list of arrivals up to that date wherein it does not appear that either the *Frances* or the *Bolton* had arrived...'. Thus the policy was issued 'lost or not lost', but this warranty was included in all printed policies at this time.[148]

Notwithstanding these limitations, it is possible to draw several conclusions from data collected by the author. Figure 2 illustrates the dramatic reduction of peace-time rates between 1620 and 1764, reflecting at least in part the institutional efficiencies and broad risk pool achieved in London over the period. The destinations were selected by Malynes in 1620, and Magens adopted them in 1753 for direct comparison. I have done the same, using archive data for 1654, 1735, and 1764. Over the period, summer rates for all destinations fell from between 3% and 8.5% to below 2%. In almost every example, prices trended consistently downwards over the period, before stabilising at between 1.25% and 1.75% in the second half of the eighteenth century. The exception is stable pricing between 1620 and 1654 for Baltic and French Atlantic destinations, although the Anglo-Dutch War, which had just ended, may have inflated these rates.

War had a clear effect both on the level and volatility of insurance prices, as rates charged by Braund for American risks in 1759 and 1764 clearly illustrate. The years are the earliest for which comprehensive London underwriting data for standard risks survives.[149] In 1759, during Atlantic naval conflicts of the Seven Years War, Braund charged ten discrete rates, including seven different rates in the month of March alone, for the voyage from London to a named American port. The destination specified does not correlate with the fluctuation of rates between 2.5% and 20%. The mean rate is 7.1%; the standard deviation 5.1%. In sharp contrast, Braund charged only three discrete rates in 1764 (2.5%, 3%, and 4%), for a mean of 3.2%, and a standard deviation of 0.76%. From March 1764 his rate for the voyage did not vary from 2.5%.

The data reveals another impact on underwriting of wartime uncertainty. In 1759 Braund insured about two dozen East India risks for the single voyage, either out or home. In 1764 he insured a similar number of East India voyages, but with the coming of peace more than half were insured for the double voyage, out and home, of at least two years' duration. The rate stabilised at 7%. Braund's data also illustrates seasonal variation in rates to European destinations, as shown in Figure 3. The

---

[148] It appears in all London policies I have examined that have been issued since 1717. ALC uncatalogued, Policy underwritten for Mrs Sarah Wilde, 27 Nov. 1818.

[149] Peter du Cane's underwriting data for 1738 and 1739 survives in manuscript but it appears that the broker through whom he acquired his business loaded the novice underwriter with non-standard risks. His records provide few details of ratings for simple voyages from London.

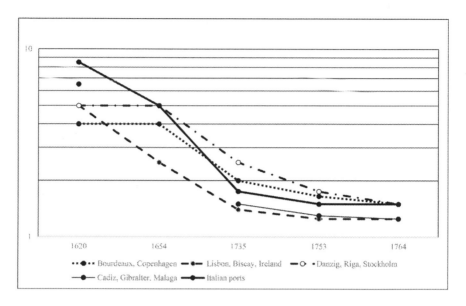

Figure 2: Peacetime cargo insurance rates (per cent), London to European and Mediterranean ports, 1620 and 1764 (logarithmic scale)

variation does not affect America and East India risks; the timings of their sailings were regulated by the seasons. This presents a further uncertainty, however. Braund underwrote India risks in August, for example, when the weather ensured that vessels did not leave London for the East. Clearly insurance was not always purchased at the outset of a voyage.

New Lloyd's

Lloyd's was reinvented in the eighteenth century, as it was transformed from a venue where underwriting took place with the support of an information network controlled by the proprietor of the venue into an institution owned and controlled by underwriters. The master of the Coffee-house went from being an entrepreneur to a profit-sharing employee. Soon after, Lloyd's adopted roles as a maker of standards for underwriting, and as a lobbying organisation for underwriters' interests. Together this significant institutional development was an important component of the changes which comprise the later eighteenth-century intervention into London marine insurance. Lloyd's became a 'self-regulating organisation'. Typically such organisations constitute a financial market which sets rules for its members, based on those members' characteristics.[150]

[150] Neal, Larry and Davis, Lance: 'The evolution of the rules and regulations of the first emerging markets: the London, New York and Paris stock exchanges, 1792–1914', *Quarterly Review of Economics and Finance*, No. 45 (2005), p. 299.

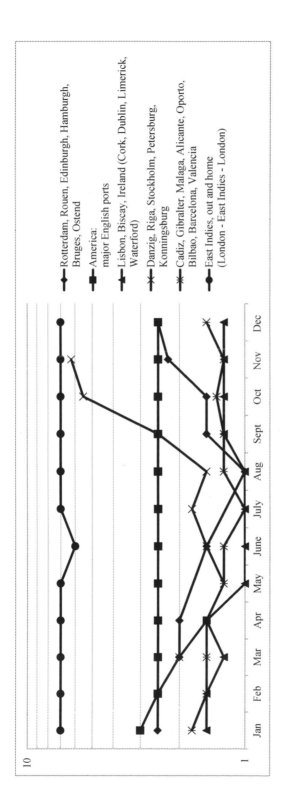

Figure 3: Seasonal insurance rate fluctuations (per cent), London to international ports, 1764 (logarithmic scale)

In 1769, a group of underwriters left Lloyd's and reformed as 'New Lloyd's Coffee House' in temporary premises at Five Pope's Head Alley, a fashionable street intersecting with Lombard Street.[151] The details of their succession have been recounted admirably in Wright and Fayle's *History of Lloyd's*. As the authors wryly observe, the adopted name shows that the defecting underwriters' intention was to supplant their former Coffee-house.[152] They successfully encouraged one of the old Lloyd's waiters, Thomas Fielding, to establish a coffee-house operation there, and the manager of old Lloyd's to retire on the same day that New Lloyd's was scheduled to open. The latter, Wright and Fayle postulate, was key to garnering the support of the Post Office, in the form of a grant to New Lloyd's of free postage for shipping intelligence, matching that of old Lloyd's.[153] They soon garnered control of the shipping intelligence network of old Lloyd's.

It is clear that Thomas Lawrence, non-executive proprietor of old Lloyd's, was not happy about these developments, and attempted to retain control both of the information network supplying *Lloyd's List* and of the clientele who took advantage of it. It appears, however, from a remarkable announcement in the *Public Advertiser* of 17 March 1769 urging customers to stay put, and for subscribers to the *List* to provide their names 'at the Bar', that Lawrence did not have the subscription lists in hand.[154] Fielding announced, three days later in the same newspaper, 'to the Merchants in general, owners, and Freighters of Ships, Insurance Brokers, &c. &c.' that New LLOYD'S COFFEE-HOUSE' was to open tomorrow.[155] Back at old Lloyd's (which briefly adopted the name Old Lloyd's), the edition of the *List* published under the old management announced that, the following week, the newspaper would continue as *New-Lloyd's List*. The competing coffee shops operated in parallel for several years. Wright and Fayle suggest that old Lloyd's closed *c*.1785,[156] but it was still trading in 1794, based on a newspaper advertisement which appeared in February that year inviting donations to support the family victims of a factory fire ('as unfortunately they had not renewed their annual insurance, owing to their uncommon press and hurry of business'), to be deposited, among other places, at 'Lloyd's Coffee-house in Lombard Street'.[157] Ultimately it was New Lloyd's which was to become the focal point of the insurance world-economy.

In all, about six dozen underwriters had departed Lloyd's to establish a competitor in new premises around the corner, which served both coffee and shipping intelligence. From New Lloyd's many, at least, of the most prominent underwriters would carry on conducting the business of underwriting. Their defection was not prompted by any of the complaints which had driven sixteenth and seventeenth century interventions into the functioning of London's insurance market. Instead,

---

[151] Gibb, *Lloyd's of London*, p. 47.

[152] Wright and Fayle, *History of Lloyd's*, p. 98.

[153] Wright and Fayle, *History of Lloyd's*, pp. 99–100.

[154] *Public Advertiser*, No. 10,728, 17 Mar. 1769, p. 1.

[155] *Public Advertiser*, No. 10,730, 20 Mar. 1769, p. 1.

[156] Wright and Fayle, *History of Lloyd's*, pp. 97–108, 122–125.

[157] *Public Advertiser*, No. 18,627, 22 Feb. 1794, p. 1.

the motivation seems to have been the rise of disreputable wagering at old Lloyd's. Heretofore, no clear-cut division had existed between insurance and wager.[158] Now, prominent merchant-insurers strove to separate themselves and their reputations from buyers and sellers of insurance who were focused solely or largely on wagering. So blurred was the line between the two activities that the bill which preceded the 1747/8 Act prohibiting the insurance of French vessels would also have prohibited 'every other Contract, or Wager, or Agreement, in the nature of a Wager' on French shipping.[159] The *London Chronicle* had reported in 1768, the year before the Lloyd's split, that

> the introduction and amazing progress of illicit gaming at Lloyd's coffee-house is, among others, a powerful and very melancholy proof of the degeneracy of the times... [and has] met with so much encouragement from many of the principal Under-writers, who are, in every other respect, useful members of society... gaming in any degree is perverting the original and useful design of that coffee-house.

Specific wagers cited in the *Chronicle* include bets upon the election, death, and even execution of named individuals, on the declaration of war with France or Spain, and on the dissolution of parliament. The unnamed author declared these insurances were 'underwrote, chiefly by Scotsmen, at the above [old Lloyd's] Coffee-house'.[160]

In a sector where reputation is critical, it is unsurprising that some underwriters, along with various insurance brokers, and men whose primary pursuits were as merchants, bankers, and shipowners, but who through those activities had an interest in insurance, felt the situation untenable, and set out to develop a new institution wherein such unscrupulous underwriting activities could be proscribed.[161] Late in 1771, seventy-nine patrons of New Lloyd's each paid £15 towards a subscription commitment of £100, with the intention of building, buying, or leasing larger premises.[162] This was the merchant-insurers' first concrete step towards forming a self-governing organisation through which to transact insurance. A meeting of fifty-one subscribers elected a committee of nine to lead the search. In November 1773, 'after many Fruitless Trials to obtain a Coffee House', they chose to lease from the Mercers' Company 'a very Roomy and Convenient place over the North West Side of the Royal Exchange at the Rent of £180 p Annum'.[163]

The choice of venue followed the intervention of a non-member of the committee, John Julius Angerstein. A Hanoverian Russia merchant, insurance underwriter and broker, adviser to William Pitt, and financier born in St Petersburg, his

---

[158] Rossi, *Insurance in Elizabethan England*, p. 10.

[159] *A Bill to prohibit Insurance on Ships belonging to France*, 1746.

[160] Cited in Malcolm, James Peller: *Anecdotes of the manners and customs of LONDON during the eighteenth century*, Second Edition, Vol. I, London: Longman, Hurst, Rees, and Orme, 1810, pp. 373–375.

[161] Wright and Fayle, *History of Lloyd's*, p. 111.

[162] GHL CLC/B/148/A/001, *Minutes of the Committee of Lloyd's*, Dec. 1771–Aug. 1804, ff. 27–28.

[163] GHL CLC/B/148/A/001, f. 34.

collection of paintings by Titian, Claude, Poussin, Raphael, Rembrandt, Rubens, Velázquez, and Van Dyck formed the basis of the National Gallery's collection.[164] Angerstein is now widely regarded as the Father of Lloyd's, of which he was a founding subscriber, but is first specifically identified in the committee minute book only as one of the 'gentlemen who attend New Lloyd's Coffeehouse'.[165] With his intervention, after two years of searching and negotiations, the committee settled New Lloyd's in the same building where the Office of Assurance had been located two hundred years earlier, and where the wording of the London insurance contract had been standardised.

Although insurance was not written exclusively at Lloyd's, the business of insuring there appears to have taken hold relatively quickly. In the 1780s the Bristol merchant William Davenport regularly addressed correspondence to his broker Anthony Kirwan at 'New Lloyd's, London', giving detailed instructions about insurance orders.[166] That said, twenty years later the multi-local nature of insurance was not entirely displaced, as shown by a handwritten policy issued in Liverpool in October 1803, which covered

> For Cash of £300 Insurance p[er] the Margaret Lace, with or without Letters of Marque, at and from Leith to the Coast of Africa & the African Islands, or the African [sic] & the Coast of Africa, during the stay & trade at any ports and places there, & from thence to the Port or Ports of Touching, Sale, Discharge, & Final Destination in the British and Foreign W Indies, the Bahamas & America, with liberty to return once into Port with a Prize or Prizes.[167]

The underwriters, for £100 each, were Moses Benson, a merchant and ship's captain who retired into slaving, James Michell, co-owner of a vessel with Benson, and Joseph Fletcher, a mariner and son of the leading slaver Caleb Fletcher.

Various resolutions in Lloyd's minute book show the ongoing process of institution-building, and reflect the evolution of the premises-committee into the governing body of a society of underwriters. These include posting in the subscribers' room, 'in large Characters on Vellum, and framed', the 'Names of all the Subscribers to New Lloyd's Coffee House'. It was further resolved that any twelve subscribers could call a general meeting of the subscribers, in order to establish new rules. At the same meeting, held 4 March 1774, the day before the move to the Royal Exchange, the subscribers agreed that

> Shameful practices which have been introduced of late years [to the] Business of Underwriting such as making Speculative Insurance on the Lives of Persons and on Government Securities – In the first Instance it is endangering the lives of the

---

[164] Palmer, Sarah: 'Angerstein, John Julius', *Oxford Dictionary of National Biography Online*, www.oxforddnb.com/view/article/549 [Accessed 3 Dec. 2021].

[165] GHL CLC/B/148/A/001, ff. 32.

[166] TNA C107/1–15, Papers of James Rogers, bankrupt (fifteen boxes). I am grateful to Dr Nick Radburn for bringing to my attention the wealth of insurance correspondence in this collection.

[167] ALC Uncatalogued, Policy underwritten for Thomas Rhodie & Co., 12 Oct. 1803 (image only).

Persons so insured, from the Idea of being Selected from Society for that inhuman purpose, which is being Virtually an Accessory in a Species of Slow Murder – In the Second Instance of Speculative Insurance on the Stocks, it is Notorious they are Calculated for the purpose of Stock Jobbing and tend to weaken the Public Credit – It is therefore hoped that the Insurers general will refuse Subscribing such Policies and that they will shew a proper Resentment against any Policy Broker who shall hereafter tender such Policy to them.[168]

Making insurance on lives or other events in which the policyholder had no insurable interest was already prohibited under law. So too was wagering on public funds through insurance. By Lloyd's resolution, this early form of hedging through derivatives was further separated from insurance, as the eighteenth-century financial revolution progressed, and specific branches of finance were more clearly defined. The resolution shows that statutory interventions cannot have been wholly effective; such contracts were unenforceable at law, but drew no further sanction. Nor is it clear that the sanction of 'proper resentment' was particularly efficacious within Lloyd's, initially at least. The society did not actually prohibit such underwriting under the threat of expulsion, despite its prohibition under statute. Although they were unenforceable at law, wagering policies were still offered at old Lloyd's. An item in the *Public Advertiser* in 1794, for example, states that 'Friday a policy was opened at Lloyd's Coffee-house, giving a premium of ten per cent. to insure a peace with America for six months'.[169]

In April or May the following year (the date is unknown because the top edge of the minute book was singed in the fire at the Royal Exchange in 1834), it was resolved that one of two rooms comprising Lloyd's 'shall be deemed the Subscribers Room', and that a waiter 'shall constantly attend the door', opening it only to 'Subscribers and their contacts'. This development, supported by letters sent to 'such Underwriters and Brokers as frequent this House and have not already Subscribed to its Establishment', encouraging them to do so, was another important step in the institutional development of Lloyd's: the exclusion of outsiders. It seems at this time, however, that the only qualification for those wishing to subscribe was the payment of a one-off fee of £15.[170] Even that was no bar: in its first decades, much of the business of the Committee of Lloyd's was focused on urging, cajoling, and encouraging frequent users of the facilities to purchase a subscription, or pay their call. The committee even posted the names of recalcitrants in the public coffee-room as 'Defaulters'.[171] They were also constrained by law. In 1762 about 150 stockbrokers at Jonathan's Coffee House had organised what was to become the London Stock Exchange. They raised a subscription of £8 per member, but when brokers excluded from Jonathan's complained, Mansfield and a City jury found that entry to an

---

[168] GHL CLC/B/148/A/001, ff. 35–36.
[169] *Public Advertiser*, No. 18, 622, 17 Feb. 1794, p. 1.
[170] GHL CLC/B/148/A/001, f. 39.
[171] Ibid., esp. f. 47.

established place of trade could not be barred through prohibitive entry fees, since to do so breached merchant custom.[172]

Information provision at Lloyd's was continuously improved, at the expense of the subscribers. From 1774 the 'Arrival and Loss Book' was displayed within the Subscribers Room. In it was recorded, on a dedicated page (or more as required), each day's news about the ends of voyages.[173] Such a register is still displayed (and updated daily by a 'waiter' with a quill pen) in the underwriting room at Lloyd's.[174] In 1779, during the Anglo-American war, the committee agreed that the subscribers would share the cost of obtaining lists of all merchant convoys and Baltic Sound lists, and at about this time – or possibly much earlier – Lloyd's struck a deal with the Post Office for receiving information from its extensive correspondent network.[175] 'Letters addressed to the Postmaster-general containing shipping information for Lloyd's Coffee-house are delivered free of postage, and have been so delivered for a period previous to the year 1788,' stated James Campbell, a secretary at the Post Office and witness before an 1837 enquiry into its management.[176] From an unknown beginning until 1788 Lloyd's had paid a flat fee of £200 for this service, which was limited to letters sent from the outports and containing information about shipping movements.

In 1792 thirty-two correspondents sent updates from twenty-eight ports. The fee was split between the Secretary and Comptroller of the Inland Office. From 1788 the fee was reduced to £100, and paid into the 'general fund'. In 1793 the charge was dropped altogether, although Lloyd's paid a penny per copy of its *List* delivered through the post. However, before publication in *Lloyd's List* shipping news was copied into the Arrival and Loss Book, the letters posted on a display board, and the information duplicated in a book in Lloyd's public coffee-room. In 1837 Thomas Chapman, a member of the Committee of Lloyd's, told a Commission of Enquiry that 'the more the information is diffused, the better pleased we are'. In 1837, the earliest record available, *Lloyd's List* had a circulation of 780 copies, of which 450 were delivered by post.[177] (So central was the Post Office to Lloyd's operations that its first dedicated building was erected in 1928 *within* the City's main Post Office building on Leadenhall Street.) Less public would have been information garnered from the inspection of vessels: multiple records of payments to surveyors indicate a centralised inspection regime from an early date, perhaps related primarily to lost vessels.[178]

At the request of the proprietor of the *Shipping Gazette*, a publication similar to *Lloyd's List* introduced in 1836, the Commissioners of Enquiry were investigating the publication and free delivery, by the Post Office since 1801, of a competing,

---

[172] Neal and Davis, 'The evolution of the rules and regulations', p. 299.

[173] Wright and Fayle, *History of Lloyd's*, pp. 121–122.

[174] I have watched it being done.

[175] GHL CLC/B/148/A/001, f. 41.

[176] *Eighth report of the commissioners appointed to inquire into the management of the Post-Office Department*, Part I, London: HMSO, 1837, p. 24.

[177] *Eighth Report, 1837*, pp. 4, 8, 22, 25, 26.

[178] GHL CLC/B/148/A/001, f. 67.

daily news sheet, the *Post-office Shipping List*. Unlike *Lloyd's List*, which covered only arrivals and sailings from foreign ports, the Post Office list covered coastal vessels. It was financed by the clerks who produced it, and its profits provided an official subsidy to the clerks' salaries. Its news was based in part on Lloyd's correspondents' submissions, but the information-sharing was said to be disclosed and mutual; for example, in the years 1833 to 1835, Lloyd's paid to the Post Office an annual 'gratuity' of £5.5s to extract shipping information from another of its publications, the *Post-office Packet Journals*.[179]

A particularly significant institutional development was made in 1779 in response to unfavourable market practices. The subscribers agreed to 'consider some Innovations in the printed part of some Policies lately Introduced in the Coffee House'. They resolved

> That no Policy be Subscribed from this time <u>knowingly</u> that may be printed in Words different from a Form now produced. – That we will not Underwrite to any Person or Persons who hereafter may tender a Policy <u>otherwise Printed</u>. – That a Committee be appointed consisting of Fifteen of the Subscribers to take into Consideration the Propriety of an Application to Parliament to determine the Printed Form of Policies of Insurance, and to Report their Opinion to another General Meeting.[180]

The majority of insurances were underwritten on printed policy forms comprising a single sheet, twenty-one inches by fifteen. The sheet was folded in half, and only the front page was printed, leaving ample space for subscribers' names, and for warranties which, as has been shown, could override the terms and conditions in the printed wording, loss particulars, and other relevant information. About two weeks later the sub-committee reported their opinion that 'the Evil being Radically Cured, there is at present no necessity for an Application to Parliament.'[181]

Lloyd's minute book does not describe the 'evil', but a contemporary commentator and underwriter, John Weskett, did so in the preliminary discourse to his 1781 volume *A complete digest of the theory, laws, and practice of insurance*. Weskett, 'of near the London-Stone Coffee House, Cannon Street', was a merchant-insurer who subscribed to Lloyd's in 1772.[182] He described two additions to the policy as a 'very extraordinary innovation'. One required underwriters to 'allow the *Balance* of our *respective Accounts* due to us from the Person or Persons to whom we shall underwrite this Policy, towards the payment' of any claims. The other stated – in small print, Weskett specified – that 'any *Insufficiency* of the Ship, or *Deviation* of the Master, unknown to the Assured, shall not prejudice this insurance.'[183]

Both clauses operated in contravention to established custom under the Law Merchant. However, as has been shown, practice could and did change, and so

---

[179] *Eighth Report, 1837*, pp. 4, 8, 22, 25, 26.

[180] Emphasis in original. GHL CLC/B/148/A/001, f. 40.

[181] GHL CLC/B/148/A/001, f. 41.

[182] Dawson, *Roll of Lloyd's*, marginal note, p. 294.

[183] Weskett, *Complete digest*, p. lii.

change the Law Merchant itself. In this case, the first policy amendment upset the longstanding cash flow arrangements, described above, between underwriter, broker, and client, by allowing insureds to set any premiums due under any policies against losses under a single policy. The second revoked the longstanding position that ignorance of the condition of an insured vessel does not exclude the insured from the requirement of disclosure at the time of underwriting, and that insurance upon vessels which deviate from their course is void. This expanded considerably the terms of cover. Weskett described the clauses as '*insidious*, and very fraudulently *foisted* into some Policies'. Underwriters, he noted, were aware that the policy form had not been altered for generations, would have assumed that any policy presented followed these conventions, and had discovered the changes only by accident. However, it is likely that brokers made the change with the support of at least some underwriters who sought competitive advantage through their offer of easier underwriting terms. Tellingly, Weskett observed that, in correcting the problem, 'More was effected at *one* meeting of the Insurers, Merchants, &c. by a *Resolution* amongst *themselves*, than could have been done by *fifty* Law Suits.'[184] To remove the need for underwriters to make sure that the policy form was as expected, the committee resolved that all policies should carry a prominent marginal note stating it was printed according to the agreed wording.[185]

The fledgling New Lloyd's had flexed its new institutional muscle to ensure that, within its own organisation at least, it was to control the evolution of underwriting practice, but the impact was broader: both the wording approved, and the practice of manually adding warranties to it, endured until the 1980s.[186] The Marine Insurance Act of 1906 includes, as a specimen, the wording of a Lloyd's policy which is almost entirely unchanged from those of 1779 and 1582. Despite this, the product supplied by London's underwriters remained flexible. Changes and amendments could be made to the language of individual policies by making handwritten additions or, later, by attaching warranties and other additional clauses. Sir David Rowland, chairman of Lloyd's from 1993 to 1997, spent the first year of his apprenticeship as a junior broker in the 1950s 'pasting' warranties into policies.[187]

The remarkable endurance of this policy wording is attributable to its flexibility, as reflected in the intended meaning and customary interpretation of each clause under the Law Merchant, and by the courts, following the intervention of Mansfield. The actual words of the policy are almost meaningless in the absence of these interpretations. However, with centuries of interpretation in place, to abandon the established policy wording would have reintroduced a panoply of ambiguities. At the same time, the interpretations were not fixed. As has been shown, when the intentions of the underwriting market shifted, however subtly, interpretations of the contract wording shifted with them, harking back to the ancient English principle of

---

[184] Weskett, *Complete digest*, pp. lii–liii.

[185] GHL CLC/B/148/A/001, f. 41.

[186] For the very minor differences between the 1779 policy and that used at Lloyd's in the twentieth century, see Wright and Fayle, *History of Lloyd's*, pp. 126–129.

[187] Personal interview, January 2013.

commercial jurisprudence, recorded by Glanvill in the twelfth century, that 'agreement prevails over the law'.[188]

Although in 1779 the Committee of New Lloyd's had deemed it unnecessary to lobby parliament to require under statute the use of its policy form throughout the realm, such legislation was to be enacted in 1795 for an entirely different reason. Under *An Act for granting His Majesty certain Stamp Duties on Sea Insurances*, the Commissioners of Stamped Vellum, Parchment, and Paper were required to provide pre-taxed, pre-stamped, pre-printed policy blanks.[189] They were to appoint 'one or more Office or Offices within the City of *London*, at some convenient place at or near the Royal Exchange' and 'a proper Officer or Officers' to distribute the blanks, which were to be printed according to contract wordings annexed to the Act. Forms of contract adopted by the Subscribers to New Lloyd's in 1779, one each for ship and goods, were the policy wordings specified, alongside those in use by the Royal Exchange and the London Assurance Companies.[190] The Stamp Duty Act was amended after the French Revolutionary and Napoleonic Wars, under acts of 1816 and 1820, but already the legislation had acted as an incubator to embed the use of the New Lloyd's policy.[191] On the negative side (according to a decidedly anti-tax commentator), the duties were 'of so onerous a nature as to compel a large quantity of the business heretofore transacted in England, to be transferred to Holland and the Hanse towns', although no evidence of this shift was offered.[192]

Pitt, speaking in support of his wartime budget, described his introduction of an *ad valorem* tax on insurance, in place of the flat tax on policies introduced under Anne, as 'not likely to be felt any where as a material inconvenience'.[193] However, a provision of the Act had an unintended consequence, which proves the danger of imposing rules upon the underwriting market. Policies were limited to 'twelve Calendar Months' duration. Thus, the maximum period for which a ship could be insured was suddenly limited to one year. Some vessels, especially East Indiamen, had routinely been insured for their entire voyage, out and back, which could be up to three years' duration (and which justified Lloyd's reporting its results three years in arrears well into the 1990s, when annual accounting was finally introduced). Indirectly, and almost certainly unintentionally, multi-year policies were no longer legal.

The Act further required that every policy must include a statement of the premium paid and the sum insured, a description of the risk insured, and the names of all of the subscribers – information already included in policies as standard practice. Unstamped policies were inadmissible in English courts, except, one presumes,

[188] See p. 57.

[189] Anno. 35 Geo. III c. 63.

[190] *Statutes at Large, Vol. XVIII, A.D. 1793–1795*, London: Andrew Straham, Law Printer, 1811, pp. 567–583.

[191] *Journals of the House of Commons, Vol. L, 1794–1795* (undated), London: HMSO, pp. 360–540.

[192] Montgomery Martin, R.: *Taxation of the British Empire*, London: Effingham Wilson, 1833, p. 191.

[193] *Parliamentary History, Vol. XXXI, A.D. 1794–1795*, London: T.C. Hansard, 1818, col. 1312.

when buyers, underwriters, or brokers who were involved in the transaction of marine insurance under unstamped policies were called to account; all faced fines of £500 for such transgressions.[194] Pitt, meanwhile, declared that 'Insurance was carried on with so much advantage in this country from the good faith that was observed by our underwriters, that many respectable merchants thought a slight additional tax was not like to hazard a diminution in the insurance… the capital annually insured in this country amounted to 120 millions sterling.' The tax, at 2s. 6d. per £100 when the cost of insurance was more than 10s. per £100, and half that on rates of 10s. or less, was expected to raise £130,000. The actual yield was £96,884 in 1797. In 1801 Pitt doubled the tax rate for all but coastal voyages, but this was reversed the following year. According to one tax commentator, the levy was effective because it was applied 'during the war, when England was practically the only country where sea risks could be insured'.[195]

At a general meeting of New Lloyd's in 1781, during the Anglo-American war, the members voted on a resolution that the committee should be 'requested to make application to Parliament to restrain Shipmasters from Ransoming their Ships and Cargoes from the Enemy'. The motion was defeated, but highlights the fact that some insurers disliked the practice of ransom.[196] Ships' masters were de facto obliged to ransom captured vessels if this was in the interests of their owners, and insurers were 'obliged to declare immediately that they will contribute towards the payment of the ransom'. Further, if a ransomed ship was lost or taken again on the same voyage, insurers were twice liable.[197]

Capture and ransom became institutionalised during the eighteenth century, and this was far more convenient than seizure for both captor and captured. However, it was perhaps less so for insurers, as the vote of the underwriters indicates. The cost of a ransom was less than that of a total loss of vessel and cargo, but the chance of a recapture negating the loss was eliminated, and efforts at evasion and resistance by crews were probably reduced.[198] Clearly, at least some merchant-insurers saw ransom as bad for their business. Lloyd's again sought parliamentary intervention to prevent fraud in 1785, when the committee ordered written 'a Draft for an Act of Parliament to oblige the Insured to insert his Name or that of their agents in all Policies of Assurance, and to be delivered to Mr. Harley', a provision proposed under bills decades earlier, although nothing seems to have come of either initiative.[199]

In 1780 Lloyd's had set aside a room for 'Arbitrators and private Business', an indication that arbitration remained of central importance, and evidence that insurance underwriting was transacted in the relative publicity of the subscribers' room.

[194] *Statutes at Large, Vol. XVIII*, pp. 567–583; *Journals of the House of Commons, Vol. L, 1794–1795* (undated), London: His Majesty's Stationery Office, pp. 360–540.

[195] *Parliamentary History*, Vol. XXXI, col. 1312; Dowell, Stephen: *A history of taxes and taxation in England*, four vols, London: Longmans, Green & Co., 1888, III, pp. 147–148.

[196] GHL CLC/B/148/A/001, ff. 43–44.

[197] Weskett, *Complete digest*, pp. 440–441.

[198] Wright and Fayle, *History of Lloyd's*, p. 154.

[199] GHL CLC/B/148/A/001, f. 48.

The committee invested the society's surplus cash in 3% consols, and appointed a full-time administrator. The premises were expanded on multiple occasions with the number of subscribers, and in 1786 the committee resolved that of those attending New Lloyd's, 'every Person writing in his own name or causing others to write for him shall be required to subscribe'.[200] The resolution shows that some underwriters were deploying the capital of others, and assuming risk in their name. This practice, present in Italy in the fifteenth century,[201] has continued in the Lloyd's market until the present day, and allows an unparalleled spread of risk. More importantly in the context of the development of London insurance, it entrenched an operational exclusivity. Those underwriting at Lloyd's, directly or through agency, would be required to be subscribers. The self-governing merchant-insurers of old were now Lloyd's underwriters, an exclusive group.[202]

Lloyd's soon began to project its institutional power to manage risks before losses occurred, through what is today described as risk management. In June 1794 the subscribers met to consider 'the Misconduct of Captains of merchant Ships under Convoy, as stated from the Lords of the Admiralty', and empowered the committee to take appropriate steps to bring to justice any merchants or captains who had 'wilfully Quitted their Convoy, or otherwise misconducted themselves while under Convoy'. The resolution was posted at 'the Customs House, & the several coffee houses round the Royal Exchange', but not just captains' behaviour was found wanting: the merchant-insurers also lobbied for improved naval support of convoys. A note to the Admiralty was prepared, with the cooperation of the insurance companies, to present a market-wide opinion. It stated that

> our fears for the Safety of the large & Rich Fleets hourly expected from the East & West Indies, whose Loss would be of the most serious import to the Nation, and would bring on inevitable ruin to that useful body of Men [the underwriters], They conceive those fears are not without foundation since they are not, with all of the means of Information they are in possession of, able to see any adequate protection at sea from this Kingdom.[203]

While this first minuted communication between Lloyd's and the Admiralty was a clear request for action, Lloyd's soon began to offer assistance, too. The week after despatching its letter requesting improved convoy support, the committee sent another note giving information about the enemy vessels involved in a capture. The Admiralty replied immediately, requesting more information, and the correspondence continued.[204] The speed and complexity of the communications shows that Lloyd's had begun to act as a voluntary intelligence arm of the state, as the merchant-insurers and the Admiralty began regularly to exchange information

---

[200] GHL CLC/B/148/A/001, ff. 48–49, 51, 71.

[201] See p. 42.

[202] GHL CLC/B/148/A/001, f. 55.

[203] Leonard, *Marine insurance and the rise of British merchant influence*; 2011. GHL CLC/B/148/A/001, ff. 58–60.

[204] GHL CLC/B/148/A/001, ff. 58–61.

about shipping movements. Thus began a long, formal relationship between Lloyd's and the Admiralty focused on shared intelligence and the maximisation of trade protection, which perhaps peaked in 1871, when the chairman of Lloyd's, George Joachim Goschen, was appointed First Lord of the Admiralty. By this time London insurance had been a component of Britain's blue-water defence strategy, and a significant cog in the mechanisms of her fiscal-military state, for two centuries.

When these interests diverged, Lloyd's sought to respond with equity. In 1795 the underwriters wrote to Pitt 'in respect to Dutch Insurances'; policies underwritten in London on Dutch vessels and cargoes 'upon the confidence of the Amity between this Country and Holland', but which had been seized by the Royal Navy and detained in British ports when the Netherlands fell under French influence as the Batavian Republic in May that year. The underwriters were concerned that they would receive total claims under the Dutch policies, should the insureds choose to 'abandon to them their property so insured under that clause in the Policy which subjects them from the restraint of Princes'. Receiving no answer, they wrote again two weeks later, and a year later to the Lords of the Treasury. Uniquely in this case, the related expenses were voted by the membership to be shared between the individual underwriters exposed to the related claims, rather than drawn from Lloyd's general funds.[205]

Much more could be said about the detail of further developments at Lloyd's following the outbreak of the French Revolutionary Wars, but by this time its basic institutional structures and roles were in place. It was a membership-based organisation of merchant-insurers and insurance brokers which existed to provide the infrastructure necessary for the business of underwriting. This included the provision of a venue, but also of information for the use of its members and others. It had become an employer of people to support that provision. It established a governance structure of an elected committee, whose major decisions had to be ratified at a general meeting of the members, which could be called at any time by a subset of those members. Lloyd's forged links with relevant bodies to advance its interests, including with the Post Office, the Admiralty, and the competing sellers, the chartered companies. It set rules to be followed by its members, censured those who did not comply, including especially the entrenching of a standardised policy form, and fostered the use of arbitration as the primary method of dispute resolution. Finally, it implemented risk management procedures which served to reduce the likelihood of losses, insured or otherwise. Notwithstanding an important philanthropic role, often linked to risk management (such as funding lifeboats), which was soon to be established, by the end of the eighteenth century the merchant-insurers had erected an institutional basis from which they could continue to trade their club good under the tenets of the Law Merchant. When outsider-buyers or -sellers were admitted, but chose not to play by the merchant-insurers' rules of the game, the common law dispute-resolution principles devised by Mansfield, and based on the same evolved Law Merchant which defined London's customary practices, were in place to resolve such problems.

[205] GHL CLC/B/148/A/001, ff. 64, 66, 74, 95.

The wars which straddled the turn of the nineteenth century gave insurance underwriting in London a final great boost. Underwriters both inside and outside Lloyd's were severely tested in 1780, when a Spanish fleet with French reinforcements assaulted the combined British East and West Indies convoy, and seized fifty-five of sixty-three vessels. Another massive loss occurred the following year, when immediately after the Dutch declaration of war Admiral Rodney seized the country's entrepôt-island of St Eustatius, and with it goods valued at £3,000,000, a great proportion of which were insured in London. Several London underwriters failed or withdrew, including many outsider-sellers who were attracted by high premiums.[206] Even today, sellers' capital floods into the insurance market when prices are high. Known today as 'naive capital', Weskett in 1781 described 'not a few Instances even of *Tradesmen, Shopkeepers*, &c. lured by the golden, but delusive Bait of *Premiums*, especially in time of *War*, drawn like Gudgeons, into the Vortex of this perilous Abyss, Insurance'. Lacking sufficient knowledge or experience to underwrite judiciously, they tended to suffer serious losses.[207] Sometimes, too, to trade in insurance is seen as a way to raise capital quickly. The London-based Americas merchant Joshua Johnson, for example, turned to underwriting only in times of need. Once, when his 'finances [were] exceedingly small', he requested of his partners 'your leaves to make insurances for any gentlemen who will favour me with their orders'.[208]

This phenomenon was not unique to London. In 1781, and again in the following year, an anonymous correspondent to *Hicky's Bengal Gazette* complained bitterly of the rise of the practice in British India:

> When I reflect on the present state of private insurance and the number of desperate and needy adventurers who, without being possessed of almost a single Rupee... plunge deeply into this alluring and attractive branch of business, I am filled with astonishment, and can't but secretly pity those who, by themselves or their Agents, trust their Property to the Merciless Winds and Waves upon such fallacious and Swindling Security... Lately you can hardly shake a Plantain Tree, but out flies an under writer, the consequence of which is that scarcely a day now passes but furnishes us with fresh accounts of some Contested Loss, by some or other of these Gentlemen.[209]

Braudel lucidly describes three conditions that may lead to such uninformed investment in insurance. High-level merchants did not specialise, and sometimes had capital 'looking vainly to be invested'. Second, merchants chased profits from sector to sector. Finally, insofar as specialisation tended to occur in commercial life, it was in money trading, of which insurance is a branch (albeit a trade in contingent money).[210] Indeed, one need not have been alien from commerce, or even from insur-

---

[206] Wright and Fayle, *History of Lloyd's*, pp. 155–158.

[207] Weskett, *Complete digest*, p. xxiii.

[208] Johnson to his partners, 6 Nov. 1771. Price, J. M. (ed.): *Joshua Johnson's letterbook, 1771–1774: letters from a merchant in London to his partners in Maryland*. London: London Record Society, 1979, p. 17.

[209] *Hicky's*, Issue 17, 20.05.1780; Issue 26, 21.07.1781.

[210] Braudel, *Afterthoughts*, pp. 60–61.

ance, to suffer through injudicious underwriting. John Walter was a coal trader who, as a merchant-insurer, had shared risk by underwriting colliers at old Lloyd's since the 1770s. He joined New Lloyd's in 1781, and dangerously extended his underwriting. Almost immediately he was, in his own words, 'weighed down, in common with about half of those who were engaged in the protection of property [ships and cargo], by the host of foes this nation had to combat in the American War'. Walter was forced from his home, sold his library, and managed to clear his debt only in 1790. Like Defoe before him, Walter changed his career (if not his name). In 1785 he launched the *Daily Universal Register*, a newspaper which, in 1789, he renamed *The Times*.[211]

Insurers and state finance in wartime

Another example of the strong links between merchants and the state is visible in the enormous role played by Members of Lloyd's and other London insurers and insurance brokers in financing Britain's participation in the French Revolutionary and Napoleonic Wars. Through this lending London marine insurers contributed significantly to the evolution of the British state towards fiscal modernity. Insurers benefit from the double use of capital: premium income collected may be invested for a return, even as it is reserved for the payment of future claims. When the British state sought to borrow through loans to finance its participation in the Continental warfare of the late eighteenth and early nineteenth centuries, marine insurers played a significant and previously unacknowledged role as purchasers of this renewed form of state debt.

Led by Angerstein, the marine insurance market was an extremely important lender in Pitt's war finance loans, which were to be raised by contractors. On 15 March 1793 Pitt wrote to the London Assurance, citing their apparent offer to subscribe £300,000 to the new loan. 'As it is my Intention to agree for the whole amount with such Persons as may be willing to take it on such terms as may be most favourable Terms for the Public, I... cannot therefore enter into any Agreement with respect to any separate Share', he stated.[212] When Pitt met with bidders 'Monday next at Eleven o'clock', the only willing contractor was the partnership Angerstein, Johnson & Devaynes. Godschall Johnson, heir to a longstanding family of West Indies planters and governors, was an associate so close to Angerstein that the insurer was godfather to his children. William Devaynes MP, a banker, five-time chairman of the East India Company, Royal Africa Company director, and undistinguished member of parliament, had worked directly with Angerstein on multiple charity projects and the trio's successful application, in 1789, to operate the first national tontine in several years. For Angerstein, the loan business was ultimately

[211] Wright and Fayle, *History of* Lloyd's, pp. 156–157; Barker, Hannah: 'Walter, John', *Oxford Dictionary of National Biography Online*, www.oxforddnb.com/view/article/28636 [Accessed 3 Dec. 2021].

[212] Pitt to the Governors and Directors of the London Assurance, 15 March 1793, reprinted in Street, G. S.: *The London Assurance, 1720–1920*, London: Williams & Norgate (for private circulation), 1920, facing p. 14.

to become an enormous side-line, as he raised vast sums for the state from his colleagues in the insurance market.[213]

The first loan for which Angerstein's subscription list survives is that of 1812. With Alexander Baring, then his current partner in loan financing, Angerstein committed to raise £10,250,000, of which he took personal responsibility for £5.135 million, a quarter of the loan total. He immediately planned to take £1.708 million onto his own account, an enormous amount for an individual. The rest he divided between 180 subscribers, including individuals and partnerships.[214]

In total, 174 discrete individuals and forty-six partnerships subscribed to Angerstein's loans of 1812 and 1813. It is plain that he turned to his familiars, from business, family, and social life, to seek subscribers, and that the underwriting members of Lloyd's comprised the bulk of them. Of the 172 individuals identified with relative confidence, ninety-three were Lloyd's underwriters, as recorded in the unique *Roll of Lloyd's*. Another sixteen had immediate family members in the market. That makes, in total, 109 loan subscribers with direct connections to Lloyd's, or slightly less than two-thirds of Angerstein's individual subscribers. Further, of forty-six partnerships that subscribed in 1812 and 1813, thirty-one include at least one partner positively identified as a member of Lloyd's. Others, such as 'Thomas Brothers', cannot be conclusively connected to the many Lloyd's members surnamed Thomas. Companies were not permitted to become underwriting members of the market, since partnerships and joint-stock companies were prohibited under the *Bubble Act* of 1720 from underwriting marine insurance risks.

Fourteen subscribers to Angerstein's loans – all members of Lloyd's – appear on a list of underwriters who were guaranteed by Angerstein eighteen years before the loan of 1812, and certainly constitute professional insurers. In 1794 Angerstein, Warren & Lock, Angerstein's insurance broking partnership, wrote to John & Francis Baring & Co. regarding an insurance they had arranged, which would provide £56,500 of cover for goods aboard the vessel *Unity*, on a voyage from Amsterdam to London. For five shillings per £100 of cover, the brokers offered 'in case of Failure ... to become your Security for Underwriters'. The list is a who's who of leading underwriters of the day, and includes Miles Peter Andrews, a partner in gunpowder merchants Pigou, Andrews & Wilkes. (Pigou was also an underwriter, and appears on the guaranteed list, but was not a loan subscriber.) The merchant and insurance broker William Bell appears, as does John Brickwood, a longstanding underwriter.

---

[213] For the full account, see Leonard, A. B.: 'Marine insurers', pp. 55–70; Grellier, J. J. and Wade, R. W.: *The terms of all the loans which have been raised for the public service*, third edition, London: John Richardson, 1812, p. 57; Newmarch, William: *On the loans raised by Mr Pitt during the first French war, 1793–1801*, London: Effingham Wilson, 1855, pp. 7–9; Cope, S. R.: 'The Goldsmids and the development of the London money market during the Napoleonic Wars', *Economica*, New Series, Vol. 9, No. 34 (May, 1942), p. 186; *Morning Chronicle*, iss. 7,428, 26 Mar. 1793; *Universal magazine of knowledge and pleasure*, 'Historical chronicle for May 1788', p. 275; 'Godschall Johnson I', *Legacies of British Slave-ownership*, www.ucl.ac.uk/lbs/person/view/2146635729 [Accessed 3 Dec. 2021].

[214] *The Times*, Issue 8,626, 13 Jun. 1812, p. 3; Grellier and Wade, *Terms of all the loans*, app. p. 9, Angerstein's subscription book, LMA F/Ang/110, frontispiece; LL Uncatalogued, *Roll of Lloyd's, 1771–1930*.

Table 6: 1812 Subscribers to Angerstein's loan, £000

Description	No.	Amount	Share
Insurance underwriters or brokers	104	£3,487	68%
Individuals with underwriters in the family	17	360	7.0%
Unrelated to insurance or no connections identified	48	1,143	22%
Unknown	4	84	1.6%
Subscriptions for others in Angerstein's name	7	61	1.2%
Total	**180**	**£5,135**	

Meanwhile loan subscriber Robert Christie, a merchant of 14 New Broad St. according to the *Post Office Annual Directory* of 1814, was a frequent underwriter, and held a Bank of England joint account with the underwriters Edward Vaux (also a subscriber), George Henkell (also guaranteed), and Thomas Parry (who appears both as guaranteed and as a loan subscriber). Guaranteed underwriters Robert Shedden and his son George, merchants of 26 Charlotte Street, Bedford Square, were subscribers, and appear frequently as underwriters in a unique policy register book now held in the vaults at Lloyd's, along with leading underwriters including Vaux, Christie, and others. Other subscribing individuals, such as the East India Company chairman Sir Henry Lushington Bt., were close to members of the list: guaranteed underwriter William Lushington was Sir Henry's brother.[215]

Absence from Lloyd's membership by no means automatically indicates that Angerstein's subscribers were not underwriters. Considerable volumes of underwriting were carried out by individuals who were not members. Angerstein himself testified in 1810 that 'other underwriters, who do not attend at Lloyd's, carry on the business of marine Insurance' at other premises.[216] Lloyd's was an exclusive club which imposed restrictions upon the business practised there, from the wording of the insurance policies permitted to the nature of the business which could be transacted in the Underwriting Room; some insurers chose to operate outside these restrictions. Direct evidence that underwriters active outside Lloyd's subscribed to Angerstein's loans is found in a policy of 27 November 1818, in my possession, under which J. Majoribanks grants cover of $50 to Mrs. Sarah Wilde's share of the vessel *Frances*, for its voyage from Quebec to Waterford. The policy reached the underwriter through the broking firm Sanderson, Brothers. Jonathan Majoribanks subscribed £3,000 to Angerstein's 1813 subscription. Insurers who did not underwrite

---

[215] Bank of England Archive, C98/182, Register of accounts 1798–1800, vol. A–C, p. 2; *Barings Archive*, WPI A1.22, Angerstein Warren & Lock to Barings & Co., 14 Oct. 1794; *Post-Office Annual Directory for 1814*, Critchett & Woods, printed by T. Maiden, London, 1814; LL L573, Policy register book, 1809–1817 (unpaginated).

[216] *Special Report of 1810*, testimony of John Julius Angerstein, p. 58.

marine insurance also appeared as subscribers, such as Thomas Dorrien, a director of the Sun Fire Office.[217]

Among the subscribers, twenty-eight individuals or partnerships have been positively identified as carrying on business as insurance brokers through reference to directories such as *Johnson's London Commercial Guide* of 1818. All of them are also identified as members of Lloyd's. It was quite usual for individuals to act both as underwriter and broker, as indeed Angerstein himself did. Others identified simply as 'brokers' or as 'stockbrokers' may also have dealt in insurance. James Bury, a stockbroker of Throgmorton Street and the Royal Exchange, is one example.

Individuals and partnerships identified as merchants in commercial directories very often were prominent underwriters or insurance brokers. For example, Joseph Marryat & Son are listed in the 1814 *Post Office Annual Directory* simply as 'Merchants', despite Marryat's leading role within Lloyd's; as an MP, he argued vociferously in Lloyd's favour in parliament. Other merchants, neither Lloyd's members nor listed as brokers in the directories, were known to Angerstein through family connections at Lloyd's. Tullie Joseph Cornthwaite, a wool broker of the Old Pay Office, Old Broad St., was not a Lloyd's member, and no evidence of underwriting by him has come to light. However, his uncle Robert Cornthwaite was a founding member of Lloyd's.

Still other subscribers are found among Angerstein's substantial insurance-buying clients, including Glyn Mills Hallifax & Co., bankers at 12 Birchin Lane, and Colonel Charles Herries, a Spain merchant in St Mary's Axe and slave trade investor. Herries was in a ship-owning partnership with Joseph Nailer and James Drummond. Nailer was an underwriting member of Lloyd's, as were many ship owners (including Angerstein), reflecting the continued mutual risk-sharing nature of underwriting, and the deep financial connection between London's merchant-insuers and the state.

The marine insurance market after the interventions

The importance of the formalisation of the institutions of Lloyd's cannot be underestimated in relation to London's enduring success as a global insurance market. The practice of recruiting multiple underwriters to insure very large risks, thus securing contingent capital from multiple sources and spreading each large risk very widely, began, as has been shown, at latest among Italian merchant-insurers during the fourteenth century.[218] Yet other than the underwriters' intervention that created New Lloyd's, no similar market was able to gain dominance in the absence of such reforms. Institutional Lloyd's led a Braudellian 'world-economy' in marine insurance, and sustained this role through the flexible participation of its institution of insiders. Its business process, based on longstanding practice, allowed this formal association of underwriters to amass and offer very large sums of contingent capital, known in today's insurance market as 'capacity'. Asked in 2002 why

---

[217] ALC uncatalogued, Policy underwritten for Sarah Wilde, 27 Nov. 1818.

[218] See pp. 40–41.

Lloyd's remained an important global insurance marketplace, Lawrence Holder, then a Member of the Council of Lloyd's (successor to the Committee of Lloyd's founded in 1769), said simply 'It's a capacity market'.[219] In other words, Lloyd's structure allowed it better to insure very large risks, relative to competitors. This phenomenon was described by Angerstein in evidence to a parliamentary select committee in 1810, when he reported that in 1807 private underwriters had insured the frigate *Diana* and its cargo for £631,800 on a voyage from Vera Cruz to England, with an additional £25,000 from one of the two London chartered companies.[220] Equally important was Lloyd's international reach, which provided risk diversification benefits. Underwriters' focus on specific branches of marine risk (American risks, for example) was 'less at Lloyd's than at any other place' because of the 'variety of business' available and 'his interest to mix the whole, that if there is a storm at one place he is safe at another'.[221] This gave London a competitive advantage over rival countries and insurance centres, where underwriting typically was fragmented between regional ports, and focused on local trade.

No similar institution had evolved in any of the other important underwriting centres in the multi-local insurance economy. Instead, these centres tended to fall from importance, or to adopt corporate underwriting, rather than nurture private underwriting through the creation of an institutional framework backed by state protection from all but corporate competition. Twentieth-century attempts in the US to create an insurance market following the Lloyd's model, such as the short-lived New York Insurance Exchange, were costly failures.[222] Private underwriting continued in the US through syndicates described as a 'Lloyds' until at least the 1960s. In 1896, a century after insurance companies were permitted to operate in the US, at least forty-five such associations were active in New York City alone, calling themselves a 'Lloyds' and accepting premiums from across the country. They ranged from 'American Lloyds' to 'Washington Lloyds', but unlike Lloyd's proper, had no central organisation. Their market role was minimal, and ultimately they too fell away.[223] Only well-organised Lloyd's of London endured.

Lloyd's had emerged from the French Revolutionary and Napoleonic Wars strengthened. Insurance penetration was nearly complete among British merchants; it was very rare to go to sea without some level of cover. Although legislation prevented the insurance of enemy vessels from 1793, London was the insurance hub of her Coalition allies. The institutional environment created by the third intervention continued to prove adequate to meet the outsider challenge, even under the stress of protracted naval hostilities, vast sums insured, and very great losses. No further significant changes were made during the period of review. However, in the wartime

---

[219] Comment made in discussion with the author.

[220] *Report from the Select Committee on Marine Insurance, Sess. 1810*, BPP (226) 1810 IV 247, reprinted 11.5.1824, London: House of Commons, testimony of J. J. Angerstein, p. 58.

[221] Ibid., p. 67.

[222] [NYIE reference].

[223] 'Lloyds Concerns; A short Account of their Pedigree and Peculiar Plans', *The Insurance Press*, New York, 4 Dec. 1895, p. 5.

environment of the turn of the century, many underwriters made large profits. Lured by these riches, entrepreneurs wished to break the duopoly of the chartered marine insurers. In response, a parliamentary inquiry probed the state of the market in 1810. MPs found it robust, and did not reverse the limitation of corporate underwriting enacted by the second intervention, but the pressure for liberalisation did not abate.[224]

In 1824 the duopoly of the chartered companies was ended, when the relevant clauses of the *Bubble Act* were repealed. That year, under pressure from entrepreneurs, parliament repealed the legislation restricting corporate underwriting in Britain. A flood of companies entered the market, and insuring for direct profit became the norm. The institutional structures of the London marine insurance market, developed over three centuries, were to face renewed challenges, and the merchant-insurers of Lloyd's saw intense new competition. London's pre-eminence in insurance was able to withstand this change because the interventions of the preceding 250 years had created institutions which ensured that good faith continued as the market's governing principle, and that buyers and sellers alike operated in an environment of certainty, whether within the exclusive Lloyd's market, outside it among the insurance companies, or, often, straddling the two to achieve maximum risk-sharing. The parallel efforts of the state and the merchant-insurers had created a system which allowed the ancient practice of Lombard Street to operate successfully in London's expanded arena of competitive international commerce, where individuals traded only for personal utility or profit. Thus, centuries of institutional development arising from interventions motivated by a common interest in sustaining the system embedded the practices which allowed London's marine insurance market to flourish.

---

[224] For a cogent summary of the events of the period, see Wright and Fayle, *History of Lloyd's*, pp. 176–318.

5.

Conclusions

Lʟondon's insurance market began as a small, cooperative venture structured for the benefit of all participants. It was maturing in the early fifteenth century, roughly a hundred years earlier than is often believed. Its smooth operation was based on the mutual interest of merchant-insurers, who typically participated on both sides of insurance transactions, and were involved primarily because they wished to avoid the financial shocks which could arise from the unavoidable perils of seaborne trade. Their reciprocal interest meant that honourable behaviour was the main guarantee that the market functioned efficiently, which left little room for sharp practice. The approach is characterised by *uberrima fides*, utmost good faith. The merchant-insurers transferred and accepted risk based on this principle. When it was not clear if a policy should respond to a loss, insureds and underwriters accepted, in good faith, the decisions of merchant arbiters. Such decisions were almost conciliar; a panel of disinterested merchant-insurers would discuss and determine, based on principles established under the uncodified Law Merchant, what the parties had reasonably intended when insurance agreements were reached. This meant that the merchant-insurers' product was flexible. Old principles were adapted to govern new circumstances, with the balance weighted to the advantage of neither the buyer nor the underwriter, but to the community of merchant-insurers. As long as everyone abided by the rules of the game, the system worked. Those who operated outside the rules could simply be excluded.

The environment demanded this approach. The evolving English legal system was ill-equipped to deal with insurance disputes, and became more so as the civil law of equity, the formal branch of jurisprudence best suited to resolving relevant questions of intention, was eroded. The typical inflexibility of statute, and of early modern English common law, meant that prescriptions set out by the state to govern market operations often had the unintended side-effect of reducing market flexibility. It seems clear that prescriptive measures, regardless of their target, are likely to have such an impact in a market which became effective and popular based on practices grounded in principles of good faith, and which traded a club good on this basis, rather than primarily for the profit of the sellers and the utility of the buyers. Such a system can function smoothly only when transactions are struck and concluded in utmost good faith.

By the later sixteenth century, the norm of transacting insurance business in good faith began to be challenged by some, as English trade changed and expanded. More individuals sought insurance, even though they were not necessarily steeped in the merchant-insurers' custom. The enlarged market also included individual participants who understood the customary rules differently, including foreign merchants from places where the governing Law Merchant was subtly different. Some new buyers were completely unaware of London's prevailing customs, and since they were not sellers, did not share a mutual interest in the merchant-insurers' approach to insurance. This group included outright fraudsters. Some sellers were not also buyers, and entered the business solely for profit. Each category of individual had reason to set aside good faith, seeking instead only direct personal gain from the underwriters' system. Such actions had the effect of reducing market efficiency by pushing up costs. The challenge was to create a framework which would allow outsiders to participate in the system, but which would preserve the merchant-insurers' practices, and retain the flexibility of their system.

Merchant-insurers and officials of the state realised that action was necessary to preserve the efficiency of the system. The former, reacting first to a rise in the number of individuals over-insuring before making multiple claims, wished to reduce loss-costs. The latter wished to preserve the system because of its contribution to the expansion of English trade, and thus to the cooperation and overlap between the merchant marine and the Royal Navy which underpinned England's blue-water strategy through merchantmen's contribution to physical defence. Insurance also contributed financially to the state. By supporting trade which generated customs revenue, a critical royal income stream, insurance was an important historical component of the structure of England's fiscal-military state. As this book has shown, insurance-buying in London was sufficiently commonplace at this time to garner the attention of the highest echelons of power, which belies the common assertion that few merchants insured until the early eighteenth century.

The Privy Council saw that the merchant-insurers' system was robust and effective, but that it was strained by the additional costs of outsiders' actions. In response, councillors launched the first intervention into the London marine insurance market, introducing both a formal tribunal which could resolve disputes outside the system, but without changing the rules of the game, and a policy registration system to impede fraud. Codification of the rules was less successful. The Law Merchant comprised principles, rather than hard-and-fast rules. When principles were interpreted in good faith against circumstances, an equitable result could be achieved in a marketplace of mutual interests, but codification limited market flexibility. The privy councillors' demands for codification were allowed to lapse, and remained in abeyance until 1906.

Preserving the certainty provided by the merchant-insurers' system was the goal of the first intervention. The market had evolved to grant merchants certainty over the cost of specific, unpredictable, but inevitable seaborne losses, by exchanging a small, fixed, regular expense for a volatile, potentially ruinous cost. The system extended dramatically the capital which a merchant could rely upon in such fortuitous situations. Utmost good faith was the mechanism which extended this certainty from the individual to the merchant-insurer community, by ensuring that the greatest possible value of losses arising from the risk pool could be insured for the lowest total premium, with minimum expenditure on transactional costs. Flexibility and certainty coexisted in the system, and had been embodied in law under the principle of equity, which progressively lost its standing over the course of the period under review. The difficulty faced by those trying to solve the cost-challenges brought to the insurance market by outsiders was to preserve the balance between flexibility and certainty.

The institutions established under the first intervention answered this difficulty relatively well. Registration made it more difficult for outsiders to escape the market's customary rules. Custom, and thus flexibility, were retained through a legal forum which was carefully constituted to blend the approaches of both the civil and the common law, alongside the Law Merchant through the Admiralty and, most importantly, the merchant-commissioners. Inflexible codification was not imposed, and the whole system effectively remained optional, since the only sanction for drawing policies outside the Office of Assurance was that they were void before the law. The system was a good solution to the challenge of preserving certainty and flexibility through institution-building for a market which relied upon action in good faith, but had to cope with individual participants who did not share this approach. The Court of Assurance operated effectively for many decades, but was weakened by a sustained common law attack on its flawed jurisdiction. Combined with the increasing number of outsiders in the market, insurance disputes were more often heard before King's Bench, which was ill-equipped to deal with them equitably, and thus to support the mutual interests of merchant-insurers, which were aligned with state interests.

English trade began to flourish in the later seventeenth century, but the cost of greater uncertainty returned to the merchant-insurers' market, as the first intervention broke down. However, the second intervention was not launched to solve this problem. Outwardly credible solutions which had been put forward, such as legislation against fraud and the nationalisation of the insurance system, were not pursued. Even in the absence of the Office and Court of Assurance, the market was functioning to the broad satisfaction of participants and the state. Instead, the intervention of financial capitalists, who had been created and enriched by the financial revolution, was intended to serve private, rather than market, interests, including those of the South Sea Company. Concern for improvement of insurance was rhetorical, and based on a problem – the mooted insecurity of individual underwriters – which had been shown by the events of 1693 to be surmountable. The intervention would be of little interest here had it not forced the continuity of the merchant-insurers' system by preventing significant competition.

Despite the growing outsider challenge, London's insurance market thrived. Prices fell as Britain entered a long era of success in trade and military ventures. Both were underpinned and underwritten by the risk-sharing mechanism honed in London by the merchant-insurers. The city became the first unchallenged international insurance leader, and although the Navigation Acts prevented foreigners from participating in British trade, London merchant-insurers shared in the mercantile gains of French, Spanish, Portuguese, Scandinavian, and other excluded traders through underwriting. Yet the costly outsider challenge remained. It was addressed, piecemeal, over the later eighteenth century. The character of this third intervention was new. During the first, the state, through the Privy Council and parliament, had responded to merchant-insurers' requests for intervention. They did so with much input from insiders such as Malynes and successive Lord Mayors, in order to preserve the insurance system which underpinned revenue-generating trade. In the second intervention the state, through MPs, ministers, placemen, and the monarch himself, connived with financial capitalists to intervene for its own gain.

The third intervention followed neither pattern. On separate occasions parliament acted in the interests both of the merchant-insurers and of the wider public, in response to requests for action. The judiciary enshrined the principles of the Law Merchant in the common law, and the merchants themselves responded by erecting organisational structures, including a self-regulating organisation, which helped them to advance their system for creating greater certainty in trade through mutual risk-sharing under principles of utmost good faith, despite the presence of outsiders in increasing numbers. Protected by the *Bubble Act*, the institution-building initiatives of the state and the merchant-insurers carried on for more than a century before the system faced serious competition, by which time it was embedded and established around the world.

The prohibition, under statute, of insurances in which the buyer had no interest did remove a measure of underwriting flexibility – the Commons could deal only in blunt instruments – but parliament's intervention set a clear boundary to delineate the nature of insurance when, it seems, the merchant-insurers could not agree. The need for an *insurable interest* before insurance could be granted became entrenched as a fundamental principle of underwriting in all branches of insurance. Much more wide-ranging, but equally foundational, was the reform of the commercial common law embarked upon by Mansfield. Earlier court decisions had failed to create certainty because they did not set out settled principles of law. Mansfield wished to resolve the problem in a way that would sustain the merchant-insurers' system, which required consideration of their practice, including the most ancient tenets of the Law Merchant, when settling principles. The common law framework his work created is equipped to handle disputes which escape the merchant-insurers' system. Common law was victorious in the jurisdiction battles; Mansfield made it much more useful for mercantile disputes.

Mansfield made scores of principle-setting decisions in insurance cases. One of the most important was in 1766, when he incorporated into English law the principle that insurance contracts were governed by *uberrima fides*. In *Carter v. Boehm*, tried at Guildhall by one of Mansfield's special merchant juries, he stated that 'Good faith forbids either party by concealing what he privately knows, to draw the other into a bargain from his ignorance of that fact, and his believing the contrary.'[1] After nearly two hundred years of occasional market strife, and various interventions intended to ensure that merchant principles continued to govern London's insurance market, this approach – peculiar because it conflicts with the legal principle *caveat emptor* – was rolled into the common law. The external enforcement systems provided by the royal courts had finally been aligned with market practice. A level of certainty was introduced which ensured that external enforcement systems would approach complex or technical questions about coverage and liability from the same basic

---

[1] *Carter* v. *Boehm*, 3 Burr. 1905 (97 Eng. Rep. 1162).

starting place. Ultimately, the principles created in law by Mansfield would provide the blueprint for insurance legislation around the world.

A working legal system for insurance was under development throughout the third intervention, but merchant-insurers tended still to prefer internal governance and dispute resolution, due to its lower cost. As outsider-buying and -selling strayed ever further from the mutually beneficial practices of the original merchant-insurers, the institution-building of the breakaway underwriters who founded New Lloyd's in 1769 went much further than originally intended. They had desired a trading environment which excluded outsiders, where their club good could be traded on the basis of utmost good faith (*uberrima fides* remains Lloyd's motto), and which operated under Law Merchant principles. To achieve this, New Lloyd's adopted rigid restrictions over how business may be conducted. Using its sanction of exclusion, it limited who could participate, fostered internal dispute resolution, and formalised information-sharing activities for the benefit of the entire market of merchant-insurers. Together these measures delivered certainty of approach and practice at minimal cost. However, Lloyd's remained a responsive marketplace with the broad flexibility to respond to insurance-buyers' needs, providing affordable certainty in the face of the perils of seaborne trade.

The insurance market interventions identified in this book shed light on the relationship between the state and the merchant community. For many centuries this had been one of mutual interest, represented by the longstanding cooperation between them, which was maintained in the interests both of security and of profit. The crown relied upon the customs income arising from trade, and inasmuch as insurance extended this trade by providing contingent capital, insurance extended the crown's income. Monarchs also relied upon the merchant marine to provide both a stream of trained sailors, and armed warships in times of conflict. Whether defensive or aggressive, the additional risks faced by merchants when participating in warfare were made more tolerable by insurance, to the benefit of royal war efforts. In this way, private capital was extended to underwrite the public projects of the state. Merchants, who from the seventeenth century participated increasingly in the mechanics of the state, relied in turn upon the monarch to protect their trade from various aggressors. Private capital was then extended more directly, when merchant-insurers stepped forward as principal lenders to the state in wartime.

Individuals often played an important role in fostering the cooperation between merchants and the state which led to successful institution-building for London's marine insurance market. It is visible in Malynes and his consultations with the Privy Council in its interventions in the late sixteenth century, in the law-reform work of Edward Vaux with Lord Justice Mansfield in the eighteenth, and in Angerstein through his fundraising work for the state among the marine insurance market practitioners in the nineteenth. Both for the state and for the merchants, cash was the immediate dividend of their institution-building efforts. They shared in the trade revenues and booty arising from their wartime activities. The longer-term benefit was survival, which would rarely have been taken for granted by either during the violent early modern era.

The first intervention revealed a credible commitment on the part of the state to ensure the continuity of the merchant-insurers' system, and the old cooperation between merchants and the state. The second marked a reversal: the principles of credible commitment and utmost good faith were overturned by individuals at almost all levels of participation, seeking to increase their personal wealth. The king in 1720 blatantly embraced the sale of monopolies, a practice which had been under attack for more than a century. The episode sheds new light on a further dimension of the financial revolution: the extensive cooperation between the state, financiers, noble landowners (looking much like early gentlemanly capitalists), and the monarch. The chartering of the London and the Royal Exchange insurance companies casts all as financial capitalists intent on extracting personal gain from the merchant-insurers' marketplace. Since the sixteenth century, merchants, politicians, and pundits combined in almost universal agreement that insurance is beneficial to trade, and thus to the mutual benefit of all. The second intervention occurred despite this consensus, and risked overturning the established insurance system.

Ensuring the rude health of the insurance market was not a constant interest of the state, but it was a persistent one during the period under review. It was driven by the pursuit of security and profit, for the safety of the nation and the coffers of the king (the latter very often simply an aspect of the former). Unlike many national competitors in Europe who hampered their insurers, the English state, through the actions of its various organisations, worked successfully to maintain the stability, solvency, and efficacy of London marine insurance throughout the period. It was a national advantage which can only have contributed positively to Britain's divergence from her Continental competitors during the eighteenth century.

Appendix:

Some London underwriters active 1690–1717

Years active	1690	1691	1692	1701	1703	1709	1710	1711	1712	1713	1714	1715	1715	1716	1716	1717	1717	Total Lines
Source	Bra	Bra	Bra	Bow	Bow	Rad	Rad	Rad	Rad	Rad	Rad	Rad	Sca	Rad	Fle	Sca	Rad	
Underwriter name																		
Acworth, Allyn	1																	1
Alie, Richard	1			1														2
Asgill, Charles												3		1				4
Ashby, John																		0
Ayles, Thomas											2							2
Baker, John										1	1	3		1			1	7
Barnard, John MP											1	3		6	1	2	1	14
Barnard, Robert														1				1
Banyand, James														1				1
Benson, Bryan												2		2				4
Bernard, Henry														1				1
Berry, John	2	1																3
Blackhall, Charles																		0
Boddington, Henry												1		2				3
Bond, Godfrey														1				1

Years active	1690	1691	1692	1701	1703	1709	1710	1711	1712	1713	1714	1715	1715	1716	1716	1717	1717	Total Lines
Source	Bra	Bra	Bra	Bow	Bow	Rad	Rad	Rad	Rad	Rad	Rad	Rad	Sca	Rad	Fle	Sca	Rad	
Bouverie, Jacob MP							2											2
BOW, R.?											1	1						2
Broughton, Andrew										1				2				3
Burrish, George																		0
Callender, ??	1																	1
Cambridge, Richard										2	2	4		12	1	1	1	23
Capellwall											2							2
Carew, Thomas	1																	1
Cepipon, Peter										2		1					1	4
Carrion, Moses					1						1				1	1		4
Chase, Richard												1						1
Churchey, William Capt														1	1	1		3
Chiswell, R(ichard)														1				1
Clarke, Thomas									1									1
Copley, George	1																	1

Years active	1690	1691	1692	1701	1703	1709	1710	1711	1712	1713	1714	1715	1715	1716	1716	1717	1717	Total Lines
Source	*Bra*	*Bra*	*Bra*	*Bow*	*Bow*	*Rad*	*Rad*	*Rad*	*Rad*	*Rad*	*Rad*	*Rad*	*Sca*	*Rad*	*Fle*	*Sca*	*Rad*	
Cowen, Humphrey	1																	1
Cretchtown, James																		0
da Costa, Ishae Telles	1	1																2
Dashwood, Thomas	1	1																2
des Bouverie, Edward	1		1															2
Dikes, Philip															1	1		2
Dishrram, William	1																	1
Eshittingham, Robert			1															1
Emmott, Chr.										2		3		2			2	9
Fletcher, John														1				1
Fellowes, W.							2			2		3		1			1	9
Foe, Daniel																		0
Foxley, David								1										1
Frome, Richard												1			1	1		3
Gideon, Samson			1															1

Years active	1690	1691	1692	1701	1703	1709	1710	1711	1712	1713	1714	1715	1715	1716	1716	1717	1717	Total Lines
Source	Bra	Bra	Bra	Bow	Bow	Rad	Rad	Rad	Rad	Rad	Rad	Rad	Sca	Rad	Fle	Sca	Rad	
Goddard, Lleydell												2		1			1	4
Godfreys										1	1							2
Godin, Dd.															1	1		2
Gonon, James			1															1
Gore, Charles							1											1
Gore, W.			1															1
Gosfright, Heanis		1																1
Gouge, Edward																	1	1
Gould, Edward										3	1							4
Greenall, William												3						3
Greene, Richard											1	3						4
Hackshaw, Robert Jr.										1	1	3		1				6
Hah, Henry	1																	1
Hall, John				1														1
Harrington, Henry	2	1																3

Years active	1690	1691	1692	1701	1703	1709	1710	1711	1712	1713	1714	1715	1715	1716	1716	1717	1717	Total Lines
Source	Bra	Bra	Bra	Bow	Bow	Rad	Rad	Rad	Rad	Rad	Rad	Rad	Sca	Rad	Fle	Sca	Rad	
Harwood, George	1																	1
Hayne, Christoph											1							1
Haydons, George												1						1
Hayton, William										1	1	4		5	1	1	2	15
Hayward, Robert												1						1
Hedges, William						1												1
Henriques, Peter			1															1
Herne, Nathaniel									1									2
Herring, Henry													1		2	1		4
Hodges, John																		0
Hopkins, Richard											1							1
Houblon, P.			1															1
Hubbock, John	1																	1
Hulls, Robert															2	2		4
Humphreys, Mr [Richard?]					1													1

Years active	1690	1691	1692	1701	1703	1709	1710	1711	1712	1713	1714	1715	1715	1716	1716	1717	1717	Total Lines
Source	Bra	Bra	Bra	Bow	Bow	Rad	Rad	Rad	Rad	Rad	Rad	Rad	Sca	Rad	Fle	Sca	Rad	
Hyam, Richard										2								2
Hyde, George											1	1						2
Inglosby, Law												2		1				3
Jackson, Ffisher											1			2				3
Jackson, Joseph Jr															1	1		2
Jackson, Richard										1	2			3				6
Jailloonal?, J.														1				1
Jammineau, Claude														1				1
Jurin, John																		0
Kadwell, John												2		3				5
Knightley, Robert			1															1
Knipe, Sir Randolph														1				1
Lambert, John											1							1
Lethieullier, Samuel	2																	2
Lock, John															2	2		4
Lock, William											1							1

Years active	1690	1691	1692	1701	1703	1709	1710	1711	1712	1713	1714	1715	1715	1716	1716	1717	1717	Total Lines
Source	Bra	Bra	Bra	Bow	Bow	Rad	Rad	Rad	Rad	Rad	Rad	Rad	Sca	Rad	Fle	Sca	Rad	
Love, John	1									1	1	3		1	1	1		9
Lunch, William										1		2		3				6
Lyde, Jeremiah											1	3		1				5
Lytton, George												2			1	1		4
Mansfield, Henry		1	1															2
Martin, J.														1				1
Meexel, Rob.	1																	1
Mercado, Abraham de											1	1						2
Merewether, John															2	2		4
Mi[t]chel[l], Rob[ert].												3		2				5
Miln, David												1		1				2
Mirande, Manuel Munez				1														1
Mocatta, Moses											1							1
Moleneux, Thomas	1																	1

Years active	1690	1691	1692	1701	1703	1709	1710	1711	1712	1713	1714	1715	1715	1716	1716	1717	1717	Total Lines
Source	Bra	Bra	Bra	Bow	Bow	Rad	Rad	Rad	Rad	Rad	Rad	Rad	Sca	Rad	Fle	Sca	Rad	
Molyneux, Nathaniel																		0
Morewood, Josiah	1																	1
Moore, John					1													1
Morley, George (Jr.)										1	1	2		1	1	1		7
Musters, Francis														1			1	2
Nash, Samuel	1	2																3
Nelson, Gilbert		4																4
Nelthorpe, Edward										1	1	2		1				5
Nelthorpe, George											1	2	1		1			5
Nunn, Jonathan											1	1		1				2
Parrauicin?, Peter			1															1
Petty, David												1						1
Phillipps, Charles							2											2
Phillipps, John							2											2
Plume, James									1									1

Years active	1690	1691	1692	1701	1703	1709	1710	1711	1712	1713	1714	1715	1715	1716	1716	1717	1717	Total Lines
Source	Bra	Bra	Bra	Bow	Bow	Rad	Rad	Rad	Rad	Rad	Rad	Rad	Sca	Rad	Fle	Sca	Rad	
Pococke, W.			1															1
Porter, James									1		1				1	1		4
Power [Poree?], Peter											1							1
le Power?	1	1																2
Praedfott, Mark																		0
Preistley, John									1	1		3						5
Prince, John	2	1																3
Radburner, John										1		3			1	1		6
Reade, John										1		1		4	1	1		8
Reade, Samuel										2		3		3				8
Roberts, George											1			1				2
Robinson, William				1														1
Rochdale, R.												1		3	1	1	1	7
Rudez [Rudge?], Edward							1			1	1	1						4
Salvador, Daniel						1												1

Years active	1690	1691	1692	1701	1703	1709	1710	1711	1712	1713	1714	1715	1715	1716	1716	1717	1717	Total Lines
Source	*Bra*	*Bra*	*Bra*	*Bow*	*Bow*	*Rad*	*Rad*	*Rad*	*Rad*	*Rad*	*Rad*	*Rad*	*Sca*	*Rad*	*Fle*	*Sca*	*Rad*	
Santini, Ni.											1							1
Sedgwick, Obediah			1															1
St Quintin, George		1																1
Stackhouse, Isaac		1																1
Steele, Ben	1																	1
Sitwell, George	1	1	1															3
Thorole (Thorold?), George									4									4
Torriano, Charles	1	3	1															5
Travers, Joseph													1		1			2
Vanderpock, Adrian	1																	1
Vanderstegen, Henry													1	1	2	1		5
Verney, John			1															1
Vernon, George															1	1		2
Wakeman, Robert				1														1
Ward, Thomas														1			1	2

Years active	1690	1691	1692	1701	1703	1709	1710	1711	1712	1713	1714	1715	1715	1716	1716	1717	1717	Total Lines
Source	Bra	Bra	Bra	Bow	Bow	Rad	Rad	Rad	Rad	Rad	Rad	Rad	Sca	Rad	Fle	Sca	Rad	
Warner, Edmond	1																	1
Williams, Jho															1	1		2
Williams, Thomas									1	1				1				3
Willys, William			1			1	2											4
Willys, Thomas																		0
Wilmer, Nathaniel				1														1
Young, Richard				1	1													2
Total lines	25	28	16	6	4	3	13	1	10	30	35	81	4	84	30	27	14	411
Total underwriters	21	22	16	6	4	3	8	1	7	22	31	39	4	44	25	23	12	157 *

* *Discrete individuals identified in column 1.*

Source codes key:

Rad	Radcliffe papers
Fle	Fletcher papers
Bow	Bowrey papers
Bra	Brasilford papers
Sca	Scattergood papers

Bibliography

Primary manuscript sources

Bank of England (BOE):

10A61/7, Humphrey Morice Papers, 1709–1731, f. 2, 'Letter to Hon. Nicholas Lechmore [Lechmere], 17 Nov. 1719.

6A49/1, Humphrey Morice Papers, 1709–1731, f. 2, 'Royall Exchange Insurance Company account with Humphrey Morice'.

C98/182, Register of accounts 1798–1800, vol. A-C, p. 2, Record of the accounts of Christie *et al.*

Barings Archive:

WPI A1.22, Angerstein Warren & Lock to Barings & Co., 14 Oct. 1794.

Bodleian Library (BOD):

MS Ballard 20 f. 141, Clarke to Dawes, 12 Mar. 1719/20.

MS Rawlinson A 478 ff. 81, Council of Trade report, 23 Jan. 1660/1.

MS Rawlinson Letters 66, *Letterbook of Joseph Cruttenden*, 3 Mar. 1709/10 to 6 Sept. 1717.

MS Tanner 74, f. 32, contemporaneous copy of a policy underwritten for Morris Abbot and Devereux Wogan on the *Tyger*, 15 Feb. 1613.

British Library (BL):

Add. Ms. 8225.a.38: *A list of the names of the subscribers…*

Add. MS 24,107: *Doctors Commons Library*, Correspondence and papers, 1694–1702, of Sir C. Hedges.

Add. Ms. 34,669–34.676: *Risk Books of John Janson, 1804–1815* (eight volumes).

Add. Ms. 43,731: *The papers of John Scattergood (1681–1723)*.

Add. Ms. 48,023, fols 246–273: the 'Booke of Orders of Assurances' (1574?).

Egerton Ms. 2395, ff. 149–151: 'Proposalls to bee presented to his Highness the Lord Protector and his Councell, for the greater encouragement of Merchants in their Navigations' (1657?).

Harleian Ms. 5103: the 'Booke of Orders' (later version).

Lansdowne MS 65 f. 104: summary of the petition of Henry Roderigues (undated).

Lansdowne MS 113 f. 9: 'Some Merchants, Notaries, and Brokers petition Sir James Hawes, Lord Mayor of London, against Rich. Candler's grant for registering policies of assurance' (undated, 1574?).

Cambridge University Library (UL):

Add. 2798, *Plumstead Letterbook*.

Essex County Records Office (ECRO):

D/DDc A16, *Journal of Peter Du Cane, 1735–1744*.
D/DRu B7, Braund, William, *Journal of Risks, 1759–1765*.

Guildhall Library (GHL):

CLC/B/148/A/001, Minutes of the Committee of Lloyd's, Dec. 1771–Aug. 1804.
CLC/B/062/MS 22,281, policy underwritten for Bartholomew Corsini, 24 Sept. 1582.
CLC/B/062/MS 22,282, insurance policies underwritten for Bartholomew Corsini (copies).

Hertfordshire Archives and Local Studies Centre (HALSC):

DE/R/B293/1–47, Business records of the Radcliffe family, policies underwritten for T. Hall and others.

Leonard, Adrian's Collection (ALC):

Uncatalogued, *Lloyd's News*, 'Numb. 20, October 15, 1696'.
Uncatalogued, Policy underwritten for Charles D'Wolfe, 29 Mar. 1794.
Uncatalogued, Policy underwritten for Wales and Field, 17 Sep. 1794.
Uncatalogued, Policy underwritten for Thomas Rhodie & Co., 12 Oct. 1803 (image only).
Uncatalogued, Policy underwritten for John Davenport, 15 Nov. 1806 (image only).
Uncatalogued, Policy underwritten for Sarah Wilde, 27 Nov. 1818.
Uncatalogued, Policy underwritten for B. Almen [?], 12 May 1836.
Uncatalogued, Policy underwritten for Jaynaraen Lukhimchund, 23 Feb. 1859 (image only).
Uncatalogued, Policies underwritten for the Baltimore Steam Packet Co. at Lloyd's and the Institute of London Underwriters, 20 Feb. 1950.

Lloyd's of London (LL):

Uncatalogued, *Risk Book of Horatio Clagett, 1807*.
Uncatalogued, *Risk Book of Edward Allfrey, 1809*.
Uncatalogued, *Risk Books of Clagett & Pratt, 1823–1824* (two volumes).
Uncatalogued, Dawson, Warren R. (Honorary Librarian to Lloyd's): *Roll of Lloyd's, 1771–1930*, London: Lloyd's of London, 1931. Although printed and bound, only two copies of this book are extant. Both remain at Lloyd's. The volume consulted (Legal Department) contains hundreds of pages of loose correspondence, clippings, and a wealth of marginalia.
L573, Policy register book, 1809–1817.

London Metropolitan Archives (LMA):

COL/AD/01/022 (MR X109/037), *Letter Book Y*, fos. 126–127.
CLC/427/MS24176/548, *The Bowrey Papers*, policy issued to Joseph Paice, 28 Oct. 1703.
CLC/063/MS32992/1, *Policy of Thomas Newton*, 27 Oct. 1760.
LMA F/Ang/110, Angerstein's loan subscription book, 1812–1816.

National Archives of Scotland (NAS):

CS96/507 f. 16, *Letterbook of Buchanan & Simson*, 1759.
GD1/618/1–2, *Ledgers of Oswald Dennistoun*, 1763–1767.

The National Archives (TNA):

High Court of the Admiralty (HCA) HCA 12/60, Examinations in the High Court of Admiralty, 6 Feb. 1645.
HCA 13/57, Examinations 1641–1642, Deposition of Edward Marckland, 18 Dec. 1641.
HCA 24/18 f. 131, policy underwritten for Tonamaso Cavalcanti and Giovanni Girale, for the account of Paulo Cicini of Messsina, 26 Nov. 1548.
HCA 24/18 f. 132, translation.
HCA 24/27 f. 147, policy underwritten for Giovanni Broke, 20 Sept. 1547.
HCA 24/27 f. 199, translation.
HCA 24/29 f. 45, policy underwritten for Anthony de Salizar, 5 Aug. 1555.
HCA 24/30 f. 151, policy underwritten for Antony Brasshet, 6 Dec. 1557.
HCA 24/30 f. 233, policy underwritten for John Mowse, 8 Mar. 1557.
HCA 24/35 f. 46, legal opinion on the Ridolphye case, undated, 1562?
HCA 24/35 f. 283, policy underwritten for Robert Ridolphye, 12 Mar. 1564.
Chancery (C) 1/914/31, *Vivalde v. Sheriff of London*.
C 3/26 f. 78, petition of John Barnes and forty-seven others, 1566.
C 33/33 ff. 103–104, *Calderaand v. Company of Assurers*, 1561.
C 66/1131 f. 41, patent granted to Richard Candeler, 21 Feb. 1575/6.
C 103/132, business papers of Thomas Hall.
C 107/1–15, Papers of James Rogers, bankrupt (fifteen boxes).
C 107/11, Risk books of Abraham Clibborn & Co., Six Vols, 1768–1769 to 1775.
C 110/152, *Brailsford v. Peers*, policies underwritten for the executors of the estate of Thomas Brailsford, 19 Sept. 1690–21 May 1692.
Privy Council (PC) 2/26, *Privy Council letter book*.
PC 2/563, *Privy Council letter book*.
State Papers (SP) 12/110/104, petition of Henry Roderigues (undated, marked 'prob. 1576').
SP 46/84/159 f. 145, policy issued to George Warner, 31 Jan. 1641/2.
Special Collections (SC) 8/111/5523, petition of Alexander Ferrantyn.

Rhode Island Historical Society (RIHS):

MSS 315, E445/44 Part 1, Reel 23, Obadiah Brown Papers, *Marine insurance book*, 1753–1762.

Primary printed and online sources

British parliamentary, state, and judicial records and calendars:

1 Ann. Stat. 2, c. 10, *An act for punishing of Accessories to Feloneys and Receivers of stolen Goods and to prevent the wilful burning and destroying of Ships*, HeinOnline, 8 Statutes of the Realm, 1702–1707, pp. 168–169.

14 Car. c. 23, *An Additional Act concerning matters of Assurance used amongst Merchants*, HeinOnline, 5 *Statutes of the Realm*, 1625–1680, pp. 418–419.

19 Geo. II c. 37.

32 Hen. VIII c. 14, par. 10, *The Mayntenaunce of the Navye*, HeinOnline, 3 Statutes of the Realm, (1509–1545), pp. 760–761.

33 Geo. III c. 27 v., *The traitorous correspondence Act*, Runnington, Charles (ed.): *The statutes at large: from the thirtieth year of the reign of King George III to the thirty-fourth year*, Vol. XII, London, 1794, pp. 308–309.

43 Eliz. c. 12, 'An Act Conc'ninge matters of Assurances, amongste Merchantes', HeinOnline, 4 Statutes of the Realm, 1547–1624, pp. 978–979.

5 & 6 Will. & Mary c. 21, *Act for granting to theire Majesties severall Dutyes upon Velum Parchment and Paper for Four Yeares towarde carryyng on the warr against France*, HeinOnline, 6 Statutes of the Realm, 1685–1694, p. 495.

6 Anne c. 68, *An Act… for granting an Equivalent to the City of London by admitting Brokers*, HeinOnline, 8 Statutes of the Realm, 1702–1707, pp. 816–817.

6 Geo I c. 18, *An Act for better securing certain Powers and Privileges, intended to be granted by His Majesty by Two Charters, for Assurance of Ships and Merchandize at Sea, and for lending Money upon Bottomry; and for restraining several extravagant and unwarrantable Practices therein mentioned.*

9 Will. III, Cap. 32, *An Act to restraine the Number and ill Pratice of Brokers and Stock-Jobbers.*

Bibl. Comunale di Treviso. MS. 996, Busta 4: 'Some extracts from a Relation of the Netherlands by Alvise Contarini, Appendix II', *Calendar of State Papers Relating to English Affairs in the Archives of Venice*, Vol. 19: 1625–1626 (1913).

Bruce, John (ed.): *Calendar of State Papers Domestic: Charles I, Vol. XCII, Feb. 1–11, 1628*, (1858); *Vol. XCV, March 1–14, 1628* (1859).

Burrell, Willliam and Marsden, R. G.: *Reports of cases determined by the High Court of Admiralty*, London: W. Clowes and Sons, 1885.

Cobbett's Parliamentary History of England, Vol. XII, A.D. 1741–1743, London: T. C. Hansard, 1812.

Dasent, John R.: *Acts of the Privy Council of England, New Series*, Vols. VII–XX, XXXI, London: HMSO, 1893–1906.

d'Ewes, Sir Simonds: 'Journal of the House of Commons: December 1601', from *Journals of all the Parliaments during the reign of Queen Elizabeth* (1682), London: History of Parliament Trust.

Eighth report of the commissioners appointed to inquire into the management of the Post-Office Department, Part I, London: His Majesty's Stationery Office, 1837.

FSA process guide to decision making on Schemes of Arrangement for insurance firms, UK Financial Services Authority, July 2007.

Green, Mary Anne Everett (ed.): *Calendar of State Papers domestic, James I, Vol. IX, 1603–1610, Aug.–Oct. 1604* (1857); *Vol. L, Dec. 1609* (1857).

Green, Mary Anne Everett (ed.): *Calendar of State Papers domestic: Charles I, Vol. XVII, Sept. 1660* (1860), *Vol. LV, May 28–31, 1662* (1861); *Vol. LVI, June 1662* (1861).

Grey, A. (ed.): *Grey's debates of the House of Commons*, Vol. X, London: T. Becket and P. A. De Hondt, 1769.

Harris, G. G. (ed.): *Trinity House of Deptford Transactions, 1609–35*, London Record Society, 1983.

History and Proceedings of the House of Commons, Vol. VI: 1714–1727, London: History of Parliament Trust, 1742.

Hoppit, Julian (ed.): *Failed legislation, 1660–1800, extracted from the Commons and Lords Journals*, London: Hambledon Press, 1997.

James II: 'By the King, *A proclamation for the better execution of the office of making and registering policys of assurance in the City of London*, The King's Printers, 1687.

Jones, Philip E. et al. (eds): *Calendar of plea and memoranda rolls preserved among the archives of the Corporation of London at the Guildhall, A.D. 1459–1482*, Cambridge: Cambridge University Press, 1961.

Journal of the Commissioners of Trade and Plantations, Vol. III: March 1714–5 to October 1718, London: HMSO, 1924.

Journal of the House of Commons: Vol. VI, 1648–1651 (1802); *Vol. XI, 1693–1697* (1803); *Vol. XIX* (1803), British History Online, www.british-history.ac.uk, London: Institute of Historical Research.

Journals of the House of Commons, Vol. XXV, 1745–1750 (1803); *Vol. L, 1794–1795* (undated), London: reprinted by order of the House of Commons, His Majesty's Stationery Office.

Lemon, John: *Calendar of State Papers, Domestic, Edward, Mary and Elizabeth, 1547–80*, Vol. XXXI, 1856.

Manuscripts of the House of Lords, 1693–1695, Vol. I, New Series, London: Her Majesty's Stationery Office, 1900.

Marsden, R. G.: *Select pleas in the Court of the Admiralty*, vols. I & II, London: Selden Society, 1897.

Parliamentary History, Vol. XIV, A.D. 1747–1753 (1813); *Vol. XXXI, A.D. 1794–1795* (1818), London: T.C. Hansard.

Pickering, Danby (ed.): *Statutes at large*, Vol. VII (1763); Vol. XV (1765), Cambridge: J. Bentham, Printer for the University, 1763.

Report from the Select Committee on Marine Insurance (Sess. 1810), 5 March 1810, House of Commons, reprinted 11 May 1824.

Statutes at large, Vol. XVIII, A.D. 1793–1795, London: Andrew Straham, Law Printer to the King, 1811.

Tawney, R. H. and Power, E. (eds), *Tudor economic documents*, three volumes, London: Longmans, Green & Co., 1924.

The special report from the committee appointed to inquire into, and examine the several subscriptions for fisheries, insurances, annuities for lives, and all other projects carried on by subscription... London: House of Commons, printed by Tonson, J., Goodwin, T., Lintot, B., and Taylor, W., 1720.

Thomas, A. H. (ed.): *Calendar of plea & memoranda roles of the City of London preserved among the archives of the Corporation of London at the Guildhall, AD 1413–1437*, Cambridge: Cambridge University Press, 1943.

Timings, E. K.: *Calendar of State Papers domestic: James II, Vol. II, Jan. 1686* (1964).

Contemporary pamphlets, broadsides, and periodicals:

Abstract of a scheme for an office: and raising one or two millions sterling by a voluntary subscription, for a fund to insure ships and merchandize at sea, &c., London: 1717, Senate House Library, University of London (SHL) Goldsmiths' Library (GL) 1717 f. 5361.

Aislabie, John: *Mr. Aislebie's second speech on his defence in the House of Lords on Thursday July 20. 1721*, London: printed for J. Roberts, 1721, BL 1392.f.17.

Anderton, William: *Remarks upon the present confederacy, and late revolution in England, &c.*, London: 1693, UL F.2.46.

A merchant: *An Essay to prove that all Insurances on Ships and Goods at Sea, beyond the interest of the assured, should be prohibited*, London: 1747, SHL GL-Kress, 8301.3.

A new year's gift for the directors, With some Account of their Plot against The Two Assurances, London: Printed for T. Bickerton, 1721, SHL GL 6026.

A subscriber to Lloyd's: *A letter to Jasper Vaux*, London: Printed for J. M. Richardson, 1810, SHL Goldsmiths-Kress 20088.

The CASE of Assurances as they now Stand: And the Evil Consequences thereof to the Nation (1700?), BL 816.m.10.116.

Daily Courant, No. 5417, 3 March 1719; No. 5640, 18 November 1719; No. 5882, 27 August 1720.

Defoe, Daniel: *The case fairly stated between the Turky Company and the Italian merchants, By a merchant*, London: J. Roberts, 1720.

Hitchcock, Robert: *A Pollitique Platt for the Development of the Fisheries*, London: 1580, cited in Tawney and Power, *Tudor economic documents*, three volumes, III, p. 253.

Johnson, Samuel (reporting, uncredited): 'Debate in the House of Clinabs, on the second reading of a bill to prevent inconveniences arising from the insurance of ships', *Gentleman's Magazine*, Vol. XII, Jan. 1742, pp. 3–15, 18–19.

'Journal of the proceedings and debates in the political club', *London Magazine, or Gentleman's Monthly Intelligencer, for March 1748*, London: R. Baldwin, 1748, pp. 105–107.

Lambe, Samuel: *Seasonable observations humbly offered to his highness the Lord Protector*, London: Printed at the authors charge, 1657.

Lloyd's News, 'Numb. 20, October 15, 1696', ALC, uncatalogued.

London Gazette, No. 2429, 21 Feb. 1688/9, No. 2482, 26 Aug. 1689/10.

Loyal Protestant and Domestick Intelligence, on NEWS both CITY and Countrey, No. 174, 29 June 1682.

Morning Chronicle, iss. 7,428, 26 Mar. 1793.

Morris, Corbyn: *An essay towards deciding the question, whether Britain be permitted by right policy to insure the ships of her enemies?* London: A. Millar, 1748.

Morris, Corbyn: *An essay towards deciding the important question, whether it be a national advantage to Britain to insure the ships of her enemies?* London: Printed by J. Robinson, 1747.

Morris, Corbyn: *An essay towards illustrating the science of insurance*, London: 1747.

Marryat, Joseph: *Observations on the report of the committee on marine insurance*, London: Printed by W. Hughes, 1810.

Praed, Peter and ten others: *The Office-Keepers Answer to a Scandalous Reflection on them by the Societies of the Mines Royal, &c.*, London: 1719?, BL SPR 357.b.3.73.

The Public Advertiser, No. 7,155, 30 Sep. 1757; No. 10,728, 17 Mar. 1769; No. 10,730, 20 Mar. 1769; No. 18,622, 17 Feb. 1794; No. 18,627, 22 Feb. 1794.

REASONS Humbly Offer'd against the Bill, intituled A Bill to prevent some Inconveniences... London: 1741/2, SHL GL Case II. 6. 7793.1.

Reasons humbly offered Against the SOCIETIES of the Mines Royal, Mineral, and Battery Works; who have undertaken to Insure Ships and Merchandizes, without a Charter, BM 357.b.3 f. 76 (c. 1719).

REASONS Humbly Offer'd By the SOCIETIES of the Mines Royal, &c. who Insure Ships and Merchandize, with the Security of a Deposited Joint-Stock, BM 816.m.10/117 f. 297 (c. 1719).

REASONS Humbly offered for the Passing of a BILL to enable divers Merchants that have been great Sufferers by the present War with France, the better to satisfy their Creditors, BL GRC 816.m.12, 16, undated (c. 1693).

Ships Arrived at, and Departed from several Ports of England, No. 257, 22 Dec. 1696, Printed for *Edward Lloyd* (Coffee-man) in *Lombard-Street*, SHL GL Box 2, broadsides.

Sydenham, William: 'PROPOSALS of William Sydenham, Esq; for the Security of Trade; and the Raising of a very considerable Sum of Mony towards the Carrying on the Present WAR with France, Humbly offered', London: 1696, SHL GL-Kress MF, 3367.44.

The Times, iss. 8,626, 13 Jun. 1812, p. 3.

T.S.: *A LETTER to a Member of Parliament by a Merchant*, London: 1720, BL SPR 357.b.3.62.

Universal magazine of knowledge and pleasure, 'Historical chronicle for May 1788', p. 275.

Weekly Journal or *British Gazetteer*, 27 August 1720.

Legal reports:

Camden v. Cowley, 1 Black. w. 417 (96 Eng. Rep. 237).

Came v Moye, K.B., 2 Siderfin 121 (82 Eng. Rep. 1290).

Carter v. Boehm, 3 Burr. 1905 (97 Eng. Rep. 1162).

Clerke v. Martin, 2 Ld. Raym. 758 (92 Eng. Rep. 6).

Delbye v. Proudfoot and Others, 1 Shower. K.B. 396 (89 Eng. Rep. 662).

Dowdale's Case, 6 Co. Rep. 46 b (77 Eng. Rep. 323).

Glover v. Black, 3 Burr. 1394 (97 Eng. Rep. 891).

Goss v. Withers, 2 Bur. 683 (97 Eng. Rep. 511).

Kaines v. Sir Robert Knightly, Skinner 54 (90 Eng. Rep. 26).

Lilly v. Ewer, 1 Dougl. 72 (99 Eng. Rep. 50).

Milles v. Fletcher, 1 Dougl. 233 (99 Eng. Rep. 151).

Merchant correspondence and records:

Balderston, Marion (ed.): *James Claypoole's letter book, London and Philadelphia, 1681–1684*, San Marino, CA: Huntington Library, 1967.

Bolton, J. L. and Bruscoli, Francesco Guidi (eds and transs), *The Ledger of Filippo Borromei and Co. of Bruges, 1438*, London: History Department, Queen Mary University, 2007: online only, www.queenmaryhistoricalresearch.org.

Hancock, David (ed.): *The letters of William Freeman, London Merchant, 1678–1685*, London: London Record Society, 2002.

Price, J. M. (ed.): *Joshua Johnson's letterbook, 1771–1774: letters from a merchant in London to his partners in Maryland*, London: London Record Society, 1979.

Roseveare, Henry (ed.): *Markets and merchants of the late seventeenth century: the Marescoe-David letters, 1668–1680*, Oxford: University Press, 1987.

Rowe Cunningham, Anne: *Letters and diary of John Rowe, Boston merchant*, Boston: W. B. Clarke, 1903.

Steckley, G. F. (ed.): *The letters of John Paige, London merchant, 1648–1658*, London: London Record Society, 1984.

Truxes, Thomas M. (ed.): *Letterbook of Greg & Cunningham, 1756–57, Merchants of New York and Belfast*, Oxford: The British Academy, 2001.

Vanes, Jean (ed.): *The ledger of John Smythe, 1538–1550*, London: HMSO, 1974.

Other published primary sources:

Anonymous, *Arbitrium redivivum, or, the law of arbitration*, by the author of *Regula placitandi*, London, 1694.

Bacon, Francis: *De Augmentis Scientiarium* (1623), in Robertson, John M. (ed.): *The philosophical works of Francis Bacon*, Abingdon: Routledge 2013.

Bacon, Francis: 'Speech on bringing in a bill concerning assurances amongst merchants' (1601), in Spedding, James (ed.): *The letters and life of Francis Bacon, Vol. III*, London: Longmans, Green, Reader and Dyer, 1868, pp. 34–35.

Cary, John: *An essay on the state of England in relation to its trade, its poor, and its taxes, for carrying on the present war against France by John Cary, merchant in Bristoll*, Bristol: W. Bonny, printer, 1695.

Child, Josiah, *A new discourse of trade*, London: T. Sowel, 1698 (first published 1692).

Defoe, Daniel: *An essay on projects* (1697), Project Gutenberg edition (unpaginated), May 2003, www.gutenberg.org/cache/epub/4087/pg4087.html, downloaded 21 Jun. 2013.

Defoe, Daniel: *A tour through the island of Great Britain divided into circuits or journeys, Volume I, eighth edition*, London: W. Strahan *et al.*, 1778 (first published 1724).

East India Company: *Court Minutes of the East India Company, 1640–1643*, Foster, William (ed.), Oxford: Clarendon Press, 1909.

Eden, Sir Frederick Morton: *On the policy and expediency of granting insurance charters*, London: Burton (printer), 1806.

Foster, William (ed.): *The English Factories in India 1651–1654: A Calendar of Documents in the India Office, Westminster*, Oxford: Clarendon Press, 1915.

Foster, William (ed.): *The English Factories in India 1655–1660: A Calendar of Documents in the India Office, Westminster,* Oxford: Clarendon Press, 1921.

Francis, Richard: *Maxims of Equity,* London: Lintot, 1727.

Hall, G. D. G. (ed.): *The treatise on the laws and customs of England commonly called Glanvill* (c. 1187–1189), London: Selden Society and Thomas Nelson & Sons, 1965.

Hatton, Edward: *Comes Commercii: or the trader's companion,* London: Chr. Coningsby, 1699.

Horwitz, H., Speck, W. A., and Gray, W. A. (eds): *London Politics 1713–1717: Minutes of a Whig club 1714–1717,* 1981, www.british-history.ac.uk/report.aspx?compid=38804.

Jados, S. (trans.): *Consulate of the Sea and related documents,* University of Alabama Press, 1975.

Jenkins, D. T. and Yoneyama, Takau (eds): *The history of insurance Vol. VIII, Marine Insurance,* London: Pickering & Chatto, 2000.

Johnstone's London commercial guide and street directory, corrected to August 31, 1817, London: Barnard & Farley, 1818.

Latham, R. and Matthews, W. (eds): *The Diary of Samuel Pepys,* Vol. IV–1663, London: Bell & Sons, 1971.

Leyborun, William: *Panarithmologia,* London: for John Dutton *et al.,* 1693.

The little London directory of 1677, reprinted London: J. C. Hotten, 1863.

Luttrell, Narcissus: *A brief historical relation of state affairs from September 1678 to April 1714,* Vol. III, Cambridge: Cambridge University Press, 2011 (reprint of Oxford University Press edition, 1857).

Magens, Nicholas: *An essay on insurances,* two volumes, London: J. Haberkorn, 1755.

Malcolm, James Peller: *Anecdotes of the manners and customs of LONDON during the eighteenth century,* Second Edition, Vol. I, London: Longman, Hurst, Rees, and Orme, 1810.

Malcolm, John: *A Memoir of Central India including Malwa,* two volumes. London: Parbury Allen & Co., 1832.

Malynes, Gerard: *Consuetudo, vel, Lex Mercatoria: or, The Ancient Law-Merchant,* London: printed for T. Basset and R. Smith, 1685 (first published 1622).

Marsden, R. G. (ed.): *Documents relating to law and custom of the sea,* Vol. 1, London: Navy Records Society, 1915.

Molloy, C.: *De jure maritimo et navali: or, A treatise of affairs maritime, and of commerce, eighth edition,* London: J. Walthoe (printer), 1744 (first published 1676).

Montgomery Martin, R.: *Taxation of the British Empire,* London: Effingham Wilson, 1833.

Mortimer, T.: *Every man his own broker, or a guide to Exchange-Alley;* tenth edition, London: G. G. J. and J. Robinson, 1785.

Park, J. A.: *A system of the law of marine insurances,* sixth edition, London: Butterworths, 1809 (first published 1787).

Postlethwayt, Malachy: *The universal dictionary of trade and commerce, vol. I., fourth edition,* London: Printed for W. Strahan and 24 others, 1774 (first published 1755).

Post-Office Annual Directory for 1814, Critchett & Woods, printed by T. Maiden, London, 1814.

Prichard, M. J. and Yale, D. E. C. (eds): *Hale and Fleetwood on Admiralty jurisdiction*, London, Selden Society.

Roccus (Rocci), Francesco: *A treatise on insurance*, (first published in Latin, 1655), in Reed Ingersoll, Joseph (ed. and trans.), *A manual of maritime law*, Philadelphia: Hopkins and Earle, 1809, pp. 85–156.

Stevens, Robert of Lloyd's: *An essay on average, and on other subjects connected with the practice of marine insurance, fourth edn*, London: Baldwin, Craddock and Joy, 1822 (first published 1813).

Stow, John: *A survey of the cities of London and Westminster (Strype's edition)* (first published 1598), London: printed for A. Churchill and nine others, 1720.

Thomas, A. H. and Thornley, I. D. (eds): *The great chronicle of London*, Gloucester: Alan Sutton, 1983.

Weskett, John (Merchant): *A complete digest of the theory, laws, and practice of insurance*, London: Printed by Frys, Couchman, & Collier, 1781.

West, William: *Simboleography, which may be termed the art, or description, of instruments and precedents*, two vols, London: Companie of Stationers, 1615.

Zouch, Richard: *The jurisdiction of the Admiralty asserted against Sir Edward Coke's Articuli admiralitatis, XXII chapter of his jurisdiction of courts*, London: Printed for Tyton, F. and Dring, T., 1663.

Secondary Sources

Books:

Allen, R. C.: *The British industrial revolution in global perspective*, Cambridge: Cambridge University Press, 2009.

Andrews, Kenneth R.: *Trade, plunder, and settlement: maritime enterprise and the genesis of the British empire, 1480–1630*, Cambridge: Cambridge University Press, 1984.

Annals of Lloyd's Register, being a sketch of the Origins, Constitution, and Progress of Lloyd's Register of British & Foreign Shipping, London: Lloyd's Register, Wyman & Sons, Printers, 1884.

Ashworth, William J.: *Customs and excise: trade, production, and consumption in England, 1640–1845*, Oxford: Oxford University Press, 2003.

Aylmer, G. E.: *The King's servants: the civil service of Charles I, 1625–1642*, London: Routledge, 1961.

Baker, Sir John: *The Oxford history of the laws of England, Volume VI, 1483–1588*, Oxford: Oxford University Press, 2003.

Bannerman, Gordon E.: *Merchants and the military in eighteenth century Britain: British army contracts and domestic supply, 1739–1763*, London: Pickering & Chatto, 2008.

Bayly, C. A.: *Rulers, townsmen and bazaars: north Indian society in the age of British expansion, 1770–1870*, Cambridge: Cambridge University Press, 1983.

Bayly, C. A.: *The Birth of the Modern World 1780–1840*, Oxford: Blackwell, 2004.

Bensa, Enrico: *Il contratto di assicurazione nel medio evo*, 1884. Translated to French, Valéry, Jules: *Histoire du contrat d'assurance au moyen age*, Paris: Ancienne Librairie Thorin et Fils, 1897.

Blackstone, William: *Commentaries on the Laws of England*, IV vols, Oxford: Clarendon Press, 1765–1769.

Borscheid, Peter and Viggo Haueter, Niels (eds): *World Insurance: The Evolution of a Global Risk Network*, Oxford: Oxford University Press, 2012.

Bowen, Huw: *Business of Empire: The East India Company and Imperial Britain, 1756–1833*, Cambridge: Cambridge University Press, 2006.

Braudel, Fernand: *Afterthoughts on material civilization and capitalism* (Ranum, P., trans.), Baltimore: Johns Hopkins University Press, 1977.

Braudel, Fernand: *A history of civilisations* (Mayne, R. trans.), London: Penguin, 1995 (1987).

Braudel, Fernand: *The Mediterranean and the Mediterranean world of Philip II*, two volumes (Reynolds, Sian: trans.), London: Harper Colophon, 1976 (1949).

Brenner, Robert: *Merchants and revolution: commercial change, political conflict, and London's overseas traders, 1550–1653*, Princeton: Princeton University Press, 1993.

Brewer, John: *The sinews of power: war, money and the English state, 1688–1783*, London: Unwin Hyman, 1989.

Burgon, John William: *The life and times of Sir Thomas Gresham*, London: R. Jennings, 1839.

Burke, John: *A genealogical and heraldic history of the commoners of Great Britain*, London: Henry Colburn, 1833.

Butel, Paul: *The Atlantic* (Grant, H. trans.), London: Routledge, 1999.

Cain, P. J. and Hopkins, A. G.: *British imperialism: Innovation and expansion, 1688–1914*, Harlow: Longman 1993.

Campbell, J.: *The lives of the chief justices of England, vol. II*, London: John Murray, 1849.

Carey, W. H. (ed.): *Good Old Days of the Honorable John Company, 1600 to 1858*, two volumes, Calcutta: R. Cambray & Co., 1906–1907.

Carswell, John: *The South Sea bubble*, London: Crescent Press, 1961.

Chaudhuri, K. N.: *Trading World of Asia and the English East India Company*, Cambridge: Cambridge University Press, 1978.

Chet, Guy: *The ocean is a wilderness: Atlantic piracy and the limits of state authority, 1688–1856*, Amherst & Boston: University of Massachusetts Press, 2014.

Clark, Geoffrey: *Betting on lives: the culture of life insurance in England, 1695–1775*, Manchester: Manchester University Press, 1995.

Clayton, G.: *British Insurance*, London: Elek Books, 1971.

Cockerell, H. A. L. and Green, Edwin: *The British insurance business 1547–1970: a guide to historical records in the United Kingdom*, London: Heinemann Educational, 1976.

Coffman, D'Maris, Leonard, Adrian, and Neal, Larry (eds): *Questioning 'credible commitment': perspectives on the rise of financial capitalism*, Cambridge: Cambridge University Press, 2013.

Cokayne, G. E. (ed.): *Complete Baronetage, Vol. II, 1625–1649 & Vol. V, 1707–1800*, Exeter: Pollard & Co., 1902, 1906.

Commission on Money and Credit: *Property and casualty insurance companies: their role as financial intermediaries*, Englewood Cliffs: Prentice-Hall Inc., 1962.

Cruickshanks, E., Handley, S., and Hayton, D. W.: *History of Parliament: The House of Commons, 1690–1715, five volumes*, Cambridge: History of Parliament Trust, 2002.

Culp, Christopher: *Risk transfer: derivatives in theory and practice*, Hoboken, NJ: Wiley & Sons, 2004.

Davis, Ralph: *The rise of the English shipping industry in the seventeenth and eighteenth centuries*, Newton Abbot: David & Charles, 1962.

Davis, Ralph: *English overseas trade, 1500–1700*, London: Macmillan, 1973.

De Roover, Raymond: *The rise and decline of the Medici Bank, 1397–1494*, New York: Norton & Co., 1966.

Del Treppo, Mario: *Els mercaders catalans i l'expansió de la corona catalano-aragonesa al segle XV*, Barcelona: Curial, 1976.

Dickson, P. G. M.: *The financial revolution in England: a study in the development of public credit*, London: Macmillan, 1967.

Dowell, Stephen: *A history of taxes and taxation in England*, four vols, London: Longmans, Green & Co., 1888.

Drew, Bernard: *The London Assurance: a second chronicle*, Plaistow: Printed for the London Assurance at the Curwen Press, 1949.

Drobak, John and Nye, John (eds), *The frontiers of the New Institutional Economics*, London: Academic Press, 1997.

Ekelund, R. B. and Tollison, R. D.: *Politicized economies: monarchy, monopoly, and mercantilism*, College Station: Texas A&M University, 1997.

Epstein, S. R.: *Freedom and Growth: The rise of states and markets in Europe, 1300–1750*, London: Routledge and LSE, 2000.

Fox Bourne, H. R.: *English merchants, memoires in illustration of the progress of British commerce*, Second Edition, Vol. I, London: Richard Bentley, 1866.

Francis, John: *History of the Bank of England, its times and traditions*, London: Willoughby & Co., 1847.

Gauci, Perry: *The politics of trade: the overseas merchant in state and society, 1660–1720*, Oxford: Oxford University Press, 2001.

Gauci, Perry: *Emporium of the World: The merchants of London, 1660–1800*, London: Hambledon Continuum, 2007.

Gershenkron, Alexander: *Economic backwardness in historical perspective*, Cambridge, MA: Belknap Press, 1962.

Gibb, D. E. W.: *Lloyd's of London, a study in individualism*, London: Macmillan & Co., 1957.

Gillingham, Howard: *Marine Insurance in Philadelphia, 1721–1800*, Philadelphia: 1933.

Glaisyer, Natasha: *The culture of commerce in England, 1660–1720*, Woodbridge: Royal Historical Society & Boydell Press, 2006.

Go, Sabine: *Marine insurance in the Netherlands 1600–1870, a comparative institutional approach*, Amsterdam: Askant, 2009.

Goldberg, Jessica: *Trade and institutions in the medieval Mediterranean: The Genzia merchants and their business world*, Cambridge: Cambridge University Press, 2012.

Golding, C. E. and King-Page, D.: *Lloyd's*, London: McGraw Hill, 1952.

Grassby, Richard: *The business community of seventeenth-century England*, Cambridge: Cambridge University Press, 1995.

Greenburg, Michael: *British Trade and the Opening of China, 1800–1842*, Cambridge: Cambridge University Press, 1951.

Greif, Avner: *Institutions and the path to the modern economy: lessons from medieval trade*, Cambridge: Cambridge University Press, 2006.

Grellier, J. J. and Wade, R. W.: *The terms of all the loans which have been raised for the public service*, third edition, London: John Richardson, 1812.

Hancock, David: *Citizens of the world: London merchants and the integration of the British Atlantic community, 1735–1785*, Cambridge: Cambridge University Press, 1995.

Harlow, Vincent: *The Founding of the Second British Empire, 1763–1793*, vol. I, London: Longmans Green & Co., 1952.

Harlow, Vincent: *The Founding of the Second British Empire, 1763–1793*, vol. II, London: Longmans Green & Co., 1963.

Harris, Tim: *Politics under the later Stuarts: party conflict in a divided society, 1660–1715*, London: Longman, 1993.

Holmes, Geoffrey: *The making of a great power: late Stuart and early Georgian Britain, 1660–1722*, London: Longman, 1993.

Holmes, G. and Szechi, D.: *Age of oligarchy: pre-industrial Britain 1722–1783*, London: Longman, 1993.

Hoppit, Julian: *Risk and Failure in English Business, 1700–1800*, Cambridge: Cambridge University Press, 1987.

Horwitz, Henry: *Parliament, policy and politics in the reign of William III*, Manchester: Manchester University Press, 1977.

Inikori, Joseph: *Africans and the industrial revolution in England: a study in international trade and economic development*, Cambridge: Cambridge University Press, 2002.

Janeway, William: *Doing capitalism in the innovation economy*, Cambridge: Cambridge University Press, 2013.

Jardine, Lisa and Stewart, Alan: *Hostage to fortune: the troubled life of Francis Bacon*, London: Victor Gollancz, 1998.

Jones, D. W.: *War and economy in the age of William III and Marlborough*, Oxford: Basil Blackwell, 1988.

Jones, W. J.: *The Elizabethan Court of Chancery*, Oxford: Clarendon Press, 1967.

Keynes, J. M.: *The collected writings of John Maynard Keynes, Vol. VIII: A treatise on probability*, Cambridge: Royal Economic Society, 1973 (1921).

Kindleberger, C. P. & Aliber, R. Z.: *Manias, panics, and crashes: a history of financial crises*, 5th edn, Hoboken: Wiley, 2005.

Knight, Frank: *Risk, uncertainty and profit*, Boston: Houghton Mifflin, 1921.

Langford, Paul: *A polite and commercial people: England 1727–1783*, Oxford: Oxford University Press, 1989.

Leonard, A. B. (ed.): *Marine insurance: origins and institutions, 1300–1850*, Basingstoke: Palgrave Macmillan, 2016.

Levack, Brian P.: *The civil lawyers in England 1601–1641: a political study*, Oxford: Clarendon Press, 1973.

Lewin, C. G.: *Pensions and insurance before 1800: A social history*, East Linton: Tuckwell Press, 2003.

Lieberman, David: *The Province of legislation determined: legal theory in eighteenth-century Britain*, Cambridge: Cambridge University Press, 1989.

Lowenfeld, H.: *Investment an Exact Science*, London: 1907.

Mann, M.: *The sources of social power, vol. I: a history of power from the beginning to A.D. 1760*, Cambridge: Cambridge University Press, 1986.

Martin, Frederick: *The history of Lloyd's and of marine insurance in Great Britain*, London: Macmillan, 1876.

McCusker, John J.: *European bills of entry and marine lists: early commercial publications and the origins of the business press*, Cambridge, MA: Harvard University Library, 1985.

McGrath, Patrick: *The merchant venturers of Bristol: A history of the Society of Merchant Venturers of the City of Bristol from its origin to the present day*, Bristol: Society of Merchant of Merchant Venturers of the City of Bristol, 1975.

Melis, Federigo: *Origini e sviluppi del assicurazione in Itali secoli XIV-XVI*, vol. I, Rome: Instituto Nazionale delle Assicurazione, 1975.

Mingay, G. E.: *English landed society in the eighteenth century*, London: Routledge, 1963.

Mitchell, B. R.: *Abstract of British historical statistics*, Cambridge: Cambridge University Press, 1962.

Montgomery, Thomas Harrison: *A history of the Insurance company of North America of Philadelphia: the oldest fire and marine insurance company in America*, Philadelphia: Press of Review Publishing and Printing Company, 1885.

Muldrew, Craig: *The economy of obligation: the culture of credit and social relations in early modern England*, Basingstoke: Palgrave, 1998.

Murphy, Anne: *The origins of English financial markets: investment and speculation before the South Sea Bubble*, Cambridge: Cambridge University Press, 2009.

Neal, Larry: *The rise of financial capitalism: international capital markets in the age of reason*, Cambridge: Cambridge University Press, 1990.

Newmarch, William: *On the loans raised by Mr Pitt during the first French war, 1793–1801*, London: Effingham Wilson, 1855.

Nightingale, Pamela: *Trade and empire in western India, 1784–1806*, Cambridge: University Press, 1970.

North, Douglass: *Institutions, institutional change and economic performance*, Cambridge: Cambridge University Press, 1990.

North, Douglass and Thomas, R. P.: *Rise of the western world: a new economic history*, Cambridge: Cambridge University Press, 1973.

Ogilvie, Sheilagh: *Institutions and European trade: merchant guilds 1000–1800*, Cambridge: Cambridge University Press, 2011.

Origo, Iris: *The merchant of Prato, Francesco di Marco Datini*, revised edition, Harmondsworth: Penguin, 1963.

Ormrod, David: *The rise of commercial empires: England and the Netherlands in the age of mercantilism, 1650–1770*, Cambridge: Cambridge University Press, 2003.

Palmer, M.: *Command at sea*, Harvard University Press, 2005.

Palmer, Sarah: *Politics, shipping, and the repeal of the navigation acts*, Manchester: University Press, 1990.

Pares, Richard: *War and trade in the West Indies, 1739–1763*, Oxford: Clarendon Press, 1963 (first published 1936).

Pares, Richard: *Yankees and Creoles: The trade between North America and the West Indies before the American Revolution*, London: Longmans, Green & Co., 1956.

Parthasarathi, Prasannan: *Why Europe grew rich, and Asia did not: global economic divergence, 1600–1800*, Cambridge: University Press, 2011.

Paul, H. J.: *The South Sea bubble: an economic history of its origins and consequences*, London: Routledge, 2011.

Pearson, Robin (ed.): *The development of international insurance*, London: Pickering & Chatto, 2010.

Plumb, J. H.: *Sir Robert Walpole: the making of a statesman*, London: Crescent Press, 1956.

Porter, Roy: *English society in the 18th century*, London: Penguin, 1982.

Power, Eileen: *The wool trade in English medieval history*, Oxford: Oxford University Press, 1941.

Ramsay, G. D.: *English overseas trade during the centuries of emergence*, London: Macmillan, 1957.

Raynes, H. E.: *A history of British insurance, second edition*, London: Pitman & Sons, 1964.

Relton, Francis Boyer: *An account of the fire insurance companies*, London: Swan Sonnenschein & Co., 1893.

Rodger, N. A. M.: *The command of the ocean: a naval history of Britain, 1649–1815*, London: Penguin, 2004.

Rogers, James Steven: *The early history of the law of bills and notes: a study of the origins of Anglo-American commercial law*, Cambridge: Cambridge University Press, 1995.

Ruwell, Mary Elizabeth: *Eighteenth-century capitalism: the formation of marine insurance companies*, New York: Garland Publishing, 1993.

Sacks, David Harris: *The widening gate: Bristol and the Atlantic economy, 1450–1700*, Berkeley: University of California Press, 1991.

Scott, William Robert: *The constitution and finance of English, Scottish, and Irish joint-stock companies to 1720, three volumes*, Gloucester, MA: Peter Smith, 1968 (first published 1912).

Semmel, Bernard: *The rise of free trade imperialism; classical political economy, the empire of free trade and imperialism 1750–1850*, Cambridge: Cambridge University Press, 1970.

Senior, William: *Doctors' Commons and the old Court of Admiralty: a short history of the civilians in England*, London: Longmans Green, 1922.

Seog, S. Hun: *The economics of risk and insurance*, Chichester: John Wiley & Sons, 2010.

Smith, Alan G.: *The emergence of a nation state: the commonwealth of England, 1529–1660*, London: Longman, 1984.

Spooner, Frank: *Risks at Sea: Amsterdam insurance and maritime Europe, 1766–1780*, Cambridge: Cambridge University Press, 1983.

Spufford, Peter: *Power and profit: the merchant in medieval Europe*, London: Thames & Hudson, 2002.

Stefani, Giuseppi: *Insurance in Venice from the origins to the end of the Serenissima, vol. I*, Amoruso, A. D. (trans.), Trieste: Assicurazioni Generali, 1958.

Street, G. S.: *The London Assurance, 1720–1920*, London: Williams & Norgate (for private circulation), 1920.

Subramanian, Lakshmi: *Indigenous capital and imperial expansion: Bombay, Surat and the west coast*, Delhi, 1996.

Supple, B. E.: *Commercial crisis and change in England 1600–1642: A study in the instability of a mercantile economy*, Cambridge: University Press, 1959.

Supple, Barry: *The Royal Exchange Assurance: A history of British insurance 1720–1970*, Cambridge: University Press, 1970.

Sutherland, Lucy: *A London merchant, 1695–1744*, London: Oxford University Press, 1933.

Sutherland, Lucy: *The East India Company in eighteenth-century politics*, Oxford: Clarendon Press, 1952.

Trenerry, C. F.: *The origin and early history of insurance, including the contract of bottomry*, London, P. S. King & Son, 1926.

Valéry, Jules: *Les contrats d'assurance au moyen âge*, Paris: Fontemoing et Cie., 1916.

Van Niekerk, J. P.: *The development of the principles of insurance law in the Netherlands: from 1500 to 1800*, two volumes, Kenwyn (Cape Town): Juta & Co., 1998.

Wadsworth, Alfred P. and Mann, J.: *The cotton trade and industrial Lancashire, 1600–1780*, Manchester: Manchester University Press, 1965.

Webster, Anthony: *The twilight of the East India Company: the evolution of Anglo-Asian commerce and politics, 1790–1860*, Woodbridge: Boydell & Brewer, 2013.

Weinreb, Ben and Hibbert, Christopher (eds): 'Lloyd's of London', *The London Encyclopaedia*, Second Edition, London: Macmillan, 1993, p. 478.

West, David: *Admiral Edward Russell and the rise of British naval supremacy*, Kinloss, Scotland: Librario, 2005.

Westall, Oliver (ed.): *The historian and the business of insurance*, Manchester: Manchester University Press, 1984.

Williams, Judith: *British commercial policy and trade expansion, 1750–1850*, Oxford: Oxford University Press, 1972.

Williams, Penry: *The later Tudors, 1547–1603*, Oxford: Oxford University Press, 1995.

Williamson, Oliver E.: *Markets and hierarchies, analysis and antitrust implications: a study in the economics of internal organization*, New York: Free Press, 1975.

Wilson, Charles: *England's apprenticeship 1603–1763*, second edition, Harlow: Longman 1984 (first published 1965).

Wilson, Charles: *Mercantilism*, London: Historical Association, 1958.

Wooddeson, Richard: *Elements of Jurisprudence, treated of in the preliminary part of a course of lectures on the laws of England*, Dublin: J. Moore, 1792.

Worsley, Commander Frank and Griffith, Captain Glyn: *The romance of Lloyd's; from coffee-house to palace*, London: Hutchinson & Co., 1932.

Wright, C. and Fayle, C. E.: *A history of Lloyd's*, London: Macmillan & Co., 1928.

Young, Rev. George: *A history of Whitby, and Streoneshalh abbey*, vol. II, Whitby: Clark & Medd, 1817.

Zahedieh, Nuala: *The capital and the colonies: London and the Atlantic economy, 1660–1700*, Cambridge: Cambridge University Press, 2010.

Zeno, Rinier: *Documenti per la storia del diritto marittimo nel secoli XIII e XIV*, Torino: Lattes & Co., 1936.

Scholarly Articles:

Acemoglu, D., Johnson, S., and Robinson, J.: 'The rise of Europe: Atlantic trade, institutional change, and economic growth', *American Economic Review*, Vol. 95, No. 3 (2005), pp. 546–579.

Achampong, F.: '*Uberrima fides* in English and American Common law: a comparative analysis', *International and Comparative Law Quarterly*, Vol. 36, April 1987.

Addobbati, A.: 'Italy 1500–1800: cooperation and competition', in Leonard, A. B. (ed.): *Marine insurance: origins and institutions, 1300–1850*, Basingstoke: Palgrave Macmillan, 2016, pp. 47–78.

Akerlof, George A.: 'The market for lemons: quality, uncertainty, and the market mechanism', *Quarterly Journal of Economics*, Vol. 84, No. 3 (1970), pp. 488–500.

Barbour, Violet: 'Marine risks and insurance in the seventeenth century', *Journal of Economic and Business History*, Vol. 1, 1928–1929, pp. 561–596.

Baugh, D. A.: 'Great Britain's "Blue-Water" policy, 1689–1815', *International History Review*, Vol. 10, No. 1 (1988), pp. 33–58.

Bayly, C. A.: 'The first age of global imperialism, c. 1760–1830', *Journal of Imperial and Commonwealth History*, Vol. 26, No. 2 (1998), pp. 28–47.

Benson, Bruce L.: 'The spontaneous evolution of commercial law', *Southern Economic Journal*, Vol. 55, No. 3 (1989), pp. 644–661.

Bindoff, S. T.: 'The greatness of Antwerp', in Elton, G. R. (ed.): *The New Cambridge Modern History, Vol. II: The Reformation*, Cambridge: Cambridge University Press, 1965, pp. 50–69.

Bogatyreva, Anastasia: 'England 1660–1720: corporate or private?', in Leonard, A. B. (ed.): *Marine insurance: origins and institutions, 1300–1850*, Basingstoke: Palgrave Macmillan, 2016, pp. 179–204.

Bosher, J. F.: 'The Paris business world and seaports under Louis XV: speculators in marine insurance', *Histoire Sociale*, XII (1979), pp. 281–297.

Bowen, H. V.: ' "The pests of human society": Stockbrokers, jobbers and speculators in mid-eighteenth-century Britain', *History*, Vol. 78 (1993), pp. 38–53.

Brenner, Robert: 'The Civil War politics of London's merchant community', *Past & Present*, No. 58 (1973), pp. 53–107.

Buchanan, James M.: 'An economic theory of clubs', *Economica*, New Series, Vol. 32, No. 125 (1965), pp. 1–14.

Casado Alonso, H.: 'Los seguros marítimos de Burgos: observatorio del comercio internacional portugués en el siglo XVI', *Revista da Faculdade de Letras*, HISTÓRIA, Porto, III Série, Vol. 4, 2003, pp. 213–242.

Clark, G. N.: 'War Trade and Trade War, 1701–1713'. *Economic History Review*, Vol. 1, No. 2 (1928), pp. 262–280.

Clark, Geoffrey: 'Insurance as an instrument of war in the 18th century', *Geneva Papers on Risk and Insurance*, Vol. 29, No. 2, April 2004, pp. 247–257.

Clark, John G.: 'Marine insurance in eighteenth-century La Rochelle', *French Historical Studies*, Vol. 10, No. 4 (1978), pp. 572–598.

Coase, R. H.: 'The nature of the firm', *Economica*, New Series, Vol. 4, No. 16 (Nov. 1937), pp. 386–405.

Cole, Arthur H.: 'Tempo of mercantile life in colonial America', *Business History Review*, Autumn 1959, Vol. 33, pp. 277–299.

Cope, S. R.: 'The Goldsmids and the development of the London money market during the Napoleonic Wars', *Economica*, New Series, Vol. 9, No. 34 (May 1942), pp. 180–206.

Crothers, A. Glenn: 'Commercial risk and capital formation in early America: Virginia merchants and the rise of American marine insurance, 1750–1815', *Business History Review*, Vol. 78, No. 4 (Winter, 2004), pp. 607–633.

Crowhurst, P.: 'Marine insurance and the trade of Rotterdam 1755–63', *Maritime History*, Vol. 2, No. 2 (1972), pp. 138–150.

Dale, Richard S., Johnson, Johnnie E. V., and Tang, Leilei: 'Financial markets can go mad: evidence of irrational behaviour during the South Sea Bubble', *Economic History Review*, Vol. 58, No. 2 (2005), pp. 233–271.

Daunton, M. J.: 'Gentlemanly capitalism and British industry 1820–1914', *Past & Present*, No. 122 (1989), pp. 119–158.

Davis, Ralph: 'English foreign trade, 1660–1700', *Economic History Review*, New Series, Vol. 7, No. 2 (1954), pp. 150–166.

de Lara, Y. G.: 'Institutions for contract enforcement and risk-sharing: From the sea loan to the commenda in late medieval Venice', *European Review of Economic History*, No. 6 (2002), pp. 257–260.

de Roover, Florence Edler: 'Early examples of marine insurance', *Journal of Economic History*, Vol. 5, No. 2 (Nov. 1945), pp. 172–200.

De ruysscher, Dave: 'Antwerp 1490–1590: insurance and speculation', in Leonard, A. B. (ed.): *Marine insurance: origins and institutions, 1300–1850*, Basingstoke: Palgrave Macmillan, 2016, pp. 79–105.

Downing, B. M.: *The military revolution and political change: origins of democracy and autocracy in early modern Europe*, Princeton: Princeton University Press, 1992.

Droback, John and Nye, John: 'Introduction', in Drobak, John and Nye, John (eds): *The frontiers of the New Institutional Economics*, London: Academic Press, 1997.

Ebert, Christopher 2011: 'Early Modern Atlantic trade and the development of maritime insurance to 1630', *Past & Present*, No. 213, pp. 87–213.

Farnell, J. E.: 'The Navigation Act of 1651, the first Dutch War, and the London merchant community', *Economic History Review*, New Series, Vol. 16, No. 3 (1964), pp. 441–442.

Fisher, F. J.: 'London's export trade in the early seventeenth century', *Economic History Review*, Vol. 3, No. 2 (1950), pp. 151–161.

Fowler, William H.: 'Marine insurance in Boston: the early years of the Boston Marine Insurance Company, 1799–1807', in Wright, Conrad Edick and Viens,

Katheryn P. (eds), *Entrepreneurs: the Boston business community, 1700–1850I*, Boston: Massachusetts Historical Society, 1997, pp. 151–180.

Gallagher, John and Robinson, Ronald: 'The imperialism of free trade', *Economic History Review*, NS Vol. 6, No. 1 (1953), pp. 1–15.

Go, Sabine: 'Amsterdam 1585–1790: emergence, dominance and decline', in Leonard, A. B. (ed.): *Marine insurance: origins and institutions, 1300–1850*, Basingstoke: Palgrave Macmillan, 2016, pp. 107–129.

Greif, Avner: 'Institutions and international trade: lessons from the commercial revolution', *American Economic Review*, Vol. 82, No. 2 (1992), pp. 128–133.

Greif, Avner: 'On the interrelations and economic implications of economic, social, political, and normative factors: reflections from two late medieval societies', in Drobak, John and Nye, John (eds): *The frontiers of the New Institutional Economics*, London: Academic Press, 1997, pp. 57–94.

Greif, Avner: 'The Maghribi traders: a reappraisal?', *Economic History Review*, Vol. 65, No. 2 (2012), pp. 445–469.

Greif, Avner, Milgrom, Paul, and Weingast, Barry R.: 'Coordination, commitment, and enforcement: the case of the merchant guild', *Journal of Political Economy*, Vol. 102, No. 4 (1994), pp. 745–776.

Habib, Irfan: 'Potentialities of capitalistic development in the economy of Mughal India', *Journal of Economic History*, Vol. 29, No. 1 (1969), pp. 32–78.

Harris, Ron: 'The Bubble Act: its passage and its effects on business', *Journal of Economic History*, Vol. 54, No. 3 (1994), pp. 610–627.

Holdsworth, W. S.: 'The early history of the contract of insurance', *Columbia Law Review*, Vol. 17, No. 2 (1917), pp. 85–113.

Hoover, Calvin: 'The sea loan in Genoa in the twelfth century', *Quarterly Journal of Economics*, Vol. 40, No. 3 (1926), pp. 495–529.

Hoppit, Julian: 'Compulsion, compensation and property rights in Britain, 1688–1833', *Past and Present*, No. 210 (2011), pp. 93–128.

Huebner, Solomon: 'The development and present status of marine insurance in the United States', *Annals of the American Academy of Political and Social Science*, Vol. 26 (1905), pp. 241–272.

Ibbetson, D.: 'Law and custom: Insurance in sixteenth-century England', *Journal of Legal History*, Vol. 29, No. 3 (2008), pp. 291–307.

John, A. H.: 'Insurance investment and the London money market of the 18th century', *Economica*, New Series, Vol. 20, No. 78 (1953), pp. 137–158.

John, A. H.: 'War and the English economy, 1700–1763', *Economic History Review*, New Series, Vol. 7, No. 3 (1955), pp. 329–344.

John, A. H.: 'The London Assurance Company and the marine insurance market of the eighteenth century', *Economica* 25 (1958), pp. 126–141.

Jones, W. J.: 'Elizabethan marine insurance: the judicial undergrowth', *Business History*, Vol. 2, No. 2 (1970), pp. 53–66.

Kenny, C. E.: 'William Leybourn, 1626–1716', *The Library*, Fifth Series, Vol. V, No. 3 (1950), pp. 159–171.

Kepler, J. S.: 'The operating potential of the London insurance market in the 1570s', *Business History* 17 (1975), pp. 44–55.

Kingston, Christopher: 'Marine insurance in Britain and America, 1720–1844: a comparative institutional analysis', *Journal of Economic History*, Vol. 67, No. 2 (2007), pp. 379–409.

Kingston, Christopher: 'Marine insurance in Philadelphia during the quasi-war with France, 1795–1801', *Journal of Economic History*, Vol. 71, No. 1 (2011), pp. 162–184.

Leonard, A. B.: 'Underwriting British trade to India and China, 1780–1835', *Historical Journal*, Vol. 55, No. 4 (2012), pp. 983–1006.

Leonard, A. B.: 'The pricing revolution in marine insurance', working paper presented to the Economic History Association, Sept. 2012, http://eh.net/eha/system/files/Leonard.pdf.

Leonard, A. B.: 'Contingent commitment: the development of English marine insurance in the context of New Institutional Economics, 1577–1720', in Coffman, D'Maris, Leonard, A. B., and Neal, Larry (eds): *Questioning 'credible commitment': Perspectives on the rise of financial capitalism*, Cambridge: Cambridge University Press, 2013, pp. 48–75.

Leonard, A. B.: 'From local to transatlantic: insuring trade in the Caribbean', in Leonard, A. B. and Pretel, D.: *The Caribbean and the Atlantic World Economy: Circuits of trade, money and knowledge, 1650–1914*, Basingstoke: Palgrave Macmillan, 2015, pp. 137–159.

Leonard, A. B.: 'Marine insurers, the City of London, and financing the Napoleonic Wars', in Hoppit, J., Needham, D., and Leonard, A. (eds): *Money and markets: essays in honour of Martin Daunton*, Woodbridge: Boydell, 2019, pp. 55–70.

Leone, Alfonso: 'Maritime insurance as a source for the history of international credit in the Middle Ages', *Journal of European Economic History*, 12 (1993), pp. 363–369.

Mallett, M. E.: 'Anglo-Florentine commercial relations, 1465–1491', *Economic History Review*, Vol. 15, No. 2 (1962), pp. 250–265.

Marlow, Richard: 'Sir Ferdinando Heyborne alias Richardson', *Musical Times*, Vol. 115, No. 1579 (1974), pp. 736–739.

McCusker, John: 'The early history of Lloyd's List', *Historical Research, the Bulletin of the Institute of Historical Research*, Vol. 64, No. 155 (1991), pp. 427–431.

Milgrom, P. R., North, D. C., and Weingast, B. R.: 'The role of institutions in the revival of trade: the Law Merchant, private judges, and the Champagne fairs', *Economics and Politics*, Vol. 2, No. 1 (1990), pp. 1–23.

Mirowski, Philip: 'The rise (and retreat) of a market: English joint stock shares in the eighteenth century', *Journal of Economic History*, Vol. 41, No. 3 (1981), pp. 559–577.

Morriss, Margaret Shove: 'Colonial trade of Maryland, 1689–1715', *Johns Hopkins University studies in historical & political science, vol. XXXII*, Baltimore: Johns Hopkins Press, 1914, pp. 446–599.

Musgrave, Peter: 'The economics of uncertainty: the structural revolution in the spice trade, 1480–1640', in *Shipping, trade, and commerce: essays in memory of Ralph Davis*, Leicester: Leicester University Press, 1981, pp. 9–22.

Nash, R. C.: 'The organization of trade and finance in the British Atlantic economy, 1600–1830', in Coclanis, Peter A.: *The Atlantic economy during the seventeenth and eighteenth centuries: organisation, operation, practice and personnel*, Columbia, SC: University of South Carolina Press, 2005, pp. 95–151.

Neal, Larry: 'How it all began: the monetary and financial architecture of Europe during the first global capital markets, 1648–1815', *Financial History Review*, Vol. 7 (2000), pp. 117–140.

Neal, Larry and Davis, Lance: 'The evolution of the rules and regulations of the first emerging markets: the London, New York and Paris stock exchanges, 1792–1914', *Quarterly Review of Economics and Finance*, No. 45 (2005), pp. 296–311.

North, Douglass: 'Institutions', *Journal of Economic Perspectives*, Vol. 5, No. 1 (1991).

North, Douglass: 'Institutions, transaction costs, and the rise of empires', in Tracy, James (ed.): *The political economy of merchant empires*, Cambridge: Cambridge University Press, 1991, pp. 22–40.

North, D. C. and Weingast, B. R.: 'Constitutions and commitment: The evolution of institutions governing public choice in England', *Journal of Economic History*, Vol. 49, No. 4 (1989), pp. 803–832.

O'Brien, P.: 'Mercantilism and imperialism in the rise and decline of the Dutch and British economies 1585–1815', *De Economist*, Vol. 148, No. 4, 2000, pp. 469–501.

O'Brien, P.: 'The nature and historical evolution of an exceptional fiscal state', *Economic History Review*, Vol. 64, No. 2 (2011), pp. 408–446.

Ogilvie, Sheilagh and Carus, A. W.: 'Institutions and economic growth in historical perspective', in Durlauf, S. and Aghion, P. (eds): *Handbook of economic growth*, Vol. 2A, Amsterdam: Elsevier, 2014, pp. 403–513.

Ogilvie, S. and Edwards, J.: 'Contract enforcement, institutions, and social capital: the Maghribi traders reappraised', *Economic History Review*, Vol. 65, No. 2 (2012), pp. 421–444.

Oldham, James C.: 'The origins of the special jury', *University of Chicago Law Review*, Vol. 50, No. 1 (1983), pp. 137–221.

Ormrod, David: 'Institutions and the environment: shipping movements in the North Sea/Baltic Zone, 1650–1800', in Unger, Richard W. (ed.): *Shipping and economic growth 1350–1850*, Leiden: Brill, 2011.

Pezzolo, Luciano and Tattara, Giuseppe: 'Una fiera senza luogo: was Bisenzone an international capital market in sixteenth-century Italy?', *Journal of Economic History*, Vol. 68, No. 4 (2008), pp. 1098–1122.

Piccinno, Luisa: 'Genoa 1340–1620: early development of marine insurance', in Leonard, A. B. (ed.): *Marine insurance: origins and institutions, 1300–1850*, Basingstoke: Palgrave Macmillan, 2016, pp. 25–46.

Pohl, H.: 'Economic powers and political powers in early modern Europe: theory and history', in Cavaciocchi, S. (ed.): *Poteri economici e poteri politici, secc. XIII-XVIII*, Florence: Le Monnier, 1999, pp. 55–78.

Price, J.: 'What did merchants do? Reflections on British overseas trade, 1660–1790', *Journal of Economic History*, Vol. 49, No. 2, *The Tasks of Economic History* (1989), pp. 267–284.

Price, J.: 'Transaction costs: a note on merchant credit and the organisation of private trade', in Tracy, J. (ed.): *The political economy of merchant empires*, Cambridge: Cambridge University Press, 1991, pp. 276–297.

Pryor, John: 'The origins of the commenda contract', *Speculum*, Vol. 52, No. 1 (1977), pp. 5–37.

Rapp, Richard T.: 'The unmaking of the Mediterranean trade hegemony: international trade rivalry and the commercial revolution', *Journal of Economic History*, Vol. 35, No. 3 (1975), pp. 499–525.

Roberts, C.: 'The constitutional significance of the financial settlement of 1690', *Historical Journal*, Vol. 20, No. 1 (1977), pp. 59–76.

Roberts, Simon: 'The study of dispute: anthropological perspectives', in Bossy, John (ed.): *Disputes and settlements: law and human relations in the west*, Cambridge: Cambridge University Press, 1983, pp. 1–24.

Rossi, Guido: 'The Book of Orders of Assurances: a civil law code in 16th century London', *Maastricht Journal*, Vol. 19, No. 2 (2012), pp. 240–261.

Rudolph, Julia: 'Jurisdictional controversy and the credibility of common law', in Coffman, D., Leonard, A., and Neal, L.: *Questioning credible commitment: perspectives on the rise of financial capitalism*, Cambridge: Cambridge University Press, 2013, pp. 104–124.

Ruffat, Michèle: 'French insurance from the *ancien régime* to 1946: shifting frontiers between state and market', *Financial History Review*, Vol. 10, No. 2 (2003), pp. 185–200.

Rupprecht, Anita: 'Excessive memories: slavery, insurance and resistance', *History Workshop Journal*, Vol. 64 (2007), pp. 6–28.

Sachs, Stephen E.: 'From St. Ives to cyberspace: the modern distortion of the medieval "Law Merchant"', *American University International Law Review*, Vol. 21, No. 5 (2006), pp. 685–812.

Saran, Paramatma: 'Insurance during medieval India', in V. S. Srivastava (ed.): *Cultural Contours of India*, New Delhi: Abhinav, 1981.

Servini, Peter: 'Henry VIII: government and politics 1529–47', in Lotherington, John (ed.): *The Tudor years*, London: Hodder & Stoughton, 1994, pp. 116–159.

Sloan, Roy: 'Elizabeth I: government of England', in Lotherington, John (ed.): *The Tudor years*, London: Hodder & Stoughton, 1994, pp. 208–238.

Smallwood, R. P. F.: 'The nature and structure of insurance markets in the Far East', *Journal of the Chartered Insurance Institute*, Vol. 59 (1962), pp. 79–94.

Spagnesi, E: 'Aspetti dell'assicurazione medievali', in Associazione Nazionale fra la imprese assicuratrici (ed.): *L'assicurazione in Italie fino al'Unita: Saggi storici in onore di Eugenio Artom*, Milan: Giuffré, 1975, pp. 3–189.

Spufford, Peter: 'From Genoa to London: the places of insurance in Europe', in Leonard, A. B. (ed.): *Marine insurance: origins and institutions, 1300–1850*, Basingstoke: Palgrave Macmillan, 2016, pp. 271–297.

Steckley, George F.: 'Merchants and the Admiralty Court during the English revolution', *American Journal of Legal History*, Vol. 22, No. 2 (1978), pp. 137–175.

Stone, Lawrence: 'Elizabethan overseas trade', *Economic History Review*, Vol. 2, No. 1 (1949), pp. 30–58.

Triandis, H. C., McCusker, C., and Hui, C. H.: 'Multimethod probes of individualism and collectivism', *Journal of Personality and Social Psychology*, Vol. 59, No. 5 (1990), pp. 1006–1020.

Vance, William Reynolds: 'The early history of insurance law', *Columbia Law Review*, Vol. 8. No. 1 (1908), pp. 1–17.

Walcott, Robert: 'The East India interest in the general election of 1700–1701', *English Historical Review*, Vol. 71, No. 279 (1956), pp. 223–239.

Westall, Oliver: 'Invisible, visible, and "direct" hands: an institutional interpretation of organisational structure and change in British general insurance', *Business History*, Vol. 39, No. 4 (1977), pp. 44–66.

Wilson, J. G. and Fiske, John (eds): 'BROOKS, Peter Chardon', in *Appleton's cyclopaedia of American biography*, Vol. 1, New York: Appleton & Co., 1887, p. 389.

Zahedieh, Nuala: 'Productivity in English Atlantic shipping in the seventeenth century: evidence from the navigation acts', in Unger, Richard W. (ed.): *Shipping and economic growth 1350–1850*, Leiden: Brill, 2011, pp. 117–134.

Other secondary sources:

Bogaterevya, Anastasia: 'Marine insurance corporations and the Parliamentary Special Report of 1720', undergraduate dissertation submitted to the Faculty of History, University of Cambridge, 2013.

Chandler, John: 'The Candelers of London', *The Home Counties Magazine*, Vol. V (1903), pp. 231–234.

Chandler, John: 'Richard Candeler of Tottenham', *The Home Counties Magazine*, Vol. II (1903), pp. 301–304.

Glasgow Herald, 'Notes & Comments', 25 Feb. 1929, p. 18.

Green, Edwin: 'Brokers and marine insurance before 1574', *CIB Link: Monthly Bulletin of the Corporation of Insurance Brokers*, No. 50, Aug. 1973.

Johnston, J. A.: *Parliament and the Navy 1688–1714*, unpublished PhD thesis, Sheffield University, 1968.

Leonard. A. B.: 'Marine insurance and the rise of British merchant influence, 1649–1748', unpublished Masters dissertation, University of Cambridge, 2011.

Leonard, A. B.: 'Wartime marine insurance and the state: insuring British shipping during WW1', unpublished conference paper, presented at *The First World War at Sea, 1914–19*, National Maritime Museum, Greenwich, 4 Jun. 2018.

Lysons, Daniel: 'Tottenham', *The environs of London: Vol. III: County of Middlesex* (1795), pp. 517–557.

O'Brien, P. K.: 'Fiscal exceptionalism: Great Britain and its European rivals from Civil War to triumph at Trafalgar and Waterloo', Working Paper No. 65/01, London School of Economics, Oct. 2001.

O'Brien, P. K. and Duran, X.: 'Total factor productivity for the Royal Navy from victory at Texal to triumph at Trafalgar', Working Paper No. 134/10, London School of Economics, Feb. 2010.

Seltmann, Astrid: 'Global Marine Insurance Report 2019', *Annual Conference Presentation*, International Union of Marine Insurers, Sept. 2019.

TheCityUK, *UK Financial and Related Professional Services: Meeting the challenges and delivering opportunities*, August 2016.

University College London, *Legacies of British Slave-ownership*, 'Godschall Johnson I', www.ucl.ac.uk/lbs/person/view/2146635729.

Multi-author online reference works:

History of Parliament Online, www.historyofparliamentonline.org, London: The History of Parliament Trust

Cruickshanks, Eveline: 'Bethell, Slingsby', www.historyofparliamentonline.org / volume/1715-1754/member/bethell-slingsby-1695-1758.

Cruickshanks, Eveline: 'Janssen, Sir Theodore', /volume/1715-1754/member/ janssen-stephen-theodore-1777.

Cruickshanks, Eveline: 'Williams, Sir John', /volume/1715-1754/member/ williams-sir-john-1676-1743.

Cruickshanks, Eveline: 'Barnard, John', volume/1715-1754/member/ barnard-john-1685-1764.

Cruickshanks, Eveline: 'Chetwynd, John', volume/1715-1754/member/ chetwynd-john-1680-1767.

Cruickshanks, Eveline: 'Chetwynd, Walter', volume/1715-1754/member/ chetwynd-walter-1677-1736.

Cruickshanks, Eveline: 'Hume, Alexander', volume/1715-1754/member/ hume-alexander-1693-1765.

Cruickshanks, Eveline: 'Willmott, Robert', volume/1715-1754/member/ willimot-robert-1746.

Cruickshanks, Eveline and Hayton, D. W.: 'Waller, Robert', volume/1690-1715/ member/waller-robert-1698.

Gauci, Perry: 'Vernon, Sir Thomas', volume/1690-1715/member/ vernon-sir-thomas-1631-1711.

Handley, Stuart: 'Hedges, Sir Charles', /volume/1690-1715/member/ hedges-sir-charles-1650-1714.

Hayton, D. W.: 'Lockwood, Richard', volume/1690-1715/member/ lockwood-richard-1676-1756.

Lea, R. S.: 'Townshend, Hon. Horatio', volume/1715-1754/member/ townshend-hon-horatio-1683-1751.

Matthews, Shirley: 'Baker, William', /volume/1715-1754/member/ baker-william-1705-70.

Sedgwick, Romney R.: 'Hume Campbell, Alexander', /volume/1715-1754/ member/hume-campbell-hon-alexander-1708-60; 'Hungerford, John', volume/1715-1754/member/hungerford-john-1658-1729.

Taylor, Lawrence and Fisher, David: 'Marryat, Joseph', volume/1790-1820/ member/marryat-joseph-1757-1824.

Watson, Paula: 'Paice, Joseph', volume/1690-1715/member/paice-joseph-1658-1735.

Oxford Dictionary of National Biography, online edition: www.oxforddnb.com, Oxford: Oxford University Press:

Barker, Hannah: 'Walter, John', www.oxforddnb.com/view/article/28636.

Boyer, Allen D.: 'Coke, Sir Edward', /article/5826.

Bryson, W. H.: 'Francis, Richard', /article/47165.

Considine, John: 'Overbury, Sir Thomas', article/20966.

de Krey, Gary: 'Hedges, Sir William', /article/12860.

Dickinson, H. T.: 'Yonge, Sir William', /article/30232.

Ellis, Kathryn: 'Onslow, Richard', /article/20794.

Gauci, Perry: 'Malynes, Gerard', /article/17912.

Glaisyer, Natasha: 'Whiston, James', /article/65789.

Halliday, Paul D.: 'Pemberton, Sir Francis', /article/21821.

Handley, Stuart: 'Dawes, Sir William', /article/7336.

Hanham, A. A.: 'Lechmere, Nicholas, Baron Lechmere', /article/16262.

Hart, James S. Jr: 'Barnardiston, Sir Samuel', /article/1461.

Lemmings, David: 'Thomson, Sir William', /article/27281.

Oldham, J.: 'Murray, William, first earl of Mansfield', /article/19655.

Palmer, Sarah: 'Angerstein, John Julius', /article/549.

Pearl, V.: 'Thomson, Maurice', /article/38061.

Speck, W. A.: 'Harley, Robert', /article/12344.

Speck, W. A. and Kilburn, Matthew: 'Promoters of the South Sea Bubble', /theme/92793.

Thomson, A.: 'Thomson, George', /article/27299.

Veale, Elspeth: 'Janssen, Sir Theodore' /article/14656.

Warmington, Andrew: 'Veel, Thomas', /article/28171.

Index

Page number suffixes indicate the following:

f figure
g glossary entry
t table.

References to notes appear in the format 15 n.47. Underwriters listed in the Appendix have been indexed where they are also discussed in the main text; for the full alphabetical list, please see the Appendix on p. 219.

Printed in the United States
by Baker & Taylor Publisher Services